Marx at the Margins

ONE WEEK LOAN

D1355018

Marx at the Margins

ON NATIONALISM, ETHNICITY, AND
NON-WESTERN SOCIETIES

Kevin B. Anderson

The University of Chicago Press   CHICAGO & LONDON

KEVIN B. ANDERSON is professor of sociology and
political science at the University of California–Santa Barbara.
He has edited four books and is the author of *Lenin, Hegel, and
Western Marxism: A Critical Study* and, with Janet Afary,
*Foucault and the Iranian Revolution: Gender and
the Seductions of Islamism.*

The University of Chicago Press, Chicago 60637
The University of Chicago Press, Ltd., London
© 2010 by The University of Chicago
All rights reserved. Published 2010
Printed in the United States of America
19 18 17 16 15 14 13 12 11 10   1 2 3 4 5

ISBN-13: 978-0-226-01982-6   (cloth)
ISBN-13: 978-0-226-01983-3   (paper)
ISBN-10: 0-226-01982-9   (cloth)
ISBN-10: 0-226-01983-7   (paper)

Library of Congress Cataloging-in-Publication Data
Anderson Kevin, 1948–
Marx at the margins : on nationalism, ethnicity, and non-western
societies / Kevin B. Anderson.
p. cm.
Includes bibliographical references and index.
ISBN-13: 978-0-226-01982-6   (cloth : alk.paper)
ISBN-10: 0-226-01982-9   (cloth : alk. paper)
ISBN-13: 978-0-226-01983-3   (pbk : alk. paper)
ISBN-10: 0-226-01983-7   (pbk. : alk. paper) 1. Marx, Karl, 1818–1883—
Political and social views. 2. Nationalism. 3. Ethnicity. I. Title
JC233.M299A544 2010
320.54—dc22   2009034187

CONTENTS

ACKNOWLEDGMENTS

During the decade and more I have worked on this project, I have received generous assistance in numerous ways from scholars in Marxist studies and other fields. Through these years, my understanding of the issues at stake in this book has benefited immensely from my association with the *Marx-Engels Gesamtausgabe*, in particular from interactions with Jürgen Rojahn, David Norman Smith, Charles Reitz, Lars Lih, Georgi Bagaturia, the late Norair Ter-Akopian, and Rolf Hecker, as well as Jürgen Herres, Malcolm Sylvers, Gerald Hubmann, Gerd Callesen, Regina Roth, and Carl-Erich Vollgraf. I also benefited from an American Council of Learned Societies Fellowship (1996–97), a travel grant from the American Philosophical Society (1996), and a Center for Humanistic Studies Fellowship at Purdue University (2004). Bert Rockman of the Department of Political Science at Purdue University and Verta Taylor of the Department of Sociology at University of California–Santa Barbara also allowed some release time from teaching, in 2007 and 2009, respectively.

Douglas Kellner, Bertell Ollman, and Frieda Afary each read and commented in important ways upon the entire manuscript. So did my partner, Janet Afary, who provided immense support and encouragement, both personal and intellectual, as she followed and encouraged this project at every step of the way. Over the years, I have also discussed this project frequently—and always fruitfully—with Peter Hudis. Louis Dupré, Donald N. Levine, and William McBride offered encouragement and suggestions at crucial junctures. The following people read and gave good suggestions on significant parts of the manuscript: David Black, Paresh Chattopadhyay, Richard Hogan, Lars Lih,

Albert Resis, Arthur Rolston, Jack Rhoads, David Roediger, Jürgen Rojahn, and Eamonn Slater. Others offered comments in response to papers on it presented at various conferences or in other settings, especially Robert Antonio, Colin Barker, Franklin Bell, Roslyn Bologh, Jordan Camp, Norman Fischer, Chris Ford, Andrew Kliman, Lauren Langman, David Mayer, Ted McGlone, David McNally, Hal Orbach, Michael Perelman, Annette Rubinstein, Lawrence Scaff, and Suzi Weissman. I would also like to thank Heather Brown, Alexander Hanna, Lisa Lubow, C. J. Pereira di Salvo, Michelle Sierzega, Rebekah Sterling, and Mir Yarfitz for research assistance. At Purdue University, Michelle Conwell provided lots of technical and secretarial support.

Over the years I worked at the following libraries, where I received particular help from several individuals: Northern Illinois University (Robert Ridinger), University of Chicago (Frank Conaway), and the International Institute of Social History in Amsterdam (Mieke Ijzermans). I also received other help with source material from Vinay Bahl, David Black, Sebastian Budgen, Paul Buhle, Paresh Chattopadhyay, Rolf Dlubek, Carl Estabrook, Eric Foner, Urszula Frydman, Rolf Hecker, Robert Hill, William McBride, Jim Obst, David Roediger, Jürgen Rojahn, David Norman Smith, and Danga Vileisis.

Earlier versions of parts this book have been presented to meetings of numerous scholarly associations, including the American Sociological Association, the Historical Materialism conferences (London and Toronto), the Socialist Scholars conferences (New York), the Left Forum conferences (New York), the Rethinking Marxism conferences (Amherst), and the Midwest Sociological Association. In addition, I would like to single out four occasions that were particularly important in the thinking through of this book in response to serious interlocutors: a colloquium at the Department of Sociology of University of Illinois at the invitation of John Lie in 1996; a talk at the Brecht Forum in New York at the invitation of Liz Mestres and Eli Messinger in 2000; a stint as a visiting scholar at the Center for Social Theory and Comparative History at University of California–Los Angeles at the invitation of Robert Brenner and Thomas Mertes in the winter and spring of 2007; and a stint as a visiting scholar at Wuhan University at the invitation of He Ping in fall 2007.

I would also like to thank John Tryneski and Rodney Powell, as well as Mary Gehl and Kristi McGuire, at the University of Chicago Press for their hard work and support through the process of publication.

Finally, I would like to dedicate this book to the memory of two outstanding thinkers who paved the way: my intellectual mentor Raya Dunayevskaya

(1910–1987), a Marxist humanist philosopher who developed original insights into Marx's writings on non-Western and precapitalist societies in her *Rosa Luxemburg, Women's Liberation and Marx's Philosophy of Revolution* (1982); and Lawrence Krader (1919–1998), the indefatigable Marx scholar who brought Marx's *Ethnological Notebooks* to light in 1972.

ABBREVIATIONS

Capital I	Karl Marx, *Capital*, volume I, translated by Ben Fowkes, Penguin edition ([1890] 1976)
Capital III	Karl Marx, *Capital*, volume III, translated by David Fernbach, Penguin edition ([1894] 1981)
Grundrisse	Karl Marx, *Grundrisse: Foundations of the Critique of Political Economy (Rough Draft)*, translated by Martin Nicolaus ([1857–58] 1973)
KML 1	*Karl Marx Library*, volume 1, edited and translated by Saul K. Padover (1971–77)
MECW 12	Karl Marx and Frederich Engels, *Collected Works*, volume 12 (1975–2004)
MEGA² II/10	*Marx-Engels Gesamtausgabe*, section II, volume 10 (1975–)
MEW 1	Karl Marx and Frederich Engels, *Werke*, volume 1 (1956–68)
Oeuvres 4	Karl Marx, *Oeuvres*, volume 4, edited with notes by Maximilien Rubel (1963–94)

In 1849, Marx was forced to move to London, where he was to dwell as a political exile until his death in 1883. Having experienced the defeat of the 1848 revolutions on the Continent, he sensed that a period of retrogression was at hand. This was confirmed by the December 1851 Bonapartist coup in France, which signaled the end of the revolutionary wave of 1848–49. If these political setbacks narrowed his horizons somewhat, his relocation to London widened them in other ways. It placed Marx at the center of the world's only truly industrial capitalist economy as he labored in the British Museum on what was to become his masterwork, *Capital*. The move to London also put him at the center of the world's largest empire, which led him to take greater account of non-Western societies and colonialism.

The deconstructionist philosopher Jacques Derrida captures well Marx's marginality as a political refugee in Victorian London, linking it to his equally marginal position within the Western intellectual tradition: "Marx remains an immigrant among us, a glorious, sacred, accursed but still clandestine immigrant as he was all his life" (1994, 174). In Britain, one of his main sources of income was his work as the chief European correspondent of the *New York Tribune*. Another was the financial support he received from his friend Friedrich Engels, also a veteran of 1848, who became a partner in his family's very successful manufacturing firm in Manchester. Frequently writing in English and French as well as his native German, Marx was a trilingual, cosmopolitan intellectual.

This book brings together two sets of writings from Marx's vast corpus, almost all of them written in London. (1) It examines his theorization of a number of non-Western societies of his day—from India to Russia and from Algeria to China—and their relation to capitalism and colonialism. (2) It also takes up his writings on movements for national emancipation, especially in Poland and Ireland, and their relation to the democratic and socialist movements of the time. Connected to the latter was his theorization of race and ethnicity in relation to class, with respect to both Black labor in America during the Civil War and Irish labor in Britain.[1]

The present study concentrates on Marx's writings on societies that were for the most part peripheral to capitalism during his lifetime. In particular, I will take up lesser-known Marx writings, like his journalism for the *New York Tribune*. I will also examine his extensive but little-known 1879–82 notebooks on non-Western and precapitalist societies, some of which are yet to be published in any language, but will be made available in the coming years through the *Marx-Engels Gesamtausgabe* (hereafter referred to as MEGA[2] and discussed in the appendix). A number of these non-Western and precapitalist societies Marx studied, like India, Indonesia, and Algeria, had been partially incorporated into capitalist modernity via colonization. Others, like Poland, Russia, and China, still stood largely outside the global capitalist system. Still others, like the United States and Ireland, were part of global capitalism, albeit at its perimeters, with Ireland relegated mainly to agriculture. Whether within the globalized capitalism of the nineteenth century but at its far edge (Ireland, the United States), or partly incorporated within global capitalism (India, Algeria, Indonesia), or just beyond it (Russia, China, Poland), all of these societies were in one way or another at the margins. Hence the title, *Marx at the Margins*.

The two major themes mentioned above stood out within Marx's writings on the above societies. (1) He emphasized that those like Russia, India, China, Algeria, and Indonesia possessed social structures markedly different from those of Western Europe. Throughout his writings, he grappled with the question of the future development of these non-Western societies. More specifically, he examined their prospects for revolution and as sites for resistance to capital. Over the years, I will argue, his perspectives on these societies evolved.[2] In the 1840s, he held to an implicitly unilinear perspective, sometimes tinged with ethnocentrism, according to which non-Western societies would necessarily be absorbed into capitalism and then modernized via colonialism and the world market. But over time, his perspective evolved toward one that was more multilinear, leaving the future development of these societies as an open question. By 1881–82, he was envisioning the possibility that Russia could modernize in a progressive noncapitalist manner, if its peasant-based revolutionary movement could link up with the working-class movements of Western Europe. I trace the evolution in his thought on this theme mainly in chapters 1, 6, and parts of 5. In a partially chronological framework, I take up the implicit unilinearism of *The Communist Manifesto* (1848) and the *Tribune* writings of the early 1850s, the multilinear theory of history carved out in the *Grundrisse* (1857–58) and the French edition of *Capital* (1872–75), and finally, through the multilinear late writings of 1879–82 on non-Western societies, among them Russia, India, and Latin America.

(2) Marx's writings on oppressed nationalities and ethnic groups—Poland, Ireland, Irish workers in Britain, and Blacks in the United States, and their relationship to the democratic and labor movements in the major capitalist countries—are the second major focus of this book. Marx discussed these issues in the *Tribune* and other newspapers, in the debates within the International Working Men's Association of the 1860s, and in *Capital*. From the 1840s onward, he consistently supported movements for the independence of Poland and Ireland, as well as the antislavery cause in the United States. But by the 1860s, with the emergence of the Civil War in America, the 1863 Polish uprising, and the Fenian movement in Ireland, his treatment of these issues took on a new urgency and underwent some alterations. They are the main focus of chapters 2, 3, 4, and parts of 5. During the 1860s, these issues became central to Marx's assessment of the working class movements of the two most powerful capitalist societies, Britain and the United States. He concluded that labor movements in core capitalist countries that failed to support adequately progressive nationalist movements on the part of those affected by their governments, or failed to combat racism toward ethnic minorities within their own societies, ran the danger of retarding or even cutting short their own development.

I will argue further that these two themes, which are at the center of this study, were not incidental to Marx's theorization of capitalism, but part of a complex analysis of the global social order of his time. Marx's proletariat was not only white and European, but also encompassed Black labor in America, as well as the Irish, not considered "white" at the time either by the dominant cultures of Britain and North America. Moreover, as capitalist modernity penetrated into Russia and Asia, undermining the precapitalist social orders of these societies, new possibilities for revolutionary change would, he held, emerge from these new locations. Here, his hopes centered on the communal social forms of the villages of India and Russia, which he saw as possible new *loci* of resistance to capital. Whether it concerned the Indian peasant or the

Russian villager, the Irish tenant farmer or immigrant worker in Britain, or the Black former slave in the southern United States, Marx kept searching for new allies of the Western working class in its struggle against capital.

Marx's positionality takes on some importance in yet another respect. While he was in a certain sense marginalized in Britain, from the beginning he refused to isolate himself within the German exile community. Instead, Marx became part of British society, keeping in contact with Chartists and other labor activists. He not only wrote in English for the *Tribune* but was also the author of a number of manifestos and addresses on the part of the International by the 1860s. Marx's life exemplified his ideal of internationalism, for by the end he was neither German nor British, but a European or even a global intellectual. It was from cosmopolitan London, the center of industry and empire, that he forged his mature critique of capital. To be sure, Marx's lifelong intellectual project centered on the critique of political economy—on the elaboration of a model of the structure of modern capitalist society and of the potential for its positive transformation through the movement for self-emancipation of the modern working class. In this book, however, I will be arguing that his writings on nationalism, ethnicity, and non-Western societies constituted an important, albeit neglected, part of that effort.

A NOTE ON MARX'S RELATIONSHIP TO ENGELS

Here at the outset, I would like to characterize briefly the Marx-Engels relationship. In this book, I will occasionally critique Engels and point to his differences with Marx. However, I do not agree with dismissive critics of Engels like Jean-Paul Sartre, who complains in his famous essay "Materialism and Revolution" (1949), of Marx's "unfortunate meeting with Engels" in 1844 ([1949] 1962, 248). Here, Sartre's verbal excess undercuts some valid critiques of Engels concerning the relationship of idealism to materialism and other issues important to dialectics. I regard many of Engels's more empirical writings as very significant contributions, especially *The Condition of the Working Class in England* (1844), a text frequently drawn on and praised by Marx that was written the very year they formed their intellectual friendship, and *The Peasant War in Germany* (1850). (These writings are highlighted in one of the most incisive counterattacks against critics of Engels [Gouldner 1980]). Engels's editing of volumes II and III of *Capital* was also an extremely important undertaking.

Nonetheless, Engels was not Marx, and unfortunately, in several areas, he placed serious obstacles in the way of grasping the fullness and originality of

Marx's contribution. This was true of his scientistic popularizations of the dialectic in works such as *Ludwig Feuerbach and the End of Classical German Philosophy* (1886). I have critiqued Engels on the dialectic in my earlier book on Lenin and Hegel (K. Anderson 1995), along the lines of what many others, such as the Hungarian Marxist philosopher Georg Lukács ([1923] 1971) and the German critical theorist Iring Fetscher (1971), had done before me.

It was also true of Engels's creation of a supposedly definitive text for *Capital*, volume I, after Marx's death, the fourth German edition (1890). As will be discussed in chapter 5, he often ignored Marx's 1872–75 French edition, a point brought out earlier—albeit sometimes one-sidedly—by the French Marx scholar Maximilien Rubel. Recently, the *Marx-Engels Gesamtausgabe* has published Marx's original drafts for volumes II and III of *Capital*, which has led to further critiques of Engels as editor of *Capital*.

Finally, it was true of Engels's *The Origin of the Family, Private Property and the State* (1884), where he evidenced a strong commitment to gender equality on the basis of anthropological findings but failed to match the subtlety of Marx's notebooks from the same period. This issue was first raised by the Marxist humanist philosopher Raya Dunayevskaya ([1982] 1991).

A NOTE ON SOURCES

Much of this study has drawn upon Marx's journalism, his organizational manifestos for the International, and his letters and unpublished notebooks.[3] His journalism for the *Tribune* and other newspapers has too often been dismissed as hackwork, yet as I will argue below, it contained significant theoretical analysis of non-Western societies, ethnicity, race, and nationalism, often in greater detail and depth than in *Capital* and his other writings on political economy. This was particularly true of his journalistic writings on India, Russia, and China, or those on race and slavery in America. Moreover, the most extensive of these journalistic writings, those for the *Tribune*, only become widely available in their entirety in their original English at the end of the 1980s, when they appeared in the *Collected Works* of Marx and Engels (hereafter referred to as MECW). Marx's organizational manifestos for the International brought out the themes of race and slavery, and to an even greater extent, his perspectives on Ireland and Poland. His letters reflected on all of the above issues. I draw upon the above sources in chapters 1 through 4, and in chapter 5 I return to the *Grundrisse* and *Capital*, where I examine the degree to which the issues of race, ethnicity, and non-Western societies found their way into Marx's core critiques of political economy. In chapter 5, I will argue that the themes of this study have a greater relationship than is usually realized—even when only as subtext—to what most would recognize as Marx's most important mature writings. His 1879–82 excerpt notebooks, many of them still unpublished in any language, will form an important part of this book, especially in chapter 6, which will examine his 1879–82 notebooks on India, Algeria, Latin America, and Indonesia. These writings occupied Marx at a time when many, including Engels, had expected him to be concentrating on what was to become volumes II and III of *Capital*, which his friend edited for publication after his death in 1883. I will argue that these 1879–82 notebooks show a new turn in his thought, toward a greater concentration on non-Western societies.

Why such a focus on relatively obscure writings rather than Marx's "major" ones? Here a few remarks are in order. It is hard to think of other modern theorists with so small a ratio of writings published during their lifetimes to those actually written. Part of this was due to Marx's poverty and ill health through most of his mature years, part to his marginalization as a political exile, and part to his constant rewriting and revising of texts. Works today considered central to the Marxian canon, such as the 1844 *Economic and Philosophical Manuscripts*, the *German Ideology*, the *Grundrisse*, and volumes II and III of *Capital*, were not published during Marx's lifetime. Therefore, the mere fact that Marx did not write a particular text for publication should be noted, but should not prevent us from considering whether it has something important to say. To be sure, what is taken to be the Marxian canon has shifted over the years. In the early twentieth century, he was viewed as a political economist and champion of the industrial worker. Since then, scholars like Louis Dupré (1983) have taken a far more expansive view of Marx, seeing him as a critic of capitalist modernity as a whole, as a dialectical and humanist philosopher, as a sociologist of alienation, and as a cultural critic. In bringing to the fore Marx's 1879–82 excerpt notebooks on non-Western societies, his earlier *Tribune* writings on these same societies, his discussion of precapitalist societies in the *Grundrisse* and the French edition of *Capital*, and other neglected Marx writings, this book seeks to shift the Marx canon further. I argue for a move toward a twenty-first-century notion of Marx as a global theorist whose social critique included notions of capital and class that were open and broad enough to encompass the particularities of nationalism, race, and ethnicity, as well as the varieties of human social and historical development, from Europe to Asia and from the Americas to Africa. Thus, I will be presenting Marx as a much more multilinear theorist of history and society than is generally supposed, as someone immersed the study of the concrete social reality of Asian societies as well as Western capitalist ones, and as a theorist who took account of nationalism and ethnicity as well as class. Further, I will be arguing that Marx was a theorist whose concept of capitalism as a social system was not an abstract universal, but instead was imbued with a rich and concrete social vision in which universality and particularity interacted within a dialectical totality.

Colonial Encounters in the 1850s: The European Impact on India, Indonesia, and China

In 1848, Marx and Engels[1] refer briefly to colonialism in *The Communist Manifesto*, pointing to the rise of the capitalist world market that "draws all, even the most barbarian, nations into civilization." Further:

> The bourgeoisie, by the rapid improvement of all instruments of production, by the immensely facilitated means of communication, draws all, even the most barbarian nations into civilization. The cheap prices of its commodities are the heavy artillery with which it batters down all Chinese walls, with which it forces the barbarians' intensely obstinate hatred of the foreigners to capitulate. It compels all nations, on pain of extinction, to adopt the bourgeois mode of production; it compels them to introduce what it calls civilization into their midst, i.e., to become bourgeois themselves. In one word, it creates a world after its own image. (MECW 6, 488)[2]

Except for the qualifier "what it calls" before the word "civilization," the above discussion, a reference to the East before moving back to European developments, seems (1) to view Western colonial incursions into Asia, including England's notorious First Opium War against China of 1839–42, as on the whole progressive and beneficial; and (2) to assume that the rest of the world would sooner or later follow in the footsteps of the more industrially advanced Western European nations.[3]

It is very important, however, to view this passage, disturbing as it is in its ethnocentrism and implicit unilinearism, in its proper context. It occurs amid the opening pages of the *Manifesto*, pages that paint a dazzling portrait of the achievements of capitalist modernization inside Europe, and that say nothing about the lot of the European workers or their revolt. The decidedly non-Marxist economist Joseph Schumpeter has rightly called these opening pages "a panegyric upon bourgeois achievement that has no equal in economic literature" (1949, 209). The bourgeoisie, write Marx and Engels, has uprooted stultifying traditional social structures. It "has pitilessly torn asunder the motley feudal ties that bound people to their 'natural superiors,'" it "has torn away from the family its sentimental veil," and it has exposed the "slothful indolence" of the "Middle Ages" (MECW 6, 486–87).[4] The bourgeoisie has not only uprooted the premodern order, however, it has also built a new society in its place: "It has been the first to show what the activity of human beings can bring about. It has accomplished wonders far surpassing Egyptian pyramids, Roman aqueducts, and Gothic cathedrals" (MECW 6, 487). Further, it "has created more massive and more colossal productive forces than have all preceding generations together" (MECW 6, 489). As is well known, these opening paragraphs of the *Manifesto* are followed by a far less flattering portrait of capitalism, one in which its inner contradictions pull it apart, first by way of the economic crises which Marx and Engels viewed as endemic to this particular social system, and second from the revolt of labor against the alienating and exploitative conditions of modern production.

Therefore, Marx and Engels's praise for Western colonialism's conquests in Asia in the *Manifesto* can be seen as part of their overall sketch of the achievements of capitalism in Western Europe and North America, a sketch that is followed by a withering critique. However, while they revisit these capitalist achievements inside Western Europe and North America, showing their contradictions, they do not do so with regard to Western colonialism in Asia. This suggests that at this time, Marx held to an implicitly unilinear model of development, according to which non-Western societies[5] would, as they were swept into the world capitalist system, soon develop similar contradictions to those of the already industrializing countries. This model was only implicit, because he gave little specific attention to non-Western societies in this period.[6]

After Marx's move to London in 1849, this gap in his worldview would begin to disappear, and, from 1853 onwards, he would devote a considerable amount of his intellectual efforts to the study of such major non-Western societies as India, Indonesia, China, and Russia, while also taking up revolutionary nationalism in Ireland and Poland as well as the dialectics of race and class in the United States. In this chapter, I will examine his writings in the 1850s on India, Indonesia, and China. Here and elsewhere, I will point to changes and developments in Marx's thinking. In so doing, I will be challenging interpretations such as those of Shlomo Avineri, who writes in the introduction to his edition of Marx's writings on colonialism: "The general tone of Marx's views on the non-European world is set in *The Communist Manifesto*" (Marx 1968, 1).

THE 1853 WRITINGS ON INDIA: QUALIFIED SUPPORT FOR COLONIALISM

Marx's 1853 writings on India have been the source of tremendous controversy, with critics of Marx pointing to them as proof of his Eurocentrism. These writings formed part of his work as a correspondent for the *New York Tribune*, an effort to which Engels also made important contributions, usually published under Marx's name. The *Tribune* articles were often accompanied by substantial letters between Marx and Engels during their composition. With a circulation of two hundred thousand, the *Tribune* was unquestionably the most important U.S. newspaper during the nineteenth century. Editorially progressive, it took a strong antislavery stance with somewhat eclectic leanings toward both utopian socialism and northern manufacturing interests. In a discussion of the origins of socialism in the United States, Socialist Party leader Eugene Debs makes the following assessment of *Tribune* founder Horace Greeley: "The power of Greeley's influence in the early history of the Socialist movement in America, when hate and persecution were aroused by the mere mention of it, has never yet been fairly recognized. . . . Horace Greeley was in the true sense a labor leader. He was the first president of Typographical Union No. 6 of New York City and took advanced ground on every question that affected the working class" (Debs 1908, 100; see also Reitz 2008). This did not exclude a certain unease about publishing Marx, however. At one point in 1853, *Tribune* editors informed their readers that "Mr. Marx has very decided opinions of his own, with some of which we are far from agreeing," while at the same time praising him as "one of the most instructive sources of information on the greatest questions of current European politics" (cited in Ledbetter 2007, xxi).

Marx served as the *Tribune*'s chief European correspondent for over a decade, from 1851 to 1862, the longest and most remunerative employment of his life. His writings for the *Tribune* constitute a far more serious and sustained affair than is generally realized. They fill most of the contents of volumes 12 through 17 of the MECW, each of which runs over five hundred pages. In this study, I will be concentrating on Marx's (and occasionally Engels's)[7] *Tribune* writings on India, China, Russia, and other non-Western societies, as well as those on Ireland and Poland. It should be noted, however, that Marx's *Tribune* writings contain even more coverage of Britain, France, Germany, Italy, Austria, and other Western European countries. They deal with parliaments and kings, with wars and revolutions, with economic crises, and with the labor movement. Many of them were reprinted in the Chartist *People's Paper* and in other British organs of the Left. To date, there has been no comprehensive analysis of Marx's *Tribune* writings, the whole of which were not even available in English (their original language) in an accessible form until they were published in the English-language MECW in the 1980s.

All too often, the *Tribune* articles have been dismissed as merely occasional pieces that distracted Marx from his writings on political economy.[8] In part, this is because of remarks in Marx's own letters disparaging his journalism. For example, in a letter of September 15, 1853, to a close colleague in the United States, the German émigré Adolph Cluss, he states that he finds "perpetual scribbling for the newspapers tiresome," and expresses the wish "to withdraw into solitude for a few months and work at my Economy" (MECW 39, 367). These private reservations during Marx's initial years with the *Tribune* should not be ignored, and his *Tribune* writings should not be ranked in importance alongside key theoretical texts, such as the *1844 Manuscripts*, the *Grundrisse*, or *Capital*. Nonetheless, Marx expended considerable scholarly and intellectual effort on his *Tribune* articles, in which he publicly expressed pride on several occasions. For example, nearly a decade after beginning to write for the *Tribune*, Marx published, as an appendix to his *Herr Vogt* (1860), a letter from the *Tribune*'s managing editor, Charles Dana, who had met Marx in Germany during the 1848 revolution. Dana's letter, dated March 8, 1860, states: "Nearly nine years ago I engaged you to write for the *New York Tribune*, and the engagement has been continued ever since. You have written for us constantly, without a single week's interruption, that I can remember; and you are not only one of the most highly valued, but one of the best paid contributors attached to the journal" (MECW 17, 323). Marx would, however, judging from his correspondence, have quarreled with the implication that he was well paid!

Although this letter was also quoted after Marx's death by no less an authority than Eleanor Marx in the preface to a volume republishing some of the *Tribune* writings on Russia and Turkey (Marx [1897] 1969), Marx's *Tribune* writings continue to be minimized or even ignored. This may be because the Continental European scholars who have dominated Marxist studies have tended to play down the importance of texts that Marx composed in English rather than German. Whether or not that is the case, the disparagement of the *Tribune* articles has contributed to a lack of attention to Marx's writings on non-Western societies, which also include his excerpt notes on books on these societies, many of them also written primarily in English. Bias in favor of texts Marx composed in German may even have distorted how volume I of *Capital* has been read, with a curious privileging of the Engels-edited 1890 edition over the last version of that work that Marx personally prepared for publication, the 1872–75 French edition.[9]

Although Marx began to publish in the *Tribune* in 1851, in that first year all of the articles published under his name were in fact written by Engels. Afterwards, Engels continued to write under Marx's name and for a while some of Marx's German drafts were translated by his friend into English, given his still relatively limited command of the language. For the first two years, their articles focused exclusively on the main countries of Western Europe such as France, Germany, Austria, and Britain,[10] but by 1853 the Russo-Turkish conflict in the Balkans and the Eastern Mediterranean threatened to place this issue, then called the "Eastern Question," at the forefront of European politics. Marx pointed to the growing importance of the Eastern Question, but admitted privately his lack of knowledge of the subject matter,[11] writing to Engels on March 10, 1853: "But this question is primarily military and geographical,[12] hence outside my *département*. So you must once more *exécuter* [do it]. What is to become of the Turkish Empire is something I have no clue about. I cannot therefore present a general perspective" (MECW 39, 288).

Marx quickly began to remedy this gap in his *Tribune* articles on India, all of them offering a general portrait of Indian society and of British rule rather than responses to immediate events. His 1853 articles on India were occasioned by the parliamentary debates over the renewal of the charter of the privately held British East India Company. The inventory of Marx's unpublished excerpt notebooks held by the International Institute of Social History in Amsterdam lists notes on dozens of titles on India, Java, Turkey, and Russia for the year 1853, among them writings by François Bernier on India and Thomas Stamford Raffles on Indonesia. In a long letter to Engels dated June 2, 1853,[13] Marx gives some indications of his library studies on India. He quotes at length "old François Bernier" (MECW 39, 332) on the military and social organization of the Mughal Empire in India, and then concludes: "Bernier rightly sees all the manifestations of the East—he mentions Turkey, Persia, and Hindustan— as having a common basis, namely the absence of private landed property. This is the real key, even to the eastern heaven" (MECW 39, 333–34).

Besides Bernier and Raffles, Marx's 1853 India articles are clearly influenced by Hegel, especially his *Philosophy of History*. Among others, the French sociologist Michael Löwy contends that this Hegelian influence led Marx to a "teleological and Eurocentric" notion of progress in these writings, something from which he later moved away (Löwy 1996, 199; see also Curtis 2009).[14] In the *Philosophy of History*, Hegel subjects Indian culture and society to a harsh critique.[15] He terms the caste system "the most degrading spiritual serfdom" (1956, 144), emphasizing as well the often-involuntary ritual suicide of widows (*sati*). In addition, and here more problematically, Hegel dismisses India as a society that "has remained stationary and fixed" (142). Due to a supposedly timeless Brahmin domination, "all political revolutions, therefore, are matters of indifference to the common Hindoo, for his lot is unchanged" (154). Thus, as a society where no real change or development had occurred, India had no real history. Even where Indian religions like Buddhism spread widely, Hegel adds, "the diffusion of Indian culture is only a dumb deedless expansion; that is, it presents no political action" (142). Likewise, Indian intellectuals, while having made great discoveries in grammar and in "Geometry, Astronomy, and Algebra" (161),[16] lack self-awareness and individual "self-consciousness," rendering them "incapable of writing History" (162). Moreover, Indian society was for Hegel essentially passive, having "achieved no foreign conquests" and having been continually "vanquished" (142). Endorsing Western colonialism as the product of historical necessity, Hegel concludes in teleological fashion that it was "the necessary fate of Asiatic Empires to be subjected to Europeans" (142). This passivity also undergirded internal despotism; in other countries, "tyranny rouses man to resentment. . . . But in India it is normal: for here there is no sense of personal independence with which a state of despotism could be compared" (161). Hegel also attacks Hindu mysticism as a form of "pure self-renouncing Idealism" (159) that created a "Dream-World," where "evil passions have their full swing" (148). This mysticism had the additional effect of making despotism and caste oppression more endurable. As the American anthropologist and Marx editor Lawrence Krader points out, however, Hegel's perspective, for all its limitations, had some advantages over previous Western theorizing about India and Asia. This is because it was more concrete and historical: "The economic order, however, was not omitted, as it had been by Montesquieu; the geographic nonsense of Montesquieu falls away in Hegel" (Krader 1975, 45).

While Marx's 1853 India articles exhibit a strong Hegelian influence, they are no mere recapitulation of Hegel. As the distinguished Indian historian Irfan Habib notes, in the most careful analysis of Marx's 1850s writings on India to date, even as early as 1853, his "conception of India was by no means an edited restatement of Hegel."[17] Habib holds that this was because, as against Hegel's focus on religion as the determinant, for Marx, "the peculiarities of Indian culture were really themselves the consequence of Indian social organization, pre-eminently the village community" (Habib 2006, xii). Up to a point, this is correct, but it does not acknowledge another key element absent in Hegel but prominent in Marx's analysis of India. This was what Marx perceived as Hinduism's deep-seated antihumanism, in his view its elevation of nature, as symbolized by sacred animals, over human beings.

Marx's first substantial publication on a non-Western society, "The British Rule in India," appeared in the *Tribune* on June 25, 1853.[18] In it, he compares India's divisions along geographic lines to those of Italy, and its victimization by British conquerors to that of Ireland. Referring to the many invasions of India, he concludes: "There cannot, however, remain any doubt but that the misery inflicted by the British on Hindostan is of an essentially different and infinitely more intensive kind than all Hindostan had to suffer before" (MECW 12, 126). Citing Raffles on Java, Marx argues that the latter's devastating description of the greed and exploitativeness of the Dutch East India Company could also be applied to what happened in India under the British East India Company.

Unlike previous conquerors, who were soon absorbed by Indian civilization, Marx writes that the British were for the first time going below "its surface," for "England has broken down the entire framework of Indian society" (MECW 12, 126). Before the British conquest, India's overall social structure "remained unaltered since its remotest antiquity" (128).[19] Britain destroyed the traditional Indian economy and social structure mainly "by the working of English steam and English free trade" (131), which displaced the traditional textile industry and "inundated the very mother country of cotton with cottons" (128). The British have "thus produced the greatest, and to speak the truth, the only social revolution ever heard of in Asia" (132).[20] The Indian historian Bipan Chandra suggests that in 1853 Marx was working with "the theoretical assumption that capitalism would create a mirror image in the colony," a position he later abandoned (1980, 402).

It is in this article that Marx also begins to sketch a concept of "Oriental despotism," which he applies to a broad range of societies, among them China, ancient Egypt, Persia, and Mesopotamia: "There have been in Asia, generally, from immemorial times, but three departments of Government; that of Finance, or the plunder of the interior; that of War, or the plunder of the exterior; and, finally, the department of Public Works" (MECW 12, 127). The economic basis of this despotism was the need for large-scale irrigation works:

Climate and territorial conditions, especially the vast tracts of desert, extending from the Sahara, through Arabia, Persia, India, and Tartary, to the most elevated Asiatic highlands, constituted artificial irrigation by canals and water-works the basis of Oriental agriculture. . . . This prime necessity of an economical and common use of water, which, in the Occident, drove private enterprise to voluntary association, as in Flanders and Italy, necessitated, in the Orient where civilization was too low and the territorial extent too vast to call into life voluntary association, the interference of the centralizing power of Government. Hence an economical function devolved upon all Asiatic Governments, the function of providing public works. (MECW 12, 127)

He adds that the British, however, unlike previous conquerors of India, "have neglected entirely" their responsibility to construct "public works," resulting in "the deterioration of an agriculture which is not capable of being conducted on the British principle of free competition" (127).

Besides public works, the second economic foundation of this pre-British "Oriental despotism" with its strong centralized state was to be found in the social structure of the Indian village: "We must not forget that these idyllic village-communities, inoffensive though they may appear, had always been the solid foundation of Oriental despotism" (MECW 12, 132). Again using material provided by Raffles, Marx argues that the economically self-sufficient Indian "village system" had, from "remotest times" (128), continued basically unaltered in the face of numerous conquests and changes of rulers at the top.[21] This resulted in a "stagnatory, and vegetative life" (132). As Avineri notes, " 'stagnation' in this context is for Marx not a mere economic and technological designation, but an anthropological determination: if man's creative ability is his distinctive trait, then stagnation is the worst adjective that may be attributed to any society" (1968, 169). Despite their many beautiful features, Marx adds, "these little communities were contaminated by distinctions of caste and by slavery" (MECW 12, 132).

Instead of "elevating man" and developing a humanist perspective, he writes that in the traditional Indian village system:

they transformed a self-developing social state into never changing natural destiny, and thus brought about a brutalizing worship of nature, exhibiting its degradation in the fact that man, the sovereign of nature, fell down on his knees in adoration of Kanuman, the monkey, and Sabbala, the cow. (MECW 12, 132)

Marx concludes his article by quoting a stanza from Goethe's *West-Eastern Divan [Diwan]* a long poem on the Turkic conqueror Timur, who had carried out an infamous massacre of the population of Delhi in 1398:

> Should this torture then torment us
> Since it brings us greater pleasure?
> Were not through the rule of Timur
> Souls devoured without measure? (MECW 12, 133)

Let us now proceed to examine Marx's use of this stanza in greater detail.

MARX, GOETHE, AND EDWARD SAID'S CRITIQUE OF EUROCENTRISM

Marx's article "The British Rule in India," especially the notion in the concluding stanza from Goethe of suffering in India bringing in the end "greater pleasure," that is, progress, has sparked some scathing criticisms, most notably in Edward Said's classic *Orientalism*: "Though Marx's humanity, his sympathy for the misery of the people, are clearly engaged" as he describes the destructiveness of British colonialism, Said holds, "in the end it is the Romantic Orientalist vision that wins out" (1978, 154). Moreover, writes Said, Marx puts forward the "ideal of regenerating a fundamentally lifeless Asia" by way of British colonialism (154). At first, Said continues, "Marx was still able to identify even a little with poor Asia," but "after he was dispatched to Goethe as a source of wisdom on the Orient," the Orientalist "labels took over" and "a wash of sentiment therefore disappeared as it encountered the unshakable definitions built up by Orientalist science, supported by 'Oriental' lore (e.g. the [Goethe's] *Diwan*)" (155). Said avers, "in article after article he returned *with increasing conviction* to the idea that even in destroying Asia, Britain was making possible there a real social revolution" (153; emphasis added). Similarly to Avineri, Said is arguing that Marx's perspectives on non-Western societies remained basically unchanged after this early period.

Certainly, Said is correct in pointing to elements of Eurocentrism in Marx's "The British Rule in India."[22] The renowned literary theorist is surely mistaken, however, when he has Marx relying on a poet, even one as brilliant as Goethe, as his "source of wisdom on the Orient."[23] The literary theorist's failure to discuss or even mention the nineteenth-century context of the stanza from Goethe is more surprising. First, in Goethe's book-length poem, *West-Eastern Divan*, initially published in 1815, the figure of Timur is almost certainly linked closely to that of Napoleon, with the parallel between the two built in part on the fact that each met defeat in an ambitious military campaign in winter—Timur's into China and Napoleon's into Russia.[24] The link to Napoleon also suggests one to the French Revolution, whose combination of creativity and destruction so inspired intellectuals of Goethe's generation.[25]

Second and more importantly, Marx continued to cite the Goethe stanza on numerous occasions, but in a different context than India, that of the dehumanization of the industrial worker. In his definitive study, *Karl Marx and World Literature* (1976), a source Said does not mention, S. S. Prawer refers to one such occasion: Marx's January 1855 *Neue Oder-Zeitung* article on the economic crisis in England. Marx writes that if capital's power were not checked, "A whole generation of workers would have lost 50 per cent of its physical strength, mental development and ability to live. The same Manchester school . . . will answer our misgivings with the words: 'Should this torture then torment us, since it brings us greater pleasure'" (cited in Prawer 1976, 248; see also MECW 13, 576).[26] Here, Marx seems hardly to agree with the sentiments expressed in these lines from Goethe, nor to lack compassion for those suffering under capitalism's "torture." Could this mean that Marx also used the Goethe stanza in his India article to characterize the British colonialist perspective rather than his own?

The German critical theorist Iring Fetscher mentions another place where Marx subsequently quoted the Goethe stanza, again on the suffering of factory workers. Fetscher maintains that this text undercuts the notion that Marx was "justifying" the type of "social revolution" that Britain was carrying out in India (1991, 113). The later use of the stanza to which Fetscher refers occurs in Marx's 1861–63 economic manuscripts,[27] as follows:

[Fifteen] men are killed every week in the English coal mines on an average. In the course of the 10 years concluding with 1861 killed about 10,000 people. Mostly by the sordid avarice of the owners of the coal mines. This generally to be remarked. The capitalistic production is—to a certain degree, when we abstract from the whole process of circulation and the immense complications of commercial and monetary transactions resulting from the basis, the value in exchange—most economical of *realized labor*, labor realized in commodities. It is a greater spendthrift than any other mode of production of man, of living labor, spendthrift not only of flesh and blood and muscles, but of brains and nerves. It is, in fact, only at the greatest waste of individual development that the

article written in this period, Marx refers in passing to the legal "suppression of the Suttee [*sati*]," the ancient Hindu practice of coercing widows to commit suicide upon the death of their husbands, as well as the "emancipation of the East India press." But he makes clear that these reforms, which he evidently applauds, were in fact nearly blocked at the upper levels of colonial administration, having been enacted by "individual Governors who had acted on their own responsibility" (MECW 12, 181).

Elsewhere during these same weeks in the summer of 1853, Marx touched on the super-exploitation of the Indian peasant, or *ryot*, under the British-created system of landownership and tenancy, superimposed on the ancient system of *zemindars* and *ryots*. Formerly, the *zemindars*, a semihereditary class of local officials, had merely collected revenue for the state from the *ryots*, keeping a portion for themselves. Under the "final settlement" of 1793 enacted by Lord Charles Cornwallis in Bengal at the behest of British prime minister William Pitt, the *zemindars* gained Western-style private ownership, with the right to evict *ryots* from land that their ancestors had cultivated for centuries and over which they had exercised possessory rights. Henceforth, there was no limit to how much the *ryot* could be squeezed from above, since a whole system of reciprocal rights and duties had been destroyed at a single stroke. Marx describes the lot of the *ryot*:

> The Ryot is subject, like the French peasant, to the extortion of the private usurer; but he has no hereditary, no permanent title in his land, like the French peasant. Like the serf he is forced to cultivation, but he is not secured against want like the serf. Like the *métayer* [sharecropper] he has to divide his produce with the State, but the State is not obliged, with regard to him, to advance the funds and the stock, as it is obliged to do with regard to the *métayer*.... The ryots—and they form 11–12ths of the whole Indian population—have been wretchedly pauperized. (MECW 12, 215)

In this article, Marx also refers to cholera epidemics in India, which he sees as resulting from extreme pauperization. He calls their spread abroad "India's revenge upon the Western world,"[31] and, ever the revolutionary humanist, adds that this development is "a striking and severe example of the solidarity of human woes and wrongs" (216).

Marx's last major article on India in this period, "The Future Results of British Rule in India," was published on August 8, 1853. He begins by arguing that India was "the predestined prey of conquest" because it was so disunited. India was "not only divided between Mahommedan and Hindoo, but between tribe and tribe, between caste and caste." Therefore, India's history "is the history of the successive conquests she has undergone." Then, with some strong Eurocentric overtones, Marx adds that "Indian society has no history at all, at least no known history," calling it an "unresisting and unchanging society" (MECW 12, 217). This phrase is possibly one of the keys to Marx's condescension toward India in this period. As he saw it in 1853, the Indians, unlike the Chinese, had allowed their great and ancient civilization to be conquered by the British in an "unresisting" manner.[32]

In the next few paragraphs, Marx discusses in glowing terms what he considers to be the modernizing effects of British colonialism on Indian society: "England has to fulfill a double mission in India: one destructive, the other regenerating—the annihilation of old Asiatic society, and the laying the material foundations of Western society in Asia" (MECW 12, 217–18). Lapsing into ethnocentrism, he writes that unlike previous conquerors of India, who were themselves "conquered by the superior civilization of their subjects," the British "were the first conquerors superior, and therefore, inaccessible to Hindoo civilization." Moreover, this was due to "an eternal law of history" (218).[33]

The British brought the telegraph, the "free press, introduced for the first time into Asiatic society," "private property in land," modern scientific education, steam power, direct and rapid communication with the West, and railroads (MECW 12, 218). Marx predicts that the railroad will become "the forerunner of modern industry" (220), which would "dissolve the hereditary divisions of labor, upon which rest the Indian castes, those decisive impediments to Indian progress and Indian power" (221). Marx also cites an East India Company official who acknowledges that the Indian people were "remarkable for a mathematical clearness of head, and talent for figures and exact sciences" (220).

Then, similarly to his use of the stanza from Goethe on Timur in his earlier article, he asks, concerning the destructive elements of British conquest: "Has [the bourgeoisie] ever effected a progress without dragging individuals and people through blood and dirt, through misery and degradation?" (MECW 12, 221).

Up to this point, Marx's article exhibits a conceptual structure similar to "The British Rule in India," in that he argues for the overall progressiveness of British colonialism. As I noted at the beginning of this chapter, this argument is similar to that of the opening pages of *The Communist Manifesto* on the achievements of capitalism in Western Europe and North America, but without, as in his discussion of the industrializing world, pointing to deep contradictions welling up from within this capitalist modernization as it reached India.

Here, in "The Future Results of British Rule in India," which concludes his 1853 series of articles on India, the structure and tone of Marx's argument shift subtly, becoming more dialectical. He begins for the first time to refer to the need for a social revolution in Britain to change colonial policy. More strikingly, he also points to the possibility of an Indian national liberation movement:

> The Indians will not reap the fruits of the new elements of society scat-
> tered among them by the British bourgeoisie, till in Great Britain itself the
> now ruling classes shall have been supplanted by the industrial proletariat,
> or till the Hindoos themselves shall have grown strong enough to throw
> off the English yoke altogether. At all events, we may safely expect to see,
> at a more or less remote period, the regeneration of that great and interest-
> ing country, whose gentle natives . . . have astonished the British officers
> by their bravery, whose country has been the source of our languages, our
> religions, and who represent the type of the ancient German in the Jat,
> and the type of the ancient Greek in the Brahmin. (MECW 12, 221)[34]

Then, he refers to "the inherent barbarism of bourgeois civilization" (221), almost reversing the ethnocentric distinction between superior and inferior civilizations with which he began the article. This is the first sign of a shift from the position of *The Communist Manifesto*.

The British historian Victor Kiernan writes that the lengthy passage cited above shows that "if Marx felt little respect for Indian society, he had no con-tempt for Indians, believing them perfectly capable to learn to run their own country" (1967, 163). Habib goes further: "In 1853 to set colonial emancipation, not just colonial reform, as an objective of the European socialist movement; and still more, to look forward to a national liberation movement ('throwing off the English yoke') attained through their struggle by the Indian people, as an event that might even precede the emancipation of the European working class—such insight and vision could belong to Marx alone" (2006, liv).

The dialectical structure of "The Future Results of British Rule in India" parallels that of *The Communist Manifesto*. As in the *Manifesto*, Marx cele-brates effusively the modernizing features of bourgeois rule, in this case Brit-ish colonialism, pointing to its undermining of caste, of *sati*, of localism, and its introduction of modern science and technology, as well as some aspects of modern political rights. Then, employing the withering critique of dialectical reason, he proceeds to note the contradictory character of that progress.[35] In the *Manifesto*, he and Engels pointed to two main contradictions inside Euro-pean capitalism, the endemic and periodic economic crises, which threatened the stability of the newly arisen capitalist society, and the rise of an oppositional working class. In the 1853 India articles, Marx predicted that British capitalism would also face a twin challenge, the rise of the British working classes (the internal crisis) and the rise of an Indian national liberation movement (the external crisis). However, while the structure of the argument is similar to that of the *Manifesto* concerning capital and labor, its content is quite different. By 1853, Marx has begun to overcome the one-sidedness of the treatment of non-Western societies in the *Manifesto*. Although Chinese (and Indian) walls continue to be battered down by what Marx still evidently considered to be the progressive effects of world trade and even colonial conquest, people from within non-Western societies are now credited with the potential of "throwing off the English yoke altogether" and self-starting the "regeneration" of their societies and cultures. This regeneration would not, however, any more than the struggle of the Western working classes, be aimed at a return to the precapitalist past. It would retain the achievements of capitalist modernity.

THE 1853 NOTES ON INDONESIA

Marx's excerpt notebooks of 1853 offer additional illumination on his thinking about India. In 1853, Marx made some fifty pages of handwritten notes on India as well as five pages on Indonesia, material that is eventually to appear in MEGA² IV/11. Given Marx's miniscule handwriting—he often squeezes nine hundred or more words onto a single page—these notes, none of which have been published in any form, would comprise around a hundred printed pages. Among them, the five pages of notes on Indonesia contain excerpts from and occasional summaries in German of Thomas Stamford Raffles's classic two-volume study, *The History of Java*, originally published in 1817. These notes are of special interest for several reasons. First, I should mention the high quality and enduring reputation of Raffles's pioneering study. It has been termed "one of the classics of South-East Asian historiography" by the British historian John Bastin in his introduction to a 1965 reprint, and a "brilliant work" by the Javanese-Dutch historian and Marx scholar Fritjof Tichelman (1983, 14). Raffles, the colonial governor during Britain's brief rule over Indonesia during the Napoleonic wars, after which the colony was returned to Dutch rule, was a man of immense intellectual curiosity as well as sympathy for the indigenous population. His position as an outsider freed him to critique what he saw as some extremely oppressive aspects of Dutch rule. Second, Marx's notes on Raffles stress those parts of the latter's work that drew comparisons to India; looking at them will therefore deepen our understanding of his India writings. Third, these 1853 notes constitute Marx's most sustained study of what is today Indonesia until the last years of his life, when he again returned to the subject.

Unlike some of his other excerpt notebooks, which contain, in addition to simple extracts from the work he is studying, summaries in his own words, critiques, and other comments, Marx's 1853 notes on Indonesia are composed almost entirely of extracts from Raffles's classic study. Nonetheless, a look at the selection, ordering, and content of the material Marx incorporated into his notes reveals something important. Marx's perspective is of course different from that of the Governor Raffles, whose outlook Tichelman summarizes as "bridging two periods: the late eighteenth century—Rousseauian influences, Wilberforce's antislavery campaign, the idea of the 'noble savage,' all of mankind being entitled to the benefits of Western civilization—and the beginning of the nineteenth century with the idea of the mission of the West to civilize barbarous overseas countries" (1983, 14–15). The latter included plans to introduce an English-style economic liberalization, never implemented due to Britain's return of Indonesia to the Dutch after the war.

Marx begins his notes not with the main text of Raffles's book, which is devoted to Indonesia's most populous island, Java, but with an appendix on the economically and politically less developed island of Bali. As Tichelman suggests, in Marx's eyes Indonesian conditions "seemed to correspond to the relationship between the ryot (landowning taxable farmer/peasant) and the zemindar in Bengal before the introduction of the permanent (land)-revenue settlement by Cornwallis" in the 1790s (1983, 16). Marx begins his notes by incorporating material pointing to Bali's isolation from large-scale ocean trade due to its lack of good harbors. The next passage he takes into his notebook describes the inhabitants of Bali who, while adhering to a form of Hinduism and suffering under the "despotism" of their village chiefs, nonetheless "still possess much of the original boldness and self-willed hardihood of the savage state" (Raffles [1817] 1965, 2:cxxxi).[36] Marx next incorporates a passage describing Balinese women: "Their women . . . here on a perfect equality with the men, and not required to perform any of the severe and degrading labors imposed upon them in Java" (cxxxi; ellipsis in Marx's notes). He also records one suggesting that while the people revere their ruler, "their minds are not broken down by numerous demands on their submission" (cxxxii). Also, although Marx's stress in the 1853 India writings was, as we have seen, on how the self-contained communal village could be a building block for "Oriental despotism," here Marx's notes seem to emphasize an earlier period, before despotic rule imposed itself on the social structure and even the "minds" of the villagers. Marx does not refer to or develop this point on the freer side of the traditional village commune in his 1853 writings on India, but it reemerges in his 1879–82 writings as a point from which progressive resistance to capital might develop.

After skipping some text on culture and religion, Marx focuses on land and property relations. He records a statement by Raffles to the effect that, as against the situation in Java, in Bali "the sovereign is not here considered as the universal landlord; on the contrary, the soil is almost invariably considered as the private property of the subject." Moreover, due to their mud-walled houses, "the principal towns are said to resemble the Hindoo towns on the continent of India" (Raffles [1817] 1965, 2:cxxxiv). Marx is also careful to record material on oppressive features of life in Bali, including opium addiction, slavery, *sati*, and the caste system, the latter including an outcast group "not permitted to reside in a village" (cxxxviii). Here the pattern of what Marx records suggests that he has a less idyllic view of Bali than did Raffles, influenced as he was by Rousseau.

Next, Marx turns to the main part of the book on Java proper. He ignores the chapters on geography and "race," focusing again on land tenure. Marx begins by taking down a passage comparing Java to India, particularly Bengal: "The relative situation, rank, and privileges of the village farmer and the native chief of Java, correspond in most instances, with those of the Ryot and Zemindar of Bengal" (Raffles [1817] 1965, 1:135). Raffles's comparison is not, however, to the India of 1853, but to that before Cornwallis's "permanent settlement" anointed the *zemindar* as a proprietary landlord. In Java, it seemed, there was a tripartite arrangement rather than Western-type exclusive property in land. First, the *ryot* had the right "to retain the land he cultivated," if the tax in money or kind was paid. This, according to Raffles, "seemed to raise his character above that of an ordinary tenant, removable at pleasure, or at the conclusion of a stipulated term" (136). Second came the *zemindar*, a tax collector with some but not all of the rights of a Western European landlord. Third came the "sovereign," who had the power to remove "both Zemindar and Ryot, in case of negligence or disobedience" (136). Thus, the *zemindars* of Java lacked exclusive property rights. Instead, rights to the land flowed out of a reciprocal arrangement among sovereign, middleman, and peasant, with the sovereign discouraged by tradition from the sudden removal of loyal *zemindars* or *ryots*.

Tichelman sums up precisely the variations in the above arrangements, which Marx follows closely in this section of his excerpt notes:

Marx's attention was primarily drawn to Javanese village relations and land tenure, including the differences between three regions: 1. the mountainous Priangan lands in the West (a relatively prosperous, not too densely populated zone with frontier features), with strong village autonomy, more or less private landownership and collective village claims on noncultivated waste land; 2. the coastal area to the North of the Priangan, Cheribon (Cirebon), where the native chiefs claimed property rights to the land, and where much land was farmed out to Chinese entrepreneurs (for sugar cultivation in particular); [3.] the northeast coast (also a commercialized area with a pre-colonial background of inter-Asian commerce and shipping) with no direct claims on property or land, to the detriment of the cultivator. (1983, 16)

Thus, except in the more isolated Priangan lands, the older and more communal property forms had been undermined by overseas trade and the capitalist forms introduced by the Dutch.

The overarching ruler was of course the Dutch East India Company, which Raffles felt free to condemn. In the following paragraph, which Marx incorporates, Raffles attacks the overall oppression of the people of Java as worse than slavery:

The Dutch Company, actuated solely by the spirit of gain, and viewing their Javan subjects with less regard or consideration than a West-India planter formerly viewed the gang upon his estate, because the latter had paid the purchase-money of human property which the other had not, employed all the pre-existing machinery of despotism, to squeeze from the people their utmost mite of contribution, the last dregs of their labour, and thus aggravated the evils of a capricious and semi-barbarous government, by working it with all the practiced ingenuity of politicians and all the monopolizing selfishness of traders. (Raffles [1817] 1965, 1:151)

Unlike Raffles, however, Marx links these practices directly to those of the British in India. In fact, he quotes the entire above paragraph in his 1853 article "The British Rule in India," discussed above, where he refers to "British Colonial Rule " as "only an imitation of the Dutch." Marx adds that "to characterize the working of the British East India Company, it is sufficient to literally repeat what Sir Stamford Raffles, the English Governor of Java, said of the old Dutch East India Company" (MECW 12, 126).

The third part of the Raffles book from which Marx records material deals with the political structure of the Javanese village, for example, the notion that in some parts of Java, the cultivators had the right to elect their village chief, something Raffles suggests was once a generalized practice throughout the island. Marx ends these excerpt notes by recording one of Raffles's footnotes. It consists of a citation from the well-known *Fifth Report* (1812) of the British House of Commons, which contained a major study of India's social structure. Marx takes down the introductory statement by Raffles to the effect that "with the exception perhaps, of the right of election, which I have not seen noticed in any account of Continental India, the constitution of the Javan village has a striking resemblance to that of the Hindus" (Raffles [1817] 1965, 1:285). The *Fifth Report's* extremely detailed description of India focuses on the various traditional village officials and their duties, including the "potail, or head inhabitant," the "tallier and the totie" who punish crimes and enforce laws, the "boundary man, who preserves the limits of the village," the regulator of the water supply, the Brahmin who performs religious rites, the "calendar-brahmin or astrologer," and the schoolmaster. The *Fifth Report*, as cited by Raffles and then Marx, goes on to suggest that this is how "the inhabitants of the country have lived from time immemorial." Even wars and invasions have changed it very little: "The inhabitants gave themselves no trouble about the breaking up and divisions of kingdoms: while the village remains entire, they care not to what power it is transferred, or to what sovereign it devolves; its internal economy remains unchanged" (Raffles [1817] 1965, 1:285; MECW 12, 131).

Marx's notes on Indonesia allow us to glimpse the hard intellectual labor he put into his *Tribune* articles on India, which were surely not hack journalism, despite what he might have on occasion suggested in despairing moments in his private correspondence. Land tenure, village self-government, and gender relations were the focus in the notes on Raffles. In looking at Java and Bali, Marx was evidently searching for data on the underlying social forms of India as well. He believed these still existed in something closer to their original version in Java, and especially Bali, at the time Raffles studied them.

ON CHINA: THE TAIPING REBELLION
AND THE OPIUM WARS

Marx's first substantial reference to China comes in 1850, in a brief discussion of the Taiping Rebellion, which forms part of a survey of world events he coauthored with Engels.[37] The Taiping Rebellion, a peasant-based antiroyalist movement that lasted from 1850 to 1864, was gigantic in scope, with the ensuing repression, civil war, and famine resulting in more than twenty million deaths (Spence 1996). The rebels propounded notions of equality, including gender equality, but their worldview also featured mystical and extremely authoritarian dimensions.

In their 1850 article, Marx and Engels describe the crisis of the old social order in China brought about by the import of cheap European manufactured goods, something they had already emphasized in *The Communist Manifesto*. However, having by now heard about the scope and depth of the Taiping Rebellion, Marx and Engels also discuss the rebels' challenge to the emperor and the Mandarins. They note their communist leanings: "Among the rebellious plebs individuals appeared who pointed to the poverty of some and the wealth of others, and who demanded, and are still demanding a different distribution of property, and even the complete abolition of private property" (MECW 10, 266). Marx and Engels were referring to reports from the German missionary Karl Gützlaff, one of the best-informed Europeans of the time on China (Spence 1996), their apparent source on the Rebellion. They waxed ironic over the fact that the pious missionary, upon his return home after two decades in China, was horrified to find communist tendencies in Europe as well.

Marx and Engels viewed the Taiping rebels' communist tendencies with some caution, writing that "Chinese socialism may admittedly be the same in relation to European socialism as Chinese philosophy in relation to Hegelian philosophy." In keeping with the language of *The Communist Manifesto*, they refer to how English imports "have brought the least perturbable kingdom on earth to the eve of a social upheaval." They then add that "European reactionaries" fleeing eastward to escape the revolution may one day, upon reaching the Great Wall of China, "read the following inscription" at the gate: "République Chinoise. Liberté, Egalité, Fraternité" (MECW 10, 267). As in the *Manifesto*, capitalism and colonialism were bringing progress to Asia, which would, Marx and Engels implied, go through a similar development to that which had already taken place in Europe, including a democratic revolution. There was a change from the perspective of the *Manifesto* on one point, however. Social progress in China was a product not only of outside intervention, but also of a largely indigenous force, the Taiping Rebellion. At the same time, and in continuity with the *Manifesto*, there was not yet even an implicit critique of colonialism.

Just before his 1853 India articles, discussed above, Marx's "Revolution in China and Europe" appeared in the *Tribune* on June 14, 1853, focusing on the effects of the opium trade and the Taiping Rebellion. It begins with a veiled reference to Hegel's speculative philosophy in an effort to show that events in China were not entirely separate from what was going on in Europe, despite differences of geography, culture, and social system:

A most profound yet fantastic speculator on the principles which govern the movements of Humanity, was wont to extol as one of the ruling secrets of nature, what he called the law of the contact of extremes. The homely proverb that "extremes meet" was, in his view, a grand and potent truth in every sphere of life. . . . Whether the "contact of extremes" be such a universal principle or not, a striking illustration of it may be seen in the effect the Chinese revolution seems likely to exercise upon the civilized world. It may seem a very strange, and a very paradoxical assertion that the next uprising of the people of Europe, and their next movement for republican freedom and economy of government, may depend more probably on what is now passing in the Celestial Empire— the very opposite of Europe,—than on any other political cause that now exists. (MECW 12, 93)

Marx points once again to the scope of the Taiping Rebellion, referring to "the chronic rebellions subsisting in China for about ten years past, now gathered together in one formidable revolution" (93). He also discussed the profound disruptions of the Chinese political and social system caused by the penetration of Western capitalism, especially in the form of the opium trade.

These twin disruptions from within and without, he argued, would soon plunge the Chinese economy into crisis—a crisis that would result in the collapse of the Chinese market for opium. The British had established a lucrative three-cornered trade by exporting opium to China from India, purchasing tea at a low price in China, and then selling the tea at a higher price in Britain. As a result, China had become so tied into the world economy that an economic crisis there could touch off a European depression. This would be, according to Marx:

the explosion of the long-prepared general crisis, which, spreading abroad, will be closely followed by political revolutions on the [European] Continent. It would be a curious spectacle, that of China spreading disorder into the Western world while the Western powers, by English, French, and American war-steamers, are conveying "order" to Shanghai, Nanking, and the mouths of the Great Canal. (MECW 12, 98)

Marx now refers to Western colonialists as "order-mongering powers" (98), a slight shift from the tone of *The Communist Manifesto*. Nonetheless, he still places considerable emphasis on the progressive effects of Western imperialism, although not to as great an extent as in the 1853 writings on India.

Moreover, even in discussing the Taiping Rebellion as an internal awakening, there is an air of ethnocentric condescension. Referring to the disruptions to the traditional social order resulting from the opium trade, he writes: "It would seem as though history had first to make this whole people drunk before it could rouse them out of their hereditary stupidity" (MECW 12, 94). The political theorist Ephraim Nimni terms the phrase "hereditary stupidity" an example of Marx's "abusive language" and "intense hostility" to many non-Western "national communities" (1994, 29). Marx's real target in this article was British imperialism and what he saw as its unconscionable opium trade, however. In this regard, as Marx editor James Ledbetter maintains, "with the possible exception of human slavery, no topic raised Marx's ire as profoundly as the opium trade with China" (Marx 2007, 1). Marx's language about "hereditary stupidity," however troubling, should not be allowed to mask this fact, nor the fact that the focus of this passage is not Chinese backwardness, but a Chinese national awakening.

Although Marx refers in 1854 to the possibility that the Taiping rebels might soon "succeed in driving the Mandshu [Manchu] dynasty out of China" (MECW 13, 41), it was only in 1856, with the outbreak of the Second Opium War, that he began to concentrate very much on China. As against the *Manifesto*, the whole tone has now changed, with the British rather than the Chinese more often in the role of "barbarians." On January 3, 1857, the *Tribune* published Marx's detailed article on Britain's extremely aggressive moves in Canton (Guangzhou) harbor after Chinese authorities had dared in October 1856 to arrest several Chinese nationals who were smuggling opium for the British. In so doing, the Chinese may have taken down a British flag from the smugglers' small harbor vessel. Concerning the British bombardment of the city to avenge this supposed insult to their flag, Marx informs his readers that "the British are in the wrong in the whole proceeding" (MECW 15, 158). After quoting Canton Governor Yeh Ming-chu's refutation of British accounts of the October incident, Marx writes that the "dialectics" of Yeh's argument "disposes so effectually of the whole question" (MECW 15, 161). He terms the British actions no more defensible than those of the notorious American invader of Nicaragua during those same years, William Walker. Marx's report includes language such as the following:

> Impatient of argument, the British Admiral hereupon forces his way into the City of Canton to the residence of the Governor, at the same time destroying the Imperial [Chinese] fleet in the river. . . . It is, perhaps, a question whether the civilized nations of the world will approve this

mode of invading a peaceful country, without previous declaration of war, for an alleged infringement of the fanciful code of diplomatic etiquette. (MECW 15, 162–63)

At the same time, Marx partially justifies the First Opium War of 1839–42 "in spite of its infamous pretext," because it included "the prospect of opening the trade with China." This Second Opium War, he writes, will only "obstruct that trade" (MECW 15, 163). Despite this backward glance to the position of the *Manifesto* with respect to the First Opium War, the overall tone of Marx's 1857 article is firmly anticolonialist. In one of several follow-up articles, he suggests that his frequent target, British prime minister Lord Henry Palmerston,[38] "planned" the whole intervention in order to prop up his sagging popularity by appealing to jingoistic sentiment in Britain (MECW 15, 218).

In a *Tribune* article published on March 22, 1857, Marx again attempts to refute "the Government journals of England and a portion of the American Press," which "have been heaping wholesale denunciations upon the Chinese" (MECW 15, 233):

The unoffending citizens and peaceful tradesmen of Canton have been slaughtered, their habitations battered to the ground, and the claims of humanity violated, on the flimsy pretence that "English life and property are endangered by the aggressive acts of the Chinese!" The British Government and the British people—at least, those who have chosen to examine the question—know how false and hollow are such charges. . . . These sweeping assertions are baseless. The Chinese have at least ninety nine injuries to complain of to one on the part of the English. How silent is the press of England upon the outrageous violations of the treaty daily practiced by foreigners living in China under British protection! We hear nothing of the illicit opium trade, which yearly feeds the British treasury at the expense of human life and morality. We hear nothing of the constant bribery of sub-officials, by means of which the Chinese Government is defrauded of its rightful revenue on incoming and outgoing merchandise. We hear nothing of the wrongs inflicted "even unto death" upon misguided and bonded emigrants sold to worse than Slavery on the coast of Peru and into Cuban bondage. We hear nothing of the bullying spirit often exercised against the timid nature of the Chinese, or of the vice introduced by foreigners at the ports open to their trade. (MECW 15, 234–35)

At the same time, as seen in the language about "timid" Chinese in the last sentence above, he continues to express a degree of condescension.

Marx writes further that the British public, "the English people at home, who look no further than the grocers where they buy their tea," are refusing to face these facts. But the truth, he concludes, was that the British were reaping untold anger: "Meanwhile, in China, the smothered fires of hatred kindled against the English during the opium war have burst into a flame of animosity, which no tenders of peace and friendship will be very likely to quench" (MECW 15, 235).

Engels followed up this point in a military analysis for the *Tribune* published in June 1857. Engels writes that the British may be facing a new situation in China wherein "a national war" might be launched "against them." Such a war would take the form of a guerrilla struggle:

> There is evidently a different spirit among the Chinese now to what they showed in the war of 1840 to '42. Then, the people were quiet; they left the Emperor's soldiers to fight the invaders, and submitted after a defeat with Eastern fatalism to the power of the enemy. But now, at least in the southern provinces, to which the contest has so far been confined, the mass of the people take an active, nay, a fanatical part in the struggle against the foreigners. They poison the bread of the European community. . . . They kidnap and kill every foreigner within their reach. . . . Civilization-mongers who throw hot shell on a defenseless city and add rape to murder, may call the system [of fighting] cowardly, barbarous, atrocious; but what matters it to the Chinese if it be only successful? Since the British treat them as barbarians, they cannot deny to them the full benefit of their barbarism. If their kidnappings, surprises, midnight massacres are what we call cowardly, the civilization-mongers should not forget that according to their own showing they could not stand against European means of destruction with their ordinary means of warfare. (MECW 15, 281)

This national struggle, combined with the Taiping Rebellion, Engels writes, suggests "that the death-hour of Old China is rapidly drawing nigh" (282), something that may bring "a new era for all Asia" (283).

A few months later, Marx, who was by then also writing on the 1857 Sepoy Uprising in India, implicitly takes back his earlier views on the First Opium War of 1839–42, this in a *Tribune* article published in September 1857. He contextualizes reports of atrocities by the Indian rebels by referring to examples of European brutality, including the following passage on the First Opium War:

> To find parallels to the Sepoy atrocities, we need not, as some London papers pretend, fall back on the middle ages, nor even wander beyond the history of contemporary England. All we want is to study the first Chinese war, an event, so to say, of yesterday. The English soldiery then committed abominations for the mere fun of it; their passions being neither sanctified by religious fanaticism nor exacerbated by hatred against an overbearing and conquering race, nor provoked by the stern resistance of a heroic enemy. The violations of women, the spittings of children, the roastings of whole villages, were then mere wanton sports, not recorded by Mandarins, but by British officers themselves. (MECW 15, 353–54)

Marx's articles on China as well as India in this period are full of reports of British brutality, with little reference to colonialism as beneficial.

A year later, in September 1858, as the war in China reached a temporary lull, Marx published in the *Tribune* two articles titled "History of the Opium Trade." In one of them, he concludes with a poetic evocation of the contradictory character of the type of modernization forced upon China by Britain's Opium Wars:

> That a giant empire, containing almost one-third of the human race, vegetating to the teeth of time, insulated by the forced exclusion of general intercourse,[39] and thus contriving to dupe itself with delusions of Celestial perfection—that such an empire should at last be overtaken by the fate on occasion of a deadly duel, in which the representative of the antiquated world appears prompted by ethical motives, while the representative of overwhelming modern society fights for the privilege of buying in the cheapest and selling in the dearest markets—this, indeed, is a sort of tragical couplet, stranger than any poet would ever have dared to fancy. (MECW 16, 16)

Here Marx's discussion recalls Hegel's treatment in the *Phenomenology of Spirit* of the fate of Antigone in Sophocles' play, something Georg Lukács takes up in an analysis of what he terms "tragedy in the realm of the ethical":

What is striking about Hegel's view of *Antigone* is the way in which the two poles of the contradiction are maintained in a tense unity: on the one hand, there is the recognition that tribal society stands higher morally and humanly than the class societies that succeed it, and that the collapse of tribal society was brought about by the release of base and evil human impulses. On the other hand, there is the equally powerful conviction that this collapse was inevitable and that it signified a definite historical advance.

Of course, China had not been a tribal or clan society for several millennia, but the echo of Hegel's argument in Marx's turns on what Lukács calls a "contradictory view of progress" (Lukács [1948] 1975, 412), wherein something very important is lost at every stage where humanity "progresses," necessary as that progress may seem.

In September 1859, as the Second Opium War heated up again with the British, now joined by the French, preparing to sack Beijing, Marx published several more articles on China in the *Tribune*. He gleefully reports that the British and French "aggressors" had suffered nearly five hundred casualties, also losing three ships in the entrance to the Peiho River as they attempted to sail toward Beijing. The jingoist "Palmerstonian press" was trumpeting these "unpleasant tidings" as it "unanimously roared for wholesale revenge." Marx ridicules British editorialists for declaring themselves "superior" to the Chinese, and for averring that the British "ought to be their masters" (MECW 16, 509). He calls such expressions nothing but the "ravings of Palmerston's penmen" (510). Palmerston, and Bonaparte as well, he writes, "want another Chinese war" to shore up their dwindling popularity at home (512).

In these articles on China published during 1857–59, Marx's thinking has begun to shift from the perspectives of the *Manifesto* or the 1853 articles on India and China in two major respects. Most obviously, he no longer lauds the supposed progressive effects of colonialism, in fact condemning British and French colonialism in the strongest terms. What could account for such a change? One factor is his growing disillusionment with capitalism, in the sense that he no longer held as strong a belief in capitalism's progressive effects. This can be seen in his April 14, 1856, "Speech at the Anniversary of *The People's Paper*," published a few days later in that Chartist organ. While Marx still proclaims that "steam, electricity, and the self-acting mule were revolutionists," the tone in 1856 is more somber, far less sanguine about capitalist progress than earlier:

On the one hand, there have started into life industrial and scientific forces, which no epoch of the former human history had ever suspected. On the other hand, there exist symptoms of decay, far surpassing the horrors recorded of the latter times of the Roman Empire. In our days, everything seems pregnant with its contrary. Machinery, gifted with the wonderful power of shortening and fructifying human labor, we behold starving and overworking it. The new-fangled sources of wealth, by some strange weird spell, are turned into sources of want. The victories of art seem bought by the loss of character. At the same pace that mankind masters nature, man seems to become enslaved to other men or to his own infamy. Even the pure light of science seems unable to shine but on the dark background of ignorance. All our invention and progress seem to result in endowing material forces with intellectual life, and in stultifying human life into a material force. (MECW 14, 655–56)

In *The Communist Manifesto*, whole pages celebrated capitalist progress before Marx and Engels began to talk of contradictions. Eight years later, the notion of capitalism's destructiveness, of its alienation and exploitation, was interwoven into the discussion of scientific and technological progress. Second, and perhaps more importantly, it should be noted that by 1859, Marx had finished writing the *Grundrisse*, where, as will be discussed in chapter five, he elaborated for the first time a more multilinear philosophy of history, wherein Asian societies had not followed the same stages from slave-based to feudal modes of production as had Western Europe.

In 1861, the *Tribune* drastically reduced its international coverage and the following year, it stopped publishing Marx altogether. He began writing for *Die Presse* of Vienna, and it is there, in July 1862, that his last substantial article on China appeared. Entitled "Chinese Affairs," it focused not on colonial intervention, but on the Taiping Rebellion, by now on the wane. Marx begins the article with a reference to the proliferation in the conservative 1850s in Europe, and especially Germany, of séances in which tables were supposedly made to levitate: "A little while before tables started to dance, China, that living fossil, began to revolutionize" (MECW 19, p. 216). Thus, while alluding to the conservatism of Chinese society, he also referred to post-1848 European political quiescence, which he contrasted with Chinese revolutionary outbursts. Later he would use a passage similar to this on China and tables dancing in the section on commodity fetishism in chapter one of *Capital*, volume I. In both instances, part of the irony is that "rationalist" Europe had in the 1850s lost its revolutionary drive and was instead swept up by mysticism, while "mystical" China was engaged not so much in mysticism as in social revolution.

As against the enthusiasm of his earlier discussions of the Taiping rebels, however, by now the tone is bleak. The Chinese rebels, he writes, "produce destruction in grotesquely detestable forms, destruction without any nucleus of new construction" (MECW 19, 216). Upon taking a town, the rebel leadership allowed its troops "to perpetuate every conceivable act of violence on women and girls." At the same time, they did not pay their troops, which encouraged pillage. As a result, executions became so common in areas ruled by the rebels that "a human head means no more than a head of cabbage to a Taiping" (217).

Here Marx is surely alluding to the discussion of the Jacobin Terror in Hegel's *Phenomenology*, where, in a well-known discussion of "absolute freedom and terror," Hegel writes that the French Revolution has become "only *negative* action . . . merely the *fury* of destruction" without a positive element, whereby death is imposed "with no more significance than cutting off a head of cabbage" ([1807] 1977, 359, 360; original emphasis). Hegel and Marx, despite their many differences concerning the French Revolution, saw it, including the Great Terror, as having produced historical progress in spite of its destructiveness. But in viewing the Taiping Rebellion in 1862, Marx mentions not progress, but "nothingness." This was because, he writes, rather than finding a basis in new emancipatory ideas, the philosophy of the Taiping rebels "is the product of a fossilized social life," the expression of what was ultimately a backward-looking movement (MECW 19, 218). Thus, Marx's writings on China end on a somber note. Both Western imperialism and the indigenous Taiping Rebellion have severely shaken the old order, but no positive, emancipatory alternative is in sight.

"INDIA IS NOW OUR BEST ALLY": THE 1857 SEPOY UPRISING

Evidence of Marx's shift toward a more anticolonialist position can also be found in his articles on the great Indian revolt of 1857–58, which broke out in the midst of the Second Opium War against China. The literary theorist Pranav Jani holds that in these later writings on India, Marx began "to theorize the self-activity and struggle of colonized Indians" (2002, 82). On May 10, 1857, a group of Indian colonial soldiers known as sepoys[40] revolted and killed their British officers. The immediate provocation was a rumor that grease for the cartridge for their rifles contained fat from beef, anathema to Hindus, and from pork, anathema to Muslims. The rebellion developed a more political form when the rebellious soldiers seized Delhi and other large cities. They placed a descendant of the Mughal emperors, Bahadur Shah, in power once again. However, the rebellion did not develop coherent goals or even a unified form, and was in many respects a basically traditionalist, decentralized outbreak of anticolonial hostility. It took the British two full years, despite their superior organization and weaponry, to suppress it. Incidents of massacre, torture, and rape of British civilians and soldiers, exaggerated and sensationalized in the Western press, became an excuse for even more horrific reprisals by the British army.

As news of the revolt reached London, Marx began an extensive series of articles on it for the *Tribune*. These articles, published during the years 1857 and 1858, with twenty-one of them written by Marx and ten at his invitation by Engels, comprise over 150 printed pages in volume 15 of the English edition of the *Collected Works* of Marx and Engels.[41] Although they constitute one of the most sustained treatments of a non-European society by Marx anywhere in his writings, they have not drawn as much attention as the 1853 articles on India.[42] Nonetheless, these articles show a major theoretical shift, away from the qualified support for British colonialism in those from 1853.

In "The Revolt in the Indian Army," published on July 15, 1857, Marx begins by noting that, like the Romans before them, the British adopted a divide-and-rule form of domination in India in which playing off "the antagonism of the various races, tribes, castes, creeds, and sovereignties" was "the vital principle of British supremacy" (MECW 15, 297). To rule over a population of two hundred million, he notes, the British created a colonial army of two hundred thousand Indians, commanded by British officers, in addition to maintaining a British force of around forty thousand men. Proceeding dialectically, Marx then points to the new contradictions and antagonisms brought about by British rule. In their colonial sepoy army, they unwittingly created for the first time a unified Indian national consciousness and organization: "British rule ... organized the first general center of resistance which the Indian people was ever possessed of. How far that native army may be relied upon is clearly shown by its recent mutinies" (297–98). In a letter to Engels of July 6, Marx gives his feelings greater vent, writing that "the Indian affair is delicious" (MECW 40, 142).

In a second article, "The Revolt in India," published on August 4, 1857, Marx points to the disorganization of the rebels occupying Delhi, predicting that they would not be able to hold out very long. He adds that what is more important is that the revolt has struck deep roots, and that "no greater mistake could be committed than to suppose that the fall of Delhi, though it may throw consternation among the ranks of the Sepoys, should suffice either to quench the rebellion, to stop its progress, or to restore the British rule" (MECW 15, 306). So deep has the hatred of British domination grown that the British now "command only the spot of ground held by their own troops" (307). In a subsequent article published on August 14, Marx reports that the rebels were managing to hold out in Delhi longer than expected. This, and the extension of the revolt through much of India, he writes, is not mainly due to military factors, for what England "considers a military mutiny is in truth a national revolt" (316).

Marx's "The Indian Revolt," which appeared on September 16, takes up the atrocities committed by the rebels, who, he writes, are "only the reflex, in concentrated form, of England's own conduct in India." These cruelties are "appalling, hideous," he adds, but they are characteristic of "wars of insurrection, of nationalities, of races, and above all of religion" (MECW 15, 353). The British press provided few details of atrocities by their own forces, but these oozed forth nonetheless in crudely racist sentences such as the following, which Marx quotes from a report in the London *Times*: "We hold court-martials on horseback, and every nigger we meet with, we either string up or shoot" (355). Marx contextualizes the sepoy atrocities against British civilians by noting similar examples from European history and from European actions in Asia:

> The cutting of noses, breasts, &c., in one word, the horrid mutilations committed by the Sepoys, are of course more revolting to European feeling than the throwing of red-hot shell on Canton dwellings by a Secretary of the Manchester Peace Society,[43] or the roasting of Arabs pent up in a cave by a French Marshal,[44] or the flaying alive of British soldiers by the cat-o'-nine-tails under drum-head court-martial,[45] or any other of the philanthropical appliances used in British penitentiary colonies. Cruelty, like every other thing, has its fashion, changing according to time and place. Caesar, the accomplished scholar, candidly narrates how he ordered many thousand Gallic warriors to have their right hands cut off. Napoleon would have been ashamed to do this. He preferred dispatching his own French regiments, suspected of republicanism, to St. Domingo, there to die of the blacks[46] and the plague. The infamous mutilations committed by the Sepoys remind one of the practices of the Christian Byzantine Empire, or the prescriptions of Charles V's criminal law,[47] or the English punishments for high treason, as still recorded

by Judge Blackstone.[48] With Hindoos, whom their religion has made virtuosi in the art of self-torturing, these tortures inflicted on the enemies of their race and creed appear quite natural, and must appear still more so to the English, who, only some years since, still used to draw revenues from the Juggernaut festivals,[49] protecting and assisting the bloody rites of a religion of cruelty. (356)

Another article published the next day details common forms of torture long used or condoned by the British in India, and then asks, "whether a people are not justified in attempting to expel the foreign conquerors who have so abused their subjects" (341).

In "The Indian Revolt" of September 16, 1857, Marx also makes an important dialectical point concerning the nature of the Indian resistance. He notes that it sprang from a part of society formed by the British, from a deep contradiction within the colonial apparatus itself:

> There is something in human history like retribution; and it is a rule of historical retribution that its instrument be forged not by the offended, but by the offender himself. The first blow dealt the French monarch proceeded from the nobility, not from the peasants. The Indian revolt does not commence with the Ryots, tortured, dishonored and stripped naked by the British, but with the Sepoys, clad, fed, petted, fatted and pampered by them. (MECW 15, 353)

In some respects, this echoed the language of *The Communist Manifesto*:

> The weapons with which the bourgeoisie felled feudalism to the ground are now turned against the bourgeoisie itself. But not only has the bourgeoisie forged the weapons that bring death to itself: it has also called into existence the men who are to wield those weapons—the modern working class—the proletarians. In proportion as the bourgeoisie, i.e., capital, is developed, in the same proportion is the proletariat, the modern working class, developed. (MECW 6, 490)

In the Sepoy Uprising, Marx was finding in colonial India something similar to capitalism's forging of the working class. Thus, the very progress of colonialism was producing its gravediggers. Such a dialectical turn had been missing with respect to Asia in the *Manifesto* and in much of the 1853 writings on India.

After Delhi finally fell in September 1857, Marx writes, in an article published on November 14, that Britain's victory was aided by "internal dissensions" between Hindus and Muslims, and between rebel soldiers and the upper classes of Delhi (MECW 15, 375). In a military analysis of the recapture of Delhi, Engels ridicules English claims of heroism, arguing that "no people, not even the French, can equal the English in self-laudation, especially when bravery is the point in question" (392).

In a letter to Engels of January 16, 1858, Marx declares tellingly with respect to the Sepoy Uprising: "India is now our best ally" (MECW 40, 249). This remarkable letter, published in full in English for the first time in 1983 in the *Collected Works* of Marx and Engels, is also the one in which Marx makes a better-known statement on the relation of his economic theory to Hegelian dialectics, at the very time he was writing the *Grundrisse*:

> I have completely demolished the theory of profit as hitherto propounded. What was of great use to me as regards *method* of treatment was Hegel's *Logic* at which I had taken another look by mere accident, Freiligrath[50] having found and made me a present of several volumes of Hegel, originally the property of Bakunin. If ever the time comes when such work is again possible, I should very much like to write 2 or 3 sheets making accessible to the common reader the *rational* aspect of the method which Hegel not only discovered but also mystified. (249)

This letter also takes up the turn to the right of Chartist leader Ernest Jones. In this sense, the revolt in India was for Marx not in a totally separate sphere from the struggles of the European workers or from his work on the *Grundrisse*, or, for that matter, Hegelian dialectics. Thus, during the conservative 1850s, he considered India's sepoy fighters to be the "best ally" of the revolutionary movement in the West at a time when the latter, as exemplified by the fate of Jones, was not moving forward.[51]

CHAPTER TWO

Russia and Poland: The Relationship of National Emancipation to Revolution

Among the various non-Western societies Marx took up in his writings, none received more attention than Russia—not even India. For much of the twentieth century, Russia came to be identified with revolution and Marxism, and also with the totalitarian regime that arose under Stalin. In the nineteenth century, however, Russia was viewed by virtually all progressives, whether socialist, anarchist, or liberal, as Europe's most conservative power. While England had developed a constitutional monarchy with a strong parliament, and while the other great powers—France, above all, but also Prussia and Austria—had experienced democratic revolutions in 1848–49, Russia alone seemed immune to revolution. Or so it appeared to Marx and others in 1848. To them, even the program of modernization begun under Tsar Peter the Great in the early eighteenth century had only strengthened what was already an extremely authoritarian regime, one that henceforth became a major player in European politics. In 1795, during the first French Revolution, Russia had worked with Austria and Prussia in a final partition of Poland, crushing a democratic movement there. Two decades later, Russian troops were decisive in defeating Napoleon and paving the way for Austrian prince Metternich's Holy Alliance. This pact united Austria, Prussia, and Russia for over three decades, from 1815 to 1848, for the purpose of preventing further revolutionary outbreaks. Then, in 1849, Tsar Nicholas I sent two hundred thousand troops into central Europe to help put Austro-Hungarian emperor Franz Josef, threatened by the revolution in Vienna and Hungary, back on the throne.

To Marx, Britain was the country where the industrial revolution had gone furthest in wiping away feudal remnants; France was where the democratic and, after 1848, the working-class uprisings had been the deepest; Germany was where the modern form of revolutionary philosophy had been born out of a critical appropriation of Hegelian idealism. In contrast, Russia was where an unchallenged autocracy remained in power, even seeming to gain strength as a counterrevolutionary force throughout Europe. Referring in May 1849 to the showdown taking place in Vienna and Hungary, where the democratic revolution was confronting Tsar Nicholas I's military intervention as well as the army of its own Austro-Hungarian Empire, Marx writes: "And in the East, a revolutionary army made up of fighters of all nationalities already confronts the alliance of old Europe represented by the Russian army, while from Paris comes the threat of a 'red republic'" (MECW 9, 454).

Marx published this statement on May 19, 1849, in the final edition of his and Engels's *Neue Rheinische Zeitung*, just before its suppression by the Prussian government. He and Engels regarded Russia as the counter-revolutionary power *par excellence*. In early 1850, Engels wrote of the weakness of the Western European reaction, maintaining that "two-thirds of the Prussians and Austrians are infected with the democratic disease." This was not the case, however, with Russia's 350,000 troops stationed right on the Polish-German border, which were "ready to march at a moment's notice," he declared ominously (MECW 10, 15). While a revolutionary movement looking to the countryside had appeared in Russia by the 1860s, Marx's daughter Eleanor Marx and Edward Aveling summed up well the attitude of European revolutionaries as late as 1897 toward the tsarist regime, writing in their introduction to a collection of Marx's 1850s writings on Russia and Turkey: "To-day the Russian government, which is no longer to-day totally synonymous with Russia, is, as it was in the 'fifties,' the greatest enemy of all advance, the greatest stronghold of reaction" (Marx [1897] 1969, viii–ix). The Russian secret police, expanded and renamed the Okhrana in 1881, was already a formidable organization in the 1850s. It not only muzzled opposition at home, but also monitored democrats and revolutionaries abroad, non-Russian as well as Russian. Marx and his generation regarded it as an omnipresent, malevolent force, similarly to how twentieth-century leftists viewed the CIA.[1]

RUSSIA AS A COUNTERREVOLUTIONARY THREAT

In the 1850s, Marx focused on Russia as a power ready to intervene again should the European revolutionary movement reassert itself, and on the absence of a Russian revolutionary movement. At this stage, Marx argued that the Russian village's communal form undergirded a despotic social and political system, as in other forms of Oriental despotism. In "Elections.—Financial Clouds.—The Duchess of Sutherland and Slavery," a *Tribune* article published on February 8, 1853, dealing with the ancient Scottish clan system and its uprooting by capitalist agriculture, he viewed this premodern system as quite similar to Russia's communal village:

> The "great man," the chieftain of the clan, is on the one hand quite as arbitrary, on the other quite as confined in his power, by consanguinity, etc., as every father of a family. To the clan, to the family, belonged the district where it had established itself, exactly as, in Russia, the land occupied by a community of peasants belongs, not to the individual peasants, but to the community. Thus the district was the common property of the family. There could be no more question, under this system, of private property, in the modern sense of the word, than there could be of comparing the social existence of the members of the clan to that of individuals living in the midst of our modern society. . . . Thus you see, the *clan* is nothing but a family organized in a military manner, quite as little defined by laws, just as closely hemmed in by traditions, as any family. But the land is the property of the family, in the midst of which differences of rank, in spite of consanguinity, do prevail as well as in all the ancient Asiatic family communities. (MECW 11, 488)

This appears to be Marx's first treatment of the sharp differences between the social structure of the villages in "despotic" Russian and those in most of modern Western Europe. As will be discussed in chapter 6, Marx changed his position by the 1870s, when he began to see the Russian communal village as a possible center of revolution. But in his Russia writings of the early 1850s, as in his 1853 writings on India, the focus was instead on what he perceived to be the almost one-dimensional character of these communal forms.

Engels, who had a particular animus toward the southern Slavs, was explicitly dismissive of the notion of the Russian commune as a base for revolution, which was a view held by many democratic Russian exiles like the future anarchist Mikhail Bakunin. This is seen in a letter to Marx on March 18, 1852: "In effect, Bakunin only came to anything because no one knew Russian. And a great deal is going to be made of the old Pan-Slavic dodge of transmogrifying the old Slav system of communal property into communism and depicting the Russian peasants as born communists" (MECW 39, 67). To Marx and Engels, Bakunin and others like Alexander Herzen were under the sway of a fuzzy-minded Russian nationalism, while other Russian exiles were actual tsarist agents (Eaton 1980).[2]

After the Crimean War began in July 1853, Marx sided openly with the Ottoman Empire and its allies Britain and France, against Russia. As mentioned above, Marx at this time considered Engels to be more knowledgeable about the Eastern Question. At Marx's invitation, Engels wrote a *Tribune* article published on April 12, 1853, on the eve of the war. It concludes with the following view of Russia:

> Russia is decidedly a conquering nation, and was so for a century, until the great movement of 1789 called into potent activity an antagonist of formidable nature. We mean the European Revolution, the explosive force of democratic ideas and man's native thirst for freedom. Since that epoch there have really been but two powers on the continent of Europe—Russia and Absolutism, the Revolution and Democracy. For the moment the Revolution seems to be suppressed, but it lives and is feared as deeply as ever. Witness the terror of the reaction at the news of the late rising at Milan.[3] But let Russia get possession of Turkey, and her strength is increased nearly half, and she becomes superior to all the rest of Europe put together. Such an event would be an unspeakable calamity to the revolutionary cause. . . . In this instance the interests of the revolutionary Democracy and of England go hand in hand. Neither can permit the Czar to make Constantinople into one of his Capitals. (MECW 12, 17)

During the Crimean War, Marx and Engels published dozens of similar articles, often berating England and France for what they considered to be an only half-hearted military effort against Russia.

Writing years later, after Marx's death, Engels called the Crimean War a "sham war" (MECW 26, 461). The chief target of these attacks against English half-heartedness was Lord Henry Palmerston, a politician Marx judged to be utterly reactionary, whether in his support for Russia, his invasions of China, his opposition to labor, or, later, his leaning toward the South during the Civil War in the United States. In a single *Tribune* article published on August 12, 1853, Marx hits out on the one hand at a pro-Palmerston newspaper, the *Morning Post*, whose editorial calling for the "flogging" of striking English workers he quotes, and on the other at Russia's "demoniac" ambitions (MECW 12, 225, 231). Although the Ottoman Empire was hardly democratic, to Marx it was not a real danger to the revolutionary movement; in fact, the weak Ottoman regime "holds Constantinople in trust for the Revolution," he concludes (MECW 12, 231). In another *Tribune* article published on September 2, 1853, Marx strongly attacks anti-Turkish and anti-Muslim racism, which in his view was leading to complacency with regard to Russia's aggressive moves: "Within the last twenty years, there had been a growing conviction that the Turks in Europe were intruders in Europe; that they were not domiciled there; that their home was Asia; that Mohammedanism could not exist in civilized states" (MECW 12, 274).[4]

In the fall of 1853, Marx published in the Chartist *People's Paper*, and later as a pamphlet, a series of articles entitled "Lord Palmerston,"[5] a text that runs some sixty pages in Marx and Engels, *Collected Works* (MECW 12, 345–406). On November 2 of the same year he writes to Engels that he has by now concluded that "for several decades Palmerston has been in the pay of Russia" (MECW 39, 395). In "Lord Palmerston," Marx recounts Palmerston's many duplicitous actions, including his public denunciation of Russian atrocities in Poland during the suppression of the 1830 uprising while simultaneously making sure that no concrete aid ever reached the Poles, and his similar behavior during the 1846 Polish uprising. Rather than an actual paid agent of the Russians, Palmerston was a conservative British aristocrat who, although he occasionally received gifts and favors from Russia, was motivated more by the view that Britain and Russia as had common interests as the two most important conservative powers in Europe.[6]

In reviewing the maneuvering of the five great powers—Britain, France, Russia, Austria, and Prussia—Engels writes in a *Tribune* article of February 2, 1854, of a "sixth power," the democratic revolution:[7]

> But we must not forget that there is a sixth power in Europe, which at given moments asserts its supremacy over the whole of the five so-called "Great" Powers and makes them tremble, every one of them. That power is the Revolution. Long silent and retired, it is now again called into action by the commercial crisis, and by the scarcity of food. From Manchester to Rome, from Paris to Warsaw and Pesth,[8] it is omnipresent, lifting up its head and awakening from its slumbers. Manifold are the symptoms of its returning life, everywhere visible in the agitation and disquietude which have seized the proletarian class. A signal only is wanted, and this sixth and greatest European power will come forward, in shining armor, and sword in hand, like Minerva from the head of the Olympian. This signal the impending European war will give, and then all calculations as to the balance of power will be upset by the addition of a new element which, ever buoyant and youthful, will as much baffle

the plans of the old European Powers, and their Generals, as it did from 1792 to 1800. (MECW 12, 557–58)

Thus, war may beget revolution.[9]

As the Crimean War ended, Marx's *Revelations of the Secret Diplomatic History of the Eighteenth Century* (1856–57), a series of articles on Russia, was published in David Urquhart's *Free Press*, a conservative weekly that regularly castigated both Palmerston and Russia. The *Secret Diplomatic History* was probably Marx's most anti-Russian work, which also made it a very controversial one for twentieth-century Marxism. Although it was republished in 1899 by Eleanor Marx and has been translated into French, the *Secret Diplomatic History* was left out of both the Russian and the East German editions of Marx's collected works (Draper 1985b) and was only with some delay published as part of volume 15 of the English-language *Collected Works* of Marx and Engels.[10] In their preface to volume 15, the editors, in a very unusual step, devote no less than five pages to criticizing Marx's "one-sided assessment and judgments" on Russian history (MECW 15, xxi). During the early days of the Cold War, two American scholars, Paul Blackstock and Bert Hoselitz, published many of the anti-Russian writings of Marx and Engels under the provocative title *The Russian Menace to Europe*, quoting in their introduction the *Secret Diplomatic History*. In that introduction, they suggest ahistorically that "the foreign policy methods of Soviet Russia have remained similar to those" of the tsars and that Marx's attacks on Russian "barbarism and tyranny" put him closer to liberalism than to Russian Communism (Blackstock and Hoselitz in Marx and Engels 1952, 11, 13).[11]

Much of the *Secret Diplomatic History* dealt with the period of Tsar Peter the Great (r. 1682–1725), during which, Marx claimed, Britain secretively betrayed its longtime Swedish allies in order to facilitate the Tsar's opening to the Baltic. Marx added that the economic benefits to Britain of these new ties to Russia had been grossly exaggerated by British officials ever since. This was because English aristocracy, increasingly beleaguered after the 1688 revolution, was searching abroad "for allies," which it found both in the Tsars and among the imperialists of the East India Company (MECW 15, 61).

Concerning Russia's internal development, Marx views the Mongol conquest as the key event setting Russia apart from the rest of Europe:

> The bloody mire of Mongolian slavery . . . forms the cradle of Muscovy, and modern Russia is but a metamorphosis of Muscovy. The Tartar yoke lasted from 1237 to 1462—more than two centuries; a yoke not only

crushing, but dishonoring and withering the very soul of the people that fell its prey. (MECW 15, 77)

Although, as seen above, Marx was not without sympathy for the sufferings of the Russian people, he characterized the Russian rulers who succeeded them as products of Mongol rule. As a result, he writes, both the Russian rulers and the Russian people retained the attitudes of slavery, both the slave's guile and the master's crushing arrogance: "It is in the terrible and abject school of Mongolian slavery that Muscovy was nursed and grew up. It gathered strength only by becoming a *virtuoso* in the craft of serfdom. Even when emancipated, Muscovy continued to perform its traditional part of the slave as master" (87).[12] As a result, he concluded, Russian modernization under Peter the Great did not bring about anything resembling the progressive achievements of Western Europe, such as urban republics, the Reformation, or the Renaissance. The more cultured and cosmopolitan Russian towns like Novgorod, when taken over by Muscovy during the late fifteenth and early sixteenth centuries, were driven backward: "It is still worthy of notice what exquisite pains were always taken by Muscovy as well as by modern Russia to execute republics. Novgorod and its colonies lead the dance; the republic of the Cossacks follows; Poland closes it." The Tsars "seemed to have snatched the chain with which the Mongols crushed Muscovy only to bind with it the Russian republics" (84).

The long reign of Peter the Great represented something new, for in his large-scale moves into the Baltics and elsewhere, he reached what Marx calls a "bold synthesis which, blending the encroaching method of the Mongol slave with the world-conquering tendencies of the Mongol master, forms the lifespring of modern Russian diplomacy" (MECW 15, 89). Peter's placement of his new capital on the Baltic Sea on the far northwestern rim of his territory (what is now St. Petersburg) was not only an effort to have contact with the West. St. Petersburg Marx holds, was at the geographic center of the territory Russia intended to conquer! By the mid-nineteenth century, Russia had taken Finland, most of Poland, and Lithuania. The fortresses in Russian-ruled Poland of the 1850s, he writes, were directed at Germany and other countries to the West. They "are more than citadels to keep a rebellious country in check. They are the same menace to the west which Petersburg, in its immediate bearing, was a hundred years ago to the north" (90). Peter attempted "to civilize Russia," Marx writes, but only in a superficial sense. The Baltic Germans of the newly conquered lands gave the Tsar "a crop of bureaucrats, schoolmasters, and drill-sergeants, who were to drill Russians into that varnish of civilization that adapts them to the technical appliances of the Western peoples, without imbuing them with their ideas" (91).

At one point in the *Secret Diplomatic History,* Marx resorts to a racial explanation, writing that it was "characteristic of the Slavonic race" to keep away from the seacoast, something Peter the Great altered (MECW 15, 88). This troubling use of race as an explanation for human behavior is very rare in Marx's writings on Russia and the southern Slavs, but unfortunately is far more common in those of Engels, as can be seen in his now infamous articles on Pan-Slavism. In April 1855, during the Crimean War, Engels published "Germany and Pan-Slavism" in the *Neue Oder-Zeitung.* In this article, he expresses the fear that, through support of Pan-Slavism, Tsar Nicholas I would be able to gain the sympathy of the Slavs of eastern and southern Europe, many of them Orthodox Christians, and use these new allies to dominate the whole of Europe. But Engels does not stop there, nor at the fact that in 1848–49 many Slavs supported either Russia or Austria against the revolutionaries. Instead, he labels the southern Slavs as a whole as counterrevolutionary.[13] He goes on to paint the entire conflict in Europe since 1848 as one between "Pan-Slavism" and the "Roman-Celtic and Germanic races, which have hitherto dominated Europe" (MECW 14, 156). These articles appear to have had Marx's general approval,[14] although one certainly cannot assume agreement on every point.

Here, Engels was continuing themes from an earlier series he had published in the *Neue Rheinische Zeitung.* In "The Magyar Struggle," published the *Neue Rheinische Zeitung* on January 13, 1849, Engels details how Austria had been able to win the Slavs over to its side in order to fight, against the revolutionary forces in Hungary, and he goes even further than in 1855 in his pejorative characterizations of the Slavs. In central and southern Europe, he writes, except for the Germans, the Poles, and the Magyars (Hungarians), "all the other large and small nationalities and peoples are destined to perish before long in the revolutionary world storm. For that reason they are now counter-revolutionary" (MECW 8, 230). Engels concludes this 1849 article by going so far as to predict "the disappearance from the face of the earth not only of reactionary classes and dynasties, but also of entire reactionary peoples. And that too is a step forward" (238). Then, in "Democratic Pan-Slavism," an anti-Bakunin polemic published on February 15–16, 1849, Engels writes that "hatred of the Russians was and still is the *primary revolutionary passion* among the Germans" and that "we know where the enemies of the revolution are concentrated, viz., in Russia and the Slav regions of Austria" (378; original emphasis). He also claims in this article to have provided "proof that the Austrian Slavs have never had a history of their own" (371) and that all real historical development in the region came from the influx of Germans, Hungarians, or Italians.[15]

It is true that Marx nowhere stooped to the type of ethnocentrism that one finds in these writings by Engels. But it is also true that Marx tended to portray Russia and its people in a one-dimensional, condescending manner in his mid-1850s writings.[16] His view of Russia began to change by 1858, once that country began to experience the tremors of revolutionary opposition. But before continuing with that story, let us examine briefly a few of Marx's writings on the Chechens and on the "Jewish Question," many of them from the same period.

ON THE CHECHENS AND THE "JEWISH QUESTION"

In his writings on the Crimean War, Marx did not perceive any revolutionary sentiment within the ethnic Russian population, but he did note frequently the determination and persistence of the Chechens and other Muslim peoples of Caucasia, who, under the leadership of the great rebel leader Shamil, had ever since the 1830s mounted a strong resistance to Russian conquest. The contemporary relevance of Marx's writings on the Chechen rebels is brought home by Marie Bennigsen Broxup, the editor of *Central Asian Survey*: "Karl Marx is not in fashion. That is too bad, because his assessments of the war in Caucasia in the nineteenth century remain an excellent source, one which could give useful historical references for those who, in the West, are so eager to give credence to Moscow's claim that 'Chechnya is an integral part of Russia'" ("Un peuple indomptable," *Le Monde*, January 4, 1995).[17]

As the Crimean War began, Marx writes in a *Tribune* article published on July 8, 1853, that while two Turkish ships had been captured by the Russians, "on the other hand, the Caucasian tribes had opened a general campaign against the Russians in which Shamyl had achieved a most brilliant victory, taking no less than 23 cannons" (MECW 12, 146). He ends his fall 1853 pamphlet "Lord Palmerston" by stating that although the covertly pro-Russian Palmerston had triumphed once again by a narrow vote in Parliament, "Those sixteen votes will neither out-voice history nor silence the mountaineers, the clashing of whose arms proves to the world that the Caucasus does not 'now belong to Russia, as stated by [Russian foreign minister] Count Nesselrode,' and as echoed by Lord Palmerston" (406).

Marx refers again to Shamil having "roundly trounced the Russians" in the letter to Engels of November 2, 1853 (MECW 39, 395). In a military analysis of the war that appeared in the *Tribune* on November 25, Engels writes that the apparent victory by the Chechens in taking "the main pass of the Caucasus, connecting Tiflis and Georgia with Russia" would open opportunities for the Ottomans to link up with Shamil (MECW 12, 455). In a follow-up article published on December 7, Engels, pointedly drawing no fundamental distinction between the Russian government and its people, writes in light of these Chechen victories: "Let us hope that . . . the Russian government and people may be taught by it to restrain their ambition and arrogance, and mind their own business hereafter" (MECW 12, 476). In over a dozen articles written during the Crimean War, Marx and Engels discuss Shamil and his fighters, as well as the failure of the Ottomans, and later, the British and the French, to assist or link up with them in a serious way.

During this period, Marx also addressed in a *Tribune* article published April 15, 1854, the relations among Muslims, Christians, and Jews in Ottoman-ruled Jerusalem. Russia was beginning to project itself internationally as the protector of the mainly Eastern Orthodox Christians within the Ottoman Empire, whether in the Balkans or in Syria, Lebanon, and Palestine. Marx points to the subordinate but protected status of the various Christian denominations in Jerusalem, and to how the Ottomans, by taking "judgment in turns favorable to the Latins, Greeks, and Armenians," played them off against one another, especially with regard to rights to the various Christian religious sites (MECW 13, 105). The Jews, he writes, were the most oppressed: "Nothing equals the misery and the sufferings of the Jews at Jerusalem, inhabiting the most filthy quarter of the town . . . the constant objects of Mussulman oppression and intolerance" (107–8). From the Christian side, Jews were being "insulted by the Greeks" and "persecuted by the Latins." Their suffering was caused not only by the Eastern Orthodox Christians and the Muslims, however, but also by the western Europeans: "To make these Jews more miserable, England and Prussia appointed, in 1840, an Anglican bishop at Jerusalem, whose avowed object is their conversion. He was dreadfully thrashed in 1845, and sneered at alike by Jews, Christians and Turks" (108).

Unfortunately, not all of Marx's discussions of Jews show as much sympathy. A considerable number of anti-Semitic characterizations crop up in his writings. For example, in the important "first thesis" on idealism and materialism in the "Theses on Feuerbach" (1845), Marx attacks Feuerbach not only on philosophical grounds as a crude materialist, but also for having developed a notion of praxis that was "defined only in its dirty-Jewish [*schmutzige jüdischen*] form of appearance" (MECW 5, 6). This text was not intended for publication, and elsewhere in the unpublished material, such as Marx's letters to Engels, even more virulent references to Jews can be found. Marx also made some extremely problematic comments on Jews in his *published* work.[18] Such references marred his otherwise penetrating critique of liberal democracy in the 1843 essay, "On the Jewish Question"(Marx [1843] 1994; see also MECW 3, 146–74), and can also be found in some of his later work, especially *Herr Vogt* (1860).[19] Several Marx scholars have argued with some justice that similar references abound in the writings of nineteenth-century secular radical intellectuals, including others of Jewish origin such as the poet Heinrich Heine (Rubel in *Oeuvres* 3; see also Draper 1978). Others have pointed to the limitations of the secular and assimilationist perspective shared by Marx and many other pre-twentieth-century writers, both Jewish and non-Jewish, who, while supporting political and civil rights for Jews, nonetheless continued to make very troubling pejorative comments about Jewish life and culture (Traverso 1994, Jacobs 1998). None, not even Marx's strongest defenders on this issue, however, have suggested that Marx made a significant positive contribution on the issue of Jews and anti-Semitism.[20]

Marx's references to Judaism and Jews were certainly problematic. They showed the downside of a universalistic secular outlook that, by condemning all religion, sometimes failed to distinguish between the impact of such attacks on a dominant religion and those on a persecuted minority one. These remarks, as problematic as they were, were for the most part occasional ones that were not typical of Marx's overall discussions of nationalism and ethnicity. (I leave aside the psychological issue of Marx's possible personal ambivalence toward his own Jewish origins.)

THE TURNING POINT OF 1858–60: "IN RUSSIA THE MOVEMENT IS PROGRESSING BETTER THAN ANYWHERE ELSE"

Marx began to change his attitude toward Russia in 1858, at a time when the new tsar, Alexander II, was discussing emancipation of the serfs and when Russian society was reeling from the tremendous human and financial losses incurred from the Crimean War. In a letter to Engels of April 29, 1858, Marx writes that "the movement for the emancipation of the serfs in Russia strikes me as important in so far as it indicates the beginning of an internal development that might run counter to the country's traditional foreign policy" (MECW 40, 310). This is Marx's first substantial reference to the possibility of major class or revolutionary conflicts inside Russia.[21]

Two months later, Marx made his new perspective on Russia public. In a *Tribune* article surveying the European scene of June 24, 1858, he evokes the possibility of a "servile war"—an uprising of the serfs—in Russia:

> There is another great power [besides England] which, ten years ago, most powerfully checked the revolutionary current. We mean Russia. This time, combustible matter has accumulated under her own feet, which a strong blast from the West may suddenly set on fire. The symptoms of a servile war are so visible in the interior of Russia, that the Provincial Governors feel themselves unable otherwise to account for the unwonted fermentation than by charging Austria with propagating through secret emissaries Socialist and revolutionary doctrines all over the land. Think only of Austria being not only suspected but publicly accused of acting as the emissary of revolution! (MECW 15, 568)

In partial continuity with his earlier positions on Russia, however, Marx suggests that Russia could not generate a revolution from its internal resources alone, and that influences from the revolutionary movement in the West (not the Austrian monarchy) would be needed to push Russia in that direction. Thus, he concludes the article by writing that "everything . . . depends on France" (568). Still, the newness of his finally acknowledging even the possibility of revolution in Russia is striking.

Marx analyzed the debates over the abolition of serfdom in Russia in a *Tribune* article of October 19, 1858. He noted that the landed aristocracy was hardly enthusiastic about Alexander II's abolition proposals. He recalls that in Prussia, abolition of serfdom came only during the Napoleonic Wars, writing that "even then the settlement was such, that the question had to be handled again in 1848, and, although in changed form, remains a question still to be settled by a revolution to come."[22] He also recalls how, during the reigns of tsars Alexander I (1801–25) and Nicholas I (1825–55), the issue of emancipation was posed "not from any motives of humanity, but from mere state reasons." He also notes that by 1848–49, Nicholas I became so frightened by the European revolution that he "turned his back on his own former schemes of emancipation and became an anxious adept of conservatism" (MECW 16, 52).

By the late 1850s, however, the new tsar, Alexander II, faced a very different situation:

> With Alexander II, it was hardly a question of choice whether or not to awaken the sleeping elements. The war, bequeathed to him by his father,

had devolved immense sacrifices upon the Russian common people. . . .
The war, moreover, led to a humiliation and a defeat, in the eyes at least
of the serfs, who cannot be supposed to be adepts in the mysteries of
diplomacy.[23] To initiate his new reign by apparent defeat and humiliation, both of them to be followed by an open breach of the promises held
out in war-time to the rustics, was an operation too dangerous even for a
Czar to venture upon. (MECW 16, 52–53)

While the nobles had dared, even in such an autocratic country as Russia, to
be less than enthusiastic,

the peasantry, with exaggerated notions even of what the Czar intended
doing for them, have grown impatient at the slow ways of their seigneurs.
The incendiary fires breaking out in several provinces are signals of distress not to be misunderstood. It is further known that in Great Russia,
as well as in the provinces formerly belonging to Poland, riots have taken
place, accompanied by terrible scenes, in consequence of which the nobility have emigrated from the country to the towns, where, under the
protection of walls and garrisons, they can bid defiance to their incensed
slaves. Under these circumstances, Alexander II has seen proper in this
state of things to convoke something like an assembly of notables. What
if his convocation should form a new starting-point in Russian history?
What if the nobles should insist upon their own political emancipation
as a condition preliminary to any concession to be made to the Czar with
respect to the emancipation of their serfs? (53)

Here Marx is pointing to nothing less than the possibility of a revolutionary
crisis in Russia, based on several new elements: (1) the regime's loss of le-
gitimacy due to the war, (2) unrest from below, and (3) a split in the dominant
classes. All of this recalled 1789. In these weeks in the fall of 1858, Engels somewhat belatedly takes up Marx's new emphasis on revolt inside Russia, writing
to Marx on October 21: "The Russian affair is turning out very well. There is
unrest in the South now, too" (MECW 40, 349).

Then, in a long article, "The Emancipation Question," published in the
Tribune on January 17, 1859, Marx analyzes in greater detail both the content
of the tsar's emancipation proposals and the overall situation in Russia. He
expresses surprise that the autocrat Alexander II has referred to "rights which
belong to the peasantry by nature," something Marx compares to the language
of the "rights of man" of 1789 (MECW 16, 141). The tsar's proposals will result

in "a pungent material loss to the aristocracy" as well as new rights for the serfs such as the ability to take aristocrats into court (142). The response of the landowners has been "procrastination" plus a demand for a "parliament of nobles" (144). Marx also points to Russia's intellectual ferment, with the founding of over a hundred new literary journals announced for 1859. He then recalls previous betrayals of promises by the tsars to free the serfs, especially that by Nicholas I after 1848.

But even though Alexander II was now "compelled to proceed seriously" toward emancipation, Marx wonders how the peasants would respond to provisions such as emancipation being subject to "twelve years probation," corvée labor, plus no specifics on the form emancipation would take (MECW 16, 146). He also refers to those parts of the plan that would undermine the *mir* or *obshchina*, the traditional Russian village commune, through an as yet unspecified form of "communal government":

> What will they say to an organization of communal government, jurisdiction and police, which takes away all the powers of democratic self-government, hitherto belonging to every Russian village community, in order to create a system of patrimonial government, vested in the hands of the landlord, and modeled upon the Prussian rural legislation of 1808 and 1809?—a system utterly repugnant to the Russian peasant, whose whole life is governed by the village association, who has no idea of individual landed property, but considers the association to be the proprietors of the soil on which he lives. (147)

He notes "that since 1842 the insurrections of serfs against their landlords and stewards have become epidemic" and that during the Crimean War these "insurrections increased enormously" (147). This is also Marx's first reference to these Russian peasant revolts in the 1840s and mid-1850s, for he did not mention them in texts such as the *Secret Diplomatic History*. Instead, he suggested then that Russia was immune to class conflict. More importantly, the above passage contains his first reference to the *mir*, not as a prop for Russian despotism, but as a possible point of revolutionary resistance.

The tsar, Marx writes, "is sure to vacillate" between pressures from the peasants and the landowners. But with the serfs' "expectations worked up to the highest pitch," they are even more likely to rise up. He makes an analogy to the most radical phase of the French Revolution, writing that if the serfs rise up in a massive way, "the Russian 1793 will be at hand; the reign of terror of these half-Asiatic serfs will be something unequalled in history; but it will be the second turning point in Russian history, and finally place real and general civilization in the place of that sham and show introduced by Peter the Great" (MECW 16, 147). Thus, it would be through revolution, now a real possibility, that Russia would finally develop and become "civilized," as it had not, in Marx's view, after Peter the Great's authoritarian modernization drive.

Marx goes even further a year later in a letter to Engels on December 19, 1859, suggesting that the unrest in Russia has "counter-balanced" the new power gained by the tsars since 1848:

> In Russia the movement is progressing better than anywhere else in Europe. On the one hand the constitutionalism of the aristocracy versus the Tsar, on the other of the peasants versus the aristocracy. Moreover, having at long last realized that the Poles have not the least inclination to be dissolved in Slav-Russian nationality, Alexander blustered frightfully. Thus the extraordinary successes of Russian diplomacy during the past 15 years, notably since 1849, are more than counter-balanced. Come the next revolution and Russia will oblige by joining in. (MECW 40, 552)

None of this, however, meant that Marx was relaxing his vigilance toward the existing Russian government as the most reactionary force in world politics. This can be seen in *Herr Vogt*, Marx's long polemical work published in 1860. In its twenty-page discussion of Russia, he writes that Tsar Alexander II might resort to "wars of conquest" abroad "as the only way to postpone the revolution within" (MECW 17, 141). He concludes that Russia stood threateningly at the gates of Germany, ready to expand westward and to suppress any serious revolutionary outbreak.

POLAND AS "'EXTERNAL' THERMOMETER" OF THE EUROPEAN REVOLUTION

Long before he began to discern the faint outline of a social upheaval inside Russia, Marx was repeatedly singling out a specific internal contradiction within the Russian, Prussian, and Austrian empires—the struggle of the Polish people to restore their national independence, eliminated by those three states in the infamous partition of 1795. His support for the Polish cause was one of the great political passions of his life. Support for Poland, like opposition to Russia, was for Marx—and much of his generation—a litmus test demarcating the democratic and revolutionary cause from its conservative opponents.

Two examples will illustrate the depth of that passion for Poland. The first one, indicative of his private opinions, is found in a letter of December 2, 1856 to Engels: "the intensity and viability of all revolutions since 1789 may be gauged with fair accuracy by their attitude towards Poland. Poland is their 'external' thermometer" (MECW 40, 85). The second example illustrates the extent to which Marx's opponents viewed him as a partisan of the Polish cause. In February 1867, when Marx was preparing to visit Germany to negotiate the contract for *Capital* with his publisher, a German newspaper reported that "Dr. Marx, who is living in London . . . seems to have been chosen to tour the continent to make propaganda for . . . the next" Polish "insurrection." Marx replied that such a report "must be a fabrication hatched by the police," prompting the newspaper to print a retraction (MECW 20, 202).

If Marx's views about Poland as " 'external' thermometer" of revolution quoted above seem surprising to today's readers, this is most often due to the general tendency to assume that Marx was only interested in working-class movements, which did not yet exist in agrarian Poland. Another source of confusion concerning Marx's views stems from how post-Marx Marxists often held different views on Poland. Rosa Luxemburg developed an outright opposition to Polish independence and an explicit critique of Marx's views. A few years earlier, Karl Kautsky, already on his way toward being recognized as the world's leading Marxist theoretician, had also distanced himself from Marx, albeit not as radically. In a letter to his colleague Viktor Adler on November 12, 1896, Kautsky writes: "On the Polish question, I am of the opinion that the old position of Marx has become untenable" (Adler 1954, 221). At least at a theoretical level Lenin attempted to reverse this, moving back toward Marx's old position.[24] But under Stalin, who partitioned Poland again during his 1939–41 pact with Hitler, anything associated with Polish nationalism came to be labeled a counterrevolutionary deviation, while many of Marx's writings on Russia and Poland were expunged from official editions.

Marx made his first substantial statement on Poland in a November 1847 speech on the anniversary of the 1830 Polish uprising. He did so at a London meeting sponsored by the Fraternal Democrats, an international organization set up by left-wing Chartists. The meeting also featured speeches by Chartist leaders Julian Harney and Ernest Jones, as well as other British, German, Belgian, and Polish labor activists and revolutionaries, including Engels. In his brief speech, Marx, using language close to that of *The Communist Manifesto*, which was then nearing completion, spoke of the rise of the bourgeoisie and the coming proletarian revolution. Since Poland was now part of the world capitalist system, its struggle must be viewed in that context:

Of all countries, England is the one where the contradiction between the proletariat and the bourgeoisie is most highly developed. The victory of the English proletarians over the English bourgeoisie is, therefore, decisive for the victory of all the oppressed over their oppressors. Hence Poland must be liberated not in Poland but in England. (MECW 6, 389)

Since the revolts in Poland of 1794, 1830, and 1846 had been crushed by its powerful neighbors Russia, Prussia, and Austria, Marx's view seemed to be, as Engels summarizes it in a newspaper report of the meeting, "that England would give the signal for the deliverance of Poland" and that therefore Poland would be liberated only when the "nations of Western Europe had won democracy" (MECW 6, 391). Marx, Engels, and their colleagues viewed the labor struggle and the democratic one as closely related. As Jürgen Rojahn (1995) has argued, in Europe well into the twentieth century, the term "democracy" was associated more with the left and with movements of labor and the poorer classes. In his speech at the same gathering, Engels echoes Marx's views but also points to the special responsibility of German revolutionaries with respect to Poland: "A nation cannot be free and at the same time continue to oppress other nations. The liberation of Germany cannot therefore take place without the liberation of Poland from German oppression" (MECW 6, 389).

In February 1848, *The Communist Manifesto* came off the press. Its celebrated statements to the effect that "the working men have no country" and that "national differences and antagonisms between peoples are daily more and more vanishing" (MECW 6, 502–3) have been interpreted, wrongly, as a rejection of all national claims or even of the very concept of nationality. However, after writing that the workers have no country, Marx and Engels add language pointing to the continuing importance of nationality issues: "We cannot take from them what they have not got . . . the proletariat must first of all acquire political supremacy, must rise to be the leading class of the nation, must constitute itself the nation" (502–3). Further, with "the supremacy of the proletariat," not only is class exploitation to end, but also "the exploitation of one nation by another" (502–3). Directly on Poland, one also finds at the end of the *Manifesto* the following programmatic declaration, the only one anywhere in the text concerning a specific national movement: "In Poland [the communists] support the party that insists on an agrarian revolution as the prime condition for national emancipation, that party which fomented the insurrection in Cracow in 1846" (518). To be sure, this implies a critique of conservative or landowner-based nationalism, and advocates "agrarian revolution," but it is also a very clear statement of support for the type of struggle waged during the 1846 Polish *national* insurrection.[25]

During the same month the *Manifesto* appeared, Marx and Engels spoke in Brussels at another Polish commemoration, this one concerning the 1846 insurrection.[26] They shared the platform with the renowned Polish revolutionary Joachim Lelewel, a leading member of the Polish Democratic Society. In his speech, Marx notes wryly that, just as Polish constitutional democrats of the 1790s were labeled Jacobins by Russia, Prussia, and Austria, so in 1846 their uprising was accused of communist tendencies: "Was it communist to have wanted to restore Polish nationality? . . . Or was the Cracow revolution communist because it wanted to set up a democratic government?" (MECW 6, 545). At a more serious level, he notes, "the revolutionaries of Cracow wanted only to abolish political distinctions between the social classes; they wanted to give equal rights to the different classes" (545). In contrast, Marx holds, communism "denies the inevitability [*nécessité de l'existence*] of classes; it proposes [*veut*] to abolish all classes, and all distinctions grounded therein" (546). In summing up this radical democratic movement, he avers:

> The men at the head of the revolutionary movement of Cracow shared the deep conviction that only a democratic Poland could be independent, and a democratic Poland was impossible without the abolition of feudal rights, without the agrarian revolution that would transform the dependent peasantry into free proprietors, modern proprietors. . . . The Cracow revolution has given a glorious example to the whole of Europe, by identifying the national cause with the democratic cause and the emancipation of the oppressed class.

He concludes that Polish freedom "has become the point of honor for all the democrats of Europe" (549).

In his speech, Engels contrasts the aristocratic leadership of the 1830 insurrection to that of 1846—the former was "a conservative revolution" (MECW 6, 550). But even in 1830, he adds, praising Lelewel:

> There was one man who vigorously attacked the narrow views of the ruling class. He proposed really revolutionary measures before whose boldness the aristocrats of the Diet recoiled. By calling the whole of ancient Poland to arms, by thus making the war for Polish independence a European war, by emancipating the Jews and the peasants, by making the latter share in

landed property, by reconstructing Poland on the basis of democracy and equality, he wanted to make the national cause the cause of freedom.... In 1830, these proposals were continually rejected by the blind self-interest of the aristocratic majority. But these principles, ripened and developed by the experience of fifteen years of servitude, we saw inscribed on the flag of the Cracow uprising.... the three foreign powers were attacked at the same time; the freeing of the peasants, agrarian reform, and the emancipation of the Jews were proclaimed, without caring for a moment whether this offended certain aristocratic interests. (550–51)

He concludes that by opposing Russia, the Poles were also undermining the major external support of the Prussian monarchy, and "henceforth the German people and the Polish people are irrevocably allied" (552).

In the summer of 1848, soon after Marx and Engels returned to Germany to take part in the revolution, they strongly protested a vote by the German national assembly to ratify Prussian annexations in Poland. These annexations took place after the Poles had risen up and been crushed by the Prussian military in April 1848. In August, at a meeting of the Cologne Democratic Society chaired by Marx, his close colleague Wilhelm Wolff, to whom he later dedicated the first volume of *Capital*, read out and had approved a stinging resolution. It concluded that "the healthy part of the German people will not and cannot take part in oppressing the Polish nation" (MECW 7, 565).

Over the next few weeks, Engels published a series of articles on Poland for the *Neue Rheinische Zeitung*, which comprise nearly fifty printed pages in the *Collected Works* of Marx and Engels. Many of these were taken up with polemics against the liberal parliamentarians, who exhibited a condescending attitude toward Poland even when they claimed to support it. Those whom Engels ridiculed included Arnold Ruge, who had worked closely with Marx in 1843–44, followed by a bitter break. Engels holds that the partition of Poland wedded Germany to Russia, strengthening the conservative Prussian landowners who sought to dominate the whole of Germany, while weakening the democratic movement:

From the moment the first robbery of Polish territory was committed Germany became dependent on Russia. Russia ordered Prussia and Austria to remain absolute monarchies, and Prussia and Austria had to obey. The efforts to gain control . . . on the part of the Prussian bourgeoisie—failed entirely because of . . . the support which Russia offered the feudalist-absolutist class in Prussia. (MECW 7, 350)

The Poles, however, showed a very different attitude.

As early as 1791, Engels argues, the question of agrarian revolution was on the agenda in Poland, with implications for the whole of eastern Europe:

> The Constitution of 1791 shows that already then the Poles clearly understood that their independence in foreign affairs was inseparable from the overthrow of the aristocracy and from the agrarian reform within the country. The big agrarian countries between the Baltic and the Black seas can free themselves from patriarchal feudal barbarism only by an agrarian revolution, which turns the peasants who are serfs or liable to compulsory labor into free landowners, a revolution which would be similar to the French revolution of 1789 in the countryside. It is to the credit of the Polish nation that it was the first of all its agricultural neighbors to proclaim this. . . . The struggle for the independence of Poland, particularly since the Cracow uprising of 1846, is at the same time a struggle of *agrarian democracy*—the only form of democracy possible in Eastern Europe—against *patriarchal feudal absolutism*. (MECW 7, 351)

Instead of continuing Germany's alliance with Russia, German democrats needed to declare war on Russia and to ally with Poland, Engels writes. He identifies strongly with the speech of Jan Janiszewski, a Polish delegate, who "refutes all earlier attacks against the Poles, makes amends for the mistakes of the supporters of the Poles, leads the debate back to the only real and just basis" (366). To conclude his series, Engels quotes Rousseau on the 1772 partition: "You have swallowed the Poles, but, by God, you shall not digest them" (381).

A year later, in the spring of 1849, Marx wrote an exposé of the Prussian monarchy for the *Neue Rheinische Zeitung*, one of his last articles before the newspaper was suppressed. Fundamentally, Marx suggests, even the much-admired Frederick the Great was no different from the others. Frederick was the "inventor of patriarchal despotism, the friend of Enlightenment with the help of floggings; . . . it is well known that he allied himself with Russia and Austria in order to carry out the rape of Poland, an act which still today, after the revolution of 1848, remains a permanent blot on German history" (MECW 9, 418–19). In 1852, after they had fled to London, Engels wrote in his *Revolution and Counter-Revolution in Germany* that the German liberals' betrayal of the Poles in the early days of the revolution not only strengthened Russia, but also "was the first means of reorganizing and strengthening that same Prussian army, which afterwards turned out the Liberal party and crushed the movement" (MECW 11, 45).

During this same period, perhaps depressed by the conservatism then prevalent in Europe, Engels suggests, in a letter to Marx of May 23, 1851, that perhaps they were overestimating the importance of the Polish struggle:

> The more I think about it, the more obvious it becomes to me that the Poles are *une nation foutue* [a nation that is finished] who can only continue to serve a purpose until such time as Russia herself becomes caught up into the agrarian revolution. From that moment Poland will have absolutely no *raison d'être* any more. The Poles' sole contribution to history has been to indulge in foolish pranks at once valiant and provocative. (MECW 38, 363)

After launching into a military analysis of the next revolution, he adds:

> Fortunately, in the *Neue Rheinische Zeitung* we assumed no positive obligations towards the Poles, save the unavoidable one of restoration combined with a suitable frontier—and even that only on the condition of there being an agrarian revolution. . . . Conclusion: To take as much away from the Poles in the West, to man their fortresses, especially Posen [Poznan], with Germans on the pretext of defense, to let them stew in their own juice . . . and, should it be possible to get the Russians moving [in a revolution], to ally oneself with the latter and compel the Poles to give way. . . . A nation which can muster 20,000 to 30,000 men at most, is not entitled to a voice. And Poland could not muster very much more. (364–65)

No reply by Marx to this outburst appears to have survived, and nowhere in his own writings does Marx express similar sentiments. Rubel, pointing to Engels's predilection for the military side of things, calls this "a diatribe worthy of the proletarian 'General'" (*Oeuvres* 4, 1352). "The General" was in fact the jocular nickname given to Engels by the Marx family, probably originating with the children. Engels, however, returned in his subsequent writings on Poland to his earlier stance of strong support for national emancipation.[27]

During the 1850s, Marx concentrated less on Polish affairs, but he devoted part of his 1853 pamphlet "Lord Palmerston" to the latter's duplicity toward Poland. Marx writes that despite his pose as a "chivalrous protector of the Poles" (MECW 12, 358), Palmerston did not lift a finger to aid them in 1830. Then, adds Marx, "when the atrocities committed by the Russians, after the fall of Warsaw, are denounced, he recommends to the house [of Commons] great tenderness towards the Emperor of Russia" (360). Marx also charges that

Palmerston helped Russia to defray the costs of its 1830 military intervention. Marx argues that in 1846 as well, Palmerston expressed public sympathy for Poland but thwarted all efforts to do anything concrete to aid her struggle.

Marx's 1855 article for the *Neue Oder-Zeitung*, "The Poland Meeting," illustrates the exile and labor milieu in which he was politically active during the 1850s. This article describes a controversy at a London gathering to support the Polish cause, a meeting that had been called by the Literary Association of the Friends of Poland. Marx portrays the Literary Association as composed of the conservative Polish émigré "[Adam] Czartoryski's supporters on the one hand and English aristocrats with a friendly disposition toward Poland on the other." The Literary Association was, he maintains, "a blind tool in the hands of Palmerston," helping him to keep "his 'anti-Russian' reputation alive" (MECW 14, 477). In the Polish exile community, the Literary Association was able to claim near-official status due to its occasional access to Palmerston and other prominent British politicians, but it was opposed fiercely by the more leftist Polish Democratic Association, the tendency with which Marx had been in contact from 1847 onwards. To their surprise, the meeting's conveners found the hall full of Chartists, anti-Russian Urquhartists, and members of the Polish Democratic Association. The Urquhartist David Collet tried to read out an amendment to the meeting's Poland support resolution, pointing to "the perfidious conduct of Lord Palmerston from 1830 to 1846." The amendment argued that Palmerston's support for Poland was "a sham and a delusion," and also accused him of conducting the Crimean War "in such a way as to avoid, as far as possible, injuring Russia" (478). Marx also mentions the eloquent intervention from the floor "of an unknown young plebeian." He concludes that the discussion in the audience made the meeting "a defeat for Palmerston" and "even more so for the class he represents" (480). Marx also complained that the pro-government English press published distorted accounts of the meeting, portraying the dissension as the work of Russian agents.

It was in this period that Marx, as discussed above, also characterizes support for Poland to be the "'external' thermometer" by which one could measure "the intensity and viability of all revolutions since 1789." In this letter to Engels of December 2, 1856, Marx adds: "This is demonstrable in detail from French history. It is conspicuous in our brief German revolutionary period, likewise in the Hungarian." The only "exception" Marx makes is for the Jacobins of 1794, who upbraided Tadeusz Kosciuszko for failing to carry out an agrarian revolution in Poland and for tolerating "aristocratic traitors to the country" (MECW 40, 85–86). A number of Marx's letters from late 1856 indicate that he was intensively studying Polish history, especially the works of Ludwik Mieroslawski and Lelewel. At this time, he sent some of his excerpt notes on Mieroslawski to Engels.

Marx and Engels coauthored a laudatory article that appeared in 1858 in Dana's *New American Cyclopaedia* on the legendary Polish military leader Jozef Bem (1795–1850). Their fervent support for Poland is evident even within the encyclopedia format. Noting that "the passion of his life was hatred of Russia," they recount Bem's early training in Napoleon's army. They also take up his distinguished leadership during the 1830 Polish uprising, but note as well some costly errors of judgment on his part during the Russian attack on Warsaw. After escaping into exile, they write, Bem came to prominence again in 1848, when "on the first appearance of revolutionary symptoms in Austrian Poland" (MECW 18, 131), he went to Vienna, and was given a command in the revolutionary forces. Later sent to defend the revolution in Hungary in 1848–49, Bem raised and trained an army and showed himself to be a master of "partisan and mountain warfare" (132). Bem also exhibited great political sensitivity to the national question, and they hold that his "policy of conciliation between the antagonist nationalities aided him in swelling his force, in a few months, to 40,000 or 50,000 men." Finally overcome by larger and better-equipped Russian and Austrian forces, Bem avoided capture in Hungary by taking refuge in the Ottoman Empire. There he converted to Islam and was given a military command by the sultan, although the Western powers pressured the Ottomans to keep him away from the Russian border. Just before dying of fever, one of Bem's last acts was that of "repressing some sanguinary excesses committed during Nov. 1850 on the Christian residents by the Mussulman populace" of Aleppo, Syria (133).[28]

THE POLISH UPRISING OF 1863: "THE ERA OF REVOLUTION HAS OPENED IN EUROPE ONCE MORE"

In late 1861, mass unrest broke out in Warsaw again, resulting in harsh repression by the Russian military. Marx followed the situation closely, commenting on it several times in letters to Engels. In a letter to Engels dated December 27, 1861, he suggests that, at a time when British public opinion was pressuring the government to support the Poles actively, Palmerston's true aim in creating a diplomatic crisis with Abraham Lincoln's government was "diversion of attention from Poland" (MECW 41, 336).[29]

In January 1863, a full-scale uprising broke out in Poland. Marx, who viewed it as the harbinger of a wider European revolution, writes Engels on February 13:

"What do you think of the Polish business? This much is certain; the era of revolution has now fairly opened in Europe once more. . . . This time, let us hope, the lava will flow from East to West" (MECW 41, 453). Before waiting for Engels's reply, and with Prussia having come to Russia's aid in suppressing the uprising, Marx proposes, in a letter from February 17, that he and Engels coauthor a "manifesto" on Poland:

> The Polish business and Prussia's intervention do indeed represent a combination that impels us to speak. . . . The [German] Workers Society here would serve well for the purpose. A manifesto should be issued in *its* name, and issued immediately. You must write the military bit—i.e., on Germany's military and political interest in the restoration of Poland. I shall write the diplomatic bit. (MECW 41, 455)

Marx also proposes that they write a larger pamphlet and submit it to a publisher in Germany. Engels accepts both proposals, but in a letter of March 24, Marx suggests a delay in order "to see events when they have reached a rather more advanced stage." He also comments on Prussia's role: "The view I have reached is this: . . . that the 'state' of Prussia (a very different creature from Germany) cannot exist either *without* Russia as she is, or *with* an independent Poland. . . . The state of Prussia must be erased from the map" (MECW 41, 461–62). During the spring of 1863, Marx made extensive excerpt notes as well as a partial draft of the Poland pamphlet, but, according to Rubel and Manale, "repeated illness kept him from finishing" (1975, 184).[30] Marx was also wary of the relatively conservative Mieroslawski's prominent role in the uprising, especially because of the latter's ties to the Bonapartist regime. As military events seemed to go against the Poles, Engels on several occasions expressed grave pessimism about the uprising's chances. However, as late as the fall of 1863, Marx seemed more optimistic about the situation, even writing to Engels on September 12 about the idea of helping to form in London a German legion to go to Poland to fight against Russia and Prussia (MECW 41, 491–93).

Also in the fall of 1863, Marx finally drafted the unsigned, short public statement on Poland that he had proposed at the beginning of the year. It was issued in November by the German Workers Educational Society in London, a group that included people active in the old Communist League of the 1840s. Seeking to raise funds for Poland among German workers abroad, the English-language flier castigated German liberal politicians for their failure to support Poland and also made connections to the Civil War in the United States:

In this fateful moment, the German working class owes it to the Poles, to foreign countries and to its own honor to raise a loud protest against the German betrayal of Poland, which is at the same time treason to Germany and to Europe. It must inscribe the *Restoration of Poland* in letters of flame on its banner, since bourgeois liberalism has erased this glorious motto from its own flag. The English working class has won immortal historical honor for itself by thwarting the repeated attempts of the ruling classes to intervene on behalf of the American slaveholders by its enthusiastic mass-meetings. . . . If police restrictions prevent the working class in Germany from conducting demonstrations on such a scale for Poland, they do not in any way force them to brand themselves in the eyes of the world as accomplices in the betrayal, through apathy and silence. (MECW 19, 297)

After the insurrection was finally crushed, Marx, in a letter to Engels of June 7, 1864, judges it to have been a major historical turning point, referring also to Russia's final defeat of the Chechen mountaineers in Caucasia:

The outrageous step the Russians have now taken in the Caucasus, watched by the rest of Europe with idiotic indifference, virtually compels them—and indeed makes it easier for them—to turn a blind eye to what is happening elsewhere. These 2 affairs, the suppression of the Polish insurrection and the annexation of the Caucasus, I regard as the two most important events to have taken place in Europe since 1815. (MECW 41, 538)

Here, the centrality of Poland and Russia to Marx's perspectives on European politics is illustrated with a dramatic flourish that may surprise readers imbued with the notion that Marx reduced all politics to class and economic questions.

Despite these bitter defeats, he writes, a new era was dawning for the socialist movement. As Riazanov ([1927] 1973) notes, since the Bonapartist police state claimed to support Poland, it allowed public meetings in France to support the 1863 insurrection. Some of these were organized by workers, who were permitted to contact like-minded British workers, the latter having organized even larger pro-Polish meetings. In July 1863, an international delegation of French workers was permitted to travel to London for a joint meeting on Poland. During these same days, London trade union leaders such as George Odger, a prominent figure in the Poland meetings, decided to form closer links with workers on the European continent. The eventual result was the founding of the International Working Men's Association, or First International, in September 1864, in which other workers and intellectuals involved in the Polish cause, among them Marx, played prominent parts.

Some weeks later, in a letter of November 29 to his uncle Lion Philips, Marx sums up briefly the relationship of Poland and the American Civil War to the birth of the First International:

> In September the Parisian workers sent a delegation to the London workers to demonstrate support for Poland. On that occasion, an international Workers' Committee was formed. The matter is not without importance because . . . in London the same people are at the head who organized the gigantic reception for [Italian revolutionary Giuseppe] Garibaldi and, by their monster meeting with [British Liberal leader John] Bright in St. James's Hall, *prevented war with the United States.* (MECW 42, 47)

In Marx's November 1864 "Inaugural Address" of the International, which became in effect its program, the main focus was on capital and labor. However, he alluded prominently to Ireland at the beginning and the end of the Address, also sketching a foreign policy for the working class, specifically mentioning the American Civil War, Poland, Russia, and Caucasia:

> It was not the wisdom of the ruling classes, but the heroic resistance to their criminal folly by the working classes of England that saved the West of Europe from plunging headlong into an infamous crusade for the perpetuation and propagation of slavery on the other side of the Atlantic. The shameless approval, mock sympathy, or idiotic indifference, with which the upper classes of Europe have witnessed the mountain fortress of the Caucasus falling a prey to, and heroic Poland being assassinated by, Russia; the immense and unresisted encroachments of that barbarous power, whose head is in St. Petersburg, and whose hands are in every Cabinet of Europe, have taught the working classes the duty to master themselves the mysteries of international politics. . . . The fight for such a foreign policy forms part of the general struggle for the emancipation of the working classes. (MECW 20, 13)

DEBATES OVER POLAND AND FRANCE
WITHIN THE INTERNATIONAL

The Polish question soon led to a series of debates and conflicts within the International, reflected in the deliberations of its London-based General Council. In the winter of 1864–65, Peter Fox, an intellectual and a prominent Poland support activist who had joined the International, presented a draft for a statement by the International on Poland which, in Marx's view, greatly exaggerated France's support for Poland over the past century.[31] In a letter to Engels dated December 10, 1864, Marx attributed this error to the "fanatical 'love' of France" often found among British radical democrats (MECW 42, 55). In December 1864 and January 1865, Marx prepared notes and gave several lengthy presentations to the International on France and Poland, as part of an effort to have Fox's draft revised. In the longest of these texts that has survived, Marx traces in great detail French policy toward Russia and Poland. He finds France's support of Poland against Russia during the eighteenth century to have been at best half-hearted. Pointing to the Seven Years' War (1756–63), in which France and Russia were allied against England and Prussia, Marx characterizes its results as follows: "That the material resources of Poland were exhausted, that Russia founded her supremacy in Germany, that Prussia was made her slave, that Catherine II [of Russia] became the most powerful sovereign in Europe, and that the *first partition of Poland* took place" (MECW 20, 314; original emphasis).

During the wars that followed the French Revolution, he writes, the Polish uprising of 1794 forced Prussia and Austria to curtail their participation in what Marx terms the "Anti-Jacobin War":[32]

> *In the spring of 1794* Kosciusko's revolutionary rising. Prussia marched at once her troops against Poland. Beaten. In *September 1794*, while forced to retreat from Warsaw, at the same time rising in Posen. Then the king of Prussia declared his intention to withdraw from the contest carried on against France. Austria also, in the autumn of 1794, detached a body of troops for Poland, by which circumstance the success of the French arms on the Rhine and so forth was secured. . . . In the very months October, *November* (1794) everywhere French successes when Kosciuszko succumbed, Praga was taken by [the Russian General Alexander] Suvorov etc., immense murdering etc. (MECW 20, 318–19; original emphasis)

While Polish actions benefited the French revolutionary regime, he adds, "Poland was blotted out under cover of the French Revolution and the Anti-

Jacobin War" by the conservative powers Russia, Prussia, and Austria (319). Marx then quotes a number of French and Polish sources, which suggested that Poland had been betrayed by the Jacobins.

Then, under Napoleon, Polish exile legions were formed. But some of them, Marx writes, were forced by 1802 to fight not in Poland but against the Haitian Revolution: "Threatened by the fire of artillery, they were embarked at Genoa and Livorno to find their graves in St. Domingo" (MECW 20, 323). Other Polish legions, however, played a great part in France's push eastward to Warsaw by 1806. Marx criticizes Napoleon's creation of a Duchy of Warsaw out of Prussian territory, rather than a full restoration of Poland, something that allowed the larger portion of Polish land partitioned in 1795 to remain in Russian hands:

> *Many large estates* in the new duchy were made a present of by Napoleon to the French generals. *Lelewel* calls this justly the *Fourth Division of Poland.* Having beaten the Prussians and the Russians by the assistance of the Poles, Napoleon disposed of Poland, as if she was a conquered country and his private property, and he disposed of her to the advantage of Russia. (MECW 20, 324; original emphasis)

In 1809, as the Poles became more adamant that their country be restored, Marx writes:

> The *Poles* now demanded the restoration of the name of *Poland* for the duchy. The Czar opposed. On *October 20, 1809,* [Jean-Baptiste] *Champagny,* [French] minister of foreign affairs, addressed a note, by order of Napoleon, to the Russian government, in which it was stated that he approved the *effacing* [of] *the name of Pole and Poland,* not only from *every public act, but even from history.* This was to prepare his proposal—after his divorce with Joséphine—for the hand of the Czar's sister. (326; original emphasis)

Marx concludes that in 1812, when Napoleon finally attacked Russia, this was "not out of any regard for Poland" but because "he was forced into it by Russia." And even then, when Napoleon finally allowed a Polish confederation to be formed, he still opposed the idea of a "national war by Poland against Russia" (327).

The draft manuscript breaks off at this point, but Marx's notes suggest that his speech to the International took the story up through the 1830 Revolution and its aftermath.[33] Continuing his attacks on Napoleon, he writes that the latter's betrayals of Poland had serious consequences for the 1812 war against Russia: "It was, therefore, not the *disaster of Napoleon* which caused him to abandon Poland, but it was his *renewed betrayal* of Poland, *that caused his disaster*" in the Russian campaign. Marx details Napoleon's refusal to allow an independent Polish army, instead dispersing the eighty thousand Polish troops into his *Grande Armée* during the war against Russia, thus refusing to allow a national war against Russia. This was similar to Napoleon's conduct during the period of his return in 1815 and defeat at Waterloo, Marx argues, when he feared a renewal of revolution in France even more than defeat: "That despot, rather than have a truly *national* and *revolutionary war* in France after his defeat at Waterloo, preferred to succumb to the Coalition" (MECW 20, 490; original emphasis).

With regard to the French Revolution of 1830 which, after the harsh Restoration years, brought the "bourgeois monarch" Louis Philippe to power, Marx argues that the 1830 "Polish insurrection had saved France from a new Anti-Jacobin War." He writes that "the Russians, on the news of the revolution, of the barricades in Paris, determined to march upon France," attempting to use a Russian-formed Polish army for this purpose (MECW 20, 492). But the outbreak of revolution in Poland, which began among those troops, forestalled any thought of Russian intervention in France. In the aftermath, however, argues Marx, Louis Philippe broke his promise to aid Poland. To buttress his views, Marx quotes from French parliamentary debates in 1831:

> The Polish nation (that is to say the *diplomatic clique*) relied on the French "compliments." An intimation was given to the Polish generals, that if they delayed attacking the Russian army for 2 months, their security would be guaranteed. The Polish generals did delay—that fatal delay, and Poland was ruined, not by the arms of Russia, but by the promises of France (and Austria).
>
> *Lafayette* communicated *against the denials of Guizot, Thiers, Périer, Sébastini,* to the chamber of deputies the documentary proofs: 1) that the Poles had broken the Russian coalition against France; 2) that Louis Philippe had caused the Poles to prolong their resistance for 2 months; 3) that it had quite been in the power of France, by one firm declaration, as they had made it on behalf of Belgium, to prevent the Prussian help which in fact decided the Russian victory.

Sitting of the Deputies of 16 January 1831:
Lafayette: "The war was prepared against us; Poland was to form the vanguard [*l'avant-garde*]; the vanguard turned against the main body." Maugin: "Who arrested the movement of Russia? It was Poland. They wanted to hurl her against us: she became our vanguard, and we are abandoning her! Well! Let her die! Her children are accustomed to dying for us." (MECW 20, 492–93; original emphasis)

Like Napoleon before him, Louis Philippe attempted to use Polish exile legions in a French colonial war, this time in Algeria. But again there was resistance by the Poles, who compared it to what Napoleon did in Haiti. Marx adds that these betrayals were those of French officials and diplomats, but that leftist revolutionaries such as Auguste Blanqui and workers' clubs "were true friends of Poland" (494).

Marx won his point within the General Council of the International. The minutes of the meeting of January 3, 1865, state that Marx "in a very able historical résumé argued that the traditional foreign policy of France had not been favorable to the restoration of the independence of Poland." A motion asking that Fox's address on Poland "be amended so as to accord with the truths of history" was passed unanimously, in a vote in which Fox seems to have concurred (*General Council of the First International* 1962, 61–62).

The French political theorist Maurice Barbier notes that concerning Poland, Marx by the 1860s "adopts a position that is the reverse of the one he held in 1847–48. Whereas in the earlier period he saw the liberation of Poland as a consequence of the proletarian revolution, henceforth he considered it to be a condition for the development of the workers movement, notably in Germany" (1992, 296). Even more was involved, however. Marx's writings on Poland in 1865–66 were debates inside the revolutionary movement, inside the International. First, he was attempting to prove to his colleagues in the International that in three key periods—the French Revolution of 1789–94, the Napoleonic era, and the Revolution of 1830—the French betrayed Poland. He was doing so in a debate within the international Left, among supporters of Poland, some of whom he considered to be imbued with illusions about France as a consistently revolutionary country. Second, he was making a broader point, one aimed at future revolutionary movements in Europe. He argued that in betraying Poland, the French revolutionaries constricted or even destroyed themselves, leading to defeat by external enemies or a too-limited revolution at home, one that did not really uproot the old system. This latter point concerned those junctures when revolutionaries in a large and powerful country such as France failed to take seriously enough the struggle of a militarily weaker, oppressed nation like Poland, and how that deficiency doomed the revolution inside the more powerful country as well as the oppressed nation. In short, he seemed to be arguing that unless democratic and class struggles could link up with those of oppressed nationalities, both would fail to realize fully their aims, if not go down to defeat. Elsewhere, he would make similar points with regard to white workers in the United States and the Black struggle, or British workers and the Irish struggle.

On March 1, 1865, the International helped to organize a large public meeting in support of the Polish cause. Although the speakers from the International included Fox, the German worker Johann Georg Eccarius, and the French intellectual Victor Le Lubez, the big British newspapers only covered the speeches by liberal politicians. When a similar incomplete report also appeared in a German-language Swiss paper, Marx published a brief reply summarizing the International's position on Poland:

> *Mr. Peter Fox* (an Englishman), on behalf of the *International Working Men's Association,* proposed "that an integral and independent Poland is an indispensable condition of democratic Europe, and that so long as this condition is unfulfilled, revolutionary triumphs on the Continent are short-lived [. . .] preludes to long periods of counter-revolutionary rule."
>
> After briefly outlining the history of the evils which had befallen Europe as a result of the loss of liberty by Poland, and of Russia's policy of conquest, Mr. P. Fox said that the stand of the *Liberal* party on this question did not coincide with that of the *democratic* society for which he was speaking. . . . The motto of the International Working Men's Association was, on the contrary: a free Europe based upon a free and independent Poland. (MECW 20, 97; original emphasis)

The above suggests that Marx had ironed out his differences with Fox and his supporters. By 1866, however, a new and more divisive dispute broke out over Poland.

DISPUTE WITH THE PROUDHONISTS OVER POLAND

At the time of Pierre Joseph Proudhon's death in 1865, Marx wrote a long article in German in which he repeated his earlier critiques of the French utopian socialist's economic theories. He added a stinging attack on Proudhon's pro-

Russia stance, writing that "his last work, written against *Poland*,[34] in which for the greater glory of the tsar he expresses moronic cynicism, must be described as ... not merely bad but base, a baseness, however, which corresponds to the petty-bourgeois point of view" (MECW 20, 32).

A year later, opposition to Marx emerged within the International among some of its French-speaking members, most of them influenced by Proudhonism. In keeping with Proudhon's view that labor should not involve itself in political issues, but stick to economic and social ones, they opposed singling out Poland for strong and specific support, and wished to concentrate on labor issues. As Riazanov notes, Marx's Proudhonist opponents were "against taking up the question of Polish independence, for they regarded it as purely political" ([1927] 1973, 168). The Proudhonists also criticized the International's organizational structure, which featured a central leadership body in London, the General Council, on which served representatives of various countries.

This dispute over Poland was to become Marx's biggest argument with the Proudhonists during the life of the First International. In a letter to Engels dated January 5, 1866, Marx writes that Poland was the key to this conflict:

A plot has been hatched against the International Association, in which connection I need your cooperation. . . . It is tied up with all that pack of Proudhonists in Brussels. . . . The real crux of the controversy is the *Polish question*. The lugs [*Bürschen*][35] have all attached themselves to the Muscovist line pursued by Proudhon and Herzen. I shall therefore send you the earlier articles ... against Poland and you must do a refutation ... (MECW 42, 212–13)

Engels agreed to write a defense of the International's position on Poland, in what was his first important contribution to the International.

In a letter to Engels of January 15, Marx quotes at length some of the attacks on the International's pro-Poland position. According to these attacks, which had appeared in a Belgian newspaper, the leadership was allowing the International to "degenerate into a committee of nationalities," a phrase intended to associate Marx and the leadership of the International with Bonapartism, which espoused a "principle of nationalities." According to the Proudhonists, Marx adds, the leaders of the International obstinately opposed "Russian influence in Europe" but ignored the fact that "Russian and Polish serfs had just been emancipated by Russia, whereas the Polish nobility and priests have always refused to grant freedom to theirs."[36] Finally, the Proudhonists had even charged that there was the danger of a Polish takeover of the International and were claiming, he reports to Engels, that "the Poles have asked to join [the General Council] *en masse* and before long will represent the overwhelming majority," plus the Poles admit openly "that they will make use of the Association to help restore their nation, without concerning themselves with the question of the emancipation of the workers" (MECW 42, 216–18).

Engels's series of articles, "What Have the Working Classes to Do with Poland?" appeared in the spring of 1866 in the *Commonwealth*, a weekly organ of the International. He begins by tracing the history of the Polish question in the European working class movement:

> Whenever the working classes have taken a part of their own in political movements, there, from the very beginning, their foreign policy was expressed in the few words—*Restoration of Poland*. This was the case with the Chartist movement so long as it existed; this was the case with the French working men long before 1848, as well as during that memorable year, when on the 15th of May they marched on to the National Assembly to the cry of "*Vive la Pologne!*"—Poland for ever! This was the case in Germany, when, in 1848 and '49, the organs of the working class[37] demanded war with Russia and the restoration of Poland. It is the case even now. (MECW 20, 152; original emphasis)

Engels also charges that, despite their expressed sympathies, "middle class politicians" had left "the Poles in the lurch in 1831, in 1846, in 1863" (152).

However, continues Engels, there is "one exception" to the near-unanimous working class support of Poland. There is found "among the working men of France a small minority who belong to the school of the late P. J. Proudhon," who, "sitting in judgment on oppressed Poland," say that her fate "serves her right" (MECW 20, 153). Engels also argues that Russia had been the main oppressor of Poland, going through the history of the partitions and of the role of Austria and Prussia as well. Engels additionally separates himself from the Bonapartist "principle of nationalities," holding that it can and is being used by Russia to gain further influence via an espousal of Pan-Slavism. Some echoes of his old position on historic versus nonhistoric peoples can be heard here, as he dismisses the Romanians as among those "who never had a history" (157). With regard to the class question inside Poland, Engels acknowledges but does not dwell upon the point that "the aristocracy *did* ruin Poland" (159). He also refers to the relative religious tolerance that had marked Polish history, especially "the asylum the Jews found there while they were being persecuted in other parts of Europe" (160).

Engels's articles had some impact on the International. Marx writes to him on May 17 that "the Poles here are waiting for the next article." He also mentions that Fox publicly criticized "the passage in which you ascribe the partitioning to the corruption of the Polish aristocracy," criticisms to which Marx says he replied (MECW 42, 277–78). Engels did not write any more on Poland at this time, however, possibly because changes in the editorship of the *Commonwealth* would have made it hard for him or Marx to publish there.

As the year 1867 opened, and in the midst of his finishing the final draft of *Capital*, Marx gave a lengthy speech on Poland to a London meeting commemorating the 1863 Polish uprising, which was sponsored by the International and the United Polish Exiles. Marx begins by tracing Poland's crucial role in safeguarding the 1830 French Revolution:

> Some 30 years ago, a Revolution broke out in France. . . . On the arrival of the awkward news, the Czar Nicholas summoned the officers of his horseguard and addressed them a short, warlike speech, culminating in the words: à cheval [to the horses], Messieurs. This was no empty threat. . . . The insurrection of Warsaw saved Europe from a second Anti-Jacobin War. (MECW 20, 196)

Again, in 1848, the same tsar, Nicholas I, was unable to interfere with the German revolution because he had to concentrate on mopping up the Polish insurrection. Marx adds:

> Only after the betrayal of the Poles by the Germans, especially the German National Assembly in Frankfurt, Russia recovered her forces and waxed strong enough to stab the Revolution of 1848 in its last asylum, Hungary. And even here, the last man who bestrode the battlefield against her was a Pole, General Bem. (197)

Then Marx recounts in great detail what he regarded as Russia's continuing aim of world conquest, referring to its fortifications in Poland, its new conquests in Caucasia and Asia, and its use of "Panslavonian propaganda" (199).

He notes that some had suggested that, by the emancipation of the serfs, Alexander II's Russia "has entered the family of civilized nations" (MECW 20, 199–200). In addition, some had argued that Prussia's rising strength or the impending European revolution were bound to limit Russia's power. Marx was dubious of these propositions. First, he declares, the emancipation of the serfs only strengthened Russia militarily and politically: "It has created a vast recruiting place for its army, broken up the common property of the Russian peasants, insulated them, and, above all, strengthened their faith in their pope-autocrat" (200). In this passage, he seems to be returning to his pre-1858 position on Russia. Second, he holds that Prussia remained dependent on Russia and that the Prussian aristocracy's rule over Polish lands gave it a feudal base from which to undermine the German revolution. Third, as to the impending European revolution, Marx suggests that it would once again face the threat of Russian intervention, just as it did in all previous revolutions since 1789.

Marx avers that Poland remained the key to the European revolution, since a Polish uprising would undermine Russia:

> There is only one alternative left for Europe. Asiatic barbarism under Muscovite leadership will burst over her head like a lawine [avalanche], or she must restore Poland, thus placing between herself and Asia 20 millions of heroes, and gaining breathing time for the accomplishment of her social regeneration. (MECW 20, 201)

With its ethnocentric language about "Asiatic barbarism," the above passage shows that as late as 1867, Marx had retained many of the essentials of his position on Russia from the 1840s and 1850s. Evidently, he saw the Russian autocracy as having weathered the crisis of the late 1850s and 1860s.

LAST WRITINGS ON POLAND

After 1867, Marx discussed Poland only occasionally, but he continued to place Polish national emancipation at the center of European revolutionary politics. In a January 1875 speech, Marx and Engels stress the "cosmopolitan" character of Polish revolutionaries, now including a reference to the Paris Commune:

> Poland . . . is the only European people that has fought and is fighting as the *cosmopolitan soldier of the revolution*. Poland shed its blood during the American War of Independence; its legions fought under the banner of the first French Republic; by its revolution of 1830 it prevented the invasion of France that had been decided by the partitioners of Poland; in 1846 in Cracow it was the first in Europe to plant the banner of social revolution; in 1848 it played an outstanding part in the revolutionary struggle in Hungary, Germany, and Italy; finally, in 1871 it supplied the Paris Commune with its best generals and most heroic soldiers. (MECW 24, 57–58; original emphasis)

The language above about the 1846 Cracow uprising as the "first in Europe to plant the banner of a social revolution" was somewhat ambiguous. At one level, it simply repeated arguments from 1848 to the effect that the 1846 uprising was a deeply democratic movement that aimed at land reform and other pressing social questions. At another level, however, the language about this being a "first" for Europe suggested something more radical, since France had experienced a major social revolution as early as 1789. Was this phrase about Europe's first social revolution an allusion to a possible socialist dimension present in Poland in 1846? The answer to this would become clearer a bit later, in their 1880 speech on Poland.

In this 1875 address, Marx and Engels detail the reciprocal affinity toward Poland on the part of the French revolutionary movement, again referring to the Paris Commune: "In Paris, in May 1848, Blanqui marched at the head of the workers against the reactionary National Assembly in order to force it to accept armed intervention for Poland; finally, in 1871, when the Parisian workers had constituted themselves as the government, they honored Poland by entrusting its sons with the military leadership of their forces" (MECW 24, 58). Marx had also stressed this point in "The Civil War in France," his celebrated pamphlet on the Paris Commune.

In a November 1880 address to a Geneva meeting on the fiftieth anniversary of the 1830 Polish revolution, Marx and Engels again emphasized Poland's centrality to the wider European revolution. They also took up the more radical 1846 revolution, which they had singled out prominently in *The Communist Manifesto* in 1848. In 1880, however, they move explicitly beyond their views of 1848 when they characterize the 1846 uprising, along with the Chartist movement in Britain, as a harbinger of the socialist revolution:

> From 1840 onwards the propertied classes of England were already forced to call out the army to resist the Chartist party, this first militant organization of the working class. Then in 1846, in the last refuge of independent Poland, Cracow, the first political revolution to proclaim socialist demands broke out. (MECW 24, 344)[38]

While Poland in 1846 is linked directly to socialism, the Chartist movement is characterized less globally, as a militant labor movement. This characterization of the 1846 Cracow uprising as the "first" revolution with "socialist demands" was new, for as discussed above, in his 1848 speech on Poland Marx had referred to its radical democratic agrarian program, but explicitly denied any socialist orientation.

This turn in Marx's thinking about the character of the 1846 uprising was very likely related to his late writings on Russia, where he was considering the possibility that a communist revolution in Russia could serve as the starting point for a wider European socialist transformation. As will be discussed in chapter 6, he first expressed these views on Russia in a March 1881 letter to the revolutionary émigré Vera Zasulich; this was only four months after the address to the Geneva meeting on Poland. While the issue of a possible communist revolution in Russia is not broached in the 1880 address on Poland, there is another difference from 1848 that bears on Russia. As against the 1840s, Russia is no longer seen as a conservative backwater. Instead, the 1880 address on Poland expresses the hope that the revolutionary efforts of Poland and its supporters would "coincide with the unparalleled efforts of our Russian brothers" (MECW 24, 344–45).

CHAPTER THREE

Race, Class, and Slavery: The Civil War as a Second American Revolution

As we have seen, new struggles broke out in Europe and North America in the 1860s, as the conservatism of the 1850s receded. For Marx, this was a period of rich creative development, as he completed and published volume I of *Capital* in 1867 and drafted most of what was to be posthumously published as volumes II and III of that work, as well as *Theories of Surplus Value*. During these same years, Marx also experienced his most intensive political activism since leaving Germany in 1849, as he helped found and lead the First International Working Men's Association, later known as the First International. New class conflicts, as well as important efforts against national and racial oppression, emerged in the 1860s in a number of countries.

In Marx's view, the 1861–65 Civil War in the United States constituted one of the century's major battles for human emancipation, one that forced white labor in both the United States and in Britain to take a stand against slavery. In the 1867 preface to *Capital*, he wrote that the Civil War was the harbinger of socialist revolutions to come. He regarded it as a social revolution that changed not only political arrangements but also class and property relations.[1] Moreover, Marx saw support for the North as a litmus test for the Left, while also siding with the radical abolitionists against the cautious Abraham Lincoln.

Although widely available through two different one-volume collections in English (Marx and Engels 1937; KML 2), Marx's Civil War writings have not received much discussion in the theoretical literature, despite his treatment in them of a hotly debated topic: the intersections of class and race. The discussion they have received offers some illumination as to why this has been the case, for these writings have sometimes been viewed as falling outside Marx's core concerns, or even his core concepts. But as I am arguing in this book, we need to adjust somewhat our view of what constituted Marx's core concepts and concerns.

In 1913, the German immigrant socialist Hermann Schlüter discussed some of Marx's writings on the Civil War in his *Lincoln, Labor, and Slavery*. While Schlüter brought to light for the first time many key issues associated with Marx and the Civil War, his study also had some important gaps, not least his avoidance of any comment on contemporary race relations.[2] They received more sustained attention during the Depression of the 1930s, when Black and white workers united as never before inside a resurgent labor movement, and as some important struggles against racism were also taking place. Bertram Wolfe, the future historian of Russia, took up Marx's Civil War writings in a 1934 pamphlet, *Marx and America*. Wolfe had recently been expelled from the Communist Party as member of its "Lovestoneite" faction, which was linked to Nikolai Bukharin's Right Opposition inside Russia. Wolfe connects the Civil War writings to a theory of American "exceptionalism," according to which the lack of a European-style class divide had given the United States a unique social structure, in which the differing status position of "native and foreign born" workers exacerbated the divide between skilled and unskilled workers found in all capitalist societies (1934, 22). Wolfe extolls Marx's notion of a Radical Reconstruction of the defeated South, which "would have involved the smashing of the Southern ruling class, breaking up their estates, distribution of the land to those who tilled it, the emancipated slaves and poor whites, and full social, economic and political equality for the negroes" (17). Unfortunately, Wolfe, like Schlüter, had almost nothing to say about contemporary race relations. In addition, the concept of American exceptionalism, which implied that Marx's major theoretical works like *Capital* did not apply to the United States, found little favor with other Marxists, although it was taken up by some outside the Marxian tradition, most notably the sociologist Seymour Martin Lipset.

A year later, the African American sociologist W. E. B. Du Bois published *Black Reconstruction in America* ([1935] 1973), a work grounded in Marx's Civil War writings. Du Bois holds that white racism had blunted labor's efforts at self-emancipation:

> The upward moving of white labor was betrayed into wars for profit based on color caste. . . . Indeed, the plight of the white working class throughout the world today is directly traceable to Negro slavery in America, on which modern commerce and industry was founded, and

which persisted to threaten free labor until it was partially overthrown in 1863. The resulting color caste founded and retained by capitalism was adopted, forwarded and approved by white labor, and resulted in subordination of colored labor to white profits the world over. Thus, the majority of the world's laborers, by the insistence of white labor, became the basis of a system of industry which ruined democracy and showed its perfect fruit in World War and Depression. ([1935] 1973, 30)

Du Bois stressed how the failure of white labor to support adequately the post–Civil War Black struggle cut short the gains of what amounted to a second American revolution. At the same time, he took up those moments where Black labor, northern radical intellectuals, and elements of white labor had coalesced to form what he termed the "abolition democracy." The latter constituted a progressive legacy for the future.[3]

By this time, Du Bois had become close to the Communist Party, whose publishing house issued *The Civil War in the United States,* a full collection of the relevant writings by Marx and Engels, in 1937. The editor, Richard Morais (who published the collection under the pseudonym Enmale—Engels-Marx-Lenin), was a labor historian and philosopher. His rather bland introduction ties Marx's Civil War writings to the contemporary battle for democracy against international fascism, and at home, against the "ultra-reactionary political groups, professional patriots and big business Bourbons," who were seeking to undermine Franklin Delano Roosevelt's New Deal (Marx and Engels 1937, xxv). According to Morais, Marx saw white labor as supporting the Black struggle, both before and after the Civil War. This avoided the issue of racism within the working class nearly completely. Morais's editing and notes were of a higher quality, however, thus making a reasonably accurate edition of the Civil War writings of Marx and Engels available to a wide public for the first time.

During World War II, while working within the Trotskyist movement, which located them to the left of the Communist Party, the Caribbean Marxist philosopher and culture critic C. L. R. James and the Russian American Marxist philosopher and economist Raya Dunayevskaya developed a new Marxist framework that placed the dialectics of race and class at the center of American history. They also argued that the Black struggle itself had shaken up American society at several crucial turning points, such as the Civil War era and the 1930s, galvanizing a coalescence of Black and white labor. In 1943, for example, James emphasized Marx's concept of an alliance among white abolitionists, white farmers of the Midwest, and African Americans. He notes that Marx in his Civil War writings "pointed out" that the "free farmers" of the Midwest "were not prepared to stand any nonsense from the South because they were not going to have the mouth of the Mississippi in the hands of a hostile power." This served to break down "bourgeois timidity" on the eve of the Civil War, James concludes (1943, 339).

Later working on her own as a Marxist humanist, Dunayevskaya took up Marx's Civil War writings at some length in *Marxism and Freedom* ([1958] 2000). First, she viewed them as part of the "American roots of Marxism." In particular, she highlighted Marx's affinity for radical abolitionism and his attacks on Lincoln's slowness to emancipate the slaves and his reluctance to use Black troops. Second, she saw Marx's Civil War writings in connection to the International: "It was under the impact of the Civil War and the response of the European workers as well as the Polish insurrection, that the First International was born" ([1958] 2000, 83). Third, she placed Marx's Civil War writings alongside his writings on the Paris Commune as examples of his theory of revolution, in the former case with an intertwining of the dimensions of race and class. Finally, she noted that the Civil War writings had important connections to *Capital* I. In addition to the brief but crucial passages on the Civil War in the text of *Capital* itself, she argued that the war and its aftermath inspired Marx to add the chapter on "The Working Day" to his masterwork. (For more discussion, see chapter 5.)[4]

Some writers in the Marxian tradition have been uneasy about Marx's unwavering support for the North despite the fact that it was dominated by big capital. If Wolfe and Morais found commonalities with liberalism in Marx's Civil War writings, and if Du Bois, James, and Dunayevskaya found a new dialectic of race and class within them, by the 1960s, others were ready to attack them as an aberration, as fundamentally un-Marxian. In 1968, the prominent Marxist historian Eugene Genovese chided "the retreat of Marx, Engels, and too many Marxists into liberalism" when it came to the Civil War ([1968] 1971, 327). In Genovese's view, Marx's "burning hatred of slavery and commitment to the Union cause interfered with his judgment" (321). In short, the Civil War writings did not conform to Genovese's reductionist notions of Marxism and therefore were not Marxist.[5]

In 1972, Saul Padover issued *The Karl Marx Library* (hereafter, referred to as KML), a new collection of Marx's writings. His volume on the United States (KML 2) contained many of the Civil War writings, with those written in German newly (and often more gracefully) translated. In his introduction, Padover sounded notes similar to Wolfe, stressing Marx's appreciation of American democracy while playing down his pungent criticisms of Lincoln. In also taking up at some length Marx's work with the *Tribune* from 1851 to 1862, Padover shed new light on the scope of Marx's engagement with the United States.[6]

Keeping in mind these varying interpretations, let us now turn directly to Marx's writings on slavery and the Civil War.

"THE SIGNAL HAS NOW BEEN GIVEN": THE CIVIL WAR AS A TURNING POINT

Marx and Engels did not mention slavery in their sketch of capitalist development in *The Communist Manifesto*. A little over a year earlier, however, in a letter of December 28, 1846, to a Russian friend, Pavel V. Annenkov, Marx suggests that slavery and capitalism were intimately connected. Writing in French, he refers to "the slavery of the Blacks [*des Noirs*] in Surinam, in Brazil, in the southern regions of North America" (MECW 38, 101). He writes further:

> Direct slavery is as much the pivot upon which our present-day industrialism turns as are machinery, credit, etc. Without slavery there would be no cotton, without cotton there would be no modern industry. It is slavery which has given value to the colonies, it is the colonies which have created world trade, and world trade is the necessary condition for large-scale machine industry. . . . Slavery is therefore an economic category of paramount importance. (101–2)[7]

The African American social theorist Cedric Robinson, who has criticized Marx's inadequacies with regard to race, acknowledges that here Marx made a "point that has not only endured but to some extent dominated attempts to characterize the relationship of slave labor to industrialization: the creation of the Negro, the fiction of a dumb beast of burden fit only for slavery, was closely associated with the economic, technical, and financial requirements of Western development from the sixteenth century on" ([1983] 2000, 81).

Marx also makes a brief reference to slavery in "Wage Labor and Capital" (1849), the first published exposition of his critique of political economy. First, he restates the common assumption of the day that Blacks were predestined for slavery: "What is a Negro slave. A man of the black race. The one explanation is as good as the other." He then adds: "A Negro is a Negro. He becomes a *slave* only in certain relationships" (MECW 9, 211).[8] However, he did not devote much attention to the topic of New World slavery until the period of the Civil War.

Marx's strong abolitionist position was not shared by all socialists, as can be seen in the attitudes of the German émigrés in the United States. In the 1840s, some like Hermann Kriege openly opposed the abolitionists; others like Wilhelm Weitling were silent on the question of slavery. By 1854, however, the newly established *Arbeiterbund* (Workers' League), led by Marx's close colleague in New York, Joseph Weydemeyer, finally spoke out against the Kansas-Nebraska Bill legalizing slavery in the West. This bill, his group stated in a resolution, "authorizes the further extension of slavery" and therefore anyone supporting it was "a traitor against the people." The resolution also declared: "We have, do now, and shall continue to protest most emphatically against white and black slavery" (cited in Schlüter [1913] 1965, 76).

Unfortunately, this rather abstract formulation too easily equated factory work, which socialists often termed "wage slavery," with what Blacks had experienced from the Atlantic slave trade and their bondage in chains in the New World. A second problem was noted by Du Bois:

> Nevertheless, when the Arbeiterbund was reorganized in December, 1857, slavery was not mentioned. When its new organ appeared in April, 1858, it said that the question of the present moment was not the abolition of slavery, but the prevention of its further extension and that Negro slavery was firmly rooted in America.... In 1859, however, a conference of the Arbeiterbund condemned all slavery in whatever form it might appear, and demanded the repeal of the Fugitive Slave Law. ([1935] 1973, 24)

Thus, the German immigrant socialists were slow to take a firm stand against slavery, in contrast to the middle-class radicals of the abolitionist movement and their Black allies.

Another context for Marx's views was the *Tribune* itself, which wrote about slavery from a strongly abolitionist standpoint. A prominent example can be found in its coverage of the famous Oberlin-Wellington rescue, in an article entitled "Kidnapping at Oberlin—The People Excited," which appeared on September 18, 1858. John Price, who had fled slavery in Kentucky, had been spirited out of Oberlin, Ohio by federal marshals operating under the Fugitive Slave Act. "In fifteen minutes, the square was alive with students and citizens armed with weapons of death," writes "R," the anonymous author of the *Tribune* article. (R's anonymity may have been intended as a protection from indictment by the federal authorities.) They drove their horses and wagons ten miles to nearby Wellington, a railroad junction where the young man of "about 19 or 20 years old" was being held for transport south. The growing crowd, which by now included "hundreds of ladies," was met by a U. S. marshal, but the assemblage questioned the validity of his legal papers. Eventually, recounts "R," they forcibly liberated Price and returned him to Oberlin:

> The whole line of our return was triumphal. Nearly every farm-house had emptied its occupants into the road to cheer and bless us, and we returned their greetings in the warmest style. At home, the whole town was out. In front of the Post Office they joined us in three terrific groans for Democracy, and three glorious cheers for Liberty. In front of the Palmer House these were repeated, and then one standing up, commanded silence and spoke as follows: "Gentlemen, we know not what may hereafter be attempted. But we want to know who can be relied on. So many of you as will here solemnly pledge yourselves to rally on the instant of an alarm, armed and ready to pursue and rescue, say 'Aye!.'" The response was enough to make a man's hair stand up. It was repeated three times. . . . Finally, it was voted with deafening unanimity that whoever laid hands on a black man in this community, no matter what color of authority, would do so at the peril of his life! If the occasion comes, it will be seen that this was no empty talk. Wo[e] to the slaveholder or Marshal that comes prowling about Oberlin hereafter! A fugitive cannot be taken from here. A number of speeches kept the crowd together until a late hour. ("Kidnapping at Oberlin—The People Excited")

This was published not as a letter or opinion piece, but as a regular news article, under the dateline "Correspondence of the N. Y. Tribune." Of course, not all *Tribune* coverage took such a militant stance.

By the 1860s, in addition to his abolitionist perspective, Marx had developed an appreciation of African Americans as revolutionary subjects. On January 11, 1860, in the aftermath of John Brown's raid on Harper's Ferry, he writes to Engels:

> In my view, the most momentous thing happening in the world today is, on the one hand, the movement among the slaves [*Sklavenbewegung*] in America, started by the death of Brown, and the movement among the slaves in Russia, on the other. . . . I have just seen in the *Tribune* that there was a new slave uprising in Missouri, naturally suppressed. But the signal has now been given. (MECW 41, 4)

The following year, after Lincoln's election, Engels writes to Marx on January 7, 1861, of increasing tensions in the States. He concludes that "slavery would appear to be rapidly nearing its end" (242).

Four months later, shortly after the firing on Fort Sumter that began hostilities, Marx writes, in a letter dated May 6, 1861, to his uncle Lion Philips, that "these acts of violence have rendered *all compromise* impossible." Presciently, he adds that the South would score early victories on the battlefield, but would not triumph in the end. He also alludes to the possibility of a "slave revolution [*Sklavenrevolution*]":

> There can be no doubt that in the beginning of the struggle, the scales will be tilted in favor of the South, where the class of propertyless white adventurers forms an inexhaustible reservoir of martial militia. But in the long run, of course, the North will win, for in case of necessity it can play the last card, that of a slave revolution. (MECW 41, 277)

Marx would return again and again to this notion that the Union needed to wage the war by revolutionary means, whether by the use of Black troops or by encouraging a slave uprising, this in contrast to what he viewed as Lincoln's lack of resolve.

Unfortunately, at this point Marx lacked an outlet for his views, the *Tribune* having cut back its international coverage in order to devote most of its pages to the war, and the socialist press in Britain and America having collapsed.[9] Beginning in October 1861, however, the *Tribune* allowed him to publish eight articles on the British response to the war and Bonaparte's intervention in Mexico, but these were the last of his articles that were to appear there. In fact, most of what Marx published on the Civil War was in German in *Die Presse*, a liberal paper published in Vienna that in June 1861 invited him to become a paid correspondent. They did not publish anything until late October, however. Therefore, one has to rely entirely on Marx's letters, mainly to Engels, for his views during the first six months of the war, from April through September 1861.

In a letter of May 29, 1861, to the statist German socialist Ferdinand Lassalle, Marx points to another theme in his Civil War writings, support for the South by Britain's dominant classes, which he attributes to economic factors: "The whole of the official press in England is, of course, in favor of the slaveholders. They are the selfsame fellows who have wearied the world with the antislave trade philanthropy. But cotton, cotton" (MECW 41, 291).

In response to Marx's request for a military analysis to help with his articles for *Die Presse*, Engels writes on June 12 that "the South had been quietly arming for years," whereas Lincoln lacked sufficient support to call up very many troops until the firing on Fort Sumter touched off a patriotic wave in the North (MECW 41, 294). Engels alludes with evident pride to the activities of their German colleagues, writing that "the reconquest of Missouri by the St. Louis Germans" would prove to be of "enormous importance to the course of the war" (296).[10] Finally, Engels points to the Union's greater than two-to-one population advantage, augmented by the fact that Southern troops would be needed to guard the slaves, some three million people. In a passage that captured well his visceral hostility to the whole culture of the slave South, he concludes:

> Man for man, there is no question that the people from the North are markedly superior to those from the South, both physically and morally. Your rowdy [*Rauflust*] Southerner has a good deal of the cowardly assassin in him. Each of them goes about armed, but only because this will enable him, during a quarrel, *to fell his antagonist before the latter expects to be attacked*. (296; original emphasis)

In his response of June 19, Marx, after thanking Engels for his letter, adds optimistically, "from the facts appearing in the *Tribune* I see that the North is now speaking of a slave war [*Sklavenkrieg*] and the abolition of slavery" (299). Lincoln's Emancipation Proclamation was still eighteen months away, however.

On July 1, 1861, in a letter to Engels, Marx developed two themes that he would carry forward in his Civil War writings. First, there was what he viewed as the pusillanimity of the North in the face of Southern fanaticism over slavery. "A closer study of these American affairs has shown me that the conflict between South and North," he writes, was delayed because the North "has degraded itself by one concession after another for fifty years" (MECW 41, 300). Marx would continue this theme in his subsequent criticisms of Lincoln.

Second, Marx analyzed class differentiation within both the North and the South. He suggests that the North began to take a stronger stand with the rise of the "northwestern" (today Midwestern) states such as Illinois and Ohio. Their large immigrant population, he writes, "richly mixed with new German and British elements, and in addition self-working[11] farmers, was naturally not as prone to intimidation as the gentlemen of Wall Street and the Quakers from Boston" (MECW 41, 300). In a reference to Kansas during the 1850s, he adds: "It was also this northwestern population that in the Kansas affair (from which the present war really is to be dated) fought at close quarters with the border ruffians" (301).[12]

As to the class composition of the South, he points to the relatively small group of three hundred thousand slaveowners, among a Southern white population of five million, calling the secession votes in the various Southern states "usurpations" by a wealthy minority (MECW 41, 301). After Engels questions this in a letter of July 3 by referring to reports of a "popular vote" for secession (304), Marx speaks, in a letter of July 5, of "the December Second character of the whole secession maneuver," a reference to the Bonapartist coup of December 2, 1851 (307). Marx argues further that "the matter has been completely misrepresented in the English papers" (305) and proceeds to do a state-by-state analysis of the voting. He notes that many southern whites initially opposed secession, but were intimidated by pro-slavery elements:

> *North Carolina* and even *Arkansas* chose Union delegates, the former even with a strong majority. They were later terrorized. . . . *Texas*, where, next to South Carolina, the biggest slavery party with the most terrorism was to be found, nevertheless, cast 11,000 votes for the Union. . . . *Alabama*. The people voted neither for secession nor for the new constitution, etc. The State Convention passed the Ordinance of Secession with 61 against 39 votes. But the 39 from the northern counties, almost entirely inhabited by whites, represented more free men than the 61. (306–7; original emphasis)

This lack of popular support for secession, argues Marx, accounted for the Bonapartist character of the secession movement, which was forced "to provoke war . . . under the slogan 'The North Against the South,'" in order to gain greater popular support (307). Marx then quotes a number of Southern newspapers such as the *Augusta Chronicle and Sentinel* of Georgia, which had noted that secession took place "without authority from the people" (308).

From this letter dated July 5, 1861 to his first article on British public opinion in the *Tribune*, written in mid-September, a period that included the major Confederate victory at Bull Run on July 21, we have nothing further from Marx on the Civil War. During these two months, he began to work intensively on his 1861–63 manuscript, which included the draft of the first volume of *Capital* I and what was to become *Theories of Surplus Value* (Draper 1985a).

On October 25, 1861, Marx's first article on the war appeared in *Die Presse*. Entitled "The North American Civil War," it offered an analysis of the conflict as a whole. He begins by refuting the reasons given in the British establishment press for denying support to the Union. He argues that slavery, not protective tariffs for Northern industry, was at the root of the war: "Secession, therefore, did not take place because Congress passed the Morrill Tariff Act; at most, Congress passed the Morrill protective tariff because secession had taken place" (MECW 19, 33). He attacks even more forcefully the notion, common in Europe at the time, that because the Union had not yet come out against it, "slavery . . . has absolutely nothing to do with this war" (33). Instead, he argues that the South initiated the war, that it made slavery into a principle of its constitution, and that its goal was the opening of the entire U.S. to slavery, hence its attacks northward in the early months of the war. The Confederacy was one cause putting itself forward as a struggle for national independence that Marx vehemently opposed, because of its utterly reactionary politics.

He detailed various concessions on the part of the North to the slave states from 1820 onwards. He then writes of how in 1857 the U.S. Supreme Court decided "the notorious Dred Scott case," according to which "every individual slaveholder is entitled to introduce slavery into hitherto free territories against the will of the majority" (MECW 19, 36–37). He also recounts the conflict in Kansas during 1854–58:

> Armed emissaries of the slaveholders, border rabble from Missouri and Arkansas, with bowie knife in one hand and revolver in the other, fell upon Kansas and by the most unheard-of atrocities sought to drive the settlers from the territory they had colonized. These raids were supported by the central government of Washington. Hence a tremendous reaction. Throughout the North, but particularly in the Northwest, a relief organization was formed to support Kansas with men, arms, and money. (38)

He argues as well that Southern slavery was an economic institution for which, the soil becoming quickly exhausted, "the acquisition of new territories becomes necessary" (39). Thus, the slaveholding South could never consent to limitations on the expansion of slavery into the territories. Additionally, it was only by such expansion, as well as the aggression involved in this process, that the interests of the small minority of slaveowners could be "squared" with those of the vast population of poor whites. This was accomplished by giving the poor whites' "turbulent impulses for action an innocuous direction and, to tame them with the prospect of themselves one day becoming slaveholders" (MECW 19, 41). Thus, the sectional conflict over slavery operated in an ideological manner to deflect the poor whites from conflict with the dominant classes of the South. As they took account of the rapid population growth in the North due to immigration, however, the dominant classes of the South had come to see that restrictions on the expansion of slavery into new territories were on the horizon. For this reason, they decided that "it was better to make the break now," he concludes (42).

In another of Marx's articles for *Die Presse*, "The Civil War in the United States," which appeared on November 7, 1861, he concentrated on two points. First, he argues that the South in reality claimed no less than three-fourths of the national territory as part of its secession: "The war of the Southern Confederacy is thus not a war of defense, but a war of conquest, a war of conquest for the extension and perpetuation of slavery" (MECW 19, 44). Second came a state-by-state survey of the social and political conditions in each of the Southern and border states, here developing and expanding the points he had made in his letter to Engels of July 1, discussed above.

Again and again, Marx suggests that the goal of the South was to dominate North America: "Thus in fact there would take place, not a dissolution of the Union, but a *reorganization* of it, a *reorganization on the basis of slavery*, under the recognized control of the slaveholding oligarchy" (MECW 19, 50; original emphasis). The result would be a new form of capitalism, openly structured upon racial and ethnic lines, in which immigrant whites would join Blacks at the bottom:

> The slave system would infect the whole Union. In the northern states, where Negro slavery is unworkable in practice, the white working class would be gradually depressed to the level of helotry. This would be in accord with the loudly proclaimed principle that only certain races are capable of freedom, and that as in the South the real labor is the lot of the Negro, so in the North it is the lot of the German and the Irishman, or their direct descendants. (51)

Finally, Marx openly criticized Lincoln for the first time in this article. The occasion was the way in which "Lincoln faintheartedly revoked [General John] Frémont's Missouri Proclamation on the emancipation of Negroes belonging to the rebels," this after protests from pro-Union slaveholders in Kentucky, who threatened to secede (51). Still, Marx concluded, the issue of emancipation had now been put forward publicly as a war aim and a strategy. He devoted an entire article to Frémont in the November 26 *Die Presse*, writing that he was "the first Northern general to have threatened the slaveholders with the emancipation of the slaves" (86).[13]

THE CIVIL WAR AND CLASS CLEAVAGE IN BRITAIN:
THE MOVEMENT AGAINST INTERVENTION

During the same period, Napoleon III, with the support of Britain and Spain, was preparing to invade Mexico to install the Austrian Prince Maximilien as emperor. Marx wrote three articles on the diplomatic maneuvering around this issue in late 1861 and early 1862, apparently worried that Napoleon III or even Palmerston planned to use Mexico as a beachhead to support the South. One of these, published in February 1862, was his last article for the *Tribune*.

Marx wrote far more on another international dimension of the Civil War, its impact on the British government and British public opinion. Padover sums up the situation in Britain in this period:

> The beginning of the conflict found British opinion divided. On the pro-Confederacy side were the aristocracy, which sympathized with the southern plantation owners; and commercial interests, which hoped for cheaper raw materials, particularly cotton, from an independent South. On the pro-Northern side were British liberals, who saw in the Civil War a struggle to preserve democracy; and the working class, which felt that the fate of free labor was at stake. Much of the London press, spearheaded by the influential *Times*, which Marx read assiduously, was pro-South. The British, led by Lord Palmerston as Prime Minister and Lord John Russell as Foreign Minister, leaned toward the Confederacy. (KML 2, 112; see also Foner 1981)

Marx's first article on the debate in Britain, "The American Question in England," published with some delay in the *Tribune* on October 11, 1861, took up the attacks on the Union side from within the British Establishment. However, as will be seen, the powerful Liberal politicians Palmerston and Russell, as well as the Tory Benjamin Disraeli, all of whom came to advocate intervention on the side of the South, were stymied by dissent from labor and the intellectual public, as well as opposition by other members of the dominant classes. In his article, Marx concedes that from the Northern standpoint, "the war has not been undertaken with a view to put down slavery," a fact often alluded to by British opponents of the Union. The South, however, not only "confessed to fight for the liberty of enslaving others," but also made the "right" to own slaves into a core principle: "The Confederate Congress boasted that its new-fangled constitution, as distinguished from the Constitution of the Washingtons,

Jeffersons, and Adams's, had recognized for the first time Slavery as a thing good in itself, a bulwark of civilization, and a divine institution" (MECW 19, 8). Marx also acknowledges that the North compromised with the South for fifty years, but he contends that by the late 1850s, the North began "to rectify the aberrations" and to "return to the true principles of its development" (10).

Another *Tribune* article, "The British Cotton Trade," published October 14, dealt with economic issues. The textile industry in Manchester was suffering terribly due to Lincoln's successful blockade of Southern shipping, which denied it raw cotton. Marx suggests that this led "the mercantile mind" to hope for one of two things. Either there would be a quick end to the war and the blockade, or Marx's old nemesis, Palmerston, prime minister once again, "would forcibly break through the blockade" (MECW 19, 18). Unfortunately for the British economic interests hoping for intervention, however, countervailing interests—vast investments in Northern industry and the fact that imports from the northern and western United States were Britain's main source of grain—militated against such a move by Palmerston. He concludes this article by taking up Ireland, the English working class, and the slaveholding South as parts of a single economic system:

> English modern industry, in general, relied upon two pivots equally monstrous. The one was the *potato* as the only means of feeding Ireland and a great part of the English working class. This pivot was swept away by the potato disease and the subsequent Irish catastrophe. A larger basis for the reproduction and maintenance of the toiling millions had then to be adopted. The second pivot of English industry was the slave-grown cotton of the United States. The present American crisis forces them to enlarge their field of supply and emancipate cotton from slave-breeding and slave-consuming oligarchies. As long as the English cotton manufactures depended on slave-grown cotton, it could be truthfully asserted that they rested on a twofold slavery, the indirect slavery of the white man in England and the direct slavery of the black man on the other side of the Atlantic. (19–20)

This latter system was now being challenged by the momentous events in America.

In a third *Tribune* article, "The London *Times* and Lord Palmerston," published October 21, 1861, Marx surmises that the British Establishment had given up any plans of intervening on the side of the South. In a fourth *Tribune* article, published on November 7, Marx writes of the strong support for the

Union among the working people of Europe. This was not only because they were antislavery, but also because European workers saw the U.S. as the most democratic society of the time, virtually the only country were even white male workers enjoyed full suffrage:

> The true people of England, of France, of Germany, of Europe, consider the cause of the United States as their own cause, as the cause of liberty, and . . . despite all paid sophistry, they consider the soil of the United States as the free soil of the landless millions of Europe, as their land of promise, now to be defended sword in hand, from the sordid grasp of the slaveholder. . . . In this contest the highest form of popular self-government till now realized is giving battle to the meanest and most shameless form of man's enslaving recorded in the annals of history. . . . Such a war . . . [is] so distinguished, by the vastness of its dimensions and the grandeur of its ends, from the groundless, wanton and diminutive wars Europe has passed through since 1849. (29–30)

Thus, he linked the Union's cause to the international struggle for democracy and revolution. Marx's subsequent article, "The Crisis in England," appeared in *Die Presse* on November 6, 1861. It detailed Britain's dependence on Southern cotton. Marx wrote that the cutoff of cotton by the Union blockade had led to a situation where "at this moment all of England trembles at the approach of the greatest economic catastrophe that has yet threatened her" (56).

Next, he turned his attention to the Trent Affair. On November 8, 1861, the U.S. warship *San Jacinto* forcibly boarded the *Trent*, a British merchant vessel, in order to arrest two Confederate diplomats on their way to London. In an article published in the *Die Presse* on December 2, Marx holds that this incident itself "brings no war in its train" (MECW 19, 89), despite what he viewed as efforts by Palmerston, the cotton barons of Liverpool, and sections of the press, to foment one. Eventually, the United States released the two Confederate envoys, and they arrived in England in January 1862. In this period, Marx wrote five more articles on the Trent Affair. He pointed out that many important members of the British Establishment opposed war with America, from the Liberals William Gladstone, John Bright, and Richard Cobden, to the Tory David Urquhart, his old ally against Russia. This blunted efforts by the leading Liberals Palmerston and Russell, as well as the Tory Disraeli, to provoke a war. Engels, who often had a more pessimistic view of the Union's prospects, worries in letter to Marx of November 27 that the United States had given Britain a *"causus belli"* (MECW 41, 329). Marx reassures him in a letter dated December 9: "There isn't going to be *war* with America, as I have said from the beginning in *Die Presse*" (MECW 41, 333).

Marx surveys the debate in Britain in a *Die Presse* article of December 31, "The Opinion of the Newspapers and the Opinion of the People." He notes that opposition to war from within the dominant classes was rooted in public opinion: "At the present moment a war with America is just as unpopular with all strata of the English people, except for the friends of cotton and the country squires, as the war cry in the press is overwhelming" (MECW 19, 128). After detailing the connections of the press to various political and economic forces, he concludes: "Palmerston wants war; the English people do not" (130).

In his next few articles, Marx reported on public meetings across Britain to oppose intervention. In "A Pro-America Meeting," an article published in *Die Presse* on January 5, 1862, Marx describes one of them. Held in Brighton on December 30, it featured the Liberal MP William Coningham, who declared: "At this moment, there is developing in the midst of the Union an *avowed policy of emancipation (Applause)*, and I express my earnest hope that no intervention on the part of the English government will be permitted (*Applause*). . . . Will you, freeborn Englishmen, allow yourselves to be embroiled in an anti-Republican war?" (MECW 19, 135; ellipsis and emphasis in original). Another speaker, the Liberal MP James White, underlined the meeting's working-class character: "It is due to the working class to mention that they are the originators of this meeting and that all the expenses of organizing it are borne by its committee." White feared "that England and France have reached an understanding to recognize the independence of the Southern states next spring" (136).[14]

Marx's article "English Public Opinion" appeared in *Die Presse* on February 1, 1862, where he notes that, due to pressure from below, "not one single public war meeting could be held in the United Kingdom" during these months, including in Ireland and Scotland. This was true "even in Manchester," he adds, despite the terrible economic cost being borne by textile workers there (MECW 19, 137). He contrasts this situation to the period of the Crimean War, when anti-Russian and pro-Polish feeling among the working classes led to "tremendous war meetings all across the country" even though, he maintains, "the *Times*, the *Post* and other Yellowplushes[15] of the London press whined for peace" (138). Now, in 1862, the establishment press has "howled for war, to be answered by peace meetings denouncing the schemes to destroy freedom [*freiheitsmörderischen*] and the proslavery sympathies of the government" (138).

In a February 2, 1862 article in *Die Presse* on "A London Workers' Meeting," Marx reports that this very large gathering voted a resolution that read in part:

This meeting considers it to be the very important duty of the workers, since they are not represented in the senate of the nation, to declare their sympathy with the United States in its gigantic struggle for maintenance of the Union, to denounce the base dishonesty and advocacy of slaveholding indulged in by *The Times* and kindred aristocratic journals, to express themselves most emphatically in favor of a policy of strictest nonintervention in the affairs of the United States, . . . to protest against the war policy of the organ of the stock-exchange swindlers,[16] and to proclaim their warmest sympathy for the endeavors of the Abolitionists to bring about a final solution of the question of slavery. (MECW 19, 156)

The resolution was sent to the American government through Charles Francis Adams, the American minister to Britain.

At a more general level, Marx salutes the British working class's history of grassroots movements around political issues, despite its still being denied voting rights:

It is well known that the working class, so preponderant a part of a society that within living memory has no longer possessed a *peasantry*, is not represented in Parliament. Nevertheless, it is not without political influence. No important innovation, no decisive measure has ever been carried out in this country without pressure from without. . . . By pressure from without the Englishman understands large, extra-parliamentary people's demonstrations, which naturally cannot be staged without the lively participation of the working class. . . . The Catholic Emancipation, the Reform Bill, the repeal of the Corn Laws, the Ten Hours Bill, the war against Russia, the rejection of Palmerston's Conspiracy Bill,[17] all were the fruit of stormy extra-parliamentary demonstrations, in which the working class, sometimes artificially incited, sometimes acting spontaneously, played the main role or—depending on circumstances—the role of spectator, now as *persona dramatis*, now as chorus. So much the more striking is the stance of the English working class toward the American Civil War. (153)

Pointing to the terrible economic plight of the workers during the cotton depression and the incitement to war by both the press and the government, Marx writes: "The working class is . . . fully conscious that the government is only waiting for the intervention cry from below to put an end to the American blockade and the distress in England. Under these circumstances, the obstinacy with which the working class keeps silent, or breaks its silence only to raise its voice against intervention and *for* the United States, is admirable" (154). In subsequent articles Marx rejoices at how the *Times* and other conservative interests were admitting that intervention over the Trent Affair had become impossible.

"A WAR OF THIS KIND MUST BE CONDUCTED IN A REVOLUTIONARY WAY"

Marx also continued to follow the debate in America over abolition. In an article entitled "Crisis Over the Slavery Issue," published in *Die Presse* on December 14, 1861, he writes that while Frémont had been dismissed, others, including Secretary of War Simon Cameron, publicly backed proposals from some Union officers for "the general arming of the slaves as a war measure" (MECW 19, 115). He also cites a Union officer's statement that "slaves of rebels will always find protection in this company and we will defend them to the last man" and that he "want[s] no men who are not Abolitionists" in his unit (116).[18] Others, including Secretary of State William Seward, who had once been strong abolitionists, had begun to hesitate, Marx complains. In another article, "American Matters," published on December 17, Marx writes of a "brilliant" speech by abolitionist Senator Charles Sumner of Massachusetts, who, he notes, "had been beaten with a stick by a Southern Senator at the time of the Kansas affair." After Sumner's speech at Cooper Union in New York, the audience voted that abolition had become "a moral, political and military necessity" (118). For both of these articles, Marx drew his source material from the *Tribune*, which he was still receiving daily as one of their correspondents. This was soon to stop too, however.

In "American Affairs," an article published on March 3, 1862, in *Die Presse*, Marx applauds Lincoln's demotion of the overall commander of the Union forces, General George McClellan. Marx writes, here again sharing the views of the American abolitionists, that McClellan was "too connected to his old comrades in the enemy camp," with whom he had attended West Point. Marx also holds that McClellan's headquarters was riddled with Confederate spies. To buttress his contention that the war needed generals more committed to its cause, he quotes a well-known 1653 speech by Oliver Cromwell concerning "how changed" his army had become, once officers loyal to the Puritan Revolution began to lead it (MECW 19, 179).

Next came the first Civil War article coauthored by Engels, "The American Civil War," a lengthy analysis published in *Die Presse* on March 26 and March

27, 1862. By this time, McClellan was coming under increasing pressure to move against the Confederate army, something he was reluctant to do, claiming that his forces needed more training. Marx and Engels begin by suggesting that the Confederacy was fighting in a "truly Bonapartist spirit" by launching a series of bold attacks, relying on the fact that its leaders had been planning war far longer than the Union's. The early Union defeats at Bull Run and elsewhere, sometimes accompanied by "panic . . . at the decisive moment," they maintain, "could surprise no one who was to some extent familiar with people's wars" (MECW 19, 187), pointing to some of the problems of the French revolutionary armies of the 1790s. With the use of the term "people's wars" and the comparison to France, Marx and Engels underline their view that the Civil War was a second American revolution. They add: "Without the considerable amount of military experience that emigrated to America as a result of the European revolutionary unrest of 1848–49, the organization of the Union Army would have taken a much longer time still" (188). Although much of the article was based on two that Engels had published in a small British military journal a few weeks earlier,[19] in the version that appeared in *Die Presse*, they make a prescient observation: "[George] Halleck and [Ulysses S.] Grant, in particular, offer good examples of resolute military leadership." They add that their leadership "deserves the highest praise" (192). Equally presciently, they foreshadow William T. Sherman's 1864 march to the sea, this two years ahead of the event: "Georgia is the key to Secessia. With the loss of Georgia, the Confederacy would be cut into two sections, which would have lost all connection with each other" (194). Marx and Engels also ridicule McClellan's military plans as, if not completely unworkable, running the danger that "the war would be prolonged indefinitely" (195).

Marx's next few articles deal with the fall of New Orleans to Union forces on May 1, 1862. In one of them, "English Humanity and America," published in *Die Presse* on June 20, he ridicules the sympathy expressed in the British Establishment for the white women of New Orleans, who had been ordered to stop insulting Union troops. After decrying the silence from the same quarters regarding "Englishwomen who are starving" in industrial Lancashire and "the cry of distress of the Irishwomen" evicted from their homes by rapacious landlords, he derides the British press reports on New Orleans: "Indeed, ladies[20]—and ladies who actually own slaves—were not even to be allowed to vent their anger and their malice on common Union troops, peasants, artisans, and other rabble with impunity! It is 'infamous'!" He contrasts this imagined insult to Napoleon III's 1851 coup, "when 'ladies' were actually shot dead, while others were raped" (MECW 19, 211). In the same article, he alludes as well to the danger that Napoleon III's intervention in Mexico, supported as it was by the British government, could aid the Confederacy.

During this period, Marx and Engels began to have some political differences over the Civil War.[21] In a letter to Marx of May 12, 1862, Engels laments "the indolence and indifference throughout the North. Where, amongst the people, is there any revolutionary energy?" (MECW 41, 364). In a letter of July 30, Engels goes further, writing that the Union's overall lack of progress would encourage some form of rotten compromise with the Confederacy. He deplores the Union's failure to come out clearly against slavery and to conduct the war "along revolutionary lines" (387). This, plus the greater talent and energy on the Confederate side, looked ominous, he concludes. Engels was to some extent reflecting the views of other German socialists, as can be seen in Marx's letter to Engels from the same day. Marx complains that Lassalle, who was staying with him in London, was totally dismissive of the Union cause: "As to America, it's totally uninteresting. The Yankees have no 'ideas.' 'Individual freedom' is only a 'negative idea,' etc. and other old, decaying, speculative rubbish of the same sort" (390).[22]

Marx makes his criticism of Engels explicit in a letter dated August 7:

> I do not entirely share your views on the American Civil War. I do not believe that all is up. The Northerners have been dominated from the beginning by the representatives of the border slave states, who pushed McClellan, that old partisan of Breckinridge,[23] to the top. The South, on the other hand, acted as a unit from the beginning. . . . In my view, all this will take another turn. The North will finally wage war seriously, adopt revolutionary methods, and overthrow the domination of the border slave statesmen. A single nigger-regiment would have a remarkable effect on Southern nerves. . . . If Lincoln does not give way (which, however, he will), there will be a revolution. . . . The long and the short of the story seems to me to be that a war of this kind must be conducted in a revolutionary way, whereas the Yankees have been trying so far to conduct it constitutionally. (MECW 41, 400)

In the block quote above, the term "nigger-regiment" is written in English in the middle of a German sentence. This is an instance of Marx using what today would be considered a very racist phrase to make an equally strong anti-racist point.[24] Ironically, it is here that Marx makes his strongest case to date on the issue of Black troops, not only for military reasons, but also for political and psychological ones. This letter is also remarkable for its unusually sharp expression of differences with Engels, this on a subject where Marx had previously deferred to his friend's expertise, military strategy.

In August 1862, Marx publishes several critiques of Lincoln's failure to abolish slavery. At the same time, Marx's overall tone remains one of confidence in the Union over the long haul, both militarily and politically. In an article entitled "Criticism of American Affairs" that appeared in *Die Presse* on August 9, he notes the pressure building on Lincoln:

> New England and the Northwest, which had supplied the main body of troops, are determined to force the government to wage the war in a revolutionary manner and to inscribe "Abolition of Slavery" on the Star-Spangled Banner as a battle slogan. . . . Up to now, we have witnessed only the first act of the Civil War, waging the war constitutionally. The second act, waging the war in a revolutionary manner, is at hand. (MECW 19, 228)

He also refers to some smaller measures leading in the direction of abolition, from the abolition of slavery in the District of Columbia and West Virginia, to the recognition by the U.S. government of "the independence of the Negro republics of Haiti and Liberia" (229). In a move toward allowing Blacks to fight for their own freedom, a newly enacted law provided that "all the slaves owned by the rebels are to be emancipated, as soon as they fall into the hands of the republican army." Marx notes that "for the first time . . . these emancipated Negroes may be militarily organized and sent into the field against the South" (228–29). In another article published two weeks later, Marx quotes some particularly venomous articles in the *Times* referring to the Southerners as "our kin" and the Northerners as "a mongrel race of robbers and oppressors," plus another reference to "an army whose officers are Yankee swindlers and whose common soldiers are German thieves." He gleefully quotes a rejoinder by the abolitionist *New York Evening Post*:[25] "Are these English squibblers, these descendants of Britons, Danes, Saxons, Celts, Normans, Dutch, of such pure blood that all other peoples appear to be mongrel compared to them?" (230–31).

Marx's next article, "Abolitionist Demonstrations in America," published in *Die Presse* on August 30, 1862, offered his strongest public critique of Lincoln.[26] He quotes at length a speech by the radical abolitionist Wendell Phillips, whom Marx describes as follows:

> For thirty years, unremittingly and in danger of his life, he has proclaimed the emancipation of the slaves as his battle cry, regardless equally of the

mockery [*Persiflage*] of the press, the enraged howls of the paid rowdies, and the conciliatory remonstrances of worried friends. He is acknowledged, even by his opponents, to be one of the greatest orators of the North, combining an iron character with powerful energy and purest conviction. (MECW 19, 233)

Marx praises the Phillips speech as "of greater importance than a battle bulletin," since it expressed a point of view being "pushed more and more into the foreground by events" (233–34).

The bulk of Marx's article consists of his translation into German of long quotations from the speech, where Phillips stated:

I do not say that McClellan is a traitor, but I say this, that if he had been a traitor from the crown of his head to the sole of his foot, he could not have served the South better than he has done since he was commander-in-chief. . . . You and I are never going to see peace, we are never to see the possibility of putting the army of this nation, whether it be made up of nineteen or thirty-four states, on a peace footing, until slavery is destroyed . . . As long as you keep a tortoise [Lincoln] at the head of the government, you are digging a pit with one hand and filling it with the other. . . . I know Lincoln. I have taken his measure in Washington. He is a first-rate *second-rate* man. (MECW 19, 234–35; original emphasis)

This speech, "The Cabinet," delivered in Massachusetts on August 1, 1862, was one of Phillips's most famous.[27] In his translation, Marx edits out some of Phillips's religious references, but otherwise his excerpts reflect the speech's general tenor accurately.

In the wake of the big Union defeat at the second battle of Bull Run on August 29–30, Engels returned to his earlier criticisms of Marx's position. He writes in a letter to Marx dated September 9, "It is too pitiful, but the fellows in the South, who, at least, know what they want, appear as heroes, compared to the flabby management of the North. Or do you still believe that the gentlemen of the North will suppress the 'Rebellion'?" (MECW 41, 415). Marx replies at some length in a letter of September 10, pointing to what he considered to be the central flaw in Engels's position, too narrow a focus on military matters:

As regards the Yankees, I am surely still of the opinion that the North will win in the end; the Civil War can, of course, go through all kinds of episodes, perhaps also including truces, and drag itself out. . . . In regard to the North's conduct of the war, nothing else could be expected from a *bourgeois* republic, where swindle has been enthroned for such a long time. But the South, an oligarchy, is better fitted for war, because it is an oligarchy, where all the productive work is done by niggers and the 4,000,000 "white trash" are filibusterers by profession.[28] Despite all that, I will wager my head that those fellows will get the shorter end of it, despite "Stonewall Jackson." It is, to be sure, possible that before that a kind of revolution will take place in the North. . . . It seems to me that you are a little too much influenced by the military aspect of things. (416)

He also reports that August Willich, their bitter opponent during the last days of the Communist League in the early 1850s, had been promoted to brigadier general in the Union army.[29]

CONTINUING DISAGREEMENTS WITH ENGELS, EVEN AS THE TIDE TURNS

In fact, events in the North were beginning to move in the direction advocated by Marx, Engels, and Phillips. The Union's narrow but important victory at the Battle of Antietam on September 17, 1862, forced the Confederate forces to give up their invasion of Maryland and retreat to Virginia. On September 22, less than a week later, Lincoln issued the preliminary Emancipation Proclamation, which was to free all slaves held in rebel states as of January 1, 1863. Buoyed by these events, Marx, in an October 12 *Die Presse* article entitled "On Events in North America," writes triumphantly that "the short campaign in Maryland has decided the fate of the American Civil War" (MECW 19, 248). Now Washington was out of danger and France and Britain would give up their plans to recognize the Confederacy, he concludes. On Lincoln, he writes:

> "*E pur si muove* [And still it moves]." Nevertheless, in world history reason does conquer.[30] More important than the Maryland campaign is Lincoln's Proclamation. The figure of Lincoln is *sui generis* in the annals of history. No initiative, no idealistic eloquence, no buskin, no historic drapery. He always presents the most important act in the most insignificant form possible. Others, when dealing with square feet of land, proclaim it a "struggle for ideas." Lincoln, even when he is dealing with ideas, proclaims their "square feet." . . . The most awesome decrees that

he hurls at the enemy, which will always remain historically remarkable, all resemble, and are intended to resemble, the trite summonses that one lawyer sends to an opposing lawyer. . . . His most recent proclamation—the Emancipation Proclamation—the most significant document in American history since the founding of the Union and one which tears up the old American Constitution, bears the same character. . . . Lincoln is not the offspring of a people's revolution. The ordinary play of the electoral system, unaware of the great tasks it was destined to fulfill, bore him to the summit—a plebeian, who made his way from stone-splitter to senator in Illinois,[31] a man without intellectual brilliance, without special greatness of character, without exceptional importance—an average man of good will. Never has the New World scored a greater victory than in the demonstration that with its political and social organization, average men of good will suffice to do that which in the Old World would have required heroes to do! Hegel once remarked that in reality comedy is above tragedy, the humor of reason above its pathos. If Lincoln does not possess the pathos of historical action, he does, as an average man of the people, possess its humor. (249–50)

Thus does Marx draw the measure of Lincoln in a new way after the Emancipation Proclamation, as someone who has developed under the pressure of events and in the context of what was by far the most democratic political system in the world at that time.

In light of these new developments, Engels seems to shift his position a little, as seen in a letter to Marx of October 16: "Militarily speaking, the North may now perhaps begin to recover a bit" (MECW 41, 419). Marx replies on October 29 with a warm invitation for him to spend the holidays in London that year. Then he returns to their debate over the Civil War. Marx notes that Lincoln had had enough confidence to make his Emancipation Proclamation "at a moment when the Confederates were pushing forward in Kentucky," something that showed "that all consideration for the loyal slaveholders of the border states has ceased" (MECW 41, 420). He also notes that, in anticipation of emancipation in the border states, not yet proclaimed, many slaveholders were already migrating south. On Lincoln, he develops some points similar to those in his article cited above: "The fury with which the Southerners have received Lincoln's acts proves their importance. All Lincoln's acts seem like the mean, pettifogging conditions that one lawyer puts to his opponent. But this does not change their historic content, and indeed it amuses me to compare them with the drapery in which a Frenchman envelops even the most insignificant point" (MECW 41, 421). In mid-November, Marx published two more articles in *Die Presse*. In one of them, he mentions his old friend Weydemeyer, referring to him as "a German officer, who has fought under the Star-Spangled Banner" and who reported that slaveowners were leaving the border states *en masse*, thus changing their political balance (MECW 19, 257). In the other one, he refers to Gladstone as having changed into "an English admirer" of the Confederacy (MECW 19, 262).

During this period, after the setbacks for Lincoln's Republican Party in the November 1862 congressional elections, Engels returns to his previous criticisms in a letter to Marx of November 5, giving a pessimistic view: "The successes of the Democrats at the polls prove that the party that is weary of war is growing. If only there were some evidence, some indication, that the masses in the North were beginning to act as in France in 1792 and 1793, everything would be splendid" (MECW 41, 423). While the Republicans lost some seats in those elections in New York and the Midwest, Lincoln retained a strong majority in the House of Representatives (102 Republicans to 75 Democrats) and an overwhelming one in the Senate (36 Republicans to 8 Democrats). Marx does not reply to Engels immediately, instead sending two desperate letters asking for money, one for the Marx family and the other for a German worker colleague in London. In his reply of November 15, when he once again sent the money, Engels continues their debate over the Civil War. As against Marx's view that Lincoln's Emancipation Proclamation was a turning point, Engels retorts that "the only apparent effect of Lincoln's emancipation so far is that the Northwest has voted Democrat for fear of being overrun by Negroes [*Negerüberschwemmung*]" (428). In a letter of November 17, however, Marx replies at some length, arguing that "in every revolutionary movement there is a sort of reaction" that challenges its forward movement at crucial junctures, here citing examples from the French Revolution (430).

Marx developed his own analysis of the election results, strikingly different from that of Engels, in a *Die Presse* article published on November 23. He acknowledges that "the elections are in fact a defeat for the Washington government." However, he argues, the defeat was only relative and was caused in part by local factors:

> The *city* of New York, with a strongly seditious Irish mob, hitherto an active participant in the slave trade, the seat of the American money market and full of owners of southern plantation mortgages, has always been decisively "Democratic," just as Liverpool is still Tory today. (MECW 19, 263)

Incorporating a point put forward by Engels, Marx also writes that racism among white ethnics, farmers, and workers was a factor:

> The Irishman sees in the Negro a dangerous competitor. The efficient farmers in Indiana and Ohio hate the Negro second only to the slave-owner. For them he is the symbol of slavery and the debasement of the working class, and the Democratic press threatens them daily with an inundation of their territories by the "nigger." (264)

The criticisms of Irish American racism in the above two quotes were particularly striking, given that Marx usually saw Irish workers and peasants in revolutionary terms, as will be discussed in chapter 4.

Marx's differences with Engels can be seen when he writes that such considerations were relatively minor compared to the larger changes taking place in this second American revolution:

> All this, however, does not touch upon the main point. At the time of Lincoln's election (1860), there was neither a Civil War nor was the question of Negro emancipation the order of the day. The Republican Party, at that time thoroughly separated from the party of the Abolitionists, aimed in the election of 1860 at nothing but a protest against the extension of slavery in the territories, but at the same time it proclaimed noninterference with that institution where it had already existed legally. If the *emancipation of the slaves* had been a campaign slogan, Lincoln would then have been absolutely defeated. Emancipation was decisively rejected. It is quite different in the case of the recently concluded elections. The Republicans made common cause with the Abolitionists. They declared themselves emphatically in favor of immediate emancipation, be it for its own sake or as a means of ending the rebellion. Once this circumstance is considered, then the pro-Administration majority in Michigan, Illinois, Massachusetts, Iowa, and Delaware, and the very considerable minority in the states of New York, Ohio, and Pennsylvania that voted for it, appear equally surprising. Before the war, such a result was impossible, even in Massachusetts. (MECW 19, 264; original emphasis)

Marx fairly crows in his next article, "The Removal of McClellan," published in *Die Presse* on November 29: "*McClellan's removal!* is Lincoln's answer to the election victory of the Democrats" (266; original emphasis). This refuted rumors that Lincoln would retreat on the Emancipation Proclamation.

Marx's next article on the Civil War, "English Neutrality—The Situation in the Southern States," appeared in *Die Presse* on December 4. It concerned the diplomatic maneuvering over British attempts to supply the Confederacy with a fleet of ships. In June 1862, a new cruiser, the CSS *Alabama*, had set sail for America over the objections of Minister Adams and was involved in attacks on Union shipping. By December, a larger number of newly built ships, some of them ironclads, were ready to sail from Liverpool for the South. It was at this point that Minister Adams sent his famous "this is war" note to Palmerston and the latter backed down, stopping the ships from leaving at the last minute. In his article, Marx quotes at length Professor Francis Newman, a Manchester liberal and Union supporter, who attacked the British Establishment's attitude toward the war: "Lord Palmerston and Lord Russell, as much as the Tory Party, are animated by a hatred of republicanism strong enough to overbear all scruples and doubts; while Mr. Gladstone, a probable future Prime Minister, avows himself an admirer of the perjured men who have leagued together to perpetuate and extend slavery" (MECW 19, 270). This was to be Marx's last article on the Civil War for *Die Presse* and the end of his regular employment as a journalist altogether.

Marx continued to analyze the war in letters, but for nearly two years, until his inaugural address to the First International in the November 1864, he had no public platform on which to do so. In a letter of January 2, 1863, to Engels, he minimizes the significance of the Union defeat at Fredericksburg in December and hails the Emancipation Proclamation, which had gone into effect the day before. In a reference to large pro-America meetings of British workers held in December during the tension over the prospect of ironclads made in Britain being shipped to the Confederacy, Marx quotes New York's antislavery mayor George Opdyke, who had replaced the pro-slavery Fernando Wood in the 1862 election: "We know that the English working classes are with us and that the governing classes of England are against us." Marx then laments the fact that workers in Germany did "not make similar demonstrations," despite the substantial participation of German immigrants in the Union army (MECW 41, 440). For his part, after a break of three weeks in their political correspondence,[32] Engels continues their debate over the Union's prospects, lamenting the Union's "moral prostration" and "inability to win" in a letter to Marx on February 19 (457).[33] A month later, in a letter of March 24, Marx wrote to Engels of America's newly aggressive stance toward Britain, which had included publishing the diplomatic correspondence from the 1861–62 Trent Affair. At this point, he seems to relish the prospect of an American "war with England, so that the self-satisfied [John Bull] would see, besides his cotton, corn [grain] also withdrawn from under his nose" (462).

TOWARD THE FIRST INTERNATIONAL

In another letter to Engels two weeks later, on April 9, 1863, Marx refers to a March 26 meeting at St. James Hall of the London Trades Union Council. Held to express solidarity with the Union, it had been chaired by John Bright, a manufacturer and Liberal Party politician:

> I attended a meeting held by Bright, at the head of the Trade Unions. He had quite the appearance of an Independent,[34] and every time he said, "In the United States no kings, no bishops," there was a burst of applause. The workers themselves spoke *excellently*, with a complete absence of all bourgeois rhetoric, and without concealing in the slightest their opposition to the capitalists (whom, moreover, Father Bright also attacked). (MECW 41, 468; original emphasis)

Among the trade unionist speakers at this large meeting were William Cremer and George Howell, future leaders of the First International, as well as the philosopher John Stuart Mill.[35]

The meeting voted to send a long message to Lincoln, which referred to the aristocracy and part of the capitalist class as enemies of freedom: "We indignantly protest against the assertion that the people of England wish for the success of the Southern states in the diabolical attempt to establish a separate government on the basis of human slavery. However much a liberty-hating aristocracy and an unscrupulous moneyocracy may desire the consummation of such a crime, we, the workingmen of London, view it with abhorrence" (Bright [1865] 1970, 191). The message to Lincoln also mentioned the common economic interests of Black and white labor: "We know that slavery in America must have an indirect but real tendency to degrade and depress labor in this country also, and for this, if for no higher reason, we should refuse our sympathy to this infamous Rebellion" (191). It expressed veiled republican sympathies as well: "Though we have felt proud of our country. . . . yet have we ever turned with glowing admiration to your great Republic, where a higher political and social freedom has been established" (191). In addition, the message spoke of political equality and labor solidarity across racial lines: "You have struck off the shackles from the poor slaves of [the District of] Columbia; you have welcomed as men, as equals under God, the colored peoples of Hayti and Liberia, and by your [Emancipation] Proclamation, . . . you have opened the gates of freedom to the millions of our negro brothers who have been deprived of their manhood by the infernal laws which have so long disgraced the civilization of America" (192). The penultimate paragraph expressed a principled opposition to slavery, even if it were to go against the immediate economic interest of British labor: "Be assured that, in following out this noble course, our earnest, our active sympathies will be with you, and that, like our brothers in Lancashire . . . we would rather perish than band ourselves in unholy alliance with the South and slavery" (192–93). This meeting and others like it constituted an historic highpoint for British labor, not only as an expression of internationalism, but also of solidarity across racial lines.

Two months later, in a letter to Marx of June 11, 1863, Engels gave a backhanded compliment to Grant. He continued to disparage the other Union generals, however, maintaining that "only Grant is performing well," here referring to the siege of Vicksburg, Mississippi (MECW 41, 478). After Lee moved into Pennsylvania, Marx writes Engels on July 6 that he considers this campaign "an act of despair," in a letter written before the North's decisive victory at Gettysburg (484).

There are no surviving comments by Marx on the war for nearly another year, but in a letter dated May 26, 1864, to Engels on the campaign to capture Richmond, Marx compliments Grant, writing, "I think that fellow knows what he's about" (MECW 41, 530). As seen by his reply of May 30, Engels remained more equivocal even at this late stage, terming the Richmond campaign "inconclusive" (531). Three months later, on September 4, Engels writes Marx that Grant's Richmond campaign seemed "on the point of collapse," although he conceded that Sherman's chances of taking Atlanta were very good. This, he admits, would be "a hard blow for the South" (559). Engels also expressed the feeling that a victory by Lincoln was highly likely in the November 1864 presidential election, in which he was opposed by McClellan, now the Democratic Party candidate. Marx replies on September 7 that he regards Lincoln's reelection as a "100 to 1" certainty (561). He also suggests that if by some chance, given the "swindle" aspect of American elections, McClellan were to win, this "would probably lead to a real *revolution*" in America. Marx adds that in 1864 Lincoln was running "on a much more radical platform" than in 1860 (562).

THE BIRTH OF THE FIRST INTERNATIONAL

In November 1864, in his "Inaugural Address" of the International Working Men's Association, or First International, whose leadership included some of the same labor activists who had organized pro-Union meetings on the Civil War, Marx inserts a mention of that campaign: "It was not the wisdom of the ruling classes, but the heroic resistance to their criminal folly by the working classes of England that saved the West of Europe from plunging headlong into an infamous crusade for the perpetuation of slavery on the other side of the Atlantic" (MECW 20, 13). Adopted at the same time, the "Provisional Rules" of the International stipulated that "all societies and individuals adhering to it" were to regulate "their conduct toward each other, and towards all men, without regard to color, creed, or nationality" (15). These texts, drafted in English, were published as a pamphlet and circulated widely in several languages.

Engels did not take part in the founding of the International and did not become very active in it until several years later. His comments on the Civil War in this period evidenced continuing skepticism about a Union victory. This was seen, for example, in a letter to Marx dated November 9, where he compared the Union military campaign to what he and Marx had regarded as the half-hearted efforts of Britain and France against Russia during the Crimean War (MECW 42, 21). Engels gives a more positive view of the Union's prospects, by now coming closer to Marx's position, in a letter to Weydemeyer of November 24, written after Sherman began his march to the sea:

> The war of yours over there is really one of the most stupendous things that one can experience. Despite the numerous stupidities [*Dummheiten*] that occurred in the Northern armies (enough in the Southern too), the tide of conquest is rolling slowly but surely onward, and, in the course of 1865, the moment will undoubtedly come when the organized resistance of the South will fold up like a pocket-knife, and the warfare turn into banditry. . . . A people's war of this kind, on both sides, has not taken place since the great states have been in existence, and it will, at all events, point the direction for the future of the whole of America for hundreds of years to come. Once slavery, the greatest shackle on the political and social development of the United States, has been broken, the country is bound to receive an impetus from which it will acquire a very different position in world history within the shortest possible time, and a use will then soon be found for the army and navy with which the war is providing it. (38–39)

This letter, with its evocation of a "people's war," and its prescient suggestion of the emergence of the United States as a world power, was his only substantial political analysis of the war after 1861.

Marx, for his part, kept stressing the revolutionary dimensions of the war and the abolition of slavery, as he had all along. In a letter to Lion Philips on November 29, 1864, he seems to agree with Engels's criticisms of the Union commanders. He quotes a letter from Weydemeyer, referring to Grant's Richmond campaign as a "blunder that has cost us hecatombs of men" (MECW 42, 48). However, his overall analysis runs in another direction: "When you think, dear Uncle, that three and a half years ago, at the time of Lincoln's election, the problem was making no further concessions to the slaveholders, while now the abolition of slavery is the avowed and in part already realized aim, you must admit that never has such a gigantic upheaval [*Riesenumwalzung*] taken place so rapidly. It will have a beneficent effect on the whole world" (48).

Marx's next effort with regard to the Civil War was to draft an address congratulating Lincoln upon his reelection on the part of the London-based General Council of the International. (Lincoln had won a solid 55 percent victory against McClellan in the 1864 presidential election.) This served to implement the notion, espoused in the Inaugural Address, that the working class needed to develop its own foreign policy.[36] As he indicates in a letter to Engels of December 2, drafting this text entailed an avoidance of "vulgar-democratic phraseology," that is, liberalism rather than socialism (MECW 42, 49). He also had to argue down a suggestion from the Left, from a French delegate who proposed that the statement be addressed to the American *people*, rather than to Lincoln. From the Right, he had to forestall a British one that it be delivered, as was customary, by a member of Parliament, which at that time had no labor representatives. According to the minutes of the December 13 weekly meeting of the General Council of the International, this latter suggestion "was strongly opposed by many Members who said Working Men should rely on themselves and not seek for extraneous aid" (MEGA² I/20, 285). William Cremer, the council's secretary, expressed the hope, based on correspondence with Minister Adams, that Adams would officially receive a forty-member workers' delegation to deliver the Address, but this did not come about (MEGA² I/20, 287–89, 1363–64). Entitled "To Abraham Lincoln, President of the United States of America," the Address stated in part:

> We congratulate the American people upon your re-election by a large majority. If resistance to the Slave Power was the reserved watchword of your first election, the triumphant warcry of your re-election is, Death

to Slavery. From the commencement of the Titanic-American strife the working men of Europe felt instinctively that the star-spangled banner carried the destiny of their class. . . . The working classes of Europe understood at once, even before the fanatic partisanship of the upper classes for the Confederate gentry had given its dismal warning, that the slave-holders' rebellion was to sound the tocsin for a general holy crusade of property against labor, and that for the men of labor, with their hopes for the future, even their past conquests were at stake in that tremendous conflict on the other side of the Atlantic. Everywhere they bore therefore patiently the hardships imposed upon them by the cotton crisis, opposed enthusiastically the pro-slavery intervention, importunities of their betters—and, from most parts of Europe, contributed their blood to the good cause. While the working men, the true political power of the North, allowed slavery to defile their own republic; while before the Negro, mastered and sold without his concurrence, they boasted it the highest prerogative of the white-skinned laborer to sell himself and choose his own master; they were unable to attain the true freedom of labor or to support their European brethren in their struggle for emancipation, but this barrier to progress has been swept off by the red sea of civil war. The working men of Europe feel sure that, as the American War of Independence initiated a new era of ascendancy for the middle class, so the American Anti-Slavery War will do for the working classes. (MECW 20, 19–20)

In many respects, the wording was similar to that from the 1863 St. James Hall meeting. But where the latter claimed to speak on behalf of British labor, this Address from the International expressed some broader concerns. First, it took up not only slavery but also the interplay of race and class inside the United States, specifically with respect to white labor's racism. Second, it linked the Civil War, which it viewed as a second American revolution, to what it saw as an impending upsurge of the working classes of Europe. The Address was sent to Adams with the signatures of Cremer and fifty-six others, including Marx, and also was published in the December 23 *London Daily News* and in several other British newspapers. Marx translated it into German for publication on January 2 in the Lassallean weekly *Der Social-Demokrat* and in other German newspapers, which, unlike the English version, named him as the author (MEGA^2 I/20, 935, 947).

Lincoln's response came by way of a letter from Minister Adams to the International, dated January 28, 1865. Adams writes that Lincoln was grateful for the support "of his fellow citizens and by so many of the friends of humanity and progress throughout the world." In a specific reference to the European working class, Adams concludes:

Nations do not exist for themselves alone, but to promote the welfare and happiness of mankind by benevolent intercourse and example. It is in this relation that the United States regard their cause in the present conflict with slavery-maintaining insurgents as the cause of human nature, and they derive new encouragement to persevere from the testimony of the workingmen of Europe that the national attitude is favored with their enlightened approval and earnest sympathies. (KML 2, 239–40)[37]

Marx was clearly elated by the warmth of Lincoln's reply, something he may not have expected after Adams had declined to receive their delegation.

Lincoln's reply was published by the *Times* on February 6. In a letter to Engels on February 10, Marx reports, "Lincoln has replied to us so courteously and to the 'Bourgeois Emancipation Society'[38] so rudely and purely formally. . . . The difference between Lincoln's answer to us and to the bourgeois has created such a sensation here that the 'Clubs' in the West End are shaking their heads over it. You can understand how much good this does our people" (MECW 42, 86).

During the next few months, with the Civil War drawing to a close, Engels acknowledged Grant's outstanding abilities, going so far as to compare his victory at Richmond to that of Napoleon at the 1807 Battle of Jena, this in a letter to Marx of May 3, 1865 (MECW 42, 153). In response to Lincoln's assassination on April 14, Marx initially expressed the view that this would increase the possibility of a more radical policy toward the Southern oligarchy after the Union's victory, both because it would harden attitudes in the North and because he thought that Andrew Johnson, now the president, would be firmer than Lincoln. Referring to Johnson's more plebeian background, he writes, in a letter to Engels dated May 1, 1865: "The *chivalry of the South* ends worthily. Lincoln's assassination was the biggest stupidity it could commit. Johnson is stern, inflexible, and, as a former poor white, has a deadly hatred for the oligarchy. He will be less ceremonious with the fellows, and because of the assassination he will find the temper of the North adequate for his intentions" (150–51; original emphasis). In a letter written on May 3 to Marx, Engels goes even further down the road of a class-based analysis of Johnson: "Johnson will insist on confiscation of the great estates, which will make the pacification and reorganization of the South more acute. Lincoln would scarcely have insisted on it" (153). While Marx was certainly correct in his assessment that the assassination would harden attitudes in the North, he was under illusions concerning Johnson's future direction. Such views were quite widespread at the time, however, even in the States, where radical abolitionists entertained similar hopes. As is well known, Johnson took the opposite track, conciliating the former slaveowners, vetoing all efforts at Radical Reconstruction, and barely escaping impeachment at the hands of radical Republicans in the Senate in 1868.

British as well as German workers reacted strongly to Lincoln's assassination. A number of large meetings took place in London in which workers expressed their sorrow and attacked the attitude of the British government toward the Confederacy. Under the impact of these events, Marx wrote another address for the International, this time to Johnson. After expressing condolences, it states in part:

> After a tremendous civil war, but which, if we consider its vast dimensions, and its broad scope, and compare it to the Old World's Hundred Years' Wars, and Thirty Years' Wars, and Twenty-Three Years' Wars,[39] can hardly be said to have lasted ninety days, yours, sir, has become the task to uproot by the law what has been felled by the sword, to preside over the arduous work of political reconstruction and social regeneration. A profound sense of your great mission will save you from any compromise with stern duties. You will never forget that, to initiate the new era of the emancipation of labor, the American people devolved the responsibilities of leadership upon two men of labor—the one Abraham Lincoln, the other Andrew Johnson. (MECW 20, 100)

The Address was published on May 20, 1865 in the *Bee-Hive*, a newspaper sympathetic to the International. It was also published on June 1 by the *Tribune*, which reported that it had been sent "by a London friend" and that they presumed it had "reached its destination" in Washington (cited in MEGA² I/20, 1112). Unsurprisingly, Johnson never replied to the International's Address, although the U.S. Embassy in London sent a perfunctory acknowledgment.

Marx soon became worried about Johnson, now characterizing him in a letter to Engels of June 24 as "extremely vacillating and weak" toward the South (MECW 42, 163). Engels too had revised his position and writes to Marx on July 15 that "if this continues, the old Secession rogues will sit in Congress within six months. Without colored suffrage, there is nothing doing, and Johnson leaves this decision to the vanquished, the ex-slaveholders" (167).

These criticisms came to a head in September 1865, when the London Conference of the International voted to send a third communication to America, this one addressed not to Johnson but "To the People of the United States of America." On September 28, according to a report later published in the London-based *Workman's Advocate*, Cremer read out the Address to a gathering of over three hundred workers and delegates from Britain, France, Germany, Poland, Belgium, and other European countries, where it was approved by acclamation.[40] The first parts of the Address applaud the Union's victory:

> We have first to congratulate you that the war is ended, and the Union preserved. The stars and stripes once rudely torn down by your own sons, again flutter in the breeze, from the Atlantic to the Pacific, never again, we hope, to be insulted by your own children, or again to wave over fields of carnage, either by civil commotion or foreign war. . . . We have next to congratulate you that the cause of these years of suffering is now removed—Slavery is no more. That dark spot upon your otherwise fair escutcheon is blotted out for ever. No more shall the salesman's hammer barter human flesh and blood in your market places, causing humanity to shudder at its cold barbarity. (*General Council of the First International* 1962, 310–11)

The letter concludes on a different note, with a diplomatic but nonetheless firm warning about the dangers ahead, were a policy of Radical Reconstruction, including full citizenship rights for Blacks, not to be put into effect immediately:

> Since we have had the honor of expressing sympathy with your sufferings, a word of encouragement for your efforts, and of congratulation for the results, permit us also to add a word of counsel for the future. As injustice to a section of your people has produced such direful results, let that cease. *Let your citizens of to-day be declared free and equal, without reserve. If you fail to give them citizens' rights, while you demand citizens' duties, there will yet remain a struggle for the future which may again stain your country with your people's blood.* The eyes of Europe and the world are fixed upon your efforts at re-construction, and enemies are ever ready to sound the knell of the downfall of republican institutions when the slightest chance is given. We warn you then, as brothers in the common cause, to remove every shackle from freedom's limb, and your victory will be complete. (311–12; emphasis added)

According to the editors of the *Marx-Engels Gesamtausgabe* (1975–), this "Address" was written by Cremer. However, Marx was present when it was read out and more importantly, had been closely involved in the preparation of all documents for the London conference (MEGA² I/20, 1501–13). The full text of the Address was first published in the *Workmen's Advocate* on October 14.

Unfortunately, this text has not received the prominence it deserves as a major statement by Marx's First International on slavery and racism in America.[41] Its sharp warning that a failure to deal decisively with the legacy of slavery could "stain your country with your people's blood" was cited prominently in *Black Reconstruction* by Du Bois, who termed it a "bold" declaration "over the signature of Marx" ([1935] 1973, 354). Du Bois cited the version published by Schlüter (1913), who gave a different rendering of the text, which he had probably retranslated into English from a German version. The language in Schlüter's version is even more forceful than in the English one, referring to the danger of "a new struggle which will once more drench your country in blood" ([1913] 1965, 200).[42]

From this point on, there is little by Marx on the Civil War and Reconstruction, except for comments in letters and some passages in *Capital* (to be discussed in chapter 5). Two years later, on August 27, 1867, he writes on behalf of the International that Johnson was "a dirty tool in the hands of the former slaveholders" (MECW 42, 414).[43] The year before, on November 12, 1866, in a letter to François Lafargue, the father of Paul Lafargue, the future husband of his daughter Laura, Marx rejoices over Johnson's battering at the hands of the radical Republicans in the 1866 Congressional elections: "You will have been as pleased as I was at President Johnson's defeat in the last elections. The workers of the North have finally understood very well that *labor in the white skin cannot emancipate itself where in the black skin it is branded*" (334; emphasis added). The last phrase also appeared in *Capital* in 1867. At a personal level for Marx and his family, it is also worth noting that Laura Marx's 1868 union with Paul Lafargue, a Franco-Cuban of mixed race, was an interracial marriage. Lafargue held major responsibilities within the International. From 1866 to 1868, he attended weekly meetings of its General Council in the capacity of the corresponding secretary for Spain. But he also functioned as a public face of the organization, in activities like making contact with workers' groups in London.[44] This too was an expression of a certain attitude toward race and class, on the part of both Marx and the International.

CHAPTER FOUR

Ireland: Nationalism, Class, and the Labor Movement

Marx's writings on Ireland, especially those around 1870, are the culmination of the interweaving of class, nationalism, race, and ethnicity also found in those on Poland and the American Civil War. Because Ireland was a locus of progressive nationalism, Marx saw it as an important source of opposition to Britain and to global capital. At the same time, Irish workers formed a subproletariat within Britain, offering an example of the interplay of class and ethnicity. Although the writings of Marx and Engels on Ireland have long been available in a collection that runs over four hundred pages (Marx and Engels 1972b), these writings have not generated as much discussion as might have been expected. This has been the case, even though they were singled out prominently by no less a figure than Lenin, this in his 1916 writings on imperialism and national liberation (Lenin [1916] 1964).

ENGELS AND MARX ON IRELAND, 1843–59: "GIVE ME TWO HUNDRED THOUSAND IRISHMEN AND I WILL OVERTHROW THE ENTIRE BRITISH MONARCHY"

Overall, Engels's contributions on Ireland are more substantial relative to those of Marx than on the other issues discussed in this study. In fact, Engels was the first of the pair to write on the subject. In 1843, even before he and Marx had begun to work together, Engels reported from London on the Irish independence movement for a Swiss newspaper. His article concerned an open-air meeting in Ireland, where the veteran nationalist Daniel O'Connell gave a speech calling for the abolition of the Union of Ireland and England. The

Union, established in 1801, had disbanded the Irish Parliament and created the United Kingdom of Great Britain and Ireland, giving Ireland 100 members out of 650 in the House of Commons. Engels is less concerned with these constitutional issues than with the militant spirit of the Irish people: "Two hundred thousand men—and what men! People who have nothing to lose, two-thirds of whom are clothed in rags, genuine proletarians and *sans-culottes* and, moreover, Irishmen, wild, headstrong, fanatical Gaels. One who has never seen Irishmen cannot know them. Give me two hundred thousand Irishmen and I will overthrow the entire British monarchy" (MECW 3, 389). At the same time, however, Engels saw two obstacles to an Irish revolutionary movement. The first was the Whig O'Connell's accommodationism toward Britain. The second was what he characterized in condescending fashion as the "half-savage" character of the Irish people themselves (390).[1]

As is well known, in his major work *The Condition of the Working Class in England: From Personal Observation and Authentic Sources* (1845),[2] Engels details the horrific conditions of life and labor faced by workers in the midst of the industrial revolution. Few, however, have noted that in this work Engels refers repeatedly to the Irish as the most oppressed sector of the working class in England. One of his guides to working-class Manchester was Mary Burns, an Irish factory worker who was to become his companion for the next two decades. In *The Condition*, he carries out a subtle analysis of the relationship of class to ethnicity, singling out Irish immigrant labor from a number of vantage points.[3] After having described the social conditions in one working class district of Manchester, Engels concludes:

> But the most horrible spot . . . is known as Little Ireland. The cottages are old, and of the smallest sort, the streets uneven, fallen into ruts and in part without drains or pavement; masses of refuse, offal and sickening filth lie among standing pools in all directions; the atmosphere, darkened and made heavy by the smoke of a dozen factory chimneys, is poisoned by the effluvia from all of these. A crowd of women and children wander round aimlessly here, as dirty as the swine that thrive upon the garbage heaps and the puddles. . . . This race must have reached the lowest stage of humanity. (MECW 4, 361)

At another point, he writes: "The Irish have introduced, too, the custom, previously unknown in England, of going barefoot. In every manufacturing town there is now to be seen a multitude of people, especially women and children, going about barefoot, and their example is gradually being adopted by the poorer English" (368). Engels not only laments this human degradation but also notes its functionality to capitalism. For the very existence of an Irish subproletariat helps capital to drive down the conditions of life and labor of the working class as a whole. Overall, Engels concludes, one is faced with "the Irishman's competing with the Englishman, and gradually forcing the rate of wages, and with it the Englishman's level of civilization, down to the Irishman's level" (377). Despite the condescending language about "race" and "civilization," Engels's pro-Irish sympathies are clear enough.

Engels also takes up Ireland itself, this in the wider context of British-dominated global capitalism. He examines the processes through which British rule and its concomitant capitalist exploitation drove large numbers of Irish people to seek work in England. He writes that "the poorer districts of Dublin are among the most hideous and repulsive to be seen in the world," even though "the Bay of Dublin is the most beautiful in the whole British Island Kingdom" (MECW 4,337). In the brief chapter "Irish Immigration," he argues: "The rapid extension of English industry could not have taken place if England had not possessed in the numerous and impoverished population of Ireland a reserve at command" (389).[4]

In a chapter titled "The Agricultural Proletariat," Engels analyzes not only English but also Irish agriculture and the latter's harshly exploitative system of tenant farming:

> The Irish people is thus held in crushing poverty, from which it cannot free itself under our present social conditions. These people live in the most wretched clay huts, scarcely good enough for cattle-pens, have scant food all winter long, or . . . they have potatoes half enough thirty weeks in the year, and the rest of the year nothing. When the time comes in the spring at which this provision reaches its end, or can no longer be used because of its sprouting, wife and children go forth to beg and tramp the country with their kettle in their hands. Meanwhile the husband, after planting potatoes for the next year, goes in search of work either in Ireland or England, and returns at the potato harvest to his family. . . . The cause of this poverty lies in the existing social conditions. (MECW 4, 558–59)

Sometimes, Engels tends toward exoticist condescension, however: "With the Irish, feeling and passion predominate; reason must bow before them" (560).

Engels penned these poignant descriptions of Irish poverty and suffering before the potato blight struck in 1845. The ensuing Great Famine of 1845–49, in which landlords continued to export large quantities of food from Ireland as peasants starved, resulted in the death of one and a half million people, with another million forced to emigrate—this out of a population of about eight million. Writing for a French newspaper in October 1847, Engels predicts an explosion: "Starving Ireland is writhing in the most terrible convulsions. The workhouses are overflowing with beggars, the ruined property owners are refusing to pay the Poor Tax, and the hungry people gather in their thousands to ransack the barns and cattle-sheds of the farmers and even the Catholic priests, who were still sacred to them a short time ago. It looks as if the Irish will not die of hunger as calmly this winter as they did last winter" (MECW 6, 309). He also points to the fivefold increase in Irish emigration to England, which, he suggests, will drive down the standard of living of the working class there still further.

After O'Connell's death in 1847, Engels predicted greater influence for more left-wing Irish leaders such as Feargus O'Connor and Bronterre O'Brien, both of whom were connected to Chartism. In an 1848 article for a German paper, Engels praises O'Connor as someone who "shows that the Irish people must fight with all their might and in close association with the English working classes and the Chartists" (MECW 6, 449). He also extols O'Connor's attempt to block Tory leader Robert Peel's Irish Coercion Bill during debates in Parliament. At this time, however, Engels holds to what the Australian historian Ian Cummins has aptly called "an Anglocentric approach to the liberation of Ireland" (1980, 108). Engels does so in the conclusion of his article: "There can be no doubt that henceforth the mass of the Irish people will unite ever more closely with the English Chartists and will act with them according to a common plan. As a result, the victory of the English democrats, and hence the liberation of Ireland, will be hastened by many years" (MECW 6, 449).

During these early years, Marx made only occasional references to Ireland, but his overall support for Irish national liberation was clear enough. For example, in a February 1848 speech commemorating the 1846 Polish uprising, Marx contrasted its program of national independence unseparated from agrarian revolution to the O'Connell-led movement to repeal the Union of Ireland and England. He charges that the Repeal movement was based upon the "narrowly nationalist party" of the Catholic landowners (MECW 6, 549). In July 1848, the more radical Young Ireland movement, which had strong links to the English Chartists, attempted an insurrection against British rule. Although neither Marx nor Engels addressed these events directly in those months, at the beginning of 1849, as the revolutionary wave was beginning to recede, Marx writes of how police serving the old regimes "once more plundered, ravished, and murdered in Poland . . . and Ireland," thus suppressing movements for national liberation (MECW 8, 214). Soon after, in *Wage-Labor and Capital* (1849), Marx refers in a synopsis of recent events in Europe to "the starving of Ireland into submission" (MECW 9, 197).

In the 1850s, after his move to London, Marx's discussions of Ireland become somewhat more substantial. In an 1852 *Tribune* article, he reports that the president of the British Board of Trade had declared that the Great Famine and the ensuing emigration reduced pauperism, to which he responds with Swiftian irony: "We must confess that 'the famine' is quite as radical a remedy against Pauperism as arsenic against rats" (MECW 11, 357). He continued this argument in a *Tribune* article published on March 22, 1853, showing that what he had in mind in discussing Ireland was also a broader critique of David Ricardo's political economy. Analyzing official statistics, Marx shows that among those emigrating from the British Isles during the years 1847–52, the overwhelming majority was Irish. He also cites the *Economist's* breezy celebration of this form of capitalist modernization: "The departure of the redundant part of the population of Ireland and the Highlands of Scotland is an indispensable preliminary to every kind of improvement. . . . The revenue of Ireland has not suffered in any degree from the famine of 1846–47, or from the emigration that has since taken place." Marx's retort again assumes an ironic tone:

> Begin with pauperizing the inhabitants of a country, and when there is no more profit to be ground out of them, when they have grown a burden on the revenue, drive them away, and sum up your Net Revenue! Such is the doctrine laid down by [David] Ricardo, in his celebrated work, *The Principle of Political Economy*. . . . Sismondi, in his *Nouveaux Principes d'Économie Politique* answers that, according to this view of the matter, the English nation would not be interested at all in the disappearance of the whole population, the King . . . remaining alone in the midst of the island, supposing only that automatic machinery enabled him to procure the amount of Net Revenue now produced by a population of 20 millions. Indeed, that grammatical entity "the national wealth" would in this case not be diminished. (529)

A month earlier, in his *Tribune* article, "The Dutchess of Sutherland and Slavery," Marx noted the involvement of his perennial target Palmerston in these developments: "The noble Viscount Palmerston, too, some years ago cleared of men his property in Ireland" (493).

Marx also took up social tensions in rural Ireland. In a February 23, 1853, *Tribune* article, he contrasts the repeal movement of the 1840s to the post-famine tenant rights movement: "The Repeal agitation was a mere political movement, and therefore, it was possible for the Catholic clergy to make use of it. . . . The Tenant-Right agitation is a deep-rooted social movement which, in its course, will produce a downright scission between the Church and the Irish Revolutionary party, and thus emancipate the people from that mental thrall-dom which has frustrated all their exertions, sacrifices, and struggles for centuries past" (MECW 11, 505). As before, he saw national emancipation through the lens of a class analysis of the internal fissures of Irish society.

Marx went more deeply into the class structure of rural Ireland in a July 11, 1853, *Tribune* article entitled "The Indian Question—Irish Tenant Right." In the part on Ireland, he noted that the absentee landowners, who were predominantly English, had the right to raise rents at will and to evict tenant farmers quite easily. If the tenant invested money and labor in improvements for which compensation was due from the landlord, a hefty rent increase could easily wipe out this gain. In reality, Marx writes, the tenant "has to pay interest for his own money to the landlord" (MECW 12, 157). In these and other ways, he continues:

> A class of absentee landlords has been enabled to pocket, not merely the labor, but also the capital, of whole generations, each generation of Irish peasants sinking a grade lower in the social scale, exactly in proportion to the exertions and sacrifices made for the raising of their condition and that of their families. If the tenant was industrious and enterprising, he became taxed in consequence of his industry and enterprise. If, on the contrary, he grew inert and negligent, he was reproached with the "abo-riginal faults of the Celtic race." He had, accordingly, no other alterna-tive left but to become a pauper—to pauperize himself by industry, or to pauperize by negligence. In order to oppose this state of things, "Tenant Right" was proclaimed in Ireland—a right of the tenant, not in the soil but in the improvements of the soil effected at his cost and charges. (158)

British policy had created the conditions that necessitated this law, Marx holds:

> England has subverted the conditions of Irish society. At first it confis-cated the land, then it suppressed the industry by "Parliamentary enact-ments," and lastly, it broke the active energy by armed force. And thus England created those abominable "conditions of society" which enable a small *caste* of rapacious lordlings to hold the land and to live upon it. Too

weak yet for revolutionizing those "social conditions," the people appeal to Parliament, demanding at least their mitigation and regulation. (159)

Marx then detailed the vociferous opposition from the landowning classes to the new tenants' rights law proposed to Parliament in June 1853. It would have granted tenants various rights, among them some compensation for improvements upon termination of a lease, but the tenants' rights bill failed to clear Parliament after two years of rancorous debate. To counter the landowners' arguments, he cites both Ricardo and Herbert Spencer, men he describes with a certain irony as being above any suspicion of communist leanings but who have nonetheless called into question the property rights of large landowners. According to Marx, Ricardo held that "private proprietorship in land . . . was a relation quite superfluous within the whole frame-work of modern production" (160–61). He also cites Spencer's *Social Statics*: "Equity, therefore, does not permit property in land, or the rest would live on the earth by sufferance only" (161).

After a hiatus of nearly two years on the subject, Marx's article "Ireland's Revenge" appeared in the *Neue Oder-Zeitung* on March 16, 1855. It concerned social and economic changes since the Great Famine. One element, he writes, was the growing social consciousness of the Irish people, who now demanded that those standing for Parliament "do what O'Connell had always avoided and refused to do, that is, to explore the real causes of the Irish malady and to make land and property relations and their reform the election slogan." Once elected to the House of Commons, however, the new politicians quickly forgot "the rights of the tenants," he complains (MECW 14, 79.) A second element in Ireland's transformation was economic, but here Marx sounds a somber note, suggesting that the social basis for a national revolution might actually be weakening: "The Irish agricultural system is being replaced by the English system, the system of small tenures by big tenures, and the modern capitalist is taking the place of the old landowner." Behind these changes, he argues, lay the experience of defeat and despair, both in the Great Famine and "the unsuccessful insurrection of 1848, which finally destroyed Ireland's faith in itself" (80).

In a September 15, 1855, article for the *Neue Oder-Zeitung* eulogizing the Irish Chartist leader Feargus O'Connor, Marx notes the presence of leftist slogans at the funeral:

Yesterday afternoon the funeral of O'Connor, the late Chartist leader, took place. A procession of 20,000 people, practically all of them from the working class, moved from Finsbury Square and Smithfield to Notting

Hill, from where the coffin was taken to Kensal Green Cemetery (one of the most magnificent burial-grounds in London). Four-horse carriages, decorated with enormous plumes in the English fashion, took their place at the head of the procession. Hard on their heels followed flag-bearers and standard-bearers. In letters of white, the black flags bore the inscription, "He lived and died for us." A gigantic red flag magnificently displayed the inscription "Alliance des peuples." A red liberty cap was swaying at the top of the main standard. . . . As the procession moved back into the city at about half past five in the afternoon it had the ironic satisfaction of meeting five detachments of constables marching out, and greeted each in turn with a "too late." Since O'Connor died as a pauper in the true sense of the word, the burial expenses were met by the working class of London. (MECW 14, 524)

In this way, Marx focuses attention on the connections of the wider democratic, labor, and socialist movements to Irish national liberation.

Engels, who had not written on Ireland since the 1840s, traveled there with his companion Mary Burns, reporting at length in a letter to Marx of May 23, 1856. He begins by remarking upon the atmosphere of total repression, which he compares unfavorably with Prussian discipline:

The "iron hand" is visible in every nook and cranny; the government meddles in everything, not a trace of so-called self-government. Ireland may be regarded as the earliest English colony and one which, by reason of proximity, is still governed in exactly the same old way; here one cannot fail to notice that the English citizen's so-called freedom is based on the oppression of the colonies. In no other country have I seen so many gendarmes, and it is in the constabulary, which is armed with carbine, bayonet and handcuffs, that the bibulous expression of your Prussian gendarme reaches its ultimate state of perfection. (MECW 40, 49)

Engels also remarks upon the depopulation of the countryside, especially in the West—the abandoned houses, the vacant pastures: "The fields are empty even of cattle; the countryside is a complete wilderness unwanted by anybody" (50). He concludes that seven centuries of English conquest and martial law have "utterly ruined the country," to the point that

[f]or all their fanatical nationalism, the fellows no longer feel at home in their own country. Ireland for the Anglo-Saxon! That is now becoming

a reality. . . . Emigration will continue until the predominantly, indeed almost exclusively Celtic nature of the population has gone to pot. . . . In this artificial manner, through systematic oppression, they have come to be a completely wretched nation and now, as everyone knows, they have the job of providing England, America, Australia, etc., with whores, day laborers, pimps, pickpockets, swindlers and other wretches. (50)

Engels sounded these despairing notes during a period when the hopes of the 1848 revolutions had receded.

After another hiatus of nearly three years concerning Ireland, Marx describes a British witch hunt against what he believed to be imagined nationalist conspirators in a January 11, 1859, *Tribune* article, "The Excitement in Ireland" (MECW 16, 134–38). The British had placed Ireland in a state of siege, enacting a reign of terror through the use of paid informers and *agents provocateurs*. While Marx correctly gauged the new level of repression, he wrongly assumed that the British were hunting shadows created by their own imagination. In fact, as the Irish historian Peter Berresford Ellis recounts, a new clandestine revolutionary movement had been formed: "The Fenians, or rather the Irish Republican Brotherhood, came into being on March 17, 1858, at a meeting in Dublin. It was a secret oathbound revolutionary movement dedicated to overthrowing English rule in Ireland by force and establishing an Irish Republic" (Ellis 1996, 130).

While none of these writings by Marx and Engels in the 1840s and 1850s offered a systematic analysis of Irish national liberation, certain basic themes were evident. (1) While they enunciated clear support for the Irish national struggle against British rule, they always counseled Irish revolutionaries to devote more attention to the internal class dynamics of Irish society. In particular, they advised a greater focus on agrarian class conflict, also pointing out that part of the landlord class was itself Irish rather than British. In this sense, they were especially critical of the upper class Catholic nationalism of O'Connell. (2) They urged Irish revolutionaries to develop the firmest unity with British workers from the mass-based Chartist movement, pointing out that the Chartists supported repeal of the Union of Ireland and England. They also noted that two Irishmen, Feargus O'Connor and Bronterre O'Brien, had served as prominent Chartist leaders. Moreover, Marx argued that O'Connell's politics had been bypassed by economic changes that had integrated Ireland more closely than ever with Britain. Thus, he urged Irish revolutionaries to follow the example of their English counterparts. (3) They also singled out Irish immigrant labor in Britain, both as an index of Irish oppression at home and as a factor in holding down the wages of English workers. Whether in Ireland or in England, they referred to the oppressive situation of Irish peasants and workers to illustrate capitalist social relations. Moreover, they argued that British rule in Ireland proved that the British state could be just as repressive as Continental regimes like Bonapartist France or Prussia. All of this fit into their larger analysis of the development of British capitalism, with Irish immigrant labor as a reserve labor pool for British industry, and Ireland itself as a crucially important agricultural colony, whose exported agricultural surplus was helping to finance Britain's industrialization.

MARX ON IRELAND DURING THE CRUCIAL YEAR 1867: "I ONCE BELIEVED THE SEPARATION OF IRELAND FROM ENGLAND TO BE IMPOSSIBLE. I NOW REGARD IT AS INEVITABLE."

As will be discussed in the next chapter, Marx took up Ireland at some length in *Capital*. After the publication of its first edition in 1867, he became increasingly involved in Irish issues through the International.[5] As we saw in chapters 1 and 2, between the 1840s and the late 1850s, Marx's perspective on India and Russia changed from a relatively uncritical modernism to one that took greater account of the internally generated emancipatory potential of these societies. In the remainder of this chapter, I will argue that after 1867, Marx's view of Ireland also underwent a transformation.

In the 1864 inaugural address to the First International, Marx refers twice to Ireland. At the beginning of the address, he charges that Britain's unparalleled economic expansion since the 1840s has not mitigated the "misery of the working masses," giving as his first example "the people of Ireland, gradually replaced by machinery in the north and by sheep-walks in the south, though even the sheep in that unhappy country are decreasing, it is true, not at so rapid a rate as the men" (MECW 20, 5). Later, he refers to attempts by Palmerston to "put down the advocates of the Irish Tenants Right Bill" (12).

During these years, the Fenian movement was gaining strength both in Ireland and among Irish immigrants in Britain and the United States. By 1865, the Fenian newspaper, *The Irish People*, was advocating an agrarian uprising as the basis of a national revolution:

Twenty years ago Thomas Davis appealed to the aristocracy to save the people with their own hands. We make no appeal to the aristocracy ... they are the willing tools of the alien government whose policy it is to slay the people, or drive them like noxious vermin from the soil. The people must save themselves. Something more even than a successful insurrection is demanded. And what is that? An entire revolution which will restore the country to its rightful owners. And who are these? The people. Every man has one simple object to accomplish. It is to rid the land of robbers, and render every cultivator of the soil his own landlord.

The Fenians yearned for "a nation which bows to no power under heaven," also criticizing openly the Catholic clergy: "Our only hope is revolution, but most bishops and many of the clergy are opposed to revolution" (cited in Ellis 1996, 133).

From its beginning, the International seems to have had some links to the Fenians, although, given the fact that the latter were part of a movement that was illegal in the British Empire, these were not always made public. There is, however, some surviving documentation of those links, as in the case of the prominent Fenian James Stephens. Stephens and other Fenian leaders were arrested in the fall of 1865, but Stephens was freed from a British prison in a March 1866 rescue carried out by Fenians from America. The somewhat erratic Stephens escaped to the United States, where he rather peremptorily declared himself the movement's supreme leader. In the spring of 1866, some six hundred Civil War veterans from a rival Fenian faction led by William Roberts crossed into Canada from near Buffalo, New York, where they raised the Irish tricolor[6] for the first time on British territory, also killing twelve British soldiers before retreating across the border. Marx seemed to regard this operation with great reservation. Some months later, in a letter to Engels of December 17, 1866, Marx reports laconically concerning the International that "one of our more dubious acquisitions was the joining (at New York) of . . . Stephens" (MECW 42, 338). Additional links are indicated by the fact that during 1865 and 1866, newspapers connected to the International published appeals from the wives of the imprisoned Fenians as well as several articles by General Council Member Peter Fox on Ireland. One of these resulted in the British government's agreement to receive a delegation on behalf of the Fenian prisoners from the International, which had complained about their harsh treatment.[7] This included permanent solitary confinement, only one letter every six months, and floggings as well as rations of bread and water for twenty-eight days for the slightest violation of prison rules.

But 1867 was the year that the Irish struggle really came to a boil. In March, crack British troops crushed a Fenian-led uprising by poorly armed Irish peasants. On September 11 in Manchester, the British caught and arrested two leading Fenians, Thomas Kelly and Timothy Deasy. Then, on September 18, other Fenians ambushed their prison van, freeing both men. A British police sergeant died of his wounds soon afterwards. These events transpired during the same week that Marx and Paul Lafargue were visiting Engels in Manchester to confer about publicizing *Capital*, which had come off the press in Hamburg on September 14. Kelly and Deasy managed to escape to America, but the police swooped down upon the Irish community in Manchester, arresting dozens and eventually putting five men on trial for murder. Three of them—the "Manchester martyrs" William Allen, Michael O'Brien, and Michael Larkin—were publicly hanged on November 23 as a drunken mob celebrated outside. Queen Victoria reflected the temper of upper-class opinion in a private communication of October 2: "These Irish are really shocking, abominable people—not like any other civilized nation" (cited in Kapp 1972, 84). Sectors of the British left and labor movement strongly condemned the trial, however, in which little credible evidence was presented. They expressed even greater outrage at the executions.

Already in June, Marx had written to Engels that he was "quite sickened" by the deplorable prison conditions for the Fenians that the British—whom he calls "swine" that nonetheless "boast of their English humanity"—had established. Invariably, the Fenian prisoners were treated as common criminals rather than as political prisoners (MECW 42, 394). He also reported that Mary O'Donovan Rossa, the wife of the prominent Fenian prisoner Jeremiah O'Donovan Rossa, had written to thank the International for its support. Five months later, during the weeks preceding the November 23 execution, the International launched a solidarity campaign. In a letter to Engels of November 2, Marx writes: "I have sought by every means at my disposal to incite the English workers to demonstrate in favor of Fenianism" (460). They joined the debate in favor of the Fenian prisoners at a meeting of the Reform League, an influential group founded by members of the International—as well as liberals—to support expansion of the suffrage. Odger, one of the labor leaders who had been so outspoken against slavery during the Civil War, was among those holding forth for the Irish at the Reform League. He soon backtracked, however, saying that he had been misunderstood. Evidently, it was easier to oppose slavery across the Atlantic than to take a stand closer to home on Ireland. This was the beginning of a division that would create a split between Marx and the English trade union leaders in 1871, during the Paris Commune.

In the November 2 letter to Engels, Marx suggests that his own views of the Irish struggle were evolving: "I once believed the separation of Ireland from England to be impossible. I now regard it as inevitable, although federation may follow upon separation" (MECW 42, 460). Then, referring to a new series of evictions of tenant farmers in Ireland, he adds: "In no other European country has foreign rule assumed this form of direct expropriation of the natives" (461).

The minutes of the November 19, 1867, public meeting of the General Council and Members and Friends of the Association on "the Fenian question" show that the majority held very strong pro-Irish views (Marx and Engels 1972b, 368). The London *Times* and two Dublin newspapers, the *Nation* and the *Irishman*, covered these proceedings. In the discussion, Hermann Jung, the International's secretary for Switzerland, received applause when he criticized those who attacked the Fenians for resorting to violence:

> Some endeavors have been made to divert the attention of the workpeople of this country with regard to the Fenians. While they are denounced as murderers, Garibaldi is held up as a great patriot; and have no lives been sacrificed in Garibaldi's movement? . . . The Irish have a right to revolt against those who drive them out of their country; the English would do the same if any foreign powers oppressed them in a similar manner. (368–69)

Eugène Dupont, the International's secretary for France, also referred to the right of revolution, but emphasized as well the progressive character of the Fenian political program: "They affirm the republican form of government, liberty of conscience, no State religion, the produce of labor to the laborer, and the possession of the soil to the people" (369).

English members of the General Council of the International were more equivocal. The union leader Benjamin Lucraft stated that violence would do no good, also criticizing the Irish workers of London for keeping aloof from the English labor movement. Another Englishman, General Council member John Weston, who was chairing the meeting, was more supportive of the Fenians: "The crime of starving the Irish was far greater than the accidental killing of one man in trying to rescue the Fenian prisoners" (Marx and Engels 1972b, 371). Marx did not take the floor, but he was the main author of an appeal from the International that was sent to the home minister the next day. It stated that the executions, if carried out, would "bear the stamp not of a judicial act, but of political revenge" (Marx and Engels 1972b, 118). Two days later, on November 21, some twenty thousand workers gathered in London to petition for mercy. Two men were reprieved at the last minute, but Allen, Larkin, and O'Brien were hanged on November 23.

Writing to Marx on November 24, a day after the hangings, Engels concludes that an irreparable breach had occurred, one that would make Irish independence inevitable:

> The Tories have really performed the ultimate act of separation between England and Ireland. . . . It was the execution of those three that will transform the liberation of Kelly and Deasy into an act of heroism, such as will now be sung at the cradle of every Irish child in Ireland, England, and America. The Irish women will see to that as surely as did the Polish womenfolk. To my knowledge, the only time that anyone has been executed for anything similar in a civilized state was the case of John Brown at Harpers Ferry. The Fenians could not wish for a better precedent. (MECW 42, 474)

Above, in a seamless web, Engels links together three issues at this core of this study: the Civil War, Poland, and Ireland.

Marx prepared a speech on Ireland for the November 26 meeting of the General Council, but again he did not speak, allowing Fox to do so instead. In a letter to Engels dated November 30, he indicates that he might have taken the floor if the Irish press had shown up again. Marx writes that, had he taken the floor, the fact of the executions only three days earlier would have "compelled" him "to unleash a revolutionary thunderbolt, instead of the intended objective analysis of the situation and the movement" (MECW 42, 485). That is why, he adds, he was not unhappy that Fox spoke, in part because he was an Englishman and it was important for the English to take a stand at that moment. However, he has difficulty with the type of resolution "the abstract Fox" (MECW 42, 485) proposed for a vote at the end of his speech, one that stressed "amity between the British and Irish nations" rather than something stronger, but Fox's resolution was tabled without apparent controversy (*General Council of the First International* 1964, 181). Another reason Marx was glad not to have spoken, he adds, was that under the circumstances of the recent executions he would have had to identify himself publicly with the Fenians more than he would have liked to have done, for he did "not enjoy getting embroiled with people like Roberts, Stephens, and the like" (MECW 42, 485).

Marx's notes for his undelivered November 26 speech, written in English, have survived. He begins on a similar note to the letter by Engels dated November 24: "Since our last meeting the object of our discussion, Fenianism, has entered a new phase. It has been baptized in blood by the English Government. The Political Executions at Manchester remind us of the fate of John Brown at

Harpers Ferry. They open a new period in the struggle between Ireland and England" (MECW 21, 189). Marx devotes considerable attention to the centralization of agricultural holdings, writing that since 1855, "1,032,694 Irishmen have been displaced by about one million cattle, pigs and sheep" (190). The result is that "the situation of the mass of the people has deteriorated, and their state is verging to a crisis similar to that of 1846. The relative surplus population [is] now as great as before the famine. . . . So result: Gradual expulsion of the natives, gradual deterioration and exhaustion of natural life, the soil" (191).

In this brief passage, Marx links together the destruction of the Irish people with the destruction of the natural environment. This new stage of Britain's capitalist penetration into Ireland was wreaking both human and ecological damage. The Irish historians Eamonn Slater and Terrence McDonough argue that this type of discussion, found here and in a few other passages on Ireland, "projects Marx not only as an historical analyst of colonialism but also, perhaps, as a theorist of environmental modernity" (2008, 170). As to Fenianism, which his notes treat very briefly, he writes that its "distinguishing character" as a "socialist, lower-class movement" meant that it was "not Catholic" but "republican," this under the influence of the Irish in America (MECW 21, 192, 193). In a letter to Engels of November 30, 1867, Marx connects the socioeconomic changes in Ireland since 1846 more explicitly to the emergence of Fenianism as a new type of resistance movement:

> What the English do not yet realize is that since 1846 the economic content and hence the political purpose of English rule in Ireland as well has entered an entirely new phase, and that for that very reason Fenianism is characterized by socialist (in the negative sense, as directed against the appropriation of the soil) leanings and as a lower orders movement. What could be more absurd than to lump together the barbarities of Elizabeth or Cromwell, who wanted to drive out the Irish by means of English colonists (in the Roman sense), and the present system, which wants to drive out the Irish by means of sheep, pigs, and oxen! . . . Clearing of the Estates of Ireland is now the sole meaning of English rule in Ireland. The *stupid* English government in London naturally knows nothing of this immense change since 1846. But the Irish do. . . . The Irish have been expressing their awareness of it in the clearest and most forcible manner. The question now is, what advice should *we* give the *English* workers? In my view, they must make *Repeal of the Union* . . . an article of their *manifesto*. This is the only *legal* and hence the only possible form of Irish emancipation which can be adopted by an *English*

party in its program. . . . What the Irish need is: 1. Self-government and independence from England. 2. Agrarian revolution. With the best will in the world the English cannot do this for them, but they can give them the legal means to do it for themselves. 3. *Protective tariffs against England.* (MECW 42, 486–87; original emphasis)

While a clear call for Irish independence was still evident, the notion that English workers would be the catalyst for change in Ireland remained, as before.[8]

The Irish situation took another dramatic turn on December 13, 1867, when Fenians placed a bomb outside Clerkenwell Gaol in London in an attempt to free some of their prisoners. The bomb misfired, instead killing a dozen English residents of the neighboring working-class community. In a letter to Engels the next day, Marx expresses dismay at this incident, which was sure to undercut English working-class support for the Irish. He also critiques the notion of conspiratorial action by small groups: "The latest Fenian exploit in Clerkenwell is a great folly. The London masses, which have shown much sympathy for Ireland, will be enraged by it and driven into the arms of the government party. One cannot expect the London proletarians to let themselves be blown up for the benefit of Fenian emissaries. Secret, melodramatic conspiracies of this kind are, in general, more or less doomed to failure" (MECW 42, 501). Engels responds on December 19 that the incident "was obviously the work of a few special fanatics; it is the misfortune of all conspiracies that they lead to acts of folly because 'we really must do something'" (505).

None of these private criticisms signified a turning away on Marx's part from the Irish cause, or even from the Fenians, however. In a letter of December 17, he informs Engels that the *Irishman*, the newspaper that had covered General Council meetings on Ireland, was "willing to print, if you write it in English," a review of *Capital*. Referring to *Capital's* section on Ireland, he adds that "Ireland must take the proper role in it, however" (MECW 42, 504).[9] Marx also mentions that he gave a lengthy public talk on Ireland before an audience of one hundred at a December 16 meeting sponsored by their colleagues in the German Workers Educational Society, this only three days after the bombing at Clerkenwell. Marx's notes for this talk have survived, as has a brief unpublished article on it drafted by Johann Georg Eccarius, who was serving as secretary to the General Council of the International.

In his notes for the speech of December 16, 1867, Marx begins by characterizing Fenianism once again as a movement that "took root (and is still really rooted) only in the mass of the people, the lower orders," as against "all earlier Irish movements," which in his view were led by the "aristocracy or middle-class men, and always the Catholic churchmen" (MECW 21, 194). He then asks why such a movement appeared when it did:

> Here is what baffles the English: they find the present regime mild compared with England's former oppression of Ireland. So why this most determined and irreconcilable form of opposition now? What I want to show—and what even those Englishmen who side with the Irish do not see—is that the [oppression] since 1846, though less barbarian in form, has been in effect destructive, leaving no alternative but Ireland's voluntary emancipation by England or life-and-death struggle. (194)

Thus, the more capitalist form of English domination since the 1846 Great Famine, although less overtly violent, had been more destructive than all previous forms of English rule over the past seven hundred years.

Next, Marx traces English attempts to conquer Ireland from the twelfth century onwards. He describes them as similar to the wars of conquest against Native Americans by later English colonists in North America: "The plan was to exterminate the Irish at least up to the River Shannon, to take their land and settle English colonists in their place" (MECW 21, 195). The nationwide Irish revolt against Cromwell in the 1640s led to a new and more thorough type of reconquest: "Bloodshed, devastation, depopulation of entire counties, removal of their inhabitants to other regions, sale of many Irish into slavery in the West Indies" (196). This had two other results: (1) Cromwell's campaign in Ireland ended the hope of a radical revolution in England itself; it "put paid to the English Republic"; and (2) it resulted in a special "Irish mistrust of the English people's party," thus driving a wedge between them and their successors on the British left (196). Subsequent English policies under the Restoration prevented the development of manufacturing in Ireland "and threw the people back on the land" (197). Marx also details the religious discrimination against Catholics and its link to the appropriation of land by the English. Inspired by the French Revolution, the 1798 Irish uprising failed because the "peasants" were "not ripe" (198). The Anglo-Irish Union of 1801 resulted, under which Irish industry was curtailed: "Every time Ireland was about to develop industrially, she was crushed and reconverted into a purely agricultural land. . . . All their accumulations were sent therefore to England for investment . . . and thus Ireland [was] forced to contribute cheap labor and cheap capital to building up 'the great works of Britain'" (200).

In the second half of his notes, Marx focuses on the period after 1846. Ireland experienced not only mass death and emigration, but also a "revolution of the old agricultural system," under which large farms were consolidated. This was not initially planned, but "soon circumstances arose whereby this became a conscious and deliberate system" (MECW 21, 201). He mentions four factors: (1) repeal of the Corn Laws led to a drop in the prices of Irish grains; (2) "reorganization" of agriculture in Ireland was a "caricature" of what had taken place in England (MECW 21, 202); (3) masses of Irish men and women were fleeing to England "in a state almost of starvation" (202); and (4) the Encumbered Estates Act of 1853 resulted in further concentration of landownership. Peasants were driven from the land, sometimes by force. Marx then details the decrease in population through emigration and the downturn in living conditions for those remaining.

In his article on the meeting, also unpublished, Eccarius gives us Marx's conclusion in a more detailed and sharper form than that found in Marx's notes, which suggests that his oral remarks may have been more pointed:

> Over 1,100,000 people have been replaced by 9,600,000 sheep. This is a thing unheard of in Europe. The Russians replace evicted Poles with Russians, not with sheep. Only under the Mongols in China was there once a discussion whether towns should be destroyed to make room for sheep. The Irish question is therefore not simply a question of nationality, but a question of land and existence. Ruin or revolution is the watchword; all the Irish are convinced that if anything is to happen at all it must happen quickly. The English should demand separation and leave it to the Irish themselves to decide the question of landownership. Everything else would be useless. (MECW 21, 318–19)

In thus comparing the effects of capitalist exploitation of Ireland to the depredations of the Mongols, Marx was making a point similar to his earlier characterization of British rule in India as an example of "the inherent barbarism of bourgeois civilization" (MECW 12, 221).

THEORIZING IRELAND AFTER THE UPHEAVALS OF 1867

In the early months of 1868, the Bonaparte regime arrested members of the International in Paris, accusing them without evidence of being at the center of an international Fenian conspiracy. In Ireland, the rather moderate paper the *Irishman* came under attack for publishing pro-Fenian material, and its editor, Richard Pigott, was sentenced to prison. In a letter to Engels of March 16, Marx intones that this type of repression "exceeds anything seen on the

Continent—except Russia. What dogs!" (MECW 42, 550). In the coming weeks, a trial of Fenians in Manchester saw an old comrade of Marx and Engels, Ernest Jones, taking the role of attorney for the defense. They had become estranged from Jones due to his move toward liberalism, and Engels, writing to Marx on April 30, 1868, criticizes Jones's "lukewarm" approach in the courtroom, which in his view allowed the prosecution to rage unchecked (MECW 43, 26). Soon after, on May 26, Michael Barrett, a Fenian convicted of participation in the Clerkenwell bombing, was hanged. He was the last person to be publicly hanged in England.

During this period, in a letter to a German member of the International, Ludwig Kugelmann, of April 6, Marx takes up the Liberal Gladstone's election strategy. Gladstone's platform included extension of the suffrage to a great portion (but not the whole) of the working classes and greater flexibility toward Ireland. Marx complains that Odger and other labor reformers within the International had attached themselves to Gladstone's campaign. Referring to Gladstone's promises to disestablish the Anglican Church in Ireland, Marx expresses the hope that this could also lead to similar moves in England, as well as to greater solidarity between Irish Catholics and Protestants. All of this could undermine the landowning classes, with important effects: "I have always felt that the social revolution must begin *seriously* from the ground, i.e., landed property" (MECW 43, 4). Marx also continues to study economic data on landlord-tenant relations, writing to Engels on October 10, 1868, that he has purchased the parliamentary *Report and Evidence on Irish Tenant Right 1867*: "Here we have a real life and death struggle between farmer and landlord as to how far rent should include, apart from the payment for land differences, also the interest on the capital invested in the land, not by the landlord but by the tenant." These, he adds, are the "real antagonisms" that form the "concealed background" to the debates by political economists (128).

In an unsigned report published in the London *Times* on September 9, 1868, on the activities of the International over the past year, Marx mentions support actions for the Fenian prisoners, including "public meetings in London for the defense of the rights of Ireland." He also details the arrests of members of the International in Paris, suggesting that Bonaparte was thereby trying to win "the good graces of the British Government" (MECW 21, 13). The Fenian prisoners continued to receive support from sections of the English working classes, judging by a hostile London *Times* article of November 23 on commemorations of the Manchester martyrs: "Yesterday, Hyde Park was again disgraced by a field day of the London 'roughs' who assembled there in the name of the murderers who were executed this day last year. . . . These murderers are called 'martyrs'.... An inflammatory handbill was distributed among the dwellers in ... the worst parts ... in the metropolis. The bill was printed in green with a deep mourning border and headed by a funeral rose" (cited in Ellis 1996, 141).

In early 1869, after he had been elected prime minister, Gladstone moved to ease tensions over Ireland. He disestablished the Anglican Church, thus ending some of the blatant religious discrimination against the majority of the Irish population. Parliament also voted a limited amnesty for some of the imprisoned Fenians, but not their leaders. Engels, who was finally able to retire from his family's manufacturing firm in Manchester after two decades as a businessman, took the first opportunity to travel to Ireland, bringing his companion Elizabeth Burns (sister of Mary, who had died in 1863) and Marx's daughter Eleanor. In a letter to Marx dated September 27, 1869, Engels delineates two major economic changes since his last visit in 1856, the depopulation of the rural areas and how, at the same time, Dublin had become a bustling and cosmopolitan port city. He also describes a "state of war," with "soldiers literally everywhere" (MECW 43, 357). Finally, he mentions that he plans to use his free time to write a book on Ireland.

In the fall of 1869, Marx seemed also to be preparing a lengthy study of Ireland and he began asking Engels about source material. After beginning his studies, Engels makes an assessment similar to Marx's earlier one on Cromwell's invasion, in a letter to Marx of October 24: "Irish history shows what a misfortune it is for one nation to subjugate another. All English abominations have their origin in the Irish Pale. I still have to bone up on the Cromwellian period, but it appears clear to me that things in England would have taken another turn but for the necessity of military rule in Ireland creating a new aristocracy" (MECW 43, 363).

During the summer and fall of 1869, the demand for amnesty for the Fenian prisoners took on new force, with one gathering in Dublin on October 10 drawing some two hundred thousand people. There were numerous petitions to the Gladstone government as well. On October 24 in London, Fenian supporters organized a demonstration that gathered some hundred thousand people, the largest leftist gathering since the days of Chartism. Marx's daughter Jenny reports on the participation of the entire Marx family in a letter to Kugelmann of October 30:

> In London the event of the week has been a Fenian demonstration got up for the purpose of praying the government for the release of the Irish prisoners. As Tussy [Eleanor] has returned from Ireland a stauncher

Irishman than ever, she did not rest until she had persuaded Moor [Marx], Mama, and me to go with her to Hyde Park, the place appointed for the meeting.[10] This Park, the biggest one in London, was one mass of men, women and children, even the trees up to their highest branches had their inhabitants. The number of persons present were by the papers estimated at somewhere about 70 thousand, but as these papers are English, this figure is no doubt too low. There were processionists carrying red, green, and white banners, with all sorts of devices, such as "Keep your powder dry!," "Disobedience to tyrants is a duty to God!" And hoisted higher than the flags were a profusion of red Jacobin caps, the bearers of which sang the *Marseillaise*—sights and sounds that must have greatly interfered with the enjoyment of the portwine at the clubs.— On the following day, Monday, all the papers made a furious onslaught on those confounded "foreigners," and cursed the day they had landed in England to demoralize John Bull by means of their bloodred flags, noisy choruses and other enormities. (MECW 43, 546–47)

Marx, in his remarks to the General Council meeting of October 26, emphasizes the participation of English workers: "The main feature of the demonstration had been ignored, it was that at least a part of the English working class had lost their prejudice against the Irish" (*General Council of the First International* 1966, 172). Jung, a strong supporter of Marx, saw wider implications for the labor movement: "England had always represented the struggle as one of race, last Sunday had shown that it was a struggle of classes" (173).

Marx also suggested that the International pass and circulate a Resolution on Ireland. According to the minutes, Lucraft, who had been more reticent during the 1867 debates, now wanted a strong resolution, since in his view English workers had been remiss in showing solidarity with their fellow workers in Ireland: "We must compel the government to do something. He as an Englishman did not believe he had done his duty. It was our business to show the Irish that it was only a class of the English that wronged them and that the same class of Irish were as bad" (*General Council of the First International* 1966, 173). The next six weeks saw another intensive debate inside the General Council over Ireland, much of it reported in *Reynolds's Newspaper*, a labor weekly.

At the November 16, 1869, General Council meeting, Marx began the debate with a speech of more than an hour on the British government and the Fenian prisoners. As recorded in the minutes, he castigated Gladstone for failing to keep his campaign promises on Ireland and for reverting to typically British high-handed tactics, such as failing to reply to a petition for amnesty bearing two hundred thousand signatures. After Gladstone had freed a few rank-and-file Fenians, he imposed humiliating conditions on the freedom of the others: "He wants them to renounce their principles, to degrade them morally" (MECW 21, 408). Marx declares further that Gladstone "wants the Irish to fall on their knees because an enlightened sovereign and Parliament have done a great act of justice," even though "they were the criminals before the Irish people" (409). Despite his claims to be a friend of Ireland, Gladstone mobilized soldiers with live ammunition on October 10 in Dublin, as government officials sought to provoke the demonstrators with last-minute restrictions on the parade route. In addition, "all tenant right meetings are broken up," Marx notes (410). At the end of his speech, which was greeted by substantial applause, he proposed the following resolution:

> Resolved, that in his reply to the Irish demands for the release of the imprisoned Irish patriots—a reply contained in his letter to Mr. O'Shea etc., etc.—Mr. Gladstone deliberately insults Irish Nation; that he clogs political amnesty with conditions alike degrading to the victims of misgovernment and the people they belong to; that having, in the teeth of his responsible position, publicly and enthusiastically cheered on the American slave-holders' Rebellion, he now steps in to preach to the Irish people the doctrine of passive obedience; that his whole proceedings with reference to the Irish Amnesty question are the true and genuine offspring of that "*policy of conquest*" by the fiery denunciation of which Mr. Gladstone ousted his Tory rivals from office; that the *General Council of the "International Working Men's Association"* express their admiration of the spirited, firm and high-souled manner in which the Irish people carry on their Amnesty movement; that these resolutions be communicated to all the branches of, and working men's bodies connected with, the "*International Working Men's Association*" in Europe and America. (MECW 21, 83)

Marx's draft sparked extended discussion in the General Council during the next few weeks, even as the mass outpourings over Ireland continued. A few days after he presented it, a demonstration called by the Reform League in Hyde Park to demand amnesty for the Fenians drew thousands of Irish and English workers, an event that also supported Irish independence.

At the November 23, 1869, General Council meeting, a heated debate took place. Odger, by now trying to stand for Parliament as a supporter of Gladstone, opposed any strong language such as "a demand for unconditional release" of the Fenian prisoners as counterproductive (*General Council of the First International* 1966, 185). Another English General Council member, Thomas Mottershead, strongly attacked Marx's resolution: "I regret that Englishmen applauded the statements of Dr. Marx, as some did last week. Ireland cannot be independent. It lies between England and France; if we relinquish our hold, it would only be asking the French to walk in" (186). A strong supporter of Gladstone, Mottershead suggested that in time amnesty would be granted. Several speakers, including Eccarius and Jung, attacked English liberals for hypocrisy in supporting the liberation of Poland but not Ireland. Weston strongly supported the resolution, however: "Gladstone in his election speeches declared that the Irish were wrongly governed; he therefore virtually justified the Fenians. When he got in he did nothing but he insulted the Irish" (189). In response to the debate, Marx argues that the purpose of the resolution was not to petition the Gladstone government: "It is a resolution of sympathy with the Irish and a review of the conduct of the government, it may bring the English and the Irish together. . . . Odger is right, if we wanted the prisoners released, this would not be the way to do it, but it is more important to make a concession to the Irish people than to Gladstone" (MECW 21, 411–412). Marx, who seemed to have a clear majority of the General Council behind him, made one concession to his opponents, however. He accepted Odger's suggestion to delete the word "deliberately" from the phrase "Gladstone deliberately insults the Irish Nation" near the beginning of the draft (MECW 21, 412).

In the intervening week, O'Donovan Rossa was elected to Parliament from his prison cell in Tipperary. In a letter to Marx of November 29, Engels expresses the hope that this would lead to a change from urban guerrilla tactics: "It launches the Fenians from empty conspiracies and the fabrication of coups on a path of action that, even if legal in appearance, is still far more revolutionary than what they have done since their abortive insurrection" (MECW 43, 387). Marx writes to Engels on November 26, calling the debate at the General Council "fiery, lively, vehement" (386). He exults that before the meeting, the labor-oriented *Reynolds's Paper* had published the draft resolution, and an account of Marx's speech, both on the front page. This, he avers, "seems to have scared those who are flirting with Gladstone" (386). Marx also points to the participation of an Irish worker, George Milner, in the debate.

At its November 30 meeting, the General Council voted unanimously to support Marx's resolution, after some additional debate. The Irishman Milner countered Odger's suggestion to go a bit easier on Gladstone by arguing that he "could not be treated differently to any other government" by the International (*General Council of the First International* 1966, 193). In a brief response to

Odger, Marx puts the issue in a wider European context, with particular reference to Poland: "If Odger's suggestions were followed the Council would put
themselves on an English party standpoint. They could not do that. The Council must show the Irish that they understood the question and the Continent
that they showed no favor to the British Government. The Council must treat
the Irish like the English would treat the Polish" (MECW 21, 412). The resolution was also published abroad in both German and French. In a letter to Engels
dated December 4, Marx sums up the debate, writing that except for Odger and
Mottershead, "the English delegates behaved excellently" (MECW 43, 392).

This resolution was a great triumph for Marx, who had worked very hard
to sensitize the British members of the General Council on Ireland. Despite
the fact that a few, like Odger, had regarded it as too strong, in the end a body
that included important representatives of British labor had unanimously approved a remarkably strong pro-Irish statement. In voting for it, the members
of the General Council broke with decades of prejudice and hostility of the
British toward the Irish. Marx, understandably proud of the resolution, saw
it as opening the possibility of a never-before achieved alliance across ethnic
and national lines among British workers, British intellectuals, Irish workers
residing in Britain, Irish peasants, and Irish intellectuals.

Another obstacle now appeared, the narrowness of Irish nationalist politics,
something that Marx now begins to attack in his private correspondence. In
the letter of December 4 to Engels, cited above, he complains that the *Irishman*
and other Irish newspapers had failed to cover the International on Ireland,
since in their view: "The 'Irish' question must be treated as something quite
distinct, excluding the outside world, and it must be *concealed* that *English*
workers sympathize *with* the Irish!" (MECW 43, 392; original emphasis). Engels responds in a December 9 letter that this avoidance of "the profane class
struggle" was "partly a calculated policy" by Irish nationalists "to maintain their
domination over the peasants," since "the Irish peasant must not be allowed
to find out that the socialist workers are his sole allies in Europe" (394). Some
months later, in a letter of July 8, 1870, Marx returns to this question, calling
Pigott, the editor of the *Irishman*, a "narrow-minded nationalist" (537).

NOTES ON IRISH ANTHROPOLOGY AND HISTORY

During this period, Marx had begun to connect Ireland to the question of
communal property. As discussed in chapters 1 and 2, in the early 1850s Marx
saw communal property as a major foundation for "Oriental despotism" in
Russia and India, or for authoritarian clan chieftains in Scotland. But his 1868

letters to Engels on Georg Maurer's studies of premodern Germanic peoples show that he had begun to view early communal forms differently. In a letter of March 14, 1868, Marx informed Engels that Maurer had shown not only that communal property was the original Germanic form, as much as in Russia or India, but also that it had persisted in parts of rural Germany until their own time. However, he chides Maurer for failing to take up the ancient Celts: "Maurer, though often referring, for instance, to Africa, Mexico, etc., knows absolutely nothing about the Celts, and therefore ascribes the development of communal property in France solely to the Germanic conquerors. As though . . . we did not possess a Celtic (Welsh) book of laws from the 11th century that is entirely communist" (549). Moreover, as Marx writes in a subsequent letter to Engels of March 25, Maurer's findings uncovered a "primitive age" that "corresponds to the socialist tendency" because its people were such "egalitarians" (MECW 42, 557).

Commenting on these letters, the French anthropologist Maurice Godelier argues that henceforth in Marx's work, "the accent is placed upon the vitality of the primitive communes and their multiple capacities of evolution" (1970, 79). Did Marx see some of these communal forms as persisting into his own century, at least within Irish culture? If so, could he have viewed them as points of resistance to Britain and to capital? This is indeed possible, but there is no direct evidence on this score in Marx's writings on Ireland. Some of Engels's writings in this period do suggest such a link, however.

Engels worked during the first half of 1870 on his history of Ireland from prehistoric times to the present. He completed only two chapters, however, covering the period up to the early eleventh century, when the Irish obtained a measure of peace after finally driving out the Vikings, but were unaware that they would soon face invasion from a much more powerful foe, England. From the beginning, Engels emphasizes the indomitable character of the Irish people, despite seven hundred years of British rule: "Even at present, the Irish are no more English, or 'West Britons,' as they are called, than the Poles are West Russians" (MECW 21, 148). By this time, Engels was reading some Celtic sources in the original, as well as Latin and Scandinavian ones. Engels's notes for other parts of the book concern English conquest and brutality, especially under Cromwell, where he emphasizes the thousands of Irish people sold into slavery in the British West Indies. Of particular interest, given his and Marx's later concerns, are several places in the notes where Engels writes of communal property, for example: "The land of the clan was communal property. In this context, . . . in Ireland it was never the Irishman, but only the Englishman who held land as private property" (284).

As they discussed Engels's book project, in a letter of May 11, 1870, Marx quotes from notes on ancient Irish law that he had made two decades earlier, when he had recorded the following historical data:

> The community of goods was accompanied by Celtic laxity in the marriage tie, already known in antiquity, at the same time, however, voting rights for women in the tribal assembly. . . . The first chapter of the book on common law deals with women: "If his wife lay with another man and he beats her, he sacrifices his claim to indemnification. . . . Sufficient grounds for divorce for a wife were the man's impotence, scabies, and bad breath." (MECW 43, 515)[11]

Marx adds immediately: "Such gallant youngsters [*galante Jungen*], these Celts!" (MECW 43, 516). This reference to more egalitarian gender relations in a preliterate society prefigures Marx's 1879–82 notebooks on non-Western and precapitalist societies, to be discussed in chapter 6.

Marx researched more recent Irish history during October and November 1869, concentrating on the period of the American and the French revolutions, up through the Anglo-Irish Union of 1801. Marx's research notes, which comprise some seventy printed pages, are mainly excerpts from historical sources, with his own occasional comments. He notes that under the impact of the American Revolution, the Protestant-dominated Irish Parliament moved to alter some of the most discriminatory laws against Catholics:

> Great fermentation produced by the American events in Ireland. Many Irish, mainly Presbyterians from Ulster, emigrate to America, enroll under the United States banners and fight against England on the other side of the Atlantic. The Catholics, who for a long time had in vain supplicated for a relaxation of the Penal Code, moved again in 1776, in louder tones. 1778: Irish Parliament relaxed the severity of the Penal Code, its worst features obliterated, Catholics were allowed to take leases of land. (MECW 21, 216)

When war broke out between England and France in 1778, Ireland was left undefended. In response, the Volunteer movement began organizing Protestants for defense against a possible invasion. However, Marx writes that this soon developed "into a truly revolutionary movement" (218). By 1790, under Wolf Tone and others, the Volunteers developed into the United Irishmen. Tone, a Presbyterian, "resolved to redress the wrongs of the Catholics" and to reform the Irish Parliament, if necessary creating "an independent republic" of Ireland (219).

Marx first concentrates on the 1780s, however, on how the Volunteers gradually developed a more inclusive view of the Irish people. As in America, British mercantilist policies had restricted local manufacturing, while flooding Ireland with British manufactured goods. Marx writes that a Volunteer-led boycott of British goods found support among the entire population, that "it flew quicker than the wind throughout the whole nation" (MECW 21, 221). Meanwhile the Volunteers, by now the numerically largest military force in the entire British Empire, announced that they would no longer obey the British Parliament and that they considered Ireland a separate kingdom within the empire. Marx quotes a 1782 declaration by one Volunteer group on Catholic emancipation: "As men, and as Irishmen, as Christians, and as Protestants, we rejoice in the relaxation of the penal laws against our Roman Catholic fellow-subjects; and that we conceive the measure to be fraught with the happiest consequences to the union and prosperity of the inhabitants of Ireland" (225). Also in 1782, the Irish Parliament, led by Henry Grattan, moved to establish Ireland as a separate kingdom within the empire and thus not subordinate to the British Parliament. However, Marx held that Grattan's equivocation at crucial moments derailed the drive for Irish independence. Meanwhile, as the Volunteers began to recruit Catholics, their numbers reached 150,000. Henry Flood's reforms, more radical than those of Grattan, were rejected by the Irish Parliament, which was packed with corrupt members who sold their votes to the aristocracy under the notorious "rotten boroughs" system.

After 1789, under the impact of the French Revolution, the Irish Parliament enacted some minor reforms. At this point, Marx began to concentrate on the career and writings of John Curran, a radical parliamentarian who was later to become the defense attorney for the United Irishmen. Curran's opponents attacked him for having as "his friends, the beggars in the streets" (MECW 21, 236). Marx records at length parliamentary debates from 1787 in which Curran points to class antagonisms and castigates the corruption of Parliament:

> Cease to utter idle complaints of inevitable effects, when you yourselves have been the causes . . . the patience of the people has been totally exhausted; their grievances (have long) been the empty song of this House, but no productive effect has ever followed. The non-residence of the landholders, the tyranny of intermediate landlords. You denied the existence of the grievance, and refused redress. . . . No wonder that the peasantry should be ripe for rebellion and revolt. . . . Not a single man of

property or consequence connected with the rebels. . . . You were called upon solemnly . . . for a proper reformation in the representation of the people: did you grant it? No; and how does it at present stand? Why, Sir, seats in this House are bought and sold. They are set up to public sale; they have become an absolute article of commerce—a traffic of the constitution. . . . Saleable rotten boroughs. (243)

Marx sums up the situation as the United Irishmen arose in the 1790s: "We remark that Catholic Emancipation and Parliamentary Reform were the two cries!" (247). He quotes at great length from various declarations of what he terms the "Irish Jacobins," on religious freedom and republicanism, for example: "Where the mode of government is not derived from all the people clearly expressed, that nation has no constitution; need we say that this is the case with Ireland; it possesses only an acting government" (249).

Marx then traces the outbreak of insurrection in 1798, which he ties closely to the success of the French armies on the Continent. At the same time, he records material on the increasing British repression, through both new laws and the creation of vigilante groups like the Yeomanry Corps. Marx excerpts Curran's last speech to Parliament, in May 1797, before he and Grattan stopped attending:

We have seen the decreasing minorities of the party who gallantly struggled to maintain the parliamentary constitution of Ireland. But they grew daily more powerless. The people looked to the United Irish Executive, to France, to arms, to Revolution. The Government persisted in refusing Reform and [Catholic Emancipation], continued the suspension of the Constitution, and incessantly augmented the despotism of their laws. . . . The Government and the United Irishmen face to face. (MECW 21, 255)

Marx holds that British Prime Minister William Pitt deliberately provoked the 1798 insurrection by his blatantly oppressive actions, such as quartering troops in peasant homes: "Free quarters rendered officers and soldiers despotic masters of the peasantry, their homes, food, property, and occasionally, their families" (257). After the insurrection was suppressed, the British began to move toward Union. In suppressing the insurrection, the British played off Protestants against Catholics. The Union of 1801 was "carried during the reign of martial law," Marx notes, with an "Irish Parliament of 1800 elected in 1797 for 8 years" (263). Marx suggests that Pitt betrayed the upper-class Catholics who had supported him once the Union was voted, but he did so in an underhanded manner: "Pitt in 1801 handed in his resignation, on pretext that the King kept not his word to Catholics. This [was] mere show. He wanted not to be minister during truce with Bonaparte. Re-entered afterwards the Ministry without stipulating any favor for Catholics" (265).

Finally, Marx traces some of the results of the 1801 Union. In his view, these were all extremely reactionary for both Britain and Ireland. Marx cites the English Radical William Cobbett's assessment that it would take sixty thousand regular army troops to hold Ireland, but then adds: "Ireland—one of the pretexts for keeping a large standing army" (MECW 21, 268). He then quotes from George Ensor's *Anti-Union: Ireland as She Ought to Be* (1831):

> Every acquisition of a nation by a nation is injurious to the liberty of both. The accessory country is a lapsed inheritance, while the people who make the acquisition are submissive to their own rulers, lest they might countenance any disturbance in the superadded nation; they submit at home for a barren, often expensive, superiority abroad . . . This is the whole story of Roman history . . . as the world fell before the Roman aristocracy, the Roman citizens were pauperized and enslaved . . . Every impeachment of liberty in one country leads to its loss in another. (MECW 21, 268)

On the outlook of the British dominant classes, Marx also cites a 1793 statement by the future king William IV to the effect that abolitionist efforts to end the slave trade should be condemned as "part of the leveling principles of the French Revolution" (268).

In a letter to Engels of December 10, 1869, Marx sums up what he had concluded from his historical research:

> You must get hold of Curran's "Speeches." . . . I meant to give it to you when you were in London. It is now circulating among the English members of the [General] Council, and God knows when I shall see it again. For the period of 1779–1800 (Union) it is of decisive importance, not only because of Curran's "Speeches" (namely in court; I regard Curran as the sole great lawyer (people's advocate) of the 18th century, and the noblest personality, while Grattan was a parliamentary rogue), but because you find all the sources about the United Irishmen. This period is of greatest interest, scientifically and dramatically. First, the dirty infamies of the English in 1588–89 repeated (perhaps even intensified) in 1788–89. Second, class movement is easily shown in the Irish movement itself. Third,

the infamous policy of Pitt. Fourth, which very much irks the English gentlemen, the proof that Ireland came to grief because in fact, from a revolutionary standpoint, the Irish were too far advanced for the English King and Church mob, while, on the other hand, English reaction in England (as in Cromwell's time) had its roots in the subjugation of Ireland. This period must be described in at least one chapter: a pillory for John Bull! (MECW 43, 398)

The last sentence refers to Engels's projected book on Ireland. He also asks Engels for source material on "common property" (398). This letter came after two months of intense involvement on Marx's part in public debates over Ireland, as well as his study of Irish history. He was now placing Ireland at the center of British revolutionary and labor politics. In both Cromwell's time and the 1790s, he now held, the collapse of revolutionary possibilities in Britain was preceded by British suppression of the Irish people.

A CHANGE OF POSITION IN 1869–70: IRELAND AS THE "LEVER" OF THE REVOLUTION

The two threads stimulating Marx's recent thinking on Ireland—debates within the International and historical research—seemed now to come together as his own perspectives on Ireland underwent a radical change. Henceforth, agrarian Ireland would in his view be very likely to play a leading role in sparking a social revolution in Britain. He states explicitly that he has changed his position, this in the December 10, 1869, letter to Engels:

> For a long time, I believed it would be possible to overthrow the Irish regime by English working class ascendancy. I always took this viewpoint in the *New York Tribune*. Deeper study has now convinced me of the opposite. The English working class will never accomplish anything before it has got rid of Ireland. The lever must be applied in Ireland. This is why the Irish question is so important for the social movement in general. (MECW 43, 398)

The American political theorist August Nimtz calls this turn "most significant since it makes clear that the revolutionary 'lever' for him, contrary to the usual Marxological claim, did not reside exclusively in the advanced industrialized capitalist world" (2000, 204).[12] Marx restated and developed his new position at some length in several other writings during late 1869 and 1870, a period in which the debate over Ireland continued to grip Britain. None of these texts in which he spells out his position bluntly and frankly were composed in English.

Two weeks earlier, in a letter of November 29, 1869, to Kugelmann, Marx spelled out his new position on Ireland in greater detail, without mentioning that it represented a change. Writing in German, he begins by explaining that his November 16 speech and the General Council Resolution on Ireland "had other grounds than simply to speak out loudly and decidedly for the oppressed Irish against their oppressors" (MECW 43, 390). Those deeper grounds bore on the possibility of radical change in England:

> I have become more and more convinced—and the thing now is to drum this conviction into the English working class—that they will never do anything decisive here in England before they separate their attitude towards Ireland quite definitely from that of the ruling classes, and not only make common cause with the Irish, but even take the initiative in dissolving the Union established in 1801, and substituting a free federal relationship for it. . . . Every movement in England itself is crippled by the dissension with the Irish, who form a very important section of the working class in England itself. (390)

Thus, English working-class consciousness was attenuated by anti-Irish prejudice.

At the level of the dominant classes, Britain was on the one hand a modern industrial country with an industrial bourgeoisie, but was on the other hand possessed of a large aristocratic landowning class, a major part of whose holdings lay in Ireland. While this situation undoubtedly strengthened the dominant classes in their struggle against the English working class, it also led in dialectical fashion to a new type of vulnerability for those very dominant classes, this one from within Ireland itself:

> The primary condition of emancipation here—the overthrow of the English landed oligarchy—remains unattainable, since its positions cannot be stormed here as long as it holds its strongly entrenched outposts in Ireland. But over there, once affairs have been laid in the hands of the Irish people themselves, . . . it will be infinitely easier there than here to abolish the landed aristocracy (to a large extent the same persons as the English landlords) since in Ireland it is not merely an economic question,

but also a national one, as the landlords there are not, as they are in England, traditional dignitaries and representatives, but the mortally-hated oppressors of the nationality. (MECW 43, 390–91)

All of this is of great importance to the European revolution, writes Marx, because due to England's position as the most developed capitalist society, "the English working class undoubtedly throws the greatest weight on the scales of social emancipation generally" (391). Yet because of the specific interaction of class and national consciousness in Britain and Ireland, Ireland "is the point where the lever must be applied" (391). The fate of the English Revolution of the 1640s bore this out, he concludes: "It is a fact that the English Republic under Cromwell met shipwreck in—Ireland. This shall not happen twice!" (391).

THE CONTROVERSY WITH BAKUNIN AND AFTER

During this period, Marx also began his long fight against the anarchist Mikhail Bakunin, which became public in January 1870 with what is now known as the General Council's Confidential Communication. Written by Marx in French and sent to all branches of the International, it strongly attacked Bakunin. As is well known, in this period, Marx was responding to Bakunin's accusation that an authoritarian and overly centralized leadership in London was running the International. One example of this, in the eyes of Bakunin and his supporters, was the fact that, unlike in other countries, the International had no separate British Federal Council. Instead, the General Council in London filled two roles simultaneously: coordinator for Britain and for the entire International.[13]

Bakunin's second critique of the General Council, which bore on Ireland, is less known. In some respects, this critique paralleled that of the Proudhonists, who had criticized from within the International its stance in favor of Polish national emancipation, for Bakunin and his supporters took issue with any kind of particular support for Irish national emancipation.[14] Bakuninists were highly suspicious of working-class involvement in political action of any kind, not only running for office, but also petitions to governments or statements designed to pressure them. An example of their position could be found in the 1868 program of Bakunin's International Alliance of Socialist Democracy, point four of which "rejects any political action that does not have as its immediate and direct aim the triumph of the workers' cause against capital" (cited in MECW 21, 208).[15]

Based on this rather formalistic premise, *L'Égalité*, a pro-Bakunin newspaper published in French in Geneva, Switzerland, published a strong attack on the General Council Resolution on Ireland in December 11, 1869, characterizing the latter as a diversion from revolutionary politics. Under the headline "Le Conseil Général," *L'Égalité* ran on its front page a French translation of Marx's November 1869 General Council resolution attacking Gladstone and applauding the "high-souled manner in which the Irish people carry out their Amnesty movement" (MECW 21, 83; "Le Conseil Général"1869). Directly under this article, also on the front page, *L'Égalité* ran its response, entitled "Refléxions," which read in part:

> It cannot be repeated often enough that the interests of the workers do not lie in attempts at *ameliorating* the governments of today, but in *eliminating* them in a radical fashion, and in replacing the present political, authoritarian, religious, and juridical state of today with a new social organization guaranteeing to each person the entire product of his labor and all the results therefrom. ("Refléxions" 1869)

Marx drafted a response to these criticisms on behalf of the General Council in the form of the aforementioned Confidential Communication, written in French and sent to all the branches of the International. The Confidential Communication was approved at a General Council meeting of January 1, 1870.[16]

While Marx's Confidential Communication takes up a number of issues related to the organizational structure of the International, about a quarter of its twelve pages are devoted to Ireland. Some of Marx's new positions on Ireland are articulated here, for example:

> Although revolutionary initiative will probably come from France, England alone can serve as the *lever* for a serious economic Revolution. It is the only country where there are no more peasants and where landed property is concentrated in a few hands. It is the only country where *the capitalist form*, that is to say, combined labor on a large scale under the authority of capitalists [*des maîtres capitalistes*], has seized hold of almost the whole of production. It is the only country where the *vast majority of the population consists of wage laborers*. . . . The English have all the *material* conditions [matière *nécessaire*] for social revolution. What they lack is *a sense of generalization and revolutionary passion*. It is only the General Council that can provide them with this, that can thus

accelerate the truly revolutionary movement in this country, and con-
sequently *everywhere*. . . . If England is the bulwark of landlordism and
European capitalism, the only point where official England can be struck
a great blow *is Ireland*. (MECW 21, 118–19; original emphasis)

In addition, while pointing to English labor's crucial place in the European
revolution, Marx was also defending the structure of the General Council, arguing that the British labor movement needed the input of exile revolutionaries like himself.

While the occasion for the Confidential Communication was to answer the
charges by Bakunin's group against the Resolution on Ireland, one can also discern here larger themes concerning the relation of national emancipation to the
labor movement. Sociologist Torben Krings writes of an "increasing dialecticiza-
tion of the issues of nationalism and internationalism" at this juncture in Marx's
work (2004, 1508). Some of the following could have applied as well to the relation of Polish national emancipation to revolution in Germany, for example:

> In the first place, Ireland is the *bulwark* of English landlordism. If it fell
> in Ireland, it would fall in England. In Ireland this is a hundred times
> easier because *the economic struggle there is concentrated exclusively on
> landed property*, because this struggle is at the same time national, and
> because the people there are more revolutionary and angry than in En-
> gland. Landlordism in Ireland is maintained solely by *the English army*.
> The moment the forced Union between the two countries ends, a social
> revolution will immediately break out in Ireland, though in *backward*
> forms. (MECW 21, 119–20; original emphasis)

Marx's second point, on the relation of national minorities to majorities
inside the working class in England, also had wider implications and would
at the time have applied, for example, to Polish immigrant labor in France and
Germany, or to Black labor in America, which is mentioned below:

> In the second place, the English bourgeoisie has . . . divided the proletar-
> iat into two hostile camps. . . . *In all the big industrial centers in England*,
> there is profound antagonism between the Irish proletarian and the En-
> glish proletarian. The common English worker hates the Irish worker as
> a competitor who lowers wages and the *standard of life*. He feels national
> and religious antipathies for him. He views him similarly to how the poor
> whites of the Southern states of North America viewed black slaves. This

antagonism among the proletarians of England is artificially nourished and kept up by the bourgeoisie. It knows that this split is the true secret of the preservation of its power. (MECW 21, 119–20; original emphasis)

Marx's Confidential Communication makes some further comments on the Irish in America, before concluding: "Thus, the position of the International Association with regard to the Irish question is very clear. Its first concern is to advance the social revolution in England. To this end the great blow must be struck in Ireland" (120).

IRELAND AND THE WIDER EUROPEAN REVOLUTION

Marx's lengthiest statement of his new view of Ireland was contained in a letter of April 9, 1870, to two German American members of the International in New York, Sigfrid Meyer and August Vogt. As in his letters to Kugelmann and Engels and the Confidential Communication, Marx describes Ireland not only as a stronghold of the English aristocracy, but also a society that was ripe for a social revolution. At the objective level, Marx first argues that the English industrial bourgeoisie has "a common interest with the English aristocracy in turning Ireland into simply pastureland to provide meat and wool at the cheapest possible price for the English market" (MECW 43, 474). However, the consolidation of agriculture in Ireland benefits English capital in a second and more crucial way, by supplying cheap labor for the English factories: "But the English bourgeoisie also has much more important interests in the present Irish economy. As a result of the steadily-increasing concentration of leaseholding, Ireland is steadily supplying its surplus for the English labor market, and thus forcing down the wages and material and moral position of the English working class" (474).

At this point, Marx moves into a discussion of the subjective factor, of those elements of England's relationship to Ireland that impact the level of class consciousness and the potential for a break with capital on the part of the English working classes. As in the Confidential Communication, but here in more depth and detail, he compares it to the racial situation in the United States:

And most important of all! All industrial and commercial centers in England now have a working class split into two hostile camps, English proletarians and Irish proletarians. The ordinary English worker hates the Irish worker as a competitor who forces down the standard of life. In relation to the Irish worker, he feels himself to be a member of the dominant nation and, therefore, makes himself a tool of his aristocrats and capitalists against Ireland, thus strengthening their domination over himself. He harbors religious, social and national prejudices against him. His attitude towards him is roughly that of the poor whites to the niggers[17] in the former slave states of the American Union. The Irishman pays him back with interest in his own money. He sees in the English worker both the accomplice and the stupid tool of English domination in Ireland. This antagonism is kept artificially alive and intensified by the press, the pulpit, the comic papers, in short by all the means at the disposal of the ruling class. This antagonism is the secret of the power-lessness of the English working class, despite its organization. It is the secret of the capitalist class's maintenance of its power. And the latter is fully conscious of this. (MECW 43, 474–75)

In this sense, mutual antagonism between two elements, the English and the Irish immigrant workers, constricted the development of class consciousness in an ethnically stratified working class.[18]

For Marx, this situation was not immutable, however. It was here that the role of an organized group such as the International became crucial, he holds, in the following summary of his intentions during the debate in the International over Ireland:

England, as the metropolis of capital, as the power that has hitherto ruled the world market, is for the present the most important country for the workers' revolution and, in addition, the only country where the material conditions of this revolution have developed to a certain state of maturity. Thus, to hasten the social revolution in England is the most important object of the International Working Men's Association. The sole means of doing so is to make Ireland independent. It is therefore, the task of the "International" to bring the conflict between England and Ireland to the forefront everywhere, and to side with Ireland publicly everywhere. The special task of the [General] Council in London is to awaken the consciousness of the English working class to the notion that, for them, the national emancipation of Ireland is not a question of abstract justice or humanitarian sentiment, but the first condition of their own social emancipation. (MECW 43, 475)

In this sense, Marx was connecting support of Ireland to what he saw as the wider European revolution. England was to be its linchpin, but Ireland was the crucial "lever" for developing revolutionary consciousness among English workers.

While the Confidential Communication and this letter go into more detail on Ireland, the British workers, and their relationship to a wider revolution against capital, the December 10, 1869, letter to Engels (and the one of November 29 to Kugelmann) stated one crucial point even more explicitly. This point, which Marx told Engels he could not reveal to his English worker colleagues, was that "the lever" of revolution, the issue that would actually open up the world situation, "must be applied in Ireland," not England (MECW 43, 399).[19] Only afterwards, could England, the center of world capitalism, be drawn into the wider revolution.

Marx's various writings on Ireland in the winter and spring of 1869–70 represent a concretization of the dialectics of class and national liberation in the struggle to uproot capitalism at a specific juncture in the history of Europe and North America. These writings illustrate his overall thinking about the relationship of societies peripheral to capitalism to those comprising its core. In this sense, they represent a broader shift in his thinking, toward the notion that struggles on the periphery of capitalism could become sparks that might very well go off in advance of the workers' revolution in the industrially developed societies. Together, these two types of struggles could bring about a radical transcendence of the capitalist system itself. Marx's writings on Ireland are the first place where he fully concretizes these notions.

At no time, however, did Marx make national self-determination into an abstract principle, separate from the issue of whether a given movement had a liberatory content. Otherwise he could have supported the Confederacy's right to independence during the Civil War. As the British political theorist Erica Benner notes astutely: "It would be wrong to infer that his support for Irish independence brought him close to endorsing a supra-historical principle of national self-determination" (1995, 192). Far from any type of identity politics, she adds, the key thing was "Marx's growing appreciation of the constructive role played by nationalism in promoting international revolution" (195).

Throughout the first half of 1870, Marx continued to occupy himself with the campaign for the release of the Fenian prisoners. In February and March, his article, "The English Government and the Fenian Prisoners," appeared in French in a Belgian organ of the International. He presents detailed information on the treatment of the prisoners, writing that "in the land of bourgeois freedom, sentences of 20 years hard labor are given for offenses that are punished by 6 months in prison in the land of the barracks," the latter a reference to Bonapartist France (MECW 21, 101). He attacks not only Gladstone's hypocrisy but also the "French Republicans" as "narrow-minded and self-ish" for concentrating "all their anger" on their own regime and keeping silent about English oppression (101).

Marx's daughter Jenny, then twenty-five years old, sought to end the silence in France about the Fenian prisoners. From February through April 1870, she published under a pseudonym an eight-part series of articles on Ireland in *La Marseillaise*, a left-of-center newspaper in Paris. With her moving reports on the conditions of the Fenian prisoners, information that up until then had been confined to the Irish papers or small English ones was now appearing in a major European daily paper. The information in these articles, especially one in which she quoted at length from a letter that O'Donovan Rossa had smuggled out of prison, was picked up by newspapers throughout Europe and the United States. This forced the British press to cover the story, although it almost always responded with pained defensiveness at this criticism from abroad. The international embarrassment caused by the articles also sparked debate in Parliament, resulting in a formal inquiry. Finally, in December 1870, Gladstone released the Fenians, on condition that they leave the United Kingdom forever.

One of Jenny Marx's articles was coauthored by her father, and it argued that the British press's silence and scorn regarding the Fenians did not represent the views of the working class. Referring to the October 24, 1869, demonstration, it states:

> Let it suffice to say that more than 200,000 men, women, and children of the English working class raised their voices in Hyde Park to demand freedom for their Irish brothers, and that the General Council of the International Working Men's Association, which has its headquarters in London and includes well-known English working-class leaders among its members, has severely condemned the treatment of the Fenian prisoners and come out in defense of the rights of the Irish people against the English government. (MECW 21, 423–24)

In their letters, both Marx and Engels expressed considerable pride in Jenny's accomplishment, with Engels and Elizabeth Burns sending her a twig of shamrock on Saint Patrick's Day. Marx also noted with pleasure that the attention that Jenny's articles had drawn to the International had resulted in the formation of its first section inside Ireland.

In the second half of 1870, however, Marx's attention moved away from Ireland, toward the Franco-Prussian War and then the Paris Commune, which erupted in the spring of 1871. The revolutionary character of the Commune and the outraged response to it in British public opinion was to split the First International irrevocably. Most of the British union leaders resigned from the General Council after Marx hailed the Commune in "The Civil War in France," which was first published in English as an "Address" of the International. These divisions undermined the International's influence over the British labor movement. The reaction against the anticlerical politics of the Commune also wiped out the small foothold that the International had gained in Ireland, where it came under attack by O'Donovan Rossa and other prominent nationalists (Collins and Abramsky 1965; Newsinger 1982). These setbacks did not, however, invalidate the general theoretical principles Marx had elaborated in 1869–70 concerning the Irish freedom struggle as a "lever" for the labor movement in Britain.

It was soon after these writings on Ireland that Marx revised *Capital*, volume I, for the 1872–75 French edition. That book and Marx's other critiques of political economy—in relationship to non-Western and precapitalist societies, and to nationalism, race, and ethnicity—are the focus of the next chapter.

CHAPTER FIVE

From the *Grundrisse* to *Capital*: Multilinear Themes

Had Marx confined his discussions of non-Western societies, nationalism, and race and ethnicity to his political and journalistic writings, these issues could more easily be dismissed as tangential to his core intellectual project. In this chapter, however, I will show how these concerns found their way into Marx's major critiques of political economy, from the *Grundrisse* to *Capital*. Moreover, I will argue that Marx's continually evolving stance toward non-Western societies helped to shape the overall argument of *Capital*, volume I, especially the too-little-known French edition of 1872–75, the last one he personally prepared for publication.

THE *GRUNDRISSE*: A MULTILINEAR PERSPECTIVE

Marx's 1857–58 *Grundrisse*, first published over fifty years after his death, is widely seen today as a major text in his critique of political economy, second only to *Capital*. Since it is a draft, not a finished work, it allows the reader, in the British historian Eric Hobsbawm's felicitous expression, to "follow Marx while he is actually thinking" (introduction to Marx 1965, 18). Raya Dunayevskaya characterizes the *Grundrisse* as

> in many respects, more total a conception than the logical, precise *Capital*. It manifests a tremendous world-historic view, not only an analysis of the existing society, but a conception of a new society based on expanding human forces. . . . Its "shapelessness" notwithstanding, its historic

sweep is what allows Marx, during the discussion of the relationship of "free" labor as alienated labor to capital, to pose the question of, and excursion into, pre-capitalist societies. ([1973] 1989, 65–66)

A year after the *Grundrisse*, in the preface to the *Contribution to the Critique of Political Economy* (1859), a published book based on a small part of the former, Marx famously refers to the six topics he intends to develop in the coming years: "I examine the system of bourgeois economy in the following order: *capital, landed property, wage-labor, the state, foreign trade, world market*" (MECW 29, 261; original emphasis). In that same 1859 preface, Marx had already divided the treatment of the first of these six topics, capital, into three parts: commodity, circulation, and capital in general. The latter tripartite list was roughly comparable to what he was to publish and revise from 1867 to 1872 as the first volume of *Capital*, and, at least in general terms, what Engels published posthumously from Marx's notes as volumes II and III.[1]

Considered at some length in a separate section of the *Grundrisse*, but only intermittently in *Capital*, was the topic of precapitalist societies. In an evocative but unfinished analysis of how early clan [*Stamm*] and communal forms of social organization were transformed into class societies, Marx examined the different course that these developments had taken in Asia as opposed to Western Europe.

Although these issues were to generate much discussion in the twentieth century under the rubric of the Asiatic mode of production, Marx never actually uses this term in the *Grundrisse*.[2] He uses the term "Oriental despotism" in his 1853 India writings, as we saw in chapter 1. In 1859, however, in the preface to the *Critique of Political Economy*, he does employ the term "Asiatic mode of production." Marx writes of "the Asiatic, ancient, feudal and modern bourgeois modes of production," which "may be designated as epochs marking progress in the economic development of society." Since he characterizes modern capitalism as "the last antagonistic form," part of "the prehistory of human society," a socialist future is also implied, as was some type of early stateless form preceding both the Asiatic and the ancient modes of production (MECW 29, 263–64). Adding these two implied modes of production would yield a sixfold list: (1) early stateless, (2) Asiatic, (3) ancient, (4) feudal, (5) bourgeois or capitalist, and (6) socialist.

Some sort of multilinearity was also implied through the insertion of an Asian form, in what otherwise would have been a unilinear model focusing on Western development, from early stateless clan societies, to the ancient

Greco-Roman class societies based on slave labor, to the feudalism of the Middle Ages, and on to bourgeois society and its successor, socialism. Some scholars of the *Grundrisse*, like Roman Rosdolsky, have insisted that Marx's list constituted a unilinear "enumeration of the successive periods of economic history" ([1968] 1977, 273), but most have agreed with Hobsbawm that any such "unilinear approach," which was also shared by orthodox Soviet Marxists, "implies a considerable simplification of Marx's thought" (introduction to Marx 1965, 60).[3] Thus, by 1857–58, Marx had developed a more complex account of historical development than the one he and Engels had elaborated a decade earlier in *The German Ideology* (1846). There, in the absence of the Asian form, stood a unilinear model based on Western European history, which ran in a straight line from "clan or tribal," to "ancient," to "feudal," and on to modern bourgeois forms of society (MECW 5, 32–35). As the political theorist Ellen Meiksins Wood suggests at a more general level, "If anything, Marx in the maturity of his critique of political economy, from the *Grundrisse* onwards, becomes less rather than more a 'determinist,' if by that is meant a thinker who treats human agents as passive receptacles of external structures or playthings of eternal laws of motion" (2008, 88).

Marx carried out his discussion on precapitalist societies in notebooks 4 and 5 of the *Grundrisse*, written between mid-December 1857 and February 1858. As we saw in chapter 1, this was the period directly following the outbreak of the Sepoy Uprising in India, during which he had begun to express a greater hostility to colonialism than in his 1853 India writings. In addition, whereas in 1853 he had characterized traditional communal forms in the Indian village as a source of "Oriental despotism," in the *Grundrisse* he described these forms neutrally, or even a bit sympathetically. In most of the *Grundrisse*, of course, Marx focused on something else, the rise of the modern Western proletariat, a working class that was formally free but largely atomized and stripped of any significant control over its means of production. In the various precapitalist societies, by contrast, individuals related to each other as "members of a community" and "as proprietors" of land. Moreover, the purpose of their labor was "not the creation of value" (*Grundrisse*, 471).[4] The earliest forms were all communal, both in their social organization and in their property relations. Marx delineated three early communal forms: Asiatic, Greco-Roman, and Germanic.

In the Asian form, early clan-based groups undergirded a communal social structure rooted in pastoralism or other types of "nomadic" existence, which preceded fixed settlement: "The *clan community* [Stammgemeinschaft], the natural community, appears not as a result of, but as a *presupposition for the communal appropriation* (temporary) *and utilization of the land*" (*Grundrisse*, 472; original emphasis). Thus, communal social organization preceded communal property. The former's "community of blood, language, customs" related "naively" to the land "as the *property of the community*" (472; original emphasis). Eventually, however, "in most of the primary *Asiatic* forms," a higher entity established itself as the landowner, and the communal villagers became that land's mere "hereditary possessors" at the local level (473). This "Oriental despotism" extracted a surplus product, which was not surplus value. At the village level, the ancient communal structures persisted, even with the rise of small-scale manufacturing, all of this underneath a single person, the despot:

> Amidst Oriental despotism and the propertylessness that seems legally to exist there, this clan or communal property exists in fact as the foundation, created mostly by a combination of manufactures and agriculture within the small commune, which thus becomes altogether self-sustaining, and contains all the conditions of reproduction and surplus production within itself. A part of their surplus labor belongs to the higher community, which exists ultimately as a *person*, and this surplus labor takes the form of tribute etc., as well as of common labor for the exaltation of the unity, partly of the real despot, partly of the imagined clan-being, the god. (473)

Throughout this discussion of Asian forms, Marx considers the "communality of labor" (473) to have been more fundamental than communal property to this social formation. In terms of historical examples of the Asian form, he casts his net very widely, here mentioning not only India, but also lands outside Asia like Romania, Mexico, and Peru. As against his 1853 writings, where he mentions only "Oriental *despotism*," he now takes a more evenhanded position, referring to the possibility of "a more *despotic* or a more *democratic* form of this communal system" (473; emphasis added).

The second precapitalist form, the Greco-Roman, he writes, was more urbanized and "the product of a more active historical life" (*Grundrisse*, 474), but it too began as a clan-based communal form. Conflict arose among the various communally organized locales, whether towns or villages, and especially for the Romans, warfare became "the great comprehensive task, the great communal labor" (474). In the Roman case, a greater degree of separation developed between "the living individual" concerning land and the community. In Rome, there was, to be sure, the *ager publicus*, public land belonging to the commune. As against the Asian forms, however, "the [landed] property of the individual" was not "directly communal property" (474–75). Nor was communal labor as central to society—aside from in warfare. Property in land existed, although only for the Roman citizen, but this contrasted with the Asian forms, where all property in land was communal and the individual was at most "only a possessor of a particular part," without juridical ownership rights (477). Although Greco-Roman society was highly urbanized, agriculture conducted by the free citizen landowner was the ideal form of economic activity, while commerce and trade were considered dishonorable, often left to freedmen and noncitizen foreigners. Moreover, where the Asian clans were basically "ancestral," the Greco-Roman ones were built around "locality" and did not view themselves as consanguineal. Ancestral clans were much older, Marx concludes, writing that "their most extreme, strictest form is the caste-order, in which one is separated from the other, without the right of intermarriage, quite different in privilege, each with an exclusive, irrevocable occupation." In this way, Marx ascribed a clan or tribal origin to the Indian caste system. This was what Greece and Rome overcame early on, however, he argues, as the "ancestral clans" were "almost everywhere pushed aside" by the "locality clans," which were somewhat more open in terms of membership (478).

Marx does not suggest here that the Asian clans were at an earlier stage than the Greco-Roman ones. Instead, a multilinear framework is strongly implied. On the whole, as the literary theorist E. San Juan Jr. writes, the notion of an Asiatic mode of production "functioned as a heuristic tool that Marx deployed to eliminate any teleological determinism or evolutionary monism in his speculative instruments of historical investigation" (2002, 63).

Marx gave far less attention to the third precapitalist form, the Germanic, which was centered in the countryside. Among the early Germanic tribes, isolated by great distances in the forests, the commune was not permanent, but rather a periodic coming together to hold a communal meeting. Here, the commune was only "a complement to individual property" (*Grundrisse*, 483). This social form became the basis of the feudal system of medieval Europe, Marx suggests.

After sketching these three forms and their sharp differences, Marx began to draw a larger distinction, between all of these precapitalist societies on the one hand and the modern bourgeois order on the other. All of the precapitalist forms had as their "economic aim" the "production of use-values" (*Grundrisse*, 485). Despite the greater individuation found in the Greco-Roman and Germanic forms, as against the Asian ones, none of them ever developed anything like "the dot-like isolation" of the modern "free worker." Nor did they develop the modern bourgeois property owner, a self-defined isolated and therefore free individual. For these earlier societies, the notion of "an isolated individual" owner of "landed property" would have been absurd. This is because property—especially in land—was mediated by a whole set of community relationships, even in the more individualized Greco-Roman or Germanic societies. Thus, Marx's main purpose seemed to be the elucidation of the structures of the modern capitalist society, through a contrast with both its predecessors in Europe and the alternative historical trajectories of Asia.

While Marx portrays these precapitalist societies in the *Grundrisse* in more neutral tones than in his earlier writings, and occasionally even in guardedly positive terms, he does not idealize them. He argues that the "lofty" ideals of these societies, which disparaged commerce, also confined them to a restricted level of economic and social development. At this point, he asks, referring to modern capitalism and its possible negation by a newer, superior social form: "Once the narrow bourgeois form has been peeled away, what is wealth other than the universality of individual needs, capacities, pleasures, productive forces etc., created through universal exchange?" These achievements of modernity stood in contrast to the *"predetermined* yardstick" of precapitalist societies, with their fixed absolutes focused upon the past. Instead, the future-oriented modern human being, he writes, is engaged in "the absolute movement of becoming." Nonetheless, this process of becoming was only a potential amid the actual capitalist world of "universal objectification as total alienation" (*Grundrisse*, 488; original emphasis).

Of all of the precapitalist forms, the Asian one was structurally at the furthest remove from modern capitalism, to which it put up a strong resistance: "The Asiatic form necessarily hangs on most tenaciously and for the longest time. This is due to its presupposition that the individual does not become independent *vis à vis* the commune; that there is a self-sustaining circle of production, unity of agriculture and manufacture, etc." (*Grundrisse*, 486). Whereas the evolution of the Greco-Roman and Germanic forms saw the breakdown of communal society, as well as a certain degree of individuation in both consciousness and social existence, including property forms, Asian societies preserved more of the older clan-based communal forms. In the Greco-Roman world, slavery and serfdom helped to break down the old communal forms, modifying these earlier social relationships by increasing the class divide among citizens and also by introducing into the community large numbers of noncitizens, a few of them very wealthy merchants, but many more of them slaves stripped of all rights. Such modifications took place within an urban, commercial civilization. As Marx saw it, slavery and serfdom did not have the same effect in Asian empires, where social relations were in many cases already despotic.

At another point in the *Grundrisse*, Marx took up slavery in a different context, the situation of the recently freed slaves of British-ruled Jamaica. These free Blacks had become self-sustaining peasants producing use-value and enjoying some leisure time, rather than proletarians producing exchange value. This was because the economic foundations for modern capitalist wage labor did not yet exist in Jamaica. Marx comments with a certain glee that the "idleness" of the former slaves displeased the white planter class, which rightly feared its own economic demise:

> *The Times* of November 1857 contains an utterly delightful cry of outrage on the part of a West-Indian plantation owner. This advocate analyzes with great moral indignation—as a plea for the re-introduction of Negro slavery—how the *Quashees* (the free niggers[5] of Jamaica) content themselves with producing only what is strictly necessary for their own consumption, and, alongside this "use value," regard loafing (indulgence and idleness) as the real luxury good; how they do not care a damn for the sugar and the fixed capital invested in the plantations, but rather observe the planters' impending bankruptcy with an ironic grin of malicious pleasure, and even exploit their acquired Christianity as an embellishment for this mood of malicious glee and indolence. They have ceased to be slaves, not in order to become wage laborers, but instead self-sustaining peasants working for their own consumption. (*Grundrisse*, 325–26)

Here again, the focus is not noncapitalist social relations as such, but the uniqueness of modern capitalism.

On the last page of the *Grundrisse*, Marx returns to the subject of communal property, terming it a "naturally arisen [*naturwüchsigen*][6] communism" found at the earliest stages of all societies, but better preserved in India than elsewhere:

> Communal property has recently been rediscovered as a special Slavic curiosity. But, in fact, India offers us a sample chart of the most diverse forms of such economic communities, more or less dissolved, but still completely recognizable; and a more thorough research into history uncovers it as the point of departure of all cultured peoples. The system of production founded on private exchange is, to begin with, the historical dissolution of this naturally arisen communism. However, a whole series of economic systems lies in turn between the modern world, where

exchange value dominates production to its whole depth and extent, and the social formations whose foundation is already formed by the dissolution of communal property, without. (*Grundrisse*, 882)

Tantalizingly, the manuscript breaks off this point.[7]

As we have seen, Marx referred to an Asiatic mode of production in the preface to the *Critique of Political Economy* (1859). In this work, he also made some remarks on communal social forms, again in the context of a broader discussion of precapitalist social formations. After considering patriarchal and feudal social relationships and arguing for their alterity with respect to modern capitalism, he brought in early communal societies. Here again, he stresses not so much communal property as communal labor, which he sees as the more fundamental aspect:

> Or finally let us take *communal labor* in its naturally arisen form as we find it among all civilized nations at the threshold of their history. . . . The communal system on which this production is based prevents the labor of an individual from becoming private labor and his product a private product; it causes individual labor to appear rather as the unmediated function of a member of the social organism. (MECW 29, 275; emphasis added)

At one level, this seemed like a unilinear perspective in which communal forms constituted the first stage of social development for all societies.

Moreover, in a footnote critiquing scholars[8] who had made a separate analytical category out of Russian communal property, he argues that this type of early social organization was very widespread, perhaps even universal:

> It is a laughable prejudice, spread abroad recently, that *naturally arisen* communal property is a specifically Slavic, or even an exclusively Russian form. It is the original form [*Urform*] that can be found among the Romans, Teutons, and Celts, and which indeed is still in existence in India, in a whole collection of diverse patterns, albeit sometimes only vestiges of them. A more careful study of the Asiatic, particularly the Indian, forms of communal property would indicate the way in which different forms of naturally arisen communal property result in different forms of its dissolution. For example, the different original types of Roman and Germanic private property can be derived from [*ableiten von*][9] various forms of Indian communal property. (MECW 29, 275; original emphasis)

However, when the above passages[10] are considered alongside the *Grundrisse*, it is pretty clear that Marx was emphasizing not only the identity of these various communal forms but also their differences. To use the language of Hegelian dialectics, he was examining differences and contradictions within apparent identities, as well as their interrelationship.[11] Here, and in more detail in the *Grundrisse*, he was stressing the variety of social forms that emerged out of the "dissolution" of "naturally arisen" communal ones, especially the structural differences between the early class societies that had emerged in India and in Rome.

Something more was at stake here, however. Marx was also changing his views concerning these communal forms. As George Lichtheim argues, this was linked to a more fundamental shift in his thinking, toward a greater hostility toward capitalism:

> While in the 1850s Marx was inclined to emphasize the progressive role of Western capitalism in disrupting Oriental stagnation, by the time he came to draft his major economic work he was less certain that traditional society embodied no positive factors. . . . We now find him remarking upon the stability of the ancient village communities, in a manner suggesting that he saw some genuine virtue in their peculiar mode of life. At the same time his hostility to capitalism had deepened. This is worth stressing as a qualification to the familiar statement that he had by the 1860s lost some of his early revolutionary ardor. . . . But at the same time he sharpened his critique of bourgeois society and the operation of capitalism as an economic system. . . . The note of indulgence has vanished, and the tone has become one of unqualified contempt. In 1847 the bourgeoisie still gained some plaudits for battering down the Chinese walls of barbarism; by 1867 even the "Asiatic mode" comes in for favorable comment, at any rate so far as the village community is concerned: it is valued as a bulwark against social disintegration. (1963, 98)

On its face, Lichtheim's notion of a growing hostility to capitalism on Marx's part sounds absurd, for such sentiments were hardly absent from *The Communist Manifesto* (1848) and other earlier works. Nonetheless, as we have seen in previous chapters, these earlier writings also exhibited more of a sense of capitalism's progressiveness vis à vis earlier social forms, whether this concerned Western feudalism or non-Western societies. By the late 1850s and early 1860s, however, Marx's perspectives on non-Western societies began to evolve. This was true of India, where he attacked British colonialism far more sharply during the 1857 Sepoy Uprising than in his 1853 writings on that country, as addressed in chapter 1. It was also true of Russia, where by 1858 he began to consider the possibility of peasant-based upheaval in a society he had previously viewed as utterly conservative from top to bottom, as discussed in chapter 2. Lichtheim added to this mix the notion of a change of position on Western capitalism itself, as Marx's thinking evolved from the *Manifesto* to *Capital*.

NON-WESTERN SOCIETIES, ESPECIALLY INDIA, IN THE 1861–65 ECONOMIC MANUSCRIPTS

The early 1860s was one of the most productive periods of Marx's life, during which he drafted thousands of pages for what were to become the three volumes of *Capital* and what is sometimes called the fourth volume, *Theories of Surplus Value*, itself three volumes in its published form. As we have seen, in this same period he wrote extensively on the American Civil War and the 1863 Polish uprising, also working to found the International in 1864. One long text, usually referred to as the "Economic Manuscript of 1861–63," stretches to five volumes in the *Collected Works* of Marx and Engels.[12] Part of it is drafts for volume I of *Capital*, and the rest is the text of what was published in the early twentieth century as *Theories of Surplus Value*. Still other manuscripts, written in 1864–65, formed the basis of what Engels published in 1894 as *Capital*, volume III. The latter had quite a bit of discussion of landed property, some of which made connections to Asian social forms. Below, I will treat all of these materials from 1861 to 1865 as a single whole, in order to view the ways in which Marx continued in his economic writings to discuss non-Western societies, especially India. I will also look more briefly at his treatment of Ireland and of slavery, particularly in the United States. Despite the fact that these are by no means the core themes of the 1861–65 economic writings, they come up more than occasionally, usually as counter-examples to modern capitalism.

At one point in the 1861–63 manuscript, as Marx is discussing the origins of modern capitalism and the transition from "feudal landownership," he mentions again the "Asiatic forms of landownership still in existence." He quickly adds that discussion of the Asiatic forms "does not belong here," being tangential to his core subject (MECW 31, 276). At another point, he compares what he calls the "natural laws" of capitalism to those of precapitalist modes of production:

> Here, it is true, it is a matter of the *natural laws of bourgeois production*, hence of the laws within which production occurs at a *particular historical stage* and under *particular historical conditions of production....*

What is involved here, therefore, is the presentation of *the nature* of this particular mode of production, hence its *natural laws*. But just as it is itself *historical*, so are its *nature* and the *laws of that nature*. The natural laws of the ancient, the Asiatic, or the feudal mode of production were essentially different. (MECW 34, 236; original emphasis)[13]

While he allows for some commonalities across these modes of production, these were extremely limited: "On the other hand, it is entirely certain that human production possesses definite *laws* or *relations* which remain the same in all forms of production. These identical characteristics are quite simple and can be summarized in a very small number of commonplace phrases" (MECW 34, 236; original emphasis). His emphasis on the uniqueness of modern capitalism was one of Marx's biggest disagreements with classical political economy.

At another point in the 1861–63 manuscript, Marx fleshes out some of the content of these similarities and differences at the level of ideology, this in a discussion of the openness of the "pure money-relation" of "capitalist and worker" in modern capitalism:

> In all states of society the class that rules (or the classes) is always the one that has possession of the objective conditions of labor, and the repositories of those conditions, in so far as they do work, do so not as workers but as proprietors, and the serving class is always the one that is either itself, as labor capacity, a possession of the proprietors (slavery), or disposes only over its labor capacity (even if, as e.g. in India, Egypt, etc., it possesses land, the proprietor of which is however the king, or a caste, etc.). But all these forms are distinguished from capital by this relation being veiled in them, by appearing as a relation of masters to servants, of free men to slaves, or demigods to ordinary mortals, etc., and existing in the consciousness of both sides as a relation of this kind. In capital alone are all political, religious, and other ideal trimmings stripped from this relation. (MECW 30, 131–32)

In volume III of *Capital*, which as mentioned above was drafted soon afterwards, Marx again underlines the uniqueness of the Asiatic mode of production, as against Western feudalism, here with regard to the effects of usury. "Usury," he writes, "has a revolutionary effect on precapitalist modes of production," helping to open the way for modern capitalism, but only "where and when other conditions . . . are present." This was not the case "in Asiatic forms," however, where usury could "persist for a long while without leading to anything more than economic decay and political corruption" (*Capital* III, 732). Here again, in addition to the relative stability of the Asian forms, his key point is the radical difference between Asian and Western European economic history.

Marx focuses on usury in British-ruled India at one point in the 1861–63 manuscript, writing that its development in rural areas had very few of the hallmarks of a capitalist development:

> Thus even the *formal capital-relation* does not take place, still less the specifically capitalist mode of production. . . . It is rather a form which makes labor sterile, places it under the most unfavorable economic conditions, and combines together capitalist exploitation without a capitalist mode of production, and the mode of production of independent small-scale property in the instruments of labor without the advantages this mode of production offers for less developed conditions. Here in fact the means of production have ceased to belong to the producer, but they are *nominally* subsumed to him, and the mode of production remains in the same relations of small independent enterprise, only the relations are *in ruins*. (MECW 34, 118–19; original emphasis)

The tone of this statement is significant, when one considers the development of Marx's thought. There is no longer the sense, as in 1853, that truly capitalist relations were beginning to develop in India, or that however painfully, some sort of progressive modernization was taking place; rather, there is a sense of reaching an historical impasse, as the old forms have disintegrated without progressive new ones being able to form and develop. Marx adds that the Indian peasant "merely vegetates in the most miserable manner," this after the old communal system has begun to "dissolve" (MECW 34, 118, 119). Marx develops this point further when, in an aside to his discussion of the tendential fall in the rate of profit, he writes that usury in the Indian village was so extortionate that what was left to the peasant was well below the minimum needed for subsistence (*Capital* III, 321).

At another point, here in his discussion of the tendency for the rate of profit to fall, a prime source of capitalist crisis during his own period, Marx also takes up countervailing factors, "how the same causes that bring about a fall in the general rate of profit provoke counter-effects that inhibit this fall" (*Capital* III, 346). Among the sources of such "counter-effects" that serve to attenuate the falling rate of profit, Marx mentions super-profits based upon colonial exploitation: "As far as capital invested in the colonies, etc. is concerned, however, the reason why this can yield higher rates of profit is that the profit rate is generally higher there on account of the lower degree of development, and so too is the exploitation of labor, through the use of slaves and coolies, etc." (345).

Also in volume III of *Capital*, Marx addresses the role of colonialism during an earlier period, at the birth of European capitalism, especially with regard to India. But here he tends to minimize the effects of colonialism on capitalist development. During the mercantile era of the sixteenth and seventeenth centuries, colonialism was only one of several factors that had contributed to capitalist modernity, as the failure of Spain and Portugal to modernize successfully demonstrated:

> The sudden expansion of the world market, the multiplication of commodities in circulation, the competition among the European nations for the seizure of Asiatic products and American treasures, the colonial system, all made a fundamental contribution towards shattering the feudal barriers to production. And yet the modern mode of production in its first period, that of manufacture, developed only where the conditions for it had been created in the Middle Ages. Compare Holland with Portugal, for example. (*Capital* III, 450)

Thus, internal factors within European society were decisive in allowing Holland to surpass Portugal in its economic development.

But this was the early stage of commercial or mercantile capitalism. Once the capitalist mode of production had become dominant on a global scale, however, mercantile Holland gave way to industrializing England. He therefore adds that it is no longer "trade that constantly revolutionizes industry, but industry that constantly revolutionizes trade. . . . Compare England and Holland, for example. Holland's decline as the dominant trading nation is the history of the subordination of commercial capital to industrial capital" (451).

It was in this latter period that the British began to dominate India fully and to make inroads into China as well. Nonetheless, there were many barriers, Marx avers, not least the remnants of the precapitalist Asian social forms:

> The obstacles that the internal solidity and articulation of precapitalist national modes of production oppose to the solvent effect of trade are strikingly apparent in the English commerce with India and China.

There the broad basis of the mode of production is formed by the union between small-scale agriculture and domestic industry, on top of which we have in the Indian case the form of village communities based on common property in the soil, which was also the original form in China. In India, moreover, the English applied their direct political and economic power, as masters and landlords, to destroying these small economic communities. (*Capital* III, 451)

The English did so very consciously, albeit cruelly and ineptly, at least in terms of modernizing India:

More than that of any other nation, the history of English economic management in India is a history of futile and actually stupid (in practice, infamous) economic experiments. In Bengal they created a caricature of English large-scale landed property; in the southeast they created a caricature of peasant smallholdings. In the northwest they did all they could to transform the Indian economic community with communal ownership of the soil into a caricature of itself. (451)

At a broader level, the penetration of mass-produced British textiles severely undermined the traditional producers, but even this did not completely destroy the village community, where the British "work of dissolution" was proceeding "very gradually." In China and Russia, where global capital lacked the "assistance" of "direct political force" as in colonized India, the change came even more slowly. In Russia in particular, Marx holds, "trade leaves the economic basis of Asiatic production quite untouched" (452). Here we find Marx making a linkage among precapitalist forms in China, India, and Russia, all of which are termed "Asiatic."[14] While these social forms resisted capitalism, this was certainly not a progressive form of resistance, nor did it alleviate in any way the suffering of the working people. Thus, the outlook Marx presented here was quite bleak: capitalism might never be able to develop these precapitalist societies, but it had severely undermined their traditional modes of production, leaving them in far worse straits.[15]

Marx critiqued a number of political economists at great length in the 1861–63 manuscript, among them Richard Jones.[16] He credits Jones with greater sensitivity to varying historical forms, thus avoiding "the illusion that capital has been in existence since the beginning of the world" (MECW 33, 320). He also used Jones as he developed his own theory of the tendential decline in the rate of profit. Jones devoted considerable attention to landed property and the theory of rent, often touching on India and other Asian societies. Jones followed François Bernier—a source for Marx's 1853 Indian writings—in seeing the state as owner of all of the land in precolonial India, which he connected to the sudden rise and fall of cities. Marx retorts: "Jones overlooks . . . the Asiatic communal system with its unity of agriculture and industry," here emphasizing the solid economic foundations of these societies (335).

At one point, Jones stimulated Marx to reflect again on the differences between India's precapitalist forms and modern capitalism, this in a discussion of "social labor," the form in which labor under capitalism appears as universal abstract labor, fit for any task in any amount:

> The original unity between the worker and the conditions of labor // abstracting from slavery, where the laborer himself belongs to the objective conditions of labor // has two main forms: the Asiatic communal system (primitive communism) and small-scale agriculture based on the family (and linked with domestic industry) in one or another form. Both are embryonic forms and both are equally unfitted to develop labor as *social* labor and the productive power of social labor. Hence the necessity for the separation, for the rupture, for the antithesis of labor and property (by which property in the conditions of production is to be understood). The most extreme form of this rupture, and the one in which the productive forces of social labor are also most powerfully developed, is capital. The original unity can be re-established only on the material foundation that capital creates and by means of the revolutions that the working class and the whole society undergo in the process of this creation. (MECW 33, 340)

Modern "social labor" thus created a radical separation between the worker and the conditions of work, including the means of production, which were now owned externally, reducing the worker to a mere bearer of labor power at the command of capital. In looking at social labor's premodern opposite, Marx sketched two noncapitalist forms of labor, which were by no means the same, that of the Asian communal villager and that of the Western European small farmer of the precapitalist period. Most significantly, as the last sentence above shows, Marx's perspective on "the Asiatic communal system" and its villages had evidently shifted a bit from the earlier stress on "Oriental despotism" and vegetative torpor. How else could Marx have written above of recovering some of the "original unity" of the precapitalist world, both the Asian and the Western precapitalist village, in a socialist society of the future, albeit in a radically different form that had a higher material foundation and a greater scope for individual development? Unfortunately, this language from the 1861–63 manuscript did not find itself into what under Engels's editorship became volume III of *Capital*.

The years of these economic writings, 1861–65, were also those of the Civil War, which brought to an end one of the largest slave systems that has ever existed under capitalism. From time to time in these writings, Marx addressed the relationship of capitalism to slavery. In the 1861–63 manuscript, he makes clear that modern plantation slavery was part of the capitalist mode of production, not a vestige of earlier ones. While "the slavery of Negroes precludes free wage labor, which is the basis of capitalist production," it was also true that "the business in which slaves are used is conducted by *capitalists*. The mode of production that they introduce has not arisen out of slavery but is grafted onto it. In this case the same person is capitalist and landowner" (MECW 31, 516).

In volume III of *Capital*, Marx took up slavery as a general category in a discussion of the role of supervision in production: "This work of supervision necessarily arises in all modes of production that are based on opposition between the worker as direct producer and the proprietor of the means of production. The greater this opposition, the greater the role that the work of supervision plays. It reaches its high point in the slave system" (*Capital* III, 507–8). Thus, slavery was at the far end of a continuum insofar as the stringency of its direct supervision of labor.

Moreover, Marx argues repeatedly, modern capitalist slavery was harsher than even its most oppressive ancient forms, because of the pressures of value creation:

> Where, for example, slavery and serfdom predominate among peoples that engage in little trade, there can be no question of overwork. It is therefore among commercial peoples that slavery and serfdom take on their most hateful form, as e.g. among the Carthaginians; this is even more pronounced among peoples that retain slavery and serfdom as the basis of their production in an epoch when they are connected with other peoples in a situation of capitalist production; thus, e.g. the southern states of the American Union. (MECW 30, 197)

If it could retain a ready supply of new labor power, the modern capitalist slave system had a tendency to work people to death, he notes, citing John Cairnes's *The Slave Power* (1862) on how slaves in the Deep South could easily be replaced "from the teeming preserves of Virginia and Kentucky." He cites Cairnes further, to the effect that in an earlier period, before the abolition of the slave trade, it became "a maxim of slave management, in slave importing countries, that the *most effective economy is that* which takes out of the human chattel *in the shortest space of time the utmost amount of exertion it is capable of putting forth*. It is in tropical culture, where annual profits often equal the whole capital of plantations, that negro life is most recklessly sacrificed" (MECW 34, 70; original emphasis).

Marx places this insight drawn from Cairnes into his general framework concerning capital:

> If labor is prolonged beyond a certain period—or labor capacity is valorized to more than a certain extent—labor capacity will be temporarily or definitively destroyed, instead of being preserved. If the capitalist sets the worker to work for e.g. 20 hours today, tomorrow he will be incapable of working the normal labor time of 12 hours or perhaps any labor time at all. If the overwork extends over a long period, the worker will perhaps only preserve himself and therefore his labor capacity for 7 years instead of the 20 or 30 years for which he might otherwise have preserved it. . . . This is still at this moment the case in Cuba, where after 12 hours in the fields the Negroes have a further two hours of manufacturing labor to perform in connection with the preparation of sugar or tobacco. (MECW 30, 182–83)

While abolition was on the horizon in the United States, in Spanish-ruled Cuba, slavery continued until 1886.

Here and elsewhere, however, Marx also makes the point that wage workers who were formally free were also being worked to death, for in this situation the manufacturers "do not even have to pay the fee-simple for the workers," but could hire them without any outlay for their labor power before the actual work was performed. This was because these workers were also part of a seemingly inexhaustible supply of labor power (MECW 34, 69). The source of that labor power for British capital included not only rural England, he writes, but also Ireland, where the destructive force of the agricultural revolution had wiped out the sources of subsistence of millions of people:

> In *England* the conversion of *arable land into pasture* since the decade prior to the middle of the 18th century through *enclosures of commons,*

the throwing together of small farms. This is still proceeding now. The *clearing of estates* has taken place again in Ireland on a very large scale since 1846. The death by hunger of 1 million Irish and the driving of another million overseas—this was a *clearing of the estate of Ireland.* Still continuing. (257–58; original emphasis)

Somewhat later, he remarks that "the flow of Irish people into the industrial districts" of England had depressed the price of labor power, far exceeding the capitalist hopes that immigration would increase competition among workers (296).

THE NARRATIVE STRUCTURE OF *CAPITAL*, VOLUME I, ESPECIALLY THE FRENCH EDITION

In Marx's masterwork, *Capital,* volume I, the abstract and impersonal power of capital is itself an historical actor, a self-developing subject. Its value form is "the dominant subject of this process" (*Capital* I, 255). The increasing hegemony of its value form over all of social life grinds down into subjection the living human subject, the worker. Moreover, Marx argues that under the domination of this humanly created but impersonal subject that is the value form, relationships between human beings take on the "fantastic form of a relation between things" (165). Rather than a false appearance behind which a pristine human essence hid, Marx writes, this subject-object reversal constitutes what human relationships "really are" under capitalism (166).

Marx delineates a second type of subjectivity as well. In a decisive chapter, "The Working Day," *Capital* chronicles the self-constitution of the working class as modern revolutionary subject out of its resistance to its dehumanization: "Suddenly, there arises the voice of the worker, which had previously been stifled by the sound and fury of the production process" (*Capital* I, 342). Marx concludes that this resistance on the part of workers would eventually result in a social conflagration, for "capitalist production begets, with the inexorability of a natural process, its own negation. This is the negation of the negation" (*Capital* I, 929). Here the book's underlying Hegelian framework was also quite evident. The "negation of the negation"—and this was a Hegelian concept that Marx surely adopted—was not an "empty negative" of pure destructiveness. Its doubling, "the positive in its negative" (Hegel [1831] 1969, 836), was concretized by Marx in this context as an affirmative, creative side of modernity that was emerging as old forms were negated in a revolutionary manner.

This undergirded a third level of Marx's argument in *Capital*. He takes up not only the possibility of worker resistance, as above, but in the first chapter of *Capital* he also sketches briefly some parameters for a postcapitalist society in a progressive sense. In this envisioning of an alternative to capitalism, Marx evokes "an association of free human beings, working with the means of production held in common" (*Capital* I, 171). Creating such a world of "freely associated human beings" would also "remove" the distorting lens or "veil" of the commodity fetish and allow members of society to see their social relations clearly for the first time since the establishment of the hegemony of the value form was established (173).

Such was the dialectical structure of the first volume of *Capital*, where the logical predominated over the historical or chronological. In fact, Marx placed the extended treatment of the historical origins of capitalism at the end of the book, under the category "Primitive Accumulation of Capital," *after* the reader had been led through a conceptual and empirical analysis of modern capitalism itself. Since the unique society that was Western capitalism had of necessity arisen from a preexisting noncapitalist one, in this case European feudalism, the issue of unilinear versus multilinear models of development was also posed.

A question arose here, as in Marx's earlier writings. Was the pathway through which modern capitalism had emerged in Western Europe and North America to be followed by all other societies, with the rest of the world simply left behind by these technologically more advanced societies? As we have seen, such a grand narrative had surely been implied in *The Communist Manifesto* two decades earlier, but Marx had altered his perspectives on non-Western societies since 1848.

Before examining this question of a grand narrative, however, a brief discussion of the development of the text of volume I of *Capital* is necessary. A major part of the argument I will put forward below hinges on the later stages of the development of the text of *Capital*, volume I, with some significant texts still largely unknown. Marx's masterwork is a symphony with variations, even a work-in-progress. Few except specialist scholars are aware that Engels not only edited volumes II and III of *Capital* from Marx's sometimes rough notes after his friend's death but also created the standard edition of volume I, a process in which he made significant editorial choices—all of this during the years 1883 to 1894. The chronology of the editions of the first volume of *Capital* on which either Marx or Engels had significant input runs as follows:

1867	First German edition	Prepared for publication by Marx with minimal input from Engels
1873	Second German edition, with considerable alterations	Prepared for publication by Marx, again with minimal input from Engels
1872–75	French edition, with considerable alterations; initially published in serial form	Translated by Joseph Roy from the second German edition, again with considerable alterations by Marx and with minimal input from Engels; last edition Marx prepared for publication
1883	Third German edition, with considerable alterations	Prepared for publication by Engels shortly after Marx's death; based on second German edition; took into account some aspects of the French edition
1886	First English edition, with some alterations	Translated from the third German edition by Samuel Moore and Edward Aveling, with considerable input from Engels; Eleanor Marx checked and corrected the numerous citations from English sources
1890	Fourth German edition, with some alterations	Standard edition to this day; prepared for publication by Engels, who took into account both the English edition and further aspects of the French edition

The most significant of these editorial choices was Engels's decision to leave aside considerable material from the 1872–75 French edition, even in the 1890 German edition, which became the standard. Yet the French edition was the last one Marx had personally prepared for publication, as he heavily edited and amended the translation by Joseph Roy. Hidden here are some theoretical differences between Marx and his friend Engels, who prepared the 1883 third German edition and the 1890 fourth German edition, both published after Marx's death. These Engelsian editions, especially the 1890 one, have been the basis for all English-language ones to date. Marx's first German edition was published in 1867, and his second German edition, with major revisions, followed in 1873. This was followed in turn by the 1872–75 French edition, translated on the basis of the 1873 German one, but very extensively edited by Marx.

One undisputed fact will illustrate the scope of these changes from 1867 all the way to 1875, and reveal the 1867 edition to have been a rather early stage of this work in progress: In the 1867 edition, the most-discussed first chapter on the commodity[17] had an entirely different form than in later editions. What was to become this chapter's section on commodity fetishism was only partially finished in 1867, and what had actually been written was divided between the first pages of the book and an appendix on value at the end. By the 1873 German edition, the text of the first chapter had become quite similar to the one we know today from the standard edition. Unfortunately, today's standard edition is also problematic, based as it is on Engels's 1890 fourth German edition. For example, MEGA² II/10, the closest thing we have to a *variorum* edition of volume I of *Capital*, contains a fifty-page appendix entitled "List of Places in the Text of the French Edition That Were Not Included in the Third and Fourth German Editions " (732–83). Many of these passages left out by Engels from the standard edition are significant, and as will be discussed below, some of them bear on the themes of this study.[18]

From the first, Engels had a different opinion of the French edition's worth than did Marx. In Marx's 1875 postface to the French edition, his last published statement on *Capital*, he stresses that "whatever the literary defects of the French edition, it possesses a scientific value independent of the original and should be consulted even by readers familiar with German" (*Capital* I, 105). Again and again in his correspondence, Marx expresses appreciation for the fact that the title page included the phrase, "completely revised by the author" (MEGA² II/7, 3). As early as May 28, 1872, Marx had written to one of the translators for the Russian edition, Nikolai Danielson, that although he had some reservations about it, he wanted to make the French edition the basis for the work's future translations:

> Although the French edition . . . has been prepared by a great expert in the two languages, he has often translated too literally. I have therefore found myself compelled to rewrite whole passages in French, to make them palatable to the French public. It will be all the easier later on to translate the book from French into English and the Romance languages. (MECW 44, 385)

Here at least, Marx's quarrel with Roy's draft translation was that it was too literal.

Engels, who read part of Roy's draft, differed strongly with Marx concerning what was wrong with Roy's work. For Engels, the problem with Roy's translation lay in what the German socialist considered—in a tone marked by a sense of German cultural superiority—to be the antidialectical character of the French language itself. After reading the draft translation of the chapter "The Working Day," Engels writes Marx on November 29, 1873:

> Yesterday I read the chapter on factory legislation in the French transla-
> tion. With all due respect for the skill with which this chapter has been

rendered into elegant French, I still felt regret at what had been lost from the beautiful chapter. Its vigor and vitality and life have gone to the devil. The chance for an ordinary writer to express himself with a certain elegance has been purchased by castrating the language. It is becoming increasingly impossible to think originally in the straitjacket of modern French. Everything striking or vital is removed if only by the need, which has become essential almost everywhere, to bow to the dictates of a pedantic formal logic and change round the sentences. I would think it a great mistake to take the French version as a model for the English translation. In English the power of expression in the original does not need to be toned down; whatever has inevitably to be sacrificed in the genuinely dialectical passages can be made up in others by the greater energy and brevity of the English language. (MECW 44, 540–41)

Marx was not convinced and replies the next day: "Now that you are taking a look at the French translation of *Capital*, I would be grateful if you could persevere with it. I think you will find that some passages are superior to the German" (MECW 44, 541). Engels replies on December 5 without conceding his basic point about the French language: "More soon on the French translation. Up to now I find that what you have *revised* is indeed better than the German, but neither French nor German has anything to do with that. Best of all is the note on Mill,[19] as to style" (545).

In the ensuing years, Marx indicated again and again in various correspondence that in any new edition of the work, the French edition was the last word, except for the very important first six chapters. In a November 15, 1878, letter to Danielson concerning a second Russian edition, Marx asked that "the translator always compare carefully the second German edition with the French one, since the latter contains many important changes and additions." He also wanted the division into parts and chapters of new editions to be based on the French edition; the most important issue here was making the discussion of primitive accumulation into a separate part eight, rather than keeping it within part seven on accumulation (MECW 45, 343).

Marx never won the argument with Engels about the French edition, however. In editing the 1883 third German edition after Marx's death, Engels indicated that he had consulted the French edition. However, he writes that he did so not for its substantive theoretical value, but only to get a sense of "what the author himself was prepared to sacrifice" for greater readability (*Capital* I, 110, preface to the 1886 English edition). Unfortunately, Engels gave no examples to buttress his claims that the French edition as a whole was a simplified one.

Here began the unsubstantiated charge, propagated widely to this day, that the 1872–75 French edition, the last one Marx prepared for publication, was somehow inferior—a more popularized version created for a less knowledgeable French public, and that the 1890 Engels-edited edition, based primarily on the second German edition of 1873, was the true version of the work.[20] To be sure, Marx sometimes indicates, for example in the 1878 letter to Danielson quoted above, that he had simplified the beginning chapters of the book in the French edition: "I was also sometimes obliged—principally in the first chapter—to 'simplify' the matter in its French version" (MECW 45, 343). In another letter to Danielson of November 28, 1878, Marx specifies that for a new Russian edition, the first six chapters[21] were "to be translated from the German text" (MECW 45, 346). These very important chapters, which included the fetishism discussion in the first chapter, nonetheless comprised only about a third of the 1873 German edition. However, in another letter during the same period, dated September 27, 1877, Marx applauds a report of an attempt (ultimately unsuccessful) to publish an Italian edition translated "from the French edition" (MECW 45, 277). As late as 1880, the American journalist John Swinton recounted, Marx had given him a copy of the French edition and stated that "it is from this that the translation into English ought to be made" (Foner 1973, 243). In his preface to the new Persian edition of *Capital*, volume I (Marx 2008), one of the few editions in any language that takes serious account of the French edition, translator Hassan Mortazavi notes that as late as a letter to Danielson on December 13, 1881, Marx was writing that he wanted to make major changes to the German edition of volume I.

Engels saw the simplifications as running through the entire text of the French edition, rather than only the first chapters. The most generous thing that could be said of Engels as editor of volume I of *Capital* is that he left us an incomplete edition, which he put forward as the definitive one. Nonetheless, in the preface to the fourth German edition of 1890, he writes that he had established "in final form [*endgültige Feststellung*], as nearly as possible, both text and footnotes" (*Capital* I, 114). Nonetheless, Engels left out Marx's preface and postface to the French edition. They did not appear in English until Dona Torr's edition (Marx 1939). A stronger criticism of Engels could be made, however, based on the notion that Marx wanted the French edition to be the standard for subsequent editions and translations, at least after the sixth chapter.

A few of the textual differences in the French edition will help to illuminate the question of a grand narrative in *Capital*. Marx surreptitiously introduced a change into the preface of the 1867 German edition when it was translated into French. In a well-known sentence on the relationship of industrialized to nonindustrialized societies, the standard English and German editions read: "The country that is more developed industrially only shows, *to the less developed*, the image of its own future" (*Capital* I, 91; emphasis added).[22]

Some of those who have attacked *Capital* as a deterministic work have seen this sentence as an example of blatant unilinearism. Teodor Shanin, the editor of a valuable book on Marx, is among those who have seen Marx's writings up through *Capital* as essentially similar to the *Manifesto* in their unilinearism. Using the above sentence as his prime example, Shanin writes that *Capital*'s "main weakness was the optimistic and unilinear determinism usually built into it" (1983b, 4).

The British Marx scholars Derek Sayer and Philip Corrigan responded at the time to Shanin by pointing out that Marx was not setting up a general global framework, but comparing England to Germany. Quoting the passage more fully, as they do, it reads:

> England is used as the main illustration of the theoretical developments I make. If, however, the German reader pharisaically shrugs his shoulders at the condition of the English industrial and agricultural workers, or optimistically comforts himself with the thought that in Germany things are not nearly so bad, I must plainly tell him: *De te fabula narratur!*[23] Intrinsically it is not a question of higher or lower degree of development of the social antagonisms that spring from the natural laws of capitalist production. It is a question of these laws themselves, of these tendencies winning their way through and working themselves out with iron necessity. The country that is the more developed industrially only shows, to the less developed, the image of its own future. (*Capital* I, 90–91)

In the next two paragraphs, Marx compared the situation in England to that in Continental Europe, especially Germany, without mentioning any non-European societies. Sayer and Corrigan conclude:

> Marx is publishing in Germany in 1867, a treatise illustrated mainly with English data. He is understandably concerned to establish its relevance to German conditions. Since Germany is a society in which capitalism has taken root already, its "normal development" can reasonably be expected to follow an "English" path. But this in no way implies any necessity for societies in which capitalist production is *not* already established to do the same. (1983, 79)

Debate over this sentence in the 1867 preface is in fact over a century old, and can be traced to some of the earliest discussions of *Capital* in Russia.

Writing in the 1930s, Leon Trotsky addresses what was already an old debate, here in the context of his theory of combined and uneven development:

> This statement of Marx which takes its point of departure methodologically not from world economy as a whole but from the single capitalist country as a type, has become less applicable in proportion as capitalist evolution has embraced all countries regardless of their previous fate and industrial level. England in her day revealed the future of France, considerably less of Germany, but not in the least of Russia and not of India. The Russian Mensheviks, however, took this conditional statement of Marx unconditionally. Backward Russia, they said, ought not to push ahead, but humbly to follow the prepared models. To this kind of "Marxism" the liberals also agreed. (Trotsky [1933] 1967, 349)[24]

These are serious answers, but they still leave open the possibility, however slight, that Marx intended to apply this notion of an "iron necessity" more widely, as he had in the *Manifesto*.

But note how the sentence in question reads in the later French edition, where Marx makes his surreptitious alteration: "The country that is more developed industrially only shows, *to those that follow it on the industrial path*, the image of its own future" ([1872–75] 1985a, 36; emphasis added).[25] Societies of Marx's time that had not yet embarked upon "the industrial path," such as Russia and India, were now explicitly bracketed out, leaving open the notion of alternative possibilities for them. I see two possibilities here. First, it could be argued that this textual alteration was a clarification on Marx's part of a position he had already arrived at by 1867. A second, more likely possibility is that this change from 1867 to 1872 is an example of the evolution of his thought away from the implicit unilinearism of the *Manifesto*, a process that had been underway since the 1850s.

The second change in the French edition that went in a similar direction was not surreptitious at all, for Marx was to refer to the new version proudly in his correspondence with Russians on more than one occasion. In an important passage in part eight on primitive accumulation in the standard Engels-edited editions, Marx discusses the rise of capitalist forms—"the transformation of feudal exploitation into capitalist exploitation" (*Capital* I, 875)—through the expropriation of the English peasantry, a period in which "great masses of men are suddenly and forcibly torn from their means of subsistence, and hurled onto the labor market as free, unprotected and rightless proletarians" (876). He concludes:

> The expropriation of the agricultural producer, of the peasant, from the soil, is the basis of the whole process. The history of this expropriation assumes different aspects in different countries, and runs through its various phases in different orders of succession, and at different historical epochs. *Only in England, which we therefore take as our example, has it the classic form.* (876; emphasis added)[26]

This concluded chapter 26, "The Secret of Primitive Accumulation," where Marx introduced the theoretical framework of the entire part on primitive accumulation. In this brief chapter, Marx mentioned only European examples, specifically the transition from feudalism to capitalism. Nonetheless, it might have been read as a global and unilinear process of capitalist development, with England exhibiting the "classic form" of this process. Given the implicitly unilinear language of *The Communist Manifesto*, this was how many have read and still read this passage, if not the whole of *Capital*.

In the French edition, Marx extended and reworked this passage considerably, expressly limiting his analysis to Western Europe. Although Marx subsequently referred more than once to the following passage from the French edition,[27] it has yet to make it into any of the standard English editions of *Capital*:

> But the basis of this whole development is the expropriation of the cultivators. *So far, it has been carried out in a radical manner only in England: therefore this country will necessarily play the leading role in our sketch. But all the countries of Western Europe are going through the same development*, although in accordance with the particular environment it changes its local color, or confines itself to a narrower sphere, or shows a less pronounced character, or follows a different order of succession. (Marx [1872–75] 1985b, 169; emphasis added)[28]

This altered text made clear, as far as Marx was concerned, that his narrative of primitive accumulation was meant as a description of Western European development, nothing more, and hardly a global grand narrative. As we will see in the next chapter, these debates especially concerned Russia in the 1870s, where revolutionaries who had read *Capital* wondered aloud whether Marx meant that their country had to pass through the same stages of development as had England. In this context, the editors of MEGA² II/10—Roland Nietzold, Wolfgang Focke, and Hannes Skambraks—suggest in their introduction: "Apparently, under the influence of his studies of agrarian relations in Russia since the beginning of the seventies, Marx modified this finding in the French edition" (MEGA² II/10, 22*).[29] Be that as it may, because Marx did not specify Russia here, the general level of new language for the French edition allows the reader to connect his qualification not only to Russia, but also to a whole range of other non-Western, nonindustrialized societies of his time.

At a minimum, these two important alterations for the 1872–75 French edition, the last one Marx personally prepared for publication, show a tightening of his argument to shield *Capital* from its critics, especially Russian Populists who wished to avoid the suffering and destruction that would have accompanied the capitalist industrialization of their country. But a stronger theoretical case can also be made concerning these alterations. It is more likely that they represent not mere clarifications, but changes in Marx's thinking, part of the long process that we have already traced in earlier chapters of this book. In particular, as discussed in chapter 4, Marx wrote in 1869 and 1870 that he had altered his position on Ireland, now advocating Irish independence as a precondition for a socialist transformation in England, as against his earlier more modernist position wherein a workers' revolution in England would have had to precede Irish independence. At a more fundamental theoretical level, we have seen earlier in this chapter how, in the *Grundrisse* and the *Critique of Political Economy*, Marx had written that Asian societies such as India needed to be analyzed separately, since their history did not fit into the stages of development that he had worked out earlier on the basis of European history. I would argue that these changes in *Capital* were part of this process of evolution in Marx's thinking. This process did not end in 1875 with the final installment of the French edition of *Capital*, however. It would continue into his late and largely unpublished writings and notes, as will be discussed in the next chapter. Before going there, however, let us view a few other aspects of *Capital*, volume I: its non-Western and precapitalist subtext, as well as its treatment of race, ethnicity, and nationalism.

SUBTEXTS OF *CAPITAL*, VOLUME I

As we have seen, in *Capital* was centered on Western development, something Marx underlined in the later French edition. Yet there was also a subtext, where non-Western and precapitalist societies put in the occasional appearance. Such societies were present throughout Marx's argument about the growth of capital, hovering in the background at crucial junctures as the "other" of Western capitalist modernity, at times helping the reader to grasp this social order's perverse uniqueness. A second aspect concerned how the very existence of these noncapitalist societies implied the possibility of alternative ways of organizing social and economic life. A third aspect revolved around the ways in which examples from these societies helped him to elaborate modern, progressive alternatives to capitalism.

In the section on commodity fetishism, Marx presents human relations under capitalism as (1) reified or thing-like and (2) containing an exploitative reality hidden by a "mystical veil or cloud" (*Capital* I, 173; German: *mystische Nebelschleier*; French: *nuage mystique*). This was the distorting lens of the commodity fetish. Noncapitalist societies, however oppressive they might be, had not perfected this veiling of social relations. Thus, he argues in the section on commodity fetishism: "The whole mystery of commodities, all the magic and necromancy that surrounds the products of labor on the basis of commodity production, vanishes therefore as soon as we come to other forms of production" (169). It "vanishes" because these earlier societies were not organized around value production. Marx proceeds to give four examples of these "other" forms. The first one was fictive, an ironical rendering of the Robinson Crusoe analogies so popular among early nineteenth century political economists. On his lonely island, Crusoe produced only use values, but used accounting methods appropriate to a developed capitalism to record his production and consumption. Nonetheless, Marx writes here social relations were "transparent," as against those of modern capitalism (170). In the latter, workers were paid the exchange value of their labor power, but capital then reaped a bonanza when it received something of far greater value, the actual value added to the production process by labor-power. The difference lay hidden under slogans like "a fair day's work for a fair day's pay."

Marx took the feudal society of the European Middle Ages as his second noncapitalist example, now with a dab of irony toward modernity's pretensions to enlightenment and openness:

> Let us now transport ourselves from Robinson's island, bathed in light, to medieval Europe, shrouded in darkness. Here, instead of the independent human being, we find everyone dependent—serfs and lords, vassals and suzerains, laymen and clerics. Personal dependence characterizes the social relations of material production. . . . There is no need for labor and its products to assume a fantastic form different from their

reality.... The social relations between individuals in the performance of their labor ... are not disguised as social relations between things, between the products of labor. (*Capital* I, 170)

Social relations might be brutally exploitative rather than free, but there was no veiling, no fetishism, under what he calls "direct relations of domination and servitude" (173).

Marx's third example, a small peasant household, might be considered a corollary to the second, or to agrarian precapitalist societies other than Western European feudalism. He considers it to be a remnant of much older social forms, already found in communal preliterate societies: "For an example of labor in common, i.e. directly associated labor, we do not need to go back to the spontaneously developed form which we find at the threshold of the history of all civilized people. We have one nearer to hand in the patriarchal rural industry of a peasant family" (*Capital* I, 171). In a long footnote, Marx quotes a passage from *Critique of Political Economy* discussed earlier in this chapter. There, he argues that "communal property" was not as some supposed, a uniquely Slavic phenomenon, but existed among the early Romans and their later "barbarian" opponents, as well as in contemporary Asia, especially India (cited in full in this volume, p. 161.) Whether then or later, the peasant family exhibited a simpler, "spontaneously developed division of labor," based on "differences of sex and age" (*Capital* I, 171). The family shared its social product on the basis of need, as conditioned by its various social hierarchies. No fetishism veiled these relationships, which were also clear and open, but they were limited by "the immaturity of the human being as an individual" in such societies (*Capital* I, 173).

It was through the mediation of these two noncapitalist examples, both of them added after the first German edition of 1867, that Marx drew the reader from the hyper-individualized and fictive Crusoe toward his final example, one of an associated form of labor that was also free. This was communism in the modern form, the *telos* of capitalist development and of the labor movement that had arisen as its negation: "Let us finally imagine, for a change, an association of free human beings, working with means of production held in common," he intones (*Capital* I, 171). After referring to earlier "ancient Asiatic,"[30] Classical-antique, and other such modes of production," each of which had a measure of commodity production, albeit in "a subordinate role" (172), he returns to his sketch of this modern communistic system. Such a system would be a free association, undergirded by social relations that would again be transparent: "The mystifying veil or cloud is not removed from the countenance of the social life-process, i.e. the process of material production, until it becomes production by freely associated human beings, and stands under their conscious and planned control" (173). In this free and transparent society, the individual would be part of a free association, rather than isolated and atomized in the modern capitalist sense.[31] Marx is careful to indicate that this return to transparency was on the basis of modernity. Precapitalist societies were sometimes transparent, but they were characterized either by "the immaturity of the human being as an individual" or by "direct relations of dominance and servitude" (173). Going beyond these naive or oppressive forms of social transparency required the "material foundation" of modern capitalism that had been the "product of a long and tormented historical development" (173).

While Marx made few mentions of China in *Capital*, an interesting one occurred in the fetishism section. In an ironical one-sentence footnote, he alluded to the period following the defeat of the 1848 revolutions in Europe. (He eliminated this footnote in the French edition.) During the quiescent 1850s, he writes, German intellectuals were drawn to séances where participants attempted to levitate tables. But during this period China's Taiping Rebellion showed an entirely different direction, one of confrontation with state powers: "One may recall that China and the tables began to dance when the rest of the world appeared to be standing still—*pour encourager les autres* [to encourage the others]" (*Capital* I, 164). This refers to a famous line from Voltaire's *Candide* (chapter 23). When Candide comes upon the public execution of a British admiral for nonfeasance, a bystander explains matter-of-factly: "It is good to execute an admiral from time to time, to encourage the others." With this phrase, Marx may have sought to bring the harsh power of revolution to mind.[32]

Among the non-Western societies discussed in first volume of *Capital*, India received the most attention. While there was no section or chapter on India as such, Marx highlighted what he considered to be that society's distinctiveness as a way of zeroing in on modern Western capitalism's uniqueness. India appeared as a subtext throughout the crucial part four, "The Production of Relative Surplus Value," where Marx analyzed the technical innovations that radically increased both labor's productivity and its level of exploitation and alienation. Marx took the reader through three forms of this process, cooperation, manufacture, and lastly, machinery and large-scale industry, which were to some extent chronological.

In the chapter titled "Cooperation," Marx focused not on small-scale or localized social cooperation, but something larger and much more authoritarian.

This was the notion that "capitalist production" began in earnest only when "each individual capital employs a comparatively large number of workers" (*Capital* I, 439). He writes of "an industrial army" organized on a hierarchical basis, with "officers (managers) and N.C.O.'s (foremen, overseers), who command during the labor process in the name of capital" (450). In describing this "purely despotic" organizational form, Marx gently mocks those political economists who saw the slave plantation as wasteful due to the high cost of supervising a hostile labor force, but who failed to notice something similar when they considered the costs of supervision "made necessary by the capitalist and therefore antagonistic character" of modern production (450).

Marx then moves to a comparison with premodern forms, into a discussion of "the colossal effects of simple cooperation," as found in "the gigantic structures erected by the ancient Egyptians, Etruscans, etc." (*Capital* I, 451). After quoting the political economist Richard Jones at length on these processes, especially in India, Marx concludes that this type of power "has in modern society been transferred to the capitalist" (452). He proceeds to delineate three historical forms of cooperation: (1) that of village India and other similar societies, characterized by "common ownership of the conditions of production" and a lack of social individuation;[33] (2) other forms, from "ancient times" to those in "modern colonies," resting on "direct domination and servitude, in most cases on slavery"; and (3) the modern capitalist form, which "presupposes from the outset the free wage laborer who sells his labor-power to capital" (452). The last of these arose out of the break-up of the medieval European guilds and village communities. Overall, it was a very different social form from the first two, "one peculiar to, and specifically distinguishing, the capitalist process of production" (453).

India also entered into his discussion at the next analytical level of relative surplus value, the chapter "The Division of Labor and Manufacture." By manufacture, Marx meant not the modern factory but more rudimentary forms that preceded the industrial revolution. This was the period of the dissolution of the medieval guilds and the gathering of skilled workers with various specialties into large workshops under the control of individual capitalists.[34] One big structural change, he holds, was that an individual worker, however skilled, no longer produced a whole commodity: "The specialized worker produces no commodities. It is only the common product of all the specialized workers that becomes a commodity" (*Capital* I, 475). On the one hand, the new manufacturing workshop was a very authoritarian institution, as against the guild workshop, where master craftsmen had controlled their means of production and thus enjoyed substantial autonomy. On the other hand, he notes, the social division of labor outside the workshop was to a great extent unregulated, without strong guilds structuring it: "While within the workshop, the iron law of proportionality subjects definite numbers of workers to definite functions, in the society outside the workshop, the play of chance and caprice results in a motley pattern of distribution of the producers and their means of production among the various branches of social labor" (476). This resulted in a contradictory situation, with "anarchy in the social division of labor and despotism in the manufacturing division of labor" (477).

Again, to get a sharper focus on the uniqueness of modern capitalist development, Marx moves his discussion to India, which he describes as a contemporary example similar to earlier European social forms:

> We find, on the contrary, in those earlier forms of society in which the separation of trades has been spontaneously developed, then crystallized, and finally made permanent by law, on the one hand, a specimen of the organization of the labor of society in accordance with an approved and authoritative plan, and on the other, the entire exclusion of division of labor in the workshop or, at the least, its development on a minute scale, sporadically and incidentally. (*Capital* I, 477)

He then launches into a detailed portrait of the traditional Indian village:

> Those small and extremely ancient Indian communities, for example, some of which continue to exist to this day, are based on the possession of the land in common, on the blending of agriculture and handicrafts and on an unalterable division of labor. . . . Most of the products are destined for direct use by the community itself, and are not commodities[35]. . . . It is the surplus alone that becomes a commodity, and a part of that surplus cannot become a commodity until it has reached the hands of the state, because from time immemorial a certain quantity of the community's production has found its way to the state as rent in kind. The form of the community varies in different parts of India. In the simplest communities, the land is tilled in common, and the produce is divided among the members. At the same time, spinning and weaving are carried on in each family as subsidiary industries. (477–78)

Marx also describes a dozen or so traditional officials and craftsmen, from the bookkeeper to the "calendar-Brahmin," and from the blacksmith to the carpenter, all of them "maintained at the expense of the whole community" (478).

This led, he concludes, to a system with a division of labor that operated quite differently from that under modern capitalism:

> The whole mechanism reveals a systematic division of labor; but a division like that in manufacture is impossible, since the smith, the carpenter, etc. find themselves faced with an unchanging market. . . . The law that regulates the division of labor in the community acts with the irresistible authority of a law of nature, while each individual craftsman, the smith, the carpenter, and so on conducts in his workshop all the operations of his handicraft in the traditional way, but *independently, and without recognizing any authority*. (*Capital* I, 478–79; emphasis added)

Thus, the Indian village system was on one level extremely conservative and restrictive, but on another level, it offered a type of freedom lost to workers under capitalism: autonomy in the actual conduct of their work. This existed because there was as yet no separation of the workers from the objective conditions of production. In this sense, the Indian craft workers—and their medieval European counterparts—exercised an important right indeed, one at the heart of the notion of what is lost when labor becomes alienated.

Here again, it seems that Marx's focus had shifted somewhat from that of the 1850s. Then, as we saw in chapter 1, he had viewed the social structure of the Indian village through the lens of the "Oriental despotism" that it undergirded. Here in *Capital,* the Indian example was not only historical, but also showed different social relations than those under capitalism.[36] Thus, after a brief description of similar autonomous powers held by the precapitalist European guilds, Marx hit the reader between the eyes with a wrenching description of modern alienated labor, where capital "seizes labor-power by its roots. It converts the worker into a crippled monstrosity by furthering his particular skill . . . through the suppression of a whole world of productive drives and inclinations" (*Capital* I, 481). This situation grew out of the fact that, rather than the autonomy of the craft worker, there was now "the autonomy of the means of production, as capital, *vis-à-vis* the worker" (480).

The lengthy fifteenth chapter, "Machinery and Large-Scale Industry" provided the third and last analytical/historical level for the discussion of relative surplus value. Here, Marx placed the reader in modern capitalism (as of the early 1870s), with large-scale factories and complex technology. At one level, Marx argues against the commonsense view that machinery reduced toil, holding instead that it increased alienation by making work into a repetitive drudgery, that it "does away with the many-sided play of the muscles, and confiscates every atom of freedom, both in bodily and intellectual activity" (*Capital* I, 548).[37] By now the machine dominated the worker, as against the tool, which had been controlled by the human being who used it. Although this level of complex technology had not yet reached India, it nonetheless affected that country from afar. For in a globalized economy, the introduction of the power-loom in Britain displaced craft workers in India. Marx describes the effects of this process in heart-rending terms:

> World history offers no spectacle more frightful than the gradual extinction of the English hand-loom weavers; this tragedy dragged on for decades, finally coming to an end in 1838. Many of the workers died of starvation, many vegetated with their families for a long period on $2^{1/2}$d. a day. In India, on the other hand, the English cotton machinery produced an acute effect. The Governor General reported as follows in 1834–5: "The misery hardly finds a parallel in the history of commerce. The bones of the cotton-weavers are bleaching the plains of India." (557–58)

Here, as in his comparison in the 1850s of the conditions of Irish and Indian peasants, each under the domination of British capital, Marx was stressing not so much the differences as the commonalities of working people's experiences under globalized capitalism.

Marx gave more attention to colonialism and globalization in part eight of *Capital*, "Primitive Accumulation," where he took up the historical emergence of capitalism out of Western feudalism.[38] By the fifteenth century, he writes, serfdom had disappeared in all but name in England, leaving a mass of "free peasant proprietors, however much the feudal trappings might disguise their absolute ownership" (*Capital* I, 877). Over the next several centuries, these formally unfree but factually free peasants were transformed into formally free but factually unfree wage laborers. At the same time, he holds, wealth in the form of capital accumulated on a vast scale, in a process marked by considerable violence: "In actual history, it is a notorious fact that conquest, enslavement, robbery, murder, in short, force, play the greatest part" in these transformations (874). While he concentrated on the experiences of English peasants, colonialism and slavery formed an important subtext (and perhaps more), one he acknowledges at key junctures: "In fact the veiled [German: *verhüllte*; French: *dissimulé*] slavery of the wage-laborers in Europe needed the unqualified slavery of the New World as its pedestal" (925). In an oft-cited paragraph, he burns his indignation onto the page:

The discovery of gold and silver in America, the extirpation, enslavement and entombment in mines of the indigenous population of that continent, the beginnings of the conquest and plunder of India, and the conversion of Africa into a preserve for the commercial hunting of blackskins,[39] are all things which characterize the rosy dawn of the era of capitalist production. These idyllic proceedings are the *chief moments* [Hauptmomente] of primitive accumulation. Hard on their heels follows the commercial war of the European nations, which has the globe as it battlefield. It begins with the revolt of the Netherlands against Spain, assumes gigantic dimensions in England's anti-Jacobin War, and is still going on in the shape of the Opium Wars against China. (915; emphasis added)

By referring to events as recent as the Second Opium War of the late 1850s, Marx was making a connection between mercantile and industrial capitalism. Interestingly, he removed completely from the French edition the second sentence, with its Hegelian language about "moments," a term referring to elements of a totality. Was this an example of what Engels had protested, the removal of dialectical language from the French edition for reasons of popularization? Perhaps. It is also possible, however, that Marx removed this sentence for more substantive reasons, to avoid merging India and the Americas—and China as well—into a single totality in which all societies could be seen as necessarily following the same pathway. If so, this deletion was in the spirit of his other alterations for the French edition discussed earlier in this chapter.

Marx also addressed the issues of globalization and colonialism in a key paragraph from the French edition that was also passed over by Engels. This was in the long chapter "The General Law of Capitalist Accumulation," which preceded the section on primitive accumulation:

But only after mechanical industry had struck root so deeply that it exerted a preponderant influence on the whole of national production; only after foreign trade began to predominate over internal trade, thanks to mechanical industry; only after the world market had successively annexed extensive areas of the New World, Asia and Australia; and finally, only after a sufficient number of industrial nations had entered the arena—only after all this had happened can one date the repeated self-perpetuating cycles, whose successive phases embrace years, and always culminate in a general crisis, which is the end of one cycle and the starting-point of another. Until now the duration of these cycles has been ten or eleven years, but there is no reason to consider this duration as a constant. On the contrary, we ought to conclude, on the basis of the laws of capitalist production as we have just expounded them, that the duration is variable, and that the length of the cycles will gradually diminish. (*Capital* I, 786)[40]

Here the context was not the past but the future, especially concerning his crisis theory, but the term primitive accumulation was not used.

In his treatment of primitive accumulation, Marx turned his attention especially to Dutch and English colonialism, both of them connected to successful capitalist development and both of them claiming moral superiority over Spanish and Portuguese versions of colonialism. On the Dutch, he intones, here citing Raffles's *History of Java*:

> The history of Dutch colonial administration—and Holland was the model capitalist nation of the seventeenth century—"is one of the most extraordinary relations of treachery, bribery, massacre, and meanness." Nothing is more characteristic than their system of stealing people in Celebes, in order to get slaves for Java. People-stealers were trained for this purpose. The thief, the interpreter, and the seller were the chief agents in the trade; the native princes were the chief sellers. The young people thus stolen were hidden in secret dungeons on Celebes, until they were ready for sending to the slave-ships. . . . Wherever [the Dutch] set foot, devastation and depopulation followed. Banjuwangi, a province of Java, numbered over 80,000 inhabitants in 1750 and only 18,000 in 1811. That is peaceful commerce! (*Capital* I, 916)

As to the English, he emphasizes that the English East India Company both "plundered" India and organized the infamous international opium trade. Nor does he spare Massachusetts, whose antislavery stance he had so admired in his Civil War writings:

> In 1703, those sober exponents of Protestantism, the Puritans of New England, by decrees of their assembly set a premium of £40 on every Indian scalp and every captured redskin; in 1720, a premium of £100 was set for every scalp; in 1744, after Massachusetts Bay had proclaimed a certain tribe as rebels, the following prices were laid down: for a male scalp 12 years and upwards, £100 in new currency, for a male prisoner

£105, for women and children prisoners £50, for the scalps of women and children £50. (917–18)

Given such evidence, Marx did not even bother to address the issue of whether colonialism benefited the colonized. Moreover, he denies that colonialism bettered the lot of the working people of the Mother Country either: "Holland, which first brought the colonial system to its full development, already stood at the zenith of its commercial greatness by 1648," by which time its people "were more over-worked, poorer, and more brutally oppressed than those of all the rest of Europe put together" (*Capital* I, 918).

Did Marx believe that the main form of primitive accumulation—through uprooting peasant and guild-based production inside Europe—brought about overall social progress? Perhaps. But here in *Capital*, he gave even this thesis surprisingly little attention. In fact, in his nearly seventy pages on primitive accumulation, I have located a single brief acknowledgement of progress. In the long run, he writes, the accumulation of capital led to "the free development of the productive forces," instead of keeping the economy "within narrow limits" that would "decree universal mediocrity."[41] This de-emphasis on the positive effects of capitalist development is further suggestive of the extent to which Marx had by now modified the progressivism of *The Communist Manifesto*.

Marx addressed colonialism in a different way in a discussion of Ireland that formed the concluding section of "The General Law of Capitalist Accumulation." As a whole, this chapter took up what Marx called changes in the organic composition of capital, especially the tendency under advanced capitalism for the amount of capital tied up in machinery and other forms of "constant capital" to predominate over that given over to labor power or "variable capital." This led to high unemployment, even during periods of relative prosperity, as technology replaced labor. This tendency was closely related to capital's centralizing tendencies, toward forms of monopoly "whose limit would be reached only when the entire social capital was united in the hands of either a single capitalist or a single capitalist company" (*Capital* I, 779).[42] He analyzed these phenomena not only in industry, but also in agriculture, here including Ireland.

Considerably expanded for the French edition, with the new material this time included by Engels in the standard edition, the section on Ireland began with some stark population figures. Considering the years 1846 to 1866, Marx notes that "Ireland has lost more than 5/16 of its people in less than twenty years" (*Capital* I, 854). The decrease in population had not alleviated the country's grinding poverty, however, because of a radical modernization of agriculture beyond anything carried out in Britain itself:

> The Irish famine of 1846 killed more than 1,000,000 people, but it killed poor devils only. It did not do the slightest damage to the wealth of the country. The exodus of the next twenty years, an exodus which still continues to increase, did not, as for instance the Thirty Years' War did, decimate the means of production along with the human beings. The Irish genius discovered an altogether new way of spiriting a poor people thousands of miles away from the scene of its misery. The exiles transplanted to the United States send sums of money home every year as traveling expenses for those left behind. Every troop that emigrates one year draws another after it the next. . . . The absolute level of the population falls every year. (861–62)

He lays the blame for this terrible human toll squarely on the drive by capital to centralize production in fewer and fewer hands: "This fall was therefore solely due to the suppression of farms of less than 15 acres, in other words it was due to their centralization" (854). Marx paints an extremely bleak picture of a dependent economy that had been used up and nearly destroyed: "Ireland is at present merely an agricultural district of England which happens to be divided by a wide stretch of water from the country for which it provides corn, wool, cattle, and industrial and military recruits" (860). It was "her true destiny, to be an English sheep-walk and cattle pasture" (869).

As in his 1867 notes for a speech to the First International that were discussed in chapter 4, Marx touches as well on how ecological destruction accompanied this terrible human toll. The new form of capitalist agriculture lurched forward, he writes, "without even allowing its cultivators the means for replacing the constituents of the exhausted soil" (*Capital* I, 860).

During the same period, Ireland became somewhat more profitable for large-scale livestock production, since "with the throwing together of small-holdings and the change from arable to pasture land, a larger part of the total product was transformed into a surplus product," even though "there was a decrease in the total product" (*Capital* I, 860). As against the British experience, he writes, little industrialization took place here, as shown by the fact that the amount of capital "employed in industry and trade accumulated only slowly during the last two decades" (861). Except for a small linen industry, even the build-up of a proletarianized urban population did not lead to any significant industrial development.[43] In several pages based on an 1870

British government report added to the French edition, he examines the lot of the urban poor:

> The first act of the agricultural revolution was to sweep away the huts situated at the place of work. This was done on the largest scale, and as if in obedience to a command from on high. Thus many laborers were compelled to seek shelter in villages and towns. There they were thrown like refuse into garrets, holes, cellars and corners, in the worst slum districts. . . . The men are now obliged to seek work from the neighboring farmers, and are only hired by the day, and therefore under the most precarious form of wage. (866)

He noted that the veracity of this damning portrait was buttressed by the fact that it was based "on the testimony of the English, blinded as the latter are by nationalist prejudices" (865).

In this new material added for the French edition, Marx also pointed to the possibility of revolution: "In view of this, it is no wonder that, according to the unanimous testimony of the inspectors, a somber discontent runs through the ranks of this class, that they long for the return of the past, loathe the present, despair of the future, give themselves up 'to the evil influence of agitators,' and have only one fixed idea, to emigrate to America" (*Capital* I, 865). He concluded the discussion on Ireland by pointing to the growth of the Fenian movement, which he had supported (albeit critically) within the First International, as we saw in chapter 4. The emigration to America had another consequence for Britain as well, for it strengthened its emergent inter-capitalist rival, the United States. He foretells Britain's decline in the dialectical tones of tragic drama:

> Like all good things in the world, this profitable mode of proceeding has its drawbacks. The accumulation of the Irish in America keeps pace with the accumulation of rents in Ireland. The Irishman, banished by the sheep and the ox, re-appears on the other side of the ocean as a Fenian. And there a young but gigantic republic rises, more and more threateningly, to face the old queen of the waves. (870)

Thus, writing only a few years after the Civil War, he discerned the rise of a new economic power, based in no small part on Irish immigrant labor.

At several key junctures in *Capital*, Marx also addressed the Civil War and the larger questions of race, labor, and slavery. The first of these was in the

1867 preface, where he refers implicitly to the impact of the Civil War on the rise of the International: "Just as the in the eighteenth century the America[n] War of Independence sounded the tocsin for the European middle class, so in the nineteenth century the American Civil War did the same for the European working class" (*Capital* I, 91). He does so a second time in the same preface, as part of a discussion of how "within the ruling classes themselves," some were beginning to recognize the need for "a radical change in the existing relations between capital and labor." He refers in this context to the fight by radical Republicans like Ohio's Benjamin Wade for the break-up of the large slave plantations, in order to make grants of forty acres and a mule to each freed slave: "At the same time, on the other side of the Atlantic Ocean, Mr. Wade, Vice-President of the United States, has declared in public meetings that, after the abolition of slavery, a radical transformation in the existing relations of capital and landed property is on the agenda" (93).[44]

Marx gives the issues of race and class greater attention in "The Working Day," a chapter of nearly eighty pages that examines the lengthening of the working day that had accompanied the rise of capitalism, as well as the counterattack by organized labor, with a shorter working day its central demand:

> After capital had taken several centuries to extend the working day to its normal maximum limit, and then beyond this to the limit of the natural day of 12 hours, there followed, with the birth of large-scale industry in the last third of the nineteenth century, an avalanche of violent and unmeasured encroachments. Every boundary set by morality and nature, age and sex, day and night, was broken down. . . . Capital was celebrating its orgies. (*Capital* I, 389–90)

In this context, the rise of capitalism represented stark retrogression rather than progress for working people. In addition, he writes, where the liberal concept of human rights was formal and abstract, a shorter working day constituted a substantive achievement for working people: "In the place of the pompous catalogue of the 'inalienable rights of man' there steps the modest Magna Carta of the legally limited working day, which at last makes clear 'when the time which the worker sells is ended, and when his own begins'" (416). For if they were working eighteen-hour days, six or seven days a week, how indeed could workers exercise their civil rights in a meaningful way?[45]

Marx incorporated into this chapter some material on the working to death of slaves in the United States and Cuba from the "Economic Manuscript of 1861–63" (see p. 170, above). However, the vast majority of the text of

"The Working Day" cannot be found in the 1861–63 draft, for it was written sometime after Marx had finished that long early draft of *Capital*—probably not until 1866.[46] In comparing the finished book to the draft, Dunayevskaya argued that the Civil War and its impact on British labor was decisive, not only for the creation of this chapter, but also for the reorganization of the text of *Capital*, volume I, as a whole. In *Capital*, as opposed to the earlier drafts of his critique of political economy, Marx made the voices and struggles of working people present in theory in a new way, while also leaving aside the long debates with other theoreticians that comprised the part of the 1861–63 manuscript published only posthumously as *Theories of Surplus Value*.

Dunayevskaya holds that Marx's activity in the International alongside the very worker activists who had championed the Union cause in Britain, at great economic sacrifice to themselves, was crucial to his decision to add a chapter on the working day:

> He is breaking with the whole concept of theory as something intellec-
> tual, a dispute between theoreticians. Instead of keeping up a running
> argument with theorists, he goes directly into the labor process itself,
> and thence to the Working Day. He no sooner relegated the history of
> theory to the end of the whole work, and began to look at the history of
> production relations, than he of necessity created a new dialectic instead
> of applying one. . . . This new dialectic led him to meet, theoretically,
> the workers' resistance inside the factory and outside of it. The result is
> the new section of *Capital*, "The Working Day." Marx, the theoretician,
> created new categories out of the impulses from the workers. It wasn't
> he, however, who decided that the Civil War in the United States was
> a holy war of labor. It was the working class of England, the very ones
> who suffered the most, who decided that. ([1958] 2000, 91; see also Welsh
> 2002)

And it is those types of voices that come to prominence in "The Working Day."

In its beginning pages, Marx refers explicitly to "the voice of the worker" for the first time (*Capital* I, 342). The chapter has two warring protagonists: the impersonal, self-aggrandizing power of capital and the working class, especially the British workers, who sacrificed so much to oppose American slavery during the 1860s. After recounting the long and ultimately successful struggle by British labor in the 1840s for the ten-hour day, he concludes:

The establishment of a normal working day is therefore the product of a protracted and more or less concealed civil war between the capitalist class and the working class. Since the contest takes place in the arena of modern industry, it is fought out first of all in the homeland of that industry—England. The English factory workers were the champions, not only of the English working class, but of the modern working class in general, just as their theorists were the first to throw down the gauntlet to the theory of the capitalists. (412–13)

While he refers to the 1840s, a continuity with the 1860s—with the Civil War and the founding of the International in London—may also have been implied in the notion of the British working class as "champions . . . of the modern working class in general."

By 1866, the eight-hour day was on the agenda. As to the impact of the Civil War on labor inside the United States, Marx makes a dramatic assertion:

In the United States of America, every independent workers' movement was paralyzed as long as slavery disfigured a part of the republic. *Labor in a white skin cannot emancipate itself where it is branded in a black skin.* However, a new life immediately arose from the death of slavery. The first fruit of the American Civil War was the eight hours agitation, which ran from the Atlantic to the Pacific, from New England to California, with the seven-league boots of a locomotive. The General Congress of Labor held at Baltimore in August 1866 declared: "The first and great necessity of the present, to free the labor of this country from capitalistic slavery, is the passing of a law by which eight hours shall be the normal working day in all the states of the American Union. We are resolved to put forth all our strength until this glorious result is attained." (*Capital* I, 414; emphasis added)

This blunt assessment of the intractably negative effects of racism on the labor movement was a theme Marx had first developed in his Civil War writings. At the same time, he sees the struggle to overcome racism as a decisive factor in the creation of a strong labor movement in America.

CHAPTER SIX

Late Writings on Non-Western and Precapitalist Societies

After the defeat of the Paris Commune in 1871, Marx focused again on forms of resistance to capital outside Western Europe and North America.[1] Three strands in his writings illustrate this turn toward agrarian non-Western societies during his last decade, 1872–83. Taken as a whole, these indicate a new turn, part of a gradual evolution in Marx's thought since the late 1850s. The first of these strands is found in the changes he introduced to the French edition of *Capital*, as discussed in the previous chapter.

The second of these strands, to be discussed in the present chapter, can be found in the 1879–82 excerpt notebooks on non-Western and precapitalist societies, some of them still unpublished in any language, which extend to over three hundred thousand words.[2] These notes on studies by other authors, many of them anthropologists, cover a wide range of societies and historical periods, including Indian history and village culture; Dutch colonialism and the village economy in Indonesia; gender and kinship patterns among Native Americans and in ancient Greece, Rome, and Ireland; and communal and private property in Algeria and Latin America.[3]

A group of shorter but better-known texts on Russia from the years 1877 to 1882 form the third strand of Marx's late writings. He started to learn Russian in 1869; his interest in that society was increased further by the wide discussion generated by the 1872 Russian translation of *Capital*, volume I. In his correspondence with the Russian exile Vera Zasulich and elsewhere, Marx began to suggest that agrarian Russia's communal villages could be a starting point for a socialist transformation, one that might avoid the brutal process of the primitive accumulation of capital. His interest in the Russian rural commune as a locus of revolution was no theory of agrarian autarky, however; to achieve a successful socialism, Russia would need connections to Western technology and above all, reciprocal relations with the Western labor movement, he held.

Except for a brief preface to an 1882 Russian edition of *The Communist Manifesto*, coauthored with Engels, Marx never published any of the results of his new research on non-Western and precapitalist societies before his death at age sixty-four in 1883.

During his last decade, he published little, as illustrated by the fact that he did not complete volumes II and III of *Capital*, which Engels edited and published after Marx's death. Marx's best-known work from this period is the *Critique of the Gotha Program* (1875), also published posthumously. Many studies of Marx's life and thought have suggested that by 1879, he had lost the capacity for serious intellectual work. The great Marx editor, David Riazanov, who launched the first MEGA in the 1920s, expresses such an attitude when he writes that by that time, "any strenuous intellectual work was a menace to his overwrought brain," this due to his "shattered health": "After 1878 [the year Marx turned 60!] he was forced to give up all work on *Capital*," but "he was still able to make notes" (Riazanov [1927] 1973, 205–6). Riazanov was almost certainly referring to the notebooks under consideration in the present chapter, among other things. Moreover, in 1925, in a report on his preparations for the first MEGA, Riazanov characterizes these excerpt notebooks as examples of "inexcusable pedantry" (1925, 399).[4] The suggestion that Marx's multilingual explorations of gender and class across a wide variety of geographical locations, cultures, and historical periods were less intellectually serious than the critique of political economy surely smacks of Eurocentrism, if not sexism. The surviving Marx correspondence does not offer a clear-cut explanation of the relationship of these late writings to the unfinished *Capital*; however, a possibility not considered by Riazanov is that Marx intended to extend the geographic scope of his critique of political economy.

More recent discussions of Marx's late writings have challenged the notion that his last years were marked by intellectual decline, although it remains the dominant one.[5] In 1972, Lawrence Krader published a careful transcription entitled *The Ethnological Notebooks of Karl Marx*.[6] This pathbreaking multilingual volume, which contained several hundred pages from Marx's notebooks from 1880 to 1882, made the extent and depth of these notebooks on non-Western and precapitalist societies, which were not included in Marx's *Collected Works* in English or German, evident for the first time. Krader published Marx's notes on anthropological works by Lewis Henry Morgan on Native Americans and ancient Greece and Rome, Henry Sumner Maine on social relations in ancient Ireland, John Budd Phear on village India, and John Lubbock on a number of preliterate societies.[7] Krader's edition of *The Ethnological Notebooks* contains only about half of Marx's 1879–82 notes on non-Western and precapitalist societies, however. The remainder, some of it not yet published in any language, concerns Marx's notes on the Russian anthropologist Maxim Kovalevsky's study of communal property in the Americas, India, and Algeria; on Indian history based on a book by the colonial civil servant Robert Sewell; on the writings of the German social historians Karl Bücher, Ludwig Friedländer, Ludwig Lange, Rudolf Jhering, and Rudolf Sohm on class, status, and gender in Rome and medieval Europe; on the British barrister J. W. B. Money's study of Indonesia (Java); on new works in physical anthropology and paleontology; on Russian-language studies of rural Russia; and finally, on Britain's moves into Egypt in the 1880s. Including those previously published by Krader, these notes would total over eight hundred printed pages.[8]

In his analysis of these notebooks, Krader (1974, 1975) stressed their relationship to Marx's earlier work on the Asiatic mode of production and their contribution to anthropological thought. The German historian Hans-Peter Harstick, who published Marx's 1879 notes on Kovalevsky's book on communal property, saw these notebooks as more of a new departure: "Marx's gaze turned from the European scene . . . toward Asia, Latin America, and North Africa" (1977, 2). Dunayevskaya ([1982] 1991, 1985) emphasized their focus on gender and the differences between Marx's notes on Morgan and what Engels developed from them in his *The Origin of the Family, Private Property, and the State* (1884).[9] Dunayevskaya's work, which attracted the attention of the feminist poet Adrienne Rich ([1991] 2001), first brought *The Ethnological Notebooks* to the attention of a wider public.

Written in an unpolished, sometimes ungrammatical mixture of English, German, and other languages, these are not draft manuscripts, but working notebooks in which Marx recorded or summarized passages from books he was studying. However, they are far more than summaries of other authors. As Dunayevskaya suggests, these notebooks "let us hear Marx think" (2002, 294). First, they show Marx as a "reader." Not only do they contain his direct or indirect critique of the assumptions or conclusions of the authors he is studying, but they also show how he connected or took apart themes and issues in the texts he was reading. Second, they indicate which themes and data he found compelling in connection with these studies of non-Western and precapitalist societies. In short, they offer a unique window into Marx's thinking at a time when he seemed to be moving in new directions.

GENDER AND SOCIAL HIERARCHY AMONG THE IROQUOIS, THE HOMERIC GREEKS, AND OTHER PRELITERATE SOCIETIES

Because Engels based *The Origin of the Family, Private Property, and the State* on them, Marx's excerpt notes on Lewis Henry Morgan's *Ancient Society* (1877) are the best known of his 1879–82 notebooks on non-Western and precapitalist societies, at least indirectly. In his pioneering book, Engels made an unusually strong argument for gender equality, challenging the prejudices not only of mainstream public opinion but also of socialist discourse, where some figures like Proudhon had expressed an untrammeled hostility to women's rights. Moreover, Engels offered an alternative to liberal feminism, since he tied women's subordination to the economic sphere, arguing that women's emancipation could not be fully achieved as long as class domination persisted. At the same time, as will be argued below, Engels's book was burdened with a deterministic framework that did not do justice to the subtlety of Marx's notes on Morgan.

In his celebrated book, Engels sees the American anthropologist Morgan as virtually a materialist in the Marxian sense, someone who "rediscovered in America, in his own way, the materialist conception of history that had been discovered by Marx forty years ago" and who "was led by this conception to the same conclusions, in the main points, as Marx."[10] Moreover, Engels writes, but without providing any evidence, that Marx "had planned to present the results of Morgan's researches" in published form (MECW 26, 131).

After surveying a number of preliterate, stateless societies as analyzed by Morgan—from the Iroquois to the early Greeks, Romans, and Germans—Engels argues that the state was a new and transitory human institution: "The state, then, has not existed from eternity. There have been societies that managed without it, that had no idea of the state and state authority" (MECW 26, 272). The gens, or clan—the non-state organizational form that Morgan had found across a wide range of preliterate cultures—structured these societies. (Marx, Engels, and Morgan all used the Roman-based terms "gentes," "gens," and "gentile" instead of "clan," the common usage of today.) Looking forward to the stateless and socialist society that he saw on the horizon, Engels concludes *The Origin of the Family* by citing Morgan's prediction of "a revival, in a higher form, of the liberty, equality and fraternity of the ancient gentes" (MECW 26, 276, Morgan 1877, 552). Striking an almost Rousseauian note, Engels maintains that the new data of anthropology had conclusively proved, when one took account of the whole period of human existence, that what was called civilization, with its hierarchies of class, property, and gender, was an atypical—and it was implied, unnatural—way of ordering human affairs. Unlike Rousseau, however, and this to his credit, Engels placed gender equality at the center of his concerns.

Engels maintains that these early egalitarian societies were "doomed to extinction" because of their low level of economic and technological development (MECW 26, 203). Sooner or later, new institutions like private property, social classes, the state, and the patriarchal family overwhelmed them. Striking a Hegelian chord concerning gender, Engels concludes that the rise of these new hierarchies marked "the world-historic defeat of the female sex," wherein women's participation in political decision-making died out, as did matrilineal forms of descent (165). Since private property, the state, and patriarchy formed a totality, Engels argues that they could likewise be overcome only by a total socialist transformation. Overall, Engels was making an economic determinist argument, according to which the development of the capitalist economy, combined with a strong workers' movement toward socialism, would reverse the world-historic defeat of the female sex, this in quasi-automatic fashion.

The Origin of the Family has come to be seen as the classic Marxist statement on gender and the family. By the mid-twentieth century, however, some feminist thinkers began to critique the book's economic determinism, which they usually linked to Marx as well. For example, the existentialist feminist Simone de Beauvoir holds, against Engels, that it is "not clear that the institution of private property must necessarily have involved the enslavement of women" ([1949] 1989, 56). As a result, the error of Engels lay in how "he tried to reduce the antagonism of the sexes to class conflict" (56, 58). But this critique of Engels, powerful as it was, also exhibited some weaknesses. For as many of its critics rooted in Marxism or structuralism have held, existentialism gives too much weight to individual subjectivity and choice, as against economic and social conditions (Marcuse [1948] 1972, Dunayevskaya [1973] 1989, Bourdieu 1977).

The publication in 1972 of Marx's notes on Morgan in Krader's *Ethnological Notebooks* created new ground for what was by then an old debate.[11] To be sure, Engels had utilized Marx's excerpts and comments on Morgan, and, as he maintains in his introduction to *The Origin of the Family*, he worked to "reproduce" those "critical notes" in his own book (MECW 26, 131). But until *The Ethnological Notebooks* first appeared, few were aware of just how comprehensive Marx's notes on Morgan had been, roughly equal in length to Engels's book. By the simple act of publishing Marx's Morgan notes alongside those on other anthropologists, whose work took up a number of non-Western societies, especially India, Krader pointed to something Engels had not taken up at all in his book: the possibility that Marx's 1880–82 notebooks were concerned not so much with the origins of social hierarchy in the distant past, as with the social relations within contemporary societies under the impact of capitalist globalization.

In his notes, Marx seemed to accept Morgan's clan-centered approach, especially the notion that the clan long preceded the family. Moreover, he seemed to agree that the family, as it developed out of the breakdown of the clan system, contained multiple forms of domination, as in Rome. In a brief remark also quoted by Engels, Marx sketches this: "The modern family contains in embryo not only *servitus* (slavery) but also *serfdom*, since from the outset it refers to *services for* agriculture. It contains within itself in miniature all the antagonisms that later develop widely in society and its state" (Marx [1880–82] 1974, 120; see also Engels in MECW 26, 166).[12]

To an extent, Marx also connected Morgan's clan-centered approach to his own materialist one. Additionally, he seemed in basic accord with Morgan's thesis concerning the relative gender equality of early clan societies. However, where Morgan and Engels focused solely on the breakdown of clan society as the source of male domination, of class society, and of the state, Marx's notebooks show a more nuanced, dialectical approach that resists such schema. To be sure, Marx seems to appreciate Morgan's view of the remarkable degree of power held by women in Iroquois society, as in the following passage he records in his notes:

> Rev. *Asher Wright*, many years a *missionary among the Senecas*, wrote to Morgan in 1873 on them: ". . . . *The women were the great power among the clans, as everywhere else.* They did not hesitate, when occasion required, *'to knock off the horns,'* as it was technically called, from the head of a chief, and send him back to the ranks of the warriors. *The original nomination of the chiefs also always rested with them.*" (Marx [1880–82] 1974, 116; original emphasis)[13]

Marx does not leave it at that, however. As Dunayevskaya asserts, Marx, unlike Engels, saw "limitations" to the type of freedom enjoyed by women in these clan societies ([1982] 1991, 182). She singles out the following passage Marx recorded from Morgan, again on the Iroquois, where women are seen to have speaking but not decision-making rights: "The *women allowed to express their wishes and opinions through an orator of their own election. Decision* given by the [male] Council" (Marx [1880–82] 1974, 162 [original emphasis]; see also Morgan 1877, 117).

Marx took up yet another core insight of Morgan, the reconceptualization of early Greco-Roman society through the lens of Iroquois clan society. The following selection, mainly a passage from Morgan on male domination in classical Greece, contains two bracketed sentences by Marx, who poses male domination there as a contradictory phenomenon, containing at least some hints of resistance:

> From beginning to end under the Greeks a principle of studied selfishness among the males, tending to lessen the appreciation of women, *scarcely found among savages*. The usages of centuries stamped upon the minds of Grecian women a sense of their inferiority. [[But the relationship to the *goddesses on Olympus* shows remembering and reflection back to an earlier, freer and more powerful position for women. Juno craving for domination, the goddess of wisdom springs from the head of Zeus, etc.]][14]. . . . The Greeks remained *barbarians* in their treatment of the female sex at the height of their civilization; their education superficial, intercourse with the opposite sex denied them, their inferiority inculcated as a principle upon them, until it *came to be accepted as a fact by the women themselves*. The wife not companion equal to her husband, *but in the relation of a daughter*. (Marx [1880–82] 1974, 121; original emphasis)[15]

As against the utterly bleak portrait of male domination in Greece in Engels and Morgan, Marx's bracketed insert makes the passage more dialectical, suggesting that Greek gender ideology was riven with deep fault lines.

Immediately following this, Marx incorporates into his notes a long passage from Morgan concerning the relatively freer position of Roman women:

> *Materfamilias* was mistress of the family; went into the streets freely without restraint from her husband, frequented with the men the theaters and festive banquets; in the house not confined to particular apartments, nor excluded from the table of the men. Roman females thus more personal dignity and independence than Greek; but *marriage* gave them *into power of the husband*; was = daughter of the husband; he had the power of correction and of life and death in case of adultery (with concurrence of the council of her gens) (Marx [1880–82] 1974, 121; original emphasis)[16]

Here and above, Marx's notes seemed to run in a different direction from Engels's formulation of a "world-historic defeat of the female sex" at the time clan society died out and was replaced by class society and state forms. Not only did Greek goddesses offer an alternative perspective within the patriarchal order, but in the later Roman society, women's position also improved somewhat, albeit with many severe restrictions remaining.[17]

Again differing somewhat from Morgan and Engels, Marx focuses upon indications of stratified hierarchy within early clan society. As Morgan interpreted the traditional accounts, the legendary early Athenian ruler Theseus had tried to undermine the egalitarianism of the clan system, this during a period long before its collapse. Morgan suggested that Theseus had attempted to set up a class system, but this had failed due to the lack of a social base within the clan society of that era. As a result, he writes, there was "in fact no transfer of power from the gentes" under Theseus (Morgan 1877, 260). Marx disagrees with Morgan on this point, viewing the early clan structures themselves as a source for the growth of social inequality:

> The statement of Plutarch, that "the *lowly and poor eagerly followed the summons of Theseus*" and the statement of *Aristotle* quoted by him, that Theseus "*was predisposed toward the people*" seem however, in spite of Morgan, to imply that the *chiefs of the gentes* etc. because of wealth etc. already engaged in *conflict of interests* with the *mass of the gentes*. (Marx [1880–82] 1974, 210; original emphasis)

Dunayevskaya sees Marx's remark on Theseus as suggesting the possibility of a nonclass form of social stratification, caste:

> Marx demonstrates that, long before the dissolution of the primitive commune, there emerged the question of ranks within the egalitarian commune. It was the beginning of the transformation into opposite— gens into caste. That is to say, within the egalitarian communal form arose the elements of its opposite—caste, aristocracy, different material interests. (1985, 214)

This is in keeping with how Marx singles out caste at another point in his notes on Morgan:

> In the situation where conquest would be added onto the gentile principle, could the gentes little by little give occasion for caste formation? . . . . As soon as *difference of rank* stands *between consanguinity of gentes*, this comes into conflict with the *gentile principle* and can rigidify the *gens* into its opposite, *caste*. (Marx [1880–82] 1974, 183; original emphasis)

Engels, who concentrated on the rise of *private* property, missed the possibility that *collectivist* forms of domination that minimized private property could also create very pronounced social hierarchies.

Had Engels taken up Morgan's chapter on the Aztecs,[18] as Marx did at some length, these distinctions might have become clearer to him. Then Engels might not have written with such assurance of Native American clan societies with "no room . . . as a rule, for the subjugation of alien tribes" (MECW 26, 203). For the Aztec confederacy was a collectivist clan society, one that Morgan termed a "military democracy," which nonetheless ruled over numerous subordinate tribes (1877, 188).

Marx continued to look at matrilineal societies in his notes on the Darwinist John Lubbock's *The Origin of Civilization and the Primitive Condition of Man* (1870). He treated Lubbock with scorn throughout these brief notes from late 1882. At several points, he mocks Lubbock's patriarchal prejudices, as in the bracketed and parenthetical comments interspersed within the following passage on Africa:

"Among many of the lower races *relationship through females is the prevalent custom*," hence "the curious (!) practice that *a man's heirs* [[but they were not then the *man's heirs*, these civilized jackasses cannot get free of their own conventionalities]] are not his own, but his *sister's children*." (105)[19] "Thus when a rich man dies in Guinea, his property, excepting the armor, descended to the *sister's son*." (Marx [1880–82] 1974, 340; Marx's emphasis)

At another point, Marx refers in parenthetical remarks to an Australian Aborigine as "the intelligent black," this in contrast to an ethnocentric anthropologist cited approvingly by Lubbock:

The *belief* in the *soul* (not identical with ghosts), *in an universal, independent and endless existence* is *confined* to the *highest* (?) *races of mankind*. The Reverend Lang in his *The Aborigines of Australia* had a friend, which friend "tried long and patiently to make a very intelligent Australian *understand* (should be called make him believe) *his existence without a body*, but the black never would keep his countenance . . . for a long time he could not believe ("he" is the intelligent black) that the "gentleman" (i.e. Reverend Lang's silly friend) *was serious*, and when he did realize it (that the gentleman was an ass in good earnest), the more serious the teacher was the more ludicrous the whole affair appeared to be." (245, 246) (Without realizing it Lubbock makes a fool of himself.) (Marx [1880–82] 1974, 349; Marx's emphasis)

He does not confine such strictures to the superficial Lubbock, however.

Marx sounds similar chords in his lengthier notes on the distinguished jurist Henry Sumner Maine's *Early History of Institutions* (1875), where he frequently chides the English scholar for his patriarchal, colonialist, and ethnocentric assumptions. As the American social theorist David Norman Smith (forthcoming) notes: "Of all Marx's writings on ethnological subjects," these "are the richest in criticism." Most of Maine's book concerned the communal social forms and the customary law of ancient Ireland, based upon the recently published Brehon laws, especially the *Senchus Mor* and the *Book of Aicill*. Maine frequently compared Irish customary law to similar legal institutions in India, where he served as a high-ranking colonial official during the 1860s.

In his first chapter, Maine argues that "the collective ownership of the soil," once widespread in Western Europe, was still a major factor in many other parts of the world (1875, 1). He refers specifically to the contemporary Slavic peoples of Eastern Europe and to India, this with some foreboding: "It is one of the facts with which the Western world will some day assuredly have to reckon, that the political ideas of so large a portion of the human race, and its ideas of property also, are inextricably bound up with the notions of family interdependency, of collective ownership, and of natural subjection to patriarchal power" (2–3). Maine attributes non-Western backwardness to the persistence of these forms. Krader holds that Maine believed "that the English could transmit the advanced form of property in land and of the State to Ireland and India" and in this regard, "Maine offered his historical jurisprudence to the service of empire" (Krader 1975, 263). While Marx was to hammer Maine repeatedly for assuming the patriarchal family as the oldest and most basic form of social organization,[20] the two writers were in agreement on one fundamental point: communal social forms in Russia and Asia represented an obstacle and a challenge to bourgeois property relations.

In taking issue with Maine's assumption that the patriarchal family came first historically, Marx writes: "Herr Maine as a blockheaded Englishman does not start with the gens, but rather with the patriarch, who becomes the Chief, etc. Height of silliness" (Marx [1880–82] 1974, 292). Marx attacks the related notion that the substantial power of women in ancient Ireland was due to later influences, like Christianity: "This Maine takes for Church influence, although it arises everywhere in the higher state of savagery, for example among Red

Indians" (288). Marx referred as well to Morgan's superior insight concerning early non-patriarchal forms.

A second element of the discussion of gender concerned *sati* and women's inheritance rights in India. Again, Marx attacked the way in which Maine, still positing the patriarchal family as the original form, sometimes explained marital property held by the wife as an innovation. Marx views this instead as the vestige of an earlier, matrilineal social order marked by "descent within the clan along the female line" (Marx [1880–82] 1974, 325). He holds the Brahmins and their treatises on law responsible for the shift.

Concerning *sati* and female inheritance, Marx brings into his notes material from Thomas Strange's *Elements of Hindu Law* (1835), which he finds more illuminating than Maine:

> The beastliness of the Brahmins reaches its height in the "*Suttee*" [*sati*] or *widow burning. Strange* considers this practice to be a "*malus usus,*"[21] not "law," since in the *Manu* and other high authorities there is no mention of it. . . . The matter is clear: the *suttee* is simply *religious murder*, in part to bring the inheritance into the hands of the (spiritual) Brahmins for the religious ceremonies for the deceased husband and in part through Brahmin legislation to transfer the inheritance of the widow to the closest in the gens, the nearer family of the *husband.* . . . Although *suttee* an innovation introduced by the Brahmins, in the Brahmin mind this *innovation* was conceived as a survival from the older barbarians (who had buried a man with his possessions)! Let it rest. (Marx [1880–82] 1974, 325–27; original emphasis)

Moreover, Marx saw all of this not in terms of Indian alterity, but in connection to Western societies, as he delved into the medieval Catholic Church's appropriation of property, albeit in a different manner than the Brahmins. He remarks that while it curtailed other rights of women, "in relation to 'proprietary right,' the wily Church certainly had an interest in securing the rights of women (the opposite interest from the Brahmins!)." This was because it wanted women to donate property (327).

Marx, like Maine, was interested in how the ancient Irish clan structures began to be transformed into a new class society, and on these issues, he occasionally expressed some affinity to Maine. He incorporated into his notes much of Maine's discussion of the breakdown of the clans in Ireland. Here again, Marx singled out the role of the pre-Christian clergy in these transformations. He also followed closely Maine's discussion of the accumulation of livestock, especially cattle, as crucial to the process class differentiation.

The transformation of the ancient clan structures into a class system eventually led to the formation of states, a topic that led to another attack by Marx on Maine. Referring to Thomas Hobbes, Jeremy Bentham, and John Austin, Maine writes that the state was predicated upon "the possession of irresistible force, not necessarily exerted but capable of being exerted" (Marx [1880–82] 1974, 328; Maine 1875, 350). Marx attacks this version of commandism, writing that "where States exist (after the primitive communities, etc.), i.e. politically organized society, the state in no way is the prince; it just seems so" (329). Instead, Marx points to the changes in the economic base as the source of the rise of the state, this in one of his longest remarks in these notebooks. One particular problem for Marx at this point is Maine's notion of the "moral," as separate from the economic base: "This 'moral' shows how little Maine understands the matter. So far as these influences (*economical* before everything else) do have a '*moral*' mode of existence, this mode is always a secondary, derived mode, never the primary one" (329; Marx's emphasis). A second problem for Marx was that the English jurist's analytical construct of state power sought to abstract out history. For example, Maine writes, in a passage not incorporated by Marx, that his "theory of sovereignty" made it possible to "class together the coercive authority of the great King of Persia, of the Athenian Demos, of the later Roman Emperors, of the Russian Czar, and of the Crown and Parliament of Great Britain" (Maine 1875, 360).[22] To Marx, such notions were ahistorical and abstract, merging together uncritically institutions from quite different modes of production.

But the biggest problem for Marx concerned Maine's Austin-derived commandist theory. I quote this passage extensively, for it reveals some late developments in Marx's theory of the state, on the basis of his anthropological studies:

> Maine ignores the much deeper aspect: that the seemingly supreme independent existence of the *state* itself is only an *illusion*, since the state in all its forms in only an excrescence of society. Just as the state only *appears* at a certain stage of social development, the state will also disappear when society reaches a stage of development that until now it has not reached. First the separation of individuality from the shackles of the group—this means the one-sided development of *individuality*. These *shackles* were originally *not despotic* (as blockhead Maine understands it)

but *comprised the social bonds of the group*, the primitive community. But the true nature of the latter can only be understood if we analyze its content—in the "last" analysis, *interests*. We find then, that these interests are common to certain social groups. They are *class interests*, which in the last analysis have *economic relations* as their basis. The state is built upon these as its basis and the existence of the state presupposes the existence of class interests ... fundamental error ... that *political superiority*, whatever its peculiar shape, and whatever the ensemble of its elements, is taken as something standing over society, resting solely upon itself. ... For example, *better armaments* depend directly on *improvements in the means of production*—these coincide directly, e.g. in hunting and fishing, with the *means of destruction*, means of war. ... A good example is the half-crazy Ivan IV.[23] While he was angry at the boyars and also at the Moscow rabble, he sought, and indeed had to, to present himself as the *representative* of *peasant interests*. (Marx [1880–82] 1974, 329–30; original emphasis)

Probably the most notable new feature above was the way Marx brought in the material from Morgan and Maine on clan societies in order to update his state theory, which remained rooted in notions of economic interest.

As we have seen, Marx's frequent attacks on Maine sometimes masked areas where he appropriated, albeit critically, some of the British jurist's data and arguments. These concerned especially (1) the rise of class differentiation within the Irish clan and (2) the rejection of the category of "feudalism" as a generic term for premodern agrarian societies. However, for the most part he portrays Maine as an ideologue defending capital and empire, rather than a real scholar.

INDIA'S COMMUNAL SOCIAL FORMS UNDER THE IMPACT OF MUSLIM AND EUROPEAN CONQUEST

Although his notes on Maine contained some discussion of India, in major parts of the 1879–82 excerpt notebooks, Marx concentrated entirely on that society. This can be seen in his lengthy notes on the young anthropologist Maxim Kovalevsky's *Communal Landownership: The Causes, Course, and Consequences of Its Decline*, published in Russian in 1879, most of which is devoted to India. It can also be seen in his equally lengthy notes on the young historian Robert Sewell's *Analytical History of India* (1870), and in those on ethnologist John Budd Phear's *The Aryan Village in India and Ceylon*

(1880). Marx's notes on the Indian subcontinent from this period comprise nearly ninety thousand words. As against the notes on Morgan, Lubbock, and Maine, however, Marx made far fewer remarks in his own voice in these India notes.

Writing mainly in German, but with some passages in Russian, Marx appears to have excerpted Kovalevsky's book on communal property in the fall of 1879, a year or two before his notes on Morgan, Maine, and Lubbock. In a letter of September 19, 1879 to Nikolai Danielson, one of the translators of *Capital* into Russian, Marx refers to the young Kovalevsky as "one of my 'scientific friends'" (MECW 45, 409). It was Kovalevsky, who saw Marx in London fairly frequently during this period, who provided him with a copy of Morgan's *Ancient Society* (Krader 1974, White 1996).[24]

In the parts of his notes on Kovalevsky dealing with India, Marx examined social relations, especially in terms of communal property, across the entirety of Indian history, covering (1) the period before the Muslim conquests, (2) that of Muslim domination, and (3) that of British colonialism. At the beginning of these excerpts, he quotes Kovalevsky to the effect that "no country" besides India has experienced so much "variety in the forms of land relations" (Marx [1879] 1975, 346).[25]

In the first part, Marx closely follows Kovalevsky's historical typology of communal forms in rural India, which consisted of three stages: (1) clan-based communities owning and tilling the land in common; (2) more differentiated village communities, where kinship did not bind together the entire village but where land was allotted to some extent on the basis of kinship; (3) village communities not organized around kinship and that periodically redivided the common land on an equal basis, the latter "a relatively late form in the history of Indian forms of landed property" (Marx [1879] 1975, 351). Somewhat later, Marx remarks that even such "individual shares of land" within a communal village "are not private property!" (362).

Given this focus on broad changes in India's communal forms, it would appear that Hindu India was for Marx no longer an "unchanging" society without any real history, as in 1853 (MECW 12, 217). Inserting his own remarks (which I have italicized) into a quote from Kovalevsky, Marx writes of social antagonisms within the early Indian village, of "the danger that threatens the system of shares determined by degree of kinship from the more distant descendants and the newly arrived settlers, inasmuch as *this antagonism indeed leads ultimately to the system* of periodic redistribution of the communal land in equal shares" (Marx [1879] 1975, 357). Thus for Marx, more than Kovalevsky, the contradiction between the older system of clan or kinship and that of equality within the broader-based communal village was the major force behind the social changes in the early Indian village.

At another level, Marx seems to have concluded that the evolution of Hindu law from the early Code of Manu onwards also facilitated the breakdown of communal property as such. This, he emphasizes, came through bequests and gifts to religious bodies, as seen in the passage below, where the parts inserted by Marx into his quotes from Kovalevsky are again italicized:

> The priestly *pack* thus plays a *central* role in the process of individualization of family property. (113). The chief sign of undivided family property is its inalienability. In order to get at this property, the legislation, which is developed under Brahmin influence, must attack this *bastion* more and more. . . . [[*Alienation by gifts everywhere the priestly hobbyhorse!*]]. . . . *Among other peoples as well, for instance in the Germanic-Roman world (vide Merovingians, Carolingians) the same rank order is also found— gifts to the priest first, preceding every other mode of alienation of immovable property.* (Marx [1879] 1975, 366–67)

In the last sentence above, Marx is again emphasizing parallels of Indian history with that of other cultures, in this instance to early medieval Europe, as against notions of Indian alterity.

While Marx seems to share much of Kovalevsky's argument concerning India's communal property, on occasion he takes issue with the young ethnologist's assumptions. For example, in response to Kovalevsky's statement that the rise of communal property in land formed the basis of "common exploitation of the soil by the members of the clans," Marx writes that cooperation, "made necessary by the conditions of the hunt, etc.," came about even before settled agriculture among "nomadic and even savage peoples" (Marx [1879] 1975, 356–57). As the Marxist humanist philosopher Peter Hudis notes, Marx rejects "Kovalevsky's identification of communal social relations with communal property forms" (2004, 63). Here again, as in the *Grundrisse*, Marx saw communal forms of production as historically prior to and more fundamental than communal property.

The second part of Marx's notes on Kovalevsky on India, which deals with the impact of Muslim rule on these earlier social relationships, calls forth one of his most explicit attacks on the notion that precolonial India was feudal. Muslim conquerors introduced the *iqta*, a form of benefice in which military leaders received land, or the income from land, in return for further military service. As against Western feudalism's fiefs, however, *iqtas* were not normally hereditary. There were also severe limits on how much land could be handed over as *iqtas*, and in most cases the Hindu subjects retained possession of their land. In an extended comment, Marx expresses exasperation over his friend Kovalevsky's interpretation of these relations as feudal:

> Because "benefices," "*farming out of offices*" [[but this is not at all *feudal*, as Rome attests]] and *commendation*[26] are found in India, Kovalevsky here finds feudalism in the Western European sense. *Kovalevsky forgets*, among other things, *serfdom*, which is not in India, and which is an essential moment. [[In regard to the *individual role of defense*, however (cf. *Palgrave*), not only of the unfree, but also the free peasants by the feudal lords (who play a role as *wardens*), this plays a limited role in India, except for the wakuf[27]]] [[of the *poetry of the soil* which the Romanic-Germanic feudalism had as its own (see Maurer), as little is found in India as in Rome. The *soil* is nowhere *noble* in India, so that it might not be alienable to commoners!]] (Marx [1879] 1975, 383; original emphasis)

This passage underlines Marx's adamant opposition to the view, sometimes held up as Marxist orthodoxy, that precapitalist class societies were uniformly "feudal." Not only was he keeping away from such notions, as he had in the *Grundrisse* two decades earlier, but he was also explicitly attacking those who maintained the "feudal" interpretation. As Harstick writes concerning this passage: "Marx argues for a differentiated examination of Asian and European history and he aims his argument . . . above all against simply carrying over concepts of social structure drawn from the Western European model into Indian or Asian social relations" (1977, 13).

Despite their differences, Marx's friend Kovalevsky—here unlike Lubbock, Maine, and Sewell, but like Morgan—also admired communal property and clan societies. In addition, the young Russian ethnologist shared much of Marx's hostility toward colonialism, here unlike even Morgan, who was silent on the matter.[28] This became clear in the third section of Marx's notes on Kovalevsky on India, which focuses on the period of British colonialism up through the 1857–58 Sepoy Uprising. Marx begins with a detailed treatment of Cornwallis's "permanent settlement" of 1793, which made the *zemindars*, formerly hereditary tax farmers for the Mughal Empire, into landlords. The *zemindars* therefore gained unrestricted capitalist-style ownership over the areas they had formerly only taxed, including the right to evict those who were now their tenants, the *ryots*, and the right to pass down these new acquisitions to their heirs. As he incorporates some excerpts from Sewell's aforementioned *Analytical*

History of India directly into his notes on Kovalevsky, Marx adds phrases such as "the scoundrel" to describe Cornwallis (Marx [1879] 1975, 385; Sewell 1870, 153). According to Sewell, one of the latter's opponents "spoke strenuously in Council [of the East India Company] against the wholesale destruction of Indian customs," a statement Marx incorporates into his notes (Marx [1879] 1975, 385; Sewell 1870, 153). But he does not incorporate Sewell's condescending description of "humbled and spiritless Hindus" accepting these changes passively (Sewell 1870, 153). Calling the British colonialists "dogs," "asses," "oxen," "blockheads," and the like, Marx describes a "general hatred of the English government" ([1879] 1975, 390–92, passim). As in 1853, he also links the situation of the *ryot* to that of the Irish peasant: "England and Ireland combined. Beautiful!" (Marx [1879] 1975, 390).

Kovalevsky discerned the continuation of communal forms in the villages, underneath the new capitalist structure. Marx records the following on this issue, inserting the italicized passage about social "atoms":

Under this system, the government has nothing to do with the totality of the communal possessors of a given village, but with hereditary users of individual parcels, whose rights cease by not paying tax punctually. Yet *between these atoms certain connections continue to exist*, distantly reminiscent of the earlier communal village landowning groups. (Marx [1879] 1975, 388; original emphasis)

This extremely important passage suggests a link between Marx's notes on India and his 1877–82 writings on Russia, discussed below. If these communal "connections" endured in India, might they not also, as in Russia, serve as points of resistance to capital?

Near the end of this discussion of the impact of British colonial rule on the communal village, Marx makes a swipe at Maine, whom he accuses of bias:

The English Indian officials and the publicists supported upon these, as *Sir H. Maine*, etc., describe the decline of common property in the Punjab as the mere result,—in spite of the loving English treatment of the archaic form,—of *economic progress*, whereas they themselves are the *chief bearers* (active) of the same—to their own danger. (Marx [1879] 1975, 394; original emphasis)

In this very interesting passage, Marx certainly shows hostility to colonialism and capitalism, and a degree of sympathy for communal social forms. But with the phrase "to their own danger," he also suggests that it was not so much the preservation of these forms as their forceful breakup in the name of "economic progress" that could unleash new social forces dangerous to British rule. The older communal forms may not have been revolutionary in and of themselves, but they could become a "danger" to the social order as they collided with capitalist modernity.

Marx probably made his sixteen thousand–word notes on Phear's *The Aryan Village in India and Ceylon* in 1881, the year after it was published.[29] Phear had served as a colonial judge in India and Ceylon (now Sri Lanka) during the 1860s and 1870s, and his book is a detailed description of village life in Bengal and Ceylon. Although Marx mainly records Phear's data, his occasional comments are illuminating. Phear expresses some sympathy for the plight of impoverished Indian villagers, but without sharing Marx's view of this as part of a stark economic polarization in which the local dominant classes and the British colonialists became rich at the villagers' expense. This is shown in a parenthetical remark Marx inserts into one of Phear's sentences: "Extreme poverty of by far the largest portion, i.e. the bulk of the population of Bengal (the richest part of India!)" (Marx [1880–82] 1974, 249).

At one point, Marx records a passage from Phear on conflicts between the *ryots* and the *zemindars*, referring also to the *mandal*, the elected village head:

> *Affray of the Zamindar's people on the Mandal* (headman of the village). . . . *The new Zamindar takes measures for enhancing rents of his ryots*; was successful at obtaining . . . increased rates from several ryots, but the *mandal of the village*, whose example most influential, sturdily held out and led the opposition. Against him the zamindar sent his retainers, with the view of capturing him and carrying him off. (p. 118, 119) Ended with the murder of a couple of people, but the mandal won. (p. 119, 120) Another case where the ryots against the *mandal* because took much the side of the zamindar in certain matters; therefore resolve in "committee" that he should be *punished and warned*, a few "charged" with thrashing him. (whereby he died) (Marx [1880–82] 1974, 261; original emphasis)

The above passage suggests a degree of class solidarity and resistance on the part of the *ryots*. Marx's selections for his notes give proportionally greater prominence to these issues than Phear's original.

Marx supplemented these anthropological studies with a chronology of Indian political and military history in his notes on Sewell's *Analytical*

History of India, made in 1879, in the same notebook as those on Kovalevsky on India. Robert Sewell, a colonial official who wrote his *Analytical History* while still in his mid-twenties, went on to publish some significant historical and archaeological works on southern India. Marx's notes on Sewell stretched to forty-two thousand words, written mainly in German, but with some passages in English. In fact, the notes on Sewell and the more anthropological ones on Kovalevsky are interspersed in Marx's handwritten notebook. If the Kovalevsky notes suggest that Marx by now believed that Indian society had a history, those on Sewell seem to suggest that a second problematic feature of the 1853 India writings was falling aside: the notion that India had always responded passively to outside conquest. This is because Marx's notes emphasize the contingent character of the Muslim and British conquests, rather than, as in 1853, the ineluctable march of large historical forces.

Although Marx made some significant comments in his own words in his notes on Sewell, these are not very frequent. Nonetheless, a close study of his notes in relation to Sewell's text offers some important indications of his evolving perspectives on India. In many cases, Marx emphasized passages that had subordinate importance in Sewell's narrative. Thus, the central thrust of his notes is often different from the work of the author from which they were drawn.

For example, while Sewell gave little attention to the period preceding the Muslim conquests, Marx emphasized this material in his notes. The following clipped passage from Sewell includes in the first sentence two words of his own, "most interesting":

> *Kingdom of Magadha* was a most interesting one. Its *Buddhist kings* wielded extensive power; they belonged for many years to the *Kshatriya caste*, until one of the *Sudra* caste—the fourth and lowest of Manu's four castes—named *Chandragupta*—called Sandracottus by the Greeks—murdered the King and made himself sovereign; he lived *in Alexander the Great's* time. Later we find *three more Sudra dynasties*, which ended with one *Andhra* in *436 A. D.* (Marx [1879–80] 1960, 54; Marx's emphasis)[30]

Marx's phrase "most interesting" may have expressed his surprise at the relative porosity of caste lines. If so, the passage may indicate an alteration of his 1853 view of caste as an insurmountable barrier that undermined social cohesion in the face of foreign invasion.

Similarly, Marx fails to incorporate into his notes a statement from Sewell with which he would likely have agreed in 1853: "The real history of India commences . . . with the invasions of the Arabs" (Sewell 1870, 10). Moreover, where Sewell tends to identify with India's Muslim conquerors, no doubt seeing the British as following their footsteps, Marx often skips over passages where Sewell praises these early conquerors.

In addition, Marx emphasizes passages where Sewell refers to Hindu resistance, while also excising parts of Sewell's text that show Hindu warriors or rulers in a more negative light. For example, Marx records passages such as the following from Sewell, emphasizing how the Hindu Maratha forces had put Mughal Emperor Aurangzeb on the defensive at the end of his reign, this before the British had gained much of a foothold in India:

> 1704. . . . In the last four years of his life whole government disorganized; *Marathas* began to recover their forts and gather strength; a terrible famine exhausted the provisions for troops and drained the treasury; soldiers mutinous over want of pay; hard pressed by the Marathas, *Aurangzeb* retreated in great confusion *to Ahmadnagar*, fell ill. (Marx [1879–80] 1960)[31]

At another point, Marx substitutes the word "clan ancestor [*Stammvater*]" for Sewell's "sovereign" in recording a description of the Maratha leadership (Marx [1879–80] 1960, 80; Sewell 1870, 122).[32] This indicates a conceptual link between these notes on Sewell and his more anthropological ones, highlighting the notion that the Marathas, who formed the most important locus of Indian resistance to both the Mughals and the British, were organized on a clan basis.

Marx also devotes considerable attention to the fact that by the late fourteenth century, just before Timur's invasion and sacking of Delhi, the Delhi sultans had begun to encounter strong resistance. Below, I have italicized Marx's insertions into passages from Sewell:

> 1351: With break-up of the Delhi Kingdom of Muhammad Tughlak, various new states came into being. About 1398 (*at the time of Timur's invasion*), the whole of India free *from Mohammedan domination*, except a few miles around Delhi. (Marx [1879–80] 1960, 25)[33]

He proceeds to record six examples of kingdoms that had asserted themselves, also writing the word "Hindu" repeatedly in the left-hand margin of his notebook.[34]

Marx does something similar in a parenthetical comment within a passage he records from Sewell concerning events fifty years later:

In 1452, the *Rajah of Jaunpur laid siege to Delhi, which led to war that
lasted for 26 years* (this is important; it shows that the native Indian
princes had become powerful enough against the old Moslem rule) and
ended in total defeat of the Rajah and *annexation of Jaunpur to Delhi.*
(Marx [1879–80] 1960, 23; original emphasis)[35]

In this instance, Marx's parenthetical insert alters the tone of Sewell's text considerably, emphasizing the lengthy resistance on the part of the "native Indian
princes," rather than their eventual defeat.[36] Again, these passages indicate a
shift from his 1853 view of Indian passivity in the face of conquest.

None of the above is meant to suggest that Marx's notes on India are anti-
Muslim, for on numerous occasions, he notes the considerable contributions
of Muslims to Indian culture and society. At one point, he writes of Mughal
Emperor Akbar, "He made *Delhi* into the greatest and finest city then existing in the world" (Marx [1879–80] 1960, 33), here giving a summary that was
more forthright than that of Sewell, who had written of Akbar's Delhi, "The
city must at this period have been *one of* the largest and handsomest in the
world" (Sewell 1870, 54; emphasis added). Marx portrays Akbar in a more
secular light than Sewell, characterizing him as "indifferent in religious matters, therefore tolerant," whereas the British historian writes: "In religious
matters Akbar was tolerant and impartial" (Marx [1879–80] 1960, 32; Sewell
1870, 52).

Marx devotes the bulk of the notes on Sewell to the period of British ascendancy, where he stresses its contingent character, and the many instances
where British power in India hung by a thread. He frequently terms the British
"blockheads" or "dogs," whom he sometimes describes as terribly frightened
in the face of Indian resistance. Throughout these notes, Marx shows a pronounced sympathy for the Marathas, while occasionally expressing disdain for
their warlordism.

Unsurprisingly, Marx often ridicules or excises from his notes passages
from Sewell portraying the British conquest of India as a heroic fight against
Asiatic barbarism. This is seen in how he excerpts Sewell's account of the
death by suffocation in 1756 of over a hundred British captives imprisoned by
a Mughal official, in what came to be known as the "Black Hole of Calcutta."
At this juncture, Marx does not incorporate into his notes phrases from Sewell
characterizing this as "one of the most horrible tragedies in the history of the
world," and so forth. Instead, he writes of "'the *Black Hole of Calcutta*,' over
which the *English hypocrites* have been making so much sham scandal to this
day" (Marx [1879–80] 1960, 65; see also Sewell 1870, 95).

Additionally, Marx takes note of how British colonialism, by introducing a most rapacious form of capitalism, had transformed ancient forms of landed property into unrestricted private property that could be acquired by money-lenders and financiers.[37] Marx takes down the following passage from Sewell, also adding some material of his own (placed in italics below). In the late eighteenth century, Muhammad Ali, a Mughal official and

> a libertine and reveller and debauchee of the worst kind, borrowed large sums from private individuals, whom he repaid by assigning to them the revenues of considerable tracts of land. The lenders (*alias English swindler usurers*) found this "very advantageous"; it established the "*vermin*"[38] at once in the position of large landowners and enabled them to amass immense fortunes by oppressing the ryots; *hence tyranny—the most unscrupulous—towards the native peasants of these upstart European (i.e. English) zemindars!* (Marx [1879–80] 1960, 90)[39]

Marx holds the English state under reformer William Pitt responsible for these developments in India.

Marx again and again singles out resistance to the British, showing sympathy for the various Maratha, Mughal, Afghan, and Sikh forces arrayed against them. At the same time, he often indicates ways in which these forces cut themselves off from possible supporters through banditry or brutality, all the while showing an utter contempt for those Indian leaders who aligned with the British. Even after the Maratha clans were finally vanquished, he still calls attention to new challenges to the British in the Northwest, from the Sikhs and the Afghans.

The British invaded Afghanistan, only to suffer a crushing defeat in 1842, with a loss of fifteen thousand soldiers and civilians as they attempted a retreat through the mountain passes. Marx records a passage from Sewell describing one point of that retreat, inserting the derisive appellation "British dogs": "*The natives* shot the 'British dogs' dead from *the heights above*, hundreds fell thus until *the end of the pass was cleared*, where only 500–600 starving and wounded men were left to continue their retreat. They too were *slaughtered like sheep* during their struggling march to the frontier" (Marx [1879–80] 1960, 136 [Marx's emphasis]; see also Sewell 1870, 240). Marx also focuses on how, in the subsequent campaigns to retake Afghanistan and the regions in between, the British on more than one occasion plundered the cities they had conquered.

Marx covers the 1857–58 Sepoy Uprising in great detail, usually leaving aside Sewell's fulsome descriptions of Indian atrocities, and concentrating instead on British ones. His clipped excerpts tended to place the rebels in a more favorable light than Sewell's text. This is seen in the following excerpt on the situation in May 1857, which Marx amends with phrases of his own, here italicized:

Rebellion spread throughout Hindustan; in 20 different places simultaneously, sepoy risings and murder of the English; chief scenes: Agra, Bareili, Moradabad. Sindhia loyal to the *"English dogs,"* not so his "troopers"; Rajah of Patiala—*for shame!*—sent large body of soldiers in aid of the English!

At Mainpuri (North-West Provinces), a young *brute of a* lieutenant, one De Kantzow, saved the treasury and fort. (Marx [1879–80] 1960, 149)[40]

Even rebel leader Nana Sahib's massacre of several hundred European civilians and soldiers at Cawnpore (Kanpur) evokes little sympathy from Marx, who makes rather clipped excerpts on this from Sewell, excising over-wrought language like "fiendish" and "treacherous demons," as well as the British historian's statement that "the horrors that revealed themselves are almost without parallel in history" (Marx [1879–80] 1960, 149–50; Sewell 1870, 268–70). At several points, Marx also replaces Sewell's term "mutineers" with "insurgents." The notes on Sewell suggest that Marx's sympathy for the Sepoy Uprising had only increased since his *Tribune* articles on these same events during the late 1850s.

COLONIALISM IN INDONESIA, ALGERIA, AND LATIN AMERICA

The notes on India contain some discussion of Islam, given the fact that that region, which comprised during the nineteenth century what are today the nations Pakistan and Bangladesh, as well as India, contained one of the world's largest Muslim populations (even though it was a minority, compared to the Hindus). Marx also took extensive notes on two predominantly Muslim societies, Indonesia (Java) and Algeria, colonized by the Netherlands and France, respectively.

Marx's notes on J. W. B. Money's *Java; or, How to Manage a Colony, Showing a Practical Solution of the Questions Now Affecting British India* (1861), concentrated on the social organization of the traditional Javanese village. Money, a British barrister born in India, visited the Dutch colony of Java during

1858, at the height of the Sepoy Uprising. His book is an unabashed panegyric to Dutch colonial rule. In Java, the Dutch had retained more of the precolonial system than had the British in India, where the Cornwallis Settlement had unleashed market forces that severely disrupted the traditional communal village. The Dutch extracted a surplus from above while allowing many aspects of traditional land tenure patterns, political organization, and communal village culture to persist. After Marx's death, Engels appears to have read Money's book, but it is unclear if he read Marx's notes as well, composed 1880–81. In a letter to Karl Kautsky of February 16, 1884, Engels views the solidity of Dutch rule as an example of a conservative "state socialism" that, "as in India and Russia" at the time, was grounded in "primitive communism" at the village level (MECW 47, 102–3). Engels's remarks were of course related to Money's core thesis concerning the stability of Dutch versus British colonial rule.

This was exactly what Marx tended to ignore in his notes on Money, however, as he concentrated instead on Money's data. Marx makes no directly critical comments on the vantage point of this rather superficial chronicler of life in Java, with the exception of an exclamation point next to a passage where Money extolled the Dutch policy of keeping modern education away from the villages. With a careful sense of objectivity, he leaves aside the most dubious parts of Money's account, while still managing to turn to his own use a book which was at that time one of the few detailed accounts of life in colonial Java by an outside observer.

Marx turned to Algeria in another part of his notes on Kovalevsky, in which he took up communal forms in both the precolonial and colonial periods. In these relatively brief seven thousand–word excerpts, he began by noting the strength of communal property in the Maghreb region. Although a considerable amount of private property in land came into existence under the Ottomans, the majority of the land in Algeria remained communal property in the hands of clans and extended families.

In the nineteenth century, French colonizers sought to change this situation, but encountered stubborn resistance. Marx singles out the role of the 1873 French National Assembly in these efforts to dismantle communal property, quoting the following from Kovalevsky, with a parenthetical remark of his own in the first sentence:

> *The formation of private landownership* (in the eyes of the French bourgeois) as the necessary condition of all progress in the political and social sphere. The further *maintenance of communal property*, "as a form that supports communist tendencies in people's minds" (*Debates of the*

National Assembly, 1873) is dangerous both for the colony and for the homeland; the distribution of *clan holdings* is encouraged, even pre-scribed, *first as a means of weakening subjugated tribes that are ever standing under impulsion to revolt*, second, as the *only way toward a further transfer of landownership* from the hands of the natives into those of the colonists. (Marx [1879] 1975, 405; Marx's emphasis)[41]

Thus, like Maine, the French legislators saw a link between indigenous communal property and the contemporary socialist movement, in that both formed major obstacles to the consolidation of bourgeois property relations, "both for the colony and the homeland."

Marx lashes out again at the French National Assembly, emphasizing that these were the so-called Rurals. "Rurals" and "assembly of shame" were derisive appellations by the French Left referring to the National Assembly at Versailles. They blamed it for having legitimated the repression of a modern communal form, the Paris Commune of 1871. Marx expresses his outrage by inserting into his excerpts several passages, italicized below, that sharpen Kovalevsky's already critical description of the Assembly:

> 1873. Hence the first concern of the *Assembly of Rurals of 1873* was to hit upon more effective measures for *stealing the land* of the Arabs. [[The debates in this *assembly of shame* concerning the project "On the Introduction of Private Property" in Algeria seek to hide the *villainy* under the cloak of the so-called eternal, inalterable laws of political economy. (224) *In these debates the "Rurals" are unanimous on the goal: destruction of collective property. The debate turns only around the method, how to bring it about.*]] (Marx [1879] 1975, 410)

Here again, Marx is drawing a connection between those who suppressed a modern "commune" set up by the workers of Paris and those who were seizing indigenous communal landholdings in Algeria. A bit later, Marx incorporates into his excerpts Kovalevsky's mention of fear on the part of the French of an anticolonial clan-based uprising. They believed this could be avoided "*by tearing away the Arabs from their natural bond to the soil* to break the last strength of the *clan unions* thus being dissolved, and thereby, any *danger of rebellion* (229)" (Marx [1879] 1975, 412; Marx's emphasis).

In yet another part of his notes on Kovalevsky, Marx takes up a much earlier form of colonialism, that of Spain in the New World, while also examining communal forms in pre-Columbian Latin America and the Caribbean. These relatively brief notes comprise some 7,500 words, written mainly in German, with some passages in Russian and Spanish. Marx begins by recording material from Kovalevsky on the transition from a herd-like existence, to clans, and to families in Native American societies. Bending Kovalevsky's text slightly in order to present the shift from clan to familial production as prior to the related changes in property forms, he writes: "With the formation of private families individual property also emerges and *only movable* at the outset" (Harstick 1977, 19).[42] Marx also incorporated text from Kovalevsky stressing the virtual absence of private property among some nomadic societies in the Americas.

Additionally, Marx focused Kovalevsky's discussion of the transition to agriculture, according to which clans settled permanently on land that they usually took by force. In Mexico, reported Kovalevsky, clan-based urban communities held land in common as *calpulli*, with their occupants termed *calli*. The land could not be sold or inherited on an individual basis. A group's ability to cultivate the land became an increasingly important factor in determining possession, thus leading to unequal shares. The *calli* closely guarded their possessory rights, strictly excluding non-clan members.

According to Kovalevsky, at another stage overlords from conquering groups like the Aztecs or the Incas used similar communal associations to administer empires. Excerpting Kovalevsky, Marx writes that "the rural population continued as before to *own the land communally,* but had to, at the same time, give up a part of its real income as payments in kind for the benefit of their rulers" (Harstick 1977, 28). This, he adds, recording another passage from the Russian ethnologist, prepared the way for "the development of the large landed estates" and created the potential for the dissolution of communal landownership, a process "accelerated by the arrival of the Spaniards" (28).

Marx's excerpts on the next period, early Spanish colonialism, expand only occasionally on Kovalevsky's own words, probably because Kovalevsky's attack on colonialism, always present in *Communal Property*, was utterly unequivocal here. Here is a representative passage, as recorded by Marx, with his inserts italicized:

The original Spanish policy of extermination of the redmen. (47) After *pillage of the gold etc. that they found, the [Amer]indians are condemned to work in the mines.* (48) With the decline of the value of gold and silver, the Spanish turn to agriculture, make the [Amer]indians into slaves in order to cultivate land for them. (1.c.) (Harstick 1977, 29)

Under this *repartimientos* system, the indigenous *caciques* or clan leaders had to furnish the Spaniards with people to be used in agricultural labor. Marx records passages on the extreme brutality of this system, where the Amerindians were hunted down if not enough were supplied up by the caciques.

Soon, under pressure from elements of the Church, the Spanish state moved to curtail the outright enslavement of the native population, as seen in this excerpt from Kovalevsky that Marx incorporates into his notes. Even here, at a point where he supports the clergy, Marx cannot resist a bit of irony toward them, inserting the word "fuss" into this excerpt from Kovalevsky:

> Hence the *fuss on the part of the monks of the Order of St. Jacob* against the enslavement of the [Amer]indians. *Hence, 1531,* bull from *Pope Paul III* declaring [Amer]indians "human beings" and therefore "free from slavery." The *Royal Council for the West Indies,* established 1524, half of which consisted of the heads of the highest clergy, declared itself for the freedom of the [Amer]indians. *Charles V* (Law of May 21, 1542) accordingly prohibited that: "no person, whether engaged in war or not, can take, apprehend, occupy, sell, exchange any Indian as a slave, nor possess him as such"; likewise, the *Law of October 26, 1546* prohibits the sale of [Amer]indians into slavery etc. (Harstick 1977, 30; Marx's emphasis)

Marx then touches on the resistance to this law by the colonists and the law's eventual enforcement. It did not lead to an actual decrease in New World slavery, however, as seen in the following passage he incorporates from Kovalevsky, inserting a pejorative phrase about the colonists, here italicized: "Resistance by the Spanish colonists against this law. (1. c.) *Fight with the latter dogs* by Las Casas, Don Juan Zumaraga and other Catholic bishops. (54) Hence the Negro slave trade as 'surrogate' for the gentlemen colonists" (30). Thus, the bishops' reforms led in the end to an increase in the African slave trade, which became the prime source of labor for the plantations of the New World.

The brutal *repartimientos* system for the Amerindians is now replaced by the *encomiendas* system. It created a sort of serfdom, in which formally free subjects living in communal villages were subject to taxes in kind and in labor, all administered by local Spanish *encomienderos.* Typically, these taxes were supposed to support one *encomiendero* and one priest per village. The new system had many paternalistic features, including requirements that the *encomienderos* were to protect the Amerindians, assist in their Christianization, and so forth. The *encomienderos* had the right to remove village elders if payments fell into arrears, something that severely undermined the communal system. While *encomienderos* could also be removed and banished for failing to fulfill their end of the bargain, the enforcement of all of these regulations was left to the Spanish colonists, something that causes Marx to exclaim: "Worthy this of the statesmen Carlos I (Charles V) and Philip II" (Harstick 1977, 32). The exactions under the encomiendas system became so severe that many Amerindians fled, or committed suicide. While the Amerindians technically owned the land through their village communes, this applied only to land actually under cultivation, which gave openings to Spaniards wishing to annex portions of it by getting it declared wasteland. These and other legal maneuvers deprived the Amerindians of much of their prime agricultural land.

Marx continues his summary and excerpts, now moving into the transition to capitalist private property, here adding a parenthetical remark in the first sentence rendering Kovalevsky's anthropological categories more precise:

> This dissolution of consanguinity (real or fictitious) led in some locations to the formation of *small-scale landed property out of the earlier communal allotments*; this in turn *passed little by little into the hands of capital-owning Europeans*—under the pressure of taxes from the encomenderos and *the system first permitted by the Spanish of lending money at interest*—Zurita says: *"under the indigenous leaders the [Amer]indians did not know usury."* (Harstick 1977, 36; original emphasis)

This sparked new, destructive conflicts within and among village communes and clans, which further eroded the power and rights of the Amerindians.

Marx ends his notes on Kovalevsky on Latin America with the following excerpt, into which he inserts a few words (italicized below):

> The survival—*in large measure*—of the rural commune is due on one hand to the [Amer]indians' preference for this type of property in land, as the one best corresponding to their level of culture; on the other hand, the lack of colonial legislation [[*in contrast to the English East Indies*]] of regulations that would give the members of the clans the possibility of selling the allotments belonging to them. (Harstick 1977, 38)

Marx's qualifier "in large measure" undercuts somewhat Kovalevsky's stress on the dissolution of these communal forms. Marx's bracketed insert about India suggests that communal forms remained stronger in Latin America than in India, probably because India had been colonized in a later period by an advanced capitalist power, Britain, which actively tried to create individual private property in the villages.

Here and elsewhere in the 1879–82 notebooks on non-Western and pre-capitalist societies, Marx was concerned with the persistence of communal forms, even into his own century, in this case after more than three centuries of colonial rule. Such considerations formed a crucial backdrop to what follows directly below, his embrace of Russia's rural commune of the 1880s as a potential source of resistance to capital.

RUSSIA: COMMUNAL FORMS AS THE "POINT OF DEPARTURE FOR A COMMUNIST DEVELOPMENT"

Many of the major themes discussed in this book reach their culmination in Marx's late writings on Russia during the years 1877 to 1882. First, it is here that Marx seems to move furthest away from the implicitly unilinear model of development espoused in *The Communist Manifesto*. Second, Marx poses more explicitly here than elsewhere the possibility that noncapitalist societies might move directly to socialism on the basis of their indigenous communal forms, without first passing through the stage of capitalism. This came with an important proviso, however, expressed by Marx and Engels in their preface to the 1882 Russian edition of the *Manifesto*: these new types of revolutions could succeed only if they were able to link up with incipient working-class revolutions in the industrially developed West.

Like the other texts discussed in this chapter, Marx's late writings on Russia included excerpt notebooks with occasional commentary in his own words. These were quite substantial. In 1875 and 1876, after having studied the Russian language for a few years, he began a lengthy set of notes from Russian sources on that country's social and political development since 1861.[43] He continued to cover Russia in other notes through the 1880s. Among these were two texts that will appear in MEGA² IV/27: a brief study of Russian agriculture and longer notes on Nikolai Kostomarov's *Historical Monographs*, the latter focusing on Stenka Razin's Cossack revolt during the late seventeenth century.

But Marx's late writings on Russia were not limited to excerpt notebooks, where his own voice was necessarily somewhat muted. They also included letters, drafts, and one published text, the aforementioned preface to *The Communist Manifesto*. Most of these writings connected communal forms, at least in Russia, to the prospects for revolution in his own time. Although these non-notebook materials on Russia are not very lengthy, about thirty pages of text in the best-known edition (Shanin 1983a), they illustrate the conclusions Marx was drawing from his studies of communal forms in Russia. At a broader level, they constitute a window into how Marx may have intended to develop the material in the 1879–82 excerpt notebooks on a variety of non-Western societies.

As mentioned earlier, Marx's renewal of interest in Russia was stimulated by the 1872 translation of *Capital* into Russian. This was its first non-German edition, and a surprisingly wide discussion followed, considering the fact that this society at the eastern edge of Europe had yet to be seriously impacted by capitalism (Resis 1970, White 1996). In the afterword to the second German edition of 1873, Marx contrasts what he sees as the ideological response by the "mealy-mouthed babblers of German vulgar economics" to the serious reviews the "excellent Russian translation" was receiving (*Capital* I, 99). In agricultural Russia, the political opposition was dominated by the Populists, who advocated an agrarian revolution that would avoid capitalism and develop Russia along different lines from the West.

In 1877, Marx drafted a response to an article on *Capital* that the sociologist and Populist leader Nikolai Mikhailovsky had published earlier that year in the Russian journal *Otechestvennye Zapiski* (Notes of the Fatherland). Mikhailovsky was sympathetic to Marx; in fact, his article took the form of a response to a harsh critique of *Capital* by another Russian, Yuli Zhukovsky.[44] What seemed to distress Marx was that in defending him, Mikhailovsky had ascribed to him a unilinear theory of human history, linked to a theory of development wherein other societies were destined to follow England into capitalism. Mikhailovsky writes:

> In the sixth chapter of *Capital* is a section entitled "So-Called Primitive Accumulation." Here, Marx has in view a historical sketch of the first steps of the capitalist process of production, but he gives us something much bigger, a whole philosophical-historical theory. This theory is of great interest in general and especially great interest for us Russians. ([1877] 1911, 167–68)[45]

Marx may also have been troubled by Mikhailovsky's open reservations concerning dialectics:

> If you take from *Capital* the heavy, clumsy, and unnecessary covering of Hegelian dialectic, then independently from the other virtues of this work we will see in it material excellently worked out for the solution of the general question of the relation of forms to the material conditions

of their existence, as well as an excellent formulation of the question in a particular sphere. (186)

Marx's draft reply to *Otechestvennye Zapiski* focused especially on Mikhailovsky's first point about *Capital* having been grounded in "a whole philosophical-historical theory."[46]

In his letter, Marx recounts that Russian affairs had occupied him greatly during the 1870s: "In order to reach an informed judgment on Russia's economic development, I learned Russian and then for many years studied official and other publications relating to the question" (Shanin 1983a, 135).[47] Marx writes, here for the first time, although without acknowledging that his position had changed, that he was open to the Populist Nikolai Chernyshevsky's argument about skipping the stage of capitalism in order to move toward socialism by another pathway: "I have come to the conclusion that if Russia continues along the pathway she has followed since 1861, she will lose the finest chance ever offered by history to a people and undergo all the fateful vicissitudes of the capitalist regime" (135). As an indication of just how tentative his argument was, Marx stated it negatively, emphasizing how the penetration of capitalist institutions into the village communes after the 1861 liberation of the serfs was rapidly closing off the alternative outlined by Chernyshevsky and other Populists.

Marx denies that he had attempted to sketch the future of Russia and other non-Western societies in *Capital*: "The chapter on primitive accumulation claims no more than to trace the path by which, in Western Europe, the capitalist economic order emerged from the womb of the feudal economic order" (Shanin 1983a, 135). To support this assertion, he cites the 1872–75 French edition, where, as discussed in the previous chapter, he had altered the text in the direction of a more multilinear perspective, writing regarding the "expropriation of the agricultural producer": "It has been accomplished in a radical manner only in England.... But all the countries of Western Europe are going through the same development" (Shanin 1983a, 135; see also Marx [1872–75] 1985b, 169).

Marx makes only a brief and implicit answer on a second point in Mikhailovsky's review, the strictures concerning "the heavy lid of Hegelian dialectics." In this regard, Marx refers to a passage near the end of the discussion of primitive accumulation in *Capital*, where he writes that the historical tendency of capitalist production "is said to consist in the fact that it 'begets its own negation with the inexorability of a natural process'; that it has itself created the elements of a new economic order" (Shanin 1983a, 135; see also *Capital* I,

929). Here, in the book's conclusion, capital was to be "negated" by the revolt of labor, a process Marx characterizes as "the negation of the negation":

> The capitalist mode of appropriation, conforming to the capitalist mode of production, constitutes the *first negation* of that individual private property that is only the corollary of independent and individual labor.[48] *But capitalist production itself begets, with the inevitability of a natural process, its own negation. This is the negation of the negation.* It does not re-establish the individual private property of the worker, but his individual property on the basis of the achievements of the capitalist era: namely cooperation and the possession in common of all the means of production, including the soil. (Marx [1872–75] 1985b, 207, emphasis added)[49]

Anti-Hegelians have often complained about Marx's use of the core Hegelian concept of negation of negation at this crucial juncture,[50] with some claiming he had dogmatically tried to prove his economic laws via Hegelian syllogisms. In his draft letter of 1877, Marx responds: "I furnish no proof at this point, for the good reason that this statement merely summarizes in brief the long expositions given previously in the chapters on capitalist production" (Shanin 1983a, 135). Thus, his recourse to Hegelian language at this juncture was not intended as a proof, but as a methodological indication informing the reader that his overall presentation of capitalist production and its eventual collapse was grounded in Hegelian dialectics, even though he had developed his discussion without any explicit reference to Hegel. Dialectics fit into *Capital*, he seemed to claim, not because he had imposed it on reality, but because reality was itself dialectical.

A third point in the letter to *Otechestvennye Zapiski* concerned a comparative historical reference. Marx writes that "if Russia is tending to become a capitalist nation like the nations of Western Europe," then and only then, (1) it would have to expropriate its peasantry and make them into unattached proletarians, and (2) be otherwise "brought into the fold of the capitalist regime," after which it would come under its "pitiless laws" (Shanin 1983a, 136). At this point, he gives an example of a trajectory of development similar to the primitive accumulation of capital, but which did not end in capitalism. This was ancient Rome:

> At various points in *Capital*, I have alluded to the fate that befell the plebeians of ancient Rome. They were originally free peasants, each tilling his own plot on his own behalf. In the course of Roman history they were

expropriated. The same movement that divorced them from their means of production and subsistence involved the formation not only of large landed property but also of big money capitals. Thus one fine morning there were, on the one side, free men stripped of everything but their labor-power, and on the other, in order to exploit their labor, owners of all the acquired wealth. What happened? The Roman proletarians became, not wage-laborers, but an idle "mob" more abject than those who used to be called *poor whites* of the southern United States; and what unfolded [*se déploya*][51] alongside them was not a capitalist but a slave mode of production. (136)[52]

Although he draws parallels between ancient Rome and the American South, the emphasis runs in another direction, toward the radical differences between Roman and modern capitalist social forms.

Marx's main point was that he had not, as Mikhailovsky had argued, developed "a whole philosophical-historical theory" of society, generalizable for all times and places:

Thus events of striking similarity, taking place in different historical contexts, led to totally disparate results. By studying each of these developments separately, one may easily discover the key to this phenomenon, but this will never be attained with the master key [*avec le passepartout*][53] of a general historico-philosophical theory, whose supreme virtue consists in being suprahistorical. (Shanin 1983a, 136)

Mikhailovsky, he complains, "insists on transforming my historical sketch of the genesis of capitalism in Western Europe into a historico-philosophical theory of the general course fatally imposed on all peoples, whatever the historical circumstances in which they find themselves placed" (136).

Thus, Marx was denying (1) that he had created a unilinear theory of history, (2) that he worked with a deterministic model of social development, or (3) that Russia in particular was bound to evolve in the manner of Western capitalism. To some extent, these arguments were new, but they grew out of the moves toward a more multilinear framework that Marx had been making ever since the *Grundrisse*.[54]

Given the general level at which Marx argued these points, it is likely that he intended these qualifications to apply not only to Russia but also to India and the other contemporary non-Western, nonindustrialized societies that he was studying during this period. India, like Russia, had communal forms in its villages, which led Krader to write of Marx's "positing of the alternatives open to the Indian and Russian rural collective institutions" (1974, 29). Indonesia, Algeria, and Latin America, also covered in the 1879–82 notebooks, had rural communal forms. Through colonialism, these societies had all been impacted by capitalism more directly than Russia. Nonetheless, one could surmise that Marx was interested in their possible anticapitalist development, somewhat along the lines that he was beginning to sketch for Russia.

The 1877 letter to *Otechestvennye Zapiski* stressed Marx's multilinear standpoint, but did not analyze Russian society any more than had *Capital*, volume I. In his March 1881 drafts of a letter to the Russian revolutionary Vera Zasulich, however, Marx began to sketch what a Russian pathway of social development might look like within the multilinear perspective put forth in the 1877 letter and the French edition of *Capital*. David Smith shows what was at stake here for Russia, whose social structure was for Marx part of the Asian social forms: "Marx's stress on the unique curve of 'Asiatic' development not only helps us to distinguish Marx's conception from the Procrustean theory of fixed evolutionary stages which masqueraded as 'Marxist materialism' for so many years, but also enables us to see that Marx's concept of postcapitalist society was just as multilinear as his conception of the past" (1995, 113). In a letter of February 16, 1881, Zasulich, who described herself as a member of Russia's "socialist party," asked Marx whether "the rural commune, freed of exorbitant tax demands, payment to the nobility and arbitrary administration, is capable of developing in a socialist direction," or whether "the commune is destined to perish" and Russian socialists needed to wait for capitalist development, the rise of a proletariat, and so forth (Shanin 1983a, 98). Marx's Russian followers held the latter view, she added, referring specifically to debates in journals like *Otechestvennye Zapiski*. Zasulich requested a reply from Marx that could be translated into Russian and published.

In his reply, dated March 8, 1881, Marx again cites the passage from the French edition of *Capital* that bracketed the discussion of primitive accumulation to Western Europe, before concluding: "The 'historical inevitability' [*fatalité*] of this course is therefore *explicitly* restricted to the *countries of Western Europe*" (Shanin 1983a, 124).[55] In Western Europe, he adds, the transition from feudal to capitalist property was "the transformation of one form of private property into another form of private property," but capitalist development would require that Russian peasants "on the contrary, transform their communal property into private property" (124). Therefore, *Capital* was agnostic on the question of Russia's future. He ends his letter with a few tentative remarks about Russia:

The special study I have made of it . . . has convinced me that the commune is the fulcrum for social regeneration in Russia. But in order that it might function as such, the deleterious influences assailing it from all sides must first be eliminated and then it must be assured the normal conditions for a spontaneous development. (124)

As in 1877, Marx was arguing that alternate pathways of development might be possible for Russia. He based his judgment in large part upon the marked differences between the social structure of the Russian village, with its communal social forms, and the medieval village of Western Europe. Moreover, he was "convinced . . . that the commune is the fulcrum for a social regeneration in Russia" (Marx in Shanin 1983a, 124).

In the much more substantial preparatory drafts of his letter, Marx covered these points in more depth, as well as other ones left out of his actual reply to Zasulich. He discusses the particularities of Russia's situation as a large country at Europe's edge: "Russia does not live in isolation from the modern world; nor has she fallen prey, like the East Indies, to a foreign conqueror" (Shanin 1983a, 106). Therefore, it might be possible to combine Russia's ancient communal forms with modern technology, this in a less exploitative manner than under capitalism.

At this point, it needs to be underlined that Marx was proposing not an autarky but a new synthesis of the archaic and the modern, one that took advantage of the highest achievements of capitalist modernity:

Thanks to the unique combination of circumstances in Russia, the rural commune, already established on a national scale, may gradually shake off its primitive characteristics and directly develop as an element of collective production on a national scale. Precisely because it is contemporaneous with capitalist production, the rural commune may appropriate for itself all the *positive achievements* and this without undergoing its frightful vicissitudes. . . . Should the Russian admirers of the capitalist system deny that such a development is theoretically possible, then I would ask them the following question: Did Russia have to undergo a long Western-style incubation of mechanical industry before it could make use of machinery, steamships, railways, etc.? Let them also explain how the Russians managed to introduce, in the twinkling of an eye, that whole machinery of exchange (banks, credit companies, etc.), which was the work of centuries in the West. (Shanin 1983a, 105–6)

The stress above was on the contradictory and dialectical character of social development, as against any unilinear determinism. At an objective level, the very existence of Western capitalist modernity meant that Russia's rural commune could draw upon its achievements. At a subjective level, this created a vastly different situation than that faced by popular movements in earlier precapitalist societies.

A second theme in the drafts, not present in the letter Marx actually sent to Zasulich, concerned the relationship of his excerpt notebooks on anthropology and on India to these reflections on Russia. He alluded, for example, to Morgan's notion that in the future, Western civilization would revive archaic communism in a higher form. Marx also stressed the persistence of communal forms across many centuries. "Recent research," he writes,

> has advanced enough in order to affirm (1) that the primitive communities had incomparably greater vitality than the Semitic, Greek, Roman, etc. societies, and, *a fortiori*,[56] that of the modern capitalist societies; (2) that the causes of their decline lie in economic conditions that prevented them from passing beyond a certain level of development, this in historical contexts not at all analogous with the present-day Russian commune. (Shanin 1983a, 107)

Marx also notes the anticommunal bias of some of the new research, again attacking Maine:

> One has to be on guard when reading the histories of primitive communities written by bourgeois authors. They do not even shrink from falsehoods. Sir Henry Maine, for example, who was an enthusiastic collaborator of the English government in carrying out its violent destruction of the Indian communes, hypocritically assures us that all of the government's noble efforts to maintain the communes succumbed to the spontaneous power of economic laws! (Shanin 1983a, 107)

Beneath this anticommunal ideological bias, as well as the real destruction carried out through the imposition of English-style private property on the Indian village, one could, Marx also argued, find evidence of the persistence of these communal forms.

Probably basing himself on his notes on Kovalevsky, Marx created a more general typology of communal forms across various societies. The earliest form, basing itself on the clan, involved not only communal distribution of land, but also "probably the land itself was worked by groups, in common" (Shanin 1983a, 118). These early communes were based upon real or fictitious consanguinity, in a clan structure: "One cannot join unless one is a natural or adopted relative" (119). At a later stage, this archaic form transitioned into the rural commune, which was based upon residency rather than kinship. It was this later form, Marx holds, that exhibits such great "natural vitality" (118). Here, "the arable land, inalienable and common property, is periodically divided among the members of the rural commune" (119).

The later "rural commune" contained an important dualism. Communal landownership held it together, Marx writes, "while at the same time, the house and yard as an individual family preserve, together with small-plot farming and private appropriation of its fruits, gave scope to an individuality incompatible with the organism of the most primitive communities" (Shanin 1983a, 120). While it constituted a source of this social form's vitality and longevity, eventually this dualism "could turn into a seed of disintegration" for the rural commune (120). Small-scale private landownership, which could be expanded, constituted one factor. Even more fundamental was the shift in labor relations that arose within this mode of production, however:

> But the key factor was fragmented labor as the source of private appropriation. It gave rise to the accumulation of movable goods, such as livestock, money, and sometimes even slaves or serfs. Such movable property, not subject to communal control, open to individual exchange with plenty of scope for trickery and chance, weighed ever more heavily upon the entire rural economy. This was what dissolved primitive economic and social equality. (120)

Such disintegration was by no means inevitable, however.

This second theme in the drafts centered on features common to Russia's rural communes and those in other times and places. To be sure, Marx had not worked out a theory of social development or revolution for Russia, let alone the often-colonized lands in Asia, Africa, or Latin America. Moreover, he explicitly contrasts politically independent Russia with colonized India: "Russia does not live in isolation from the modern world; nor has she fallen prey, like the East Indies, to a foreign conqueror" (Shanin 1983a, 106). This contrast was not absolute, but relative, however, for there were also many commonalities, chief among them the presence of rural communes in the villages of these two large agrarian societies. This meant that in India as in Russia, the development of modern capitalist private property would of necessity involve a transition not from quasi-private feudal peasant property, but from communal property. Recall that in the 1877 draft and these writings of 1881, Marx restricted the laws of primitive accumulation in *Capital* to the lands of Western Europe, not to those lands and their colonies. At this historical juncture, did Marx place India and other non-Western societies outside the logic of capitalist modernity, at least to some extent?

When Marx's historical typology of communal forms in the 1881 drafts is placed alongside his 1879 notes on Sewell and Kovalevsky on India, another question arises, that of India's communal forms as potential sites of resistance to colonialism and to capital. The notes on Kovalevsky suggested that communal forms in colonized India and Algeria, as well as Latin America, still possessed some vitality, albeit not as much as Marx was ascribing to those in Russia. Recall that Marx added a passage (here italicized) to an excerpt from Kovalevsky on this point with regard to post-Cornwallis India: "*Yet between these atoms certain connections continue to exist*, distantly reminiscent of the earlier communal village landowning groups" (Marx [1879] 1975, 388; original emphasis). Recall also that Marx's notes on Sewell highlighted the continuous resistance of the Indian people to their conquerors, Muslim and British, notes he interspersed with those on Kovalevsky, which centered on those very communal forms.

A third theme in the drafts for the letter to Zasulich concerned the prospects for revolution in Russia and the form that revolution might assume. Here, Marx weighed the Russian communal form's strengths against the threats it faced from capital and the state. While the Russian communes possessed a certain vitality, they were also isolated in villages scattered across "the country's huge expanse," with the "central despotism" of the state towering over them (Shanin 1983a, 103). But although the existing state fostered their isolation, this "could easily be overcome once the government fetters have been cast off" (103). This could not happen without a revolution, however: "Thus, only a general uprising can break the isolation of the 'rural commune,' the lack of connection between the different communes, in short, its existence as a localized microcosm that denies it the historical initiative" (112).

Such a revolution would not be easy to achieve, as time was running out for the rural commune: "What threatens the life of the Russian commune is neither an historical inevitability nor a theory; it is oppression by the state and exploitation by capitalist intruders made powerful, at the expense of the peasants, by this same state" (Shanin 1983a, 104–5). At an international level, however, other objective factors operated in a more positive direction: "the *contemporaneity* of Western production, which dominates the world market, enables Russia to incorporate into the commune all the positive achievements of the capitalist system, without passing under its humiliating tribute [*fourches caudines*]"[57] (110). Moreover, the isolation of the communes could be alleviated through a greater democratization, removing the centralized state as an overlord: "All that is necessary is to replace the volost, a government institution, with a peasant assembly chosen by the communes themselves—an economic and administrative body serving their own interests" (111). This would parallel the process already taking place in the West, where the capitalist system found itself, "both in Western Europe and the United States, in conflict with the working masses, with science, and with the very productive forces it engenders—in short, in a crisis that will end through its own elimination, through the return of modern societies to a higher form of an 'archaic' type of collective ownership and production" (111).

It is important to note that here, for the first time in his late writings on Russia, Marx was referring to a major external subjective factor, the presence in Western Europe and North America of a self-conscious, organized working class movement. Alongside the objective achievements of capitalist modernity, this subjective factor would also be able to impact Russia.

What would be the character of the Russian revolution and how would it affect that society's future development?

> To save the Russian commune, a Russian revolution is needed. Moreover, the Russian government and the "new pillars of society" are doing their utmost to prepare the masses for such a catastrophe. If the revolution takes place at an opportune moment, if it concentrates all its forces[58] to ensure the free unfolding [*essor libre*][59] of the rural commune, the latter will soon develop itself as a regenerating element of Russian society and as an element of superiority over those countries enslaved by the capitalist regime. (Shanin 1983a, 116–17)

This was a clear enough statement concerning Russia's indigenous revolutionary potential. But even such a ringing endorsement of the possibility of a peasant-based, noncapitalist social order should not be seen as an argument for a freestanding Russian socialism, for as shown elsewhere in the drafts of the letter to Zasulich, Marx held that such a new system could arise only in the context of a wider social transformation involving the Western working classes.

The last part of Marx's late writings on Russia was a preface, coauthored by Engels, to the 1882 second Russian edition of *The Communist Manifesto*.

It was also Marx's last publication before his death in March 1883. Drafted in German and dated January 21, 1882, it was translated into Russian and published almost immediately in *Narodnya Volya* (People's Will), a Populist journal, and again later that year in a new translation of the *Manifesto* by Georgi Plekhanov.[60] Marx and Engels begin their preface by noting that neither Russia nor the United States figured very much in the original edition, and not at all in the section on communist movements. They then develop a brief analysis of the growing crisis in the United States due to the squeezing out of the small independent farmer by capital. As to Russia, they note the rise of a serious revolutionary movement at a time when the rest of Europe was relatively quiescent: "Russia forms the vanguard [*Vorhut*] of revolutionary action in Europe" (Shanin 1983a, 139).

What form would a Russian revolution take? Marx and Engels weigh the revolutionary possibilities within the communal form of the Russian village, with its *obshchina* or *mir*.

> Can the Russian obshchina, a form, albeit heavily eroded, of the primeval communal ownership of the land, pass directly into the higher, communist form of communal ownership? Or must it first go through the same process of dissolution that marks the West's historical development? Today there is only one possible answer: If the Russian revolution becomes the signal for a proletarian revolution in the West, so that the two complement each other, then Russia's peasant communal landownership may serve as the point of departure for a communist development. (Shanin 1983a, 139)

Two points stand out here. (1) The final sentence clarifies a point to which Marx had alluded in the drafts of the letter to Zasulich: a Russian revolution based upon its agrarian communal forms would be a necessary, but not a sufficient condition for the development of a modern communism. What was also needed was help from an outside subjective factor, a revolution on the part of the Western working classes.[61] Only this would allow the achievements of capitalist modernity to be shared with autocratic and technologically backward Russia, rather than employed to exploit it. Subjective factors could work in the other direction as well, however: A Russian revolution would not need to follow one in the West; in fact, it could be "the point of departure" for such an uprising. (2) Another point implicit in the drafts of the letter to Zasulich was also clarified here: a Russian revolution could lead to a "communist development."[62] Russia would not need to go through an independent capitalist development to reap the fruits of modern socialism, provided that its revolution became the spark for a working class uprising in the more democratic and technologically developed world. This was a different and more radical claim than that he had made in the 1850s concerning a Chinese economic crisis sparking a European one and thus a revolution, or with regard to the Sepoy rebels in India as allies of the Western working classes. In the 1850s, he saw the national resistance movements in China and India as, at most, carrying the potential for a democratic transformation in those lands. In the 1870s, he saw an Irish national revolution, which would not have been communist in character, as a precondition for a communist transformation in Britain. In the late writings on Russia, however, he was arguing that a modern communist transformation was possible in an agrarian, technologically backward land like Russia, if it could ally itself with a revolution on the part of the Western working classes, and thus gain access on a cooperative basis to the fruits of Western modernity.[63]

Did Marx discern similar possibilities in places like India as well, whose communal forms he was also studying in this period? He never addressed this question explicitly. In the Zasulich drafts, as we have seen, he sometimes stresses Russia's uniqueness, at other times its commonalities with regard to India and other colonized non-Western societies. Nonetheless, I would argue, based on the preponderance of the evidence in the excerpt notebooks discussed in this chapter, that Marx did not intend to limit his new reflections about moving toward a communist revolution on the basis of indigenous communal forms to Russia alone.

This journey into Marx's writings on nationalism, race, ethnicity, and non-Western societies has, I hope, revealed the multidimensional character of his overall intellectual projects, especially in his later years. Marx's critique of capital, it has been shown, was far broader than is usually supposed. To be sure, he concentrated on the labor-capital relation within Western Europe and North America, but at the same time, he expended considerable time and energy on the analysis of non-Western societies, as well as that of race, ethnicity, and nationalism. While some of these writings show a problematically unilinear perspective and, on occasion, traces of ethnocentrism, the overall trajectory of Marx's writings on these issues moves in a different direction. The foregoing discussion has shown Marx to have created a multilinear and non-reductionist theory of history, to have analyzed the complexities and differences of non-Western societies, and to have refused to bind himself into a single model of development or revolution.

In 1848, Marx and Engels set out a theoretical model of capitalist society and its core contradictions in so prescient a manner that even today the descriptive power of *The Communist Manifesto* has no equal. In the *Manifesto*, they also espoused an implicitly and problematically unilinear concept of social progress. Precapitalist societies, especially China, which they characterized in ethnocentric terms as a "most barbarian" society, were destined to be forcibly penetrated and modernized by this new and dynamic social system. In his 1853 articles for the *New York Tribune*, Marx extended these perspectives to India, extolling what he then saw as the progressive features of British colonialism, as against India's caste-ridden and "unchanging" traditional social order. In this sense, he argued, India was a society without history, except for the history of its foreign conquerors, from Arab to British. Moreover, he held, Indian society had failed to resist these conquests, due to both its caste divisions and the society's general passivity. The communal social relations and communal property of the Indian village offered a solid foundation for the resultant "Oriental despotism." All of this left India particularly open to British colonialism, which in any case brought progress in its wake. Postcolonial and postmodern thinkers, most notably Edward Said, have criticized *The Communist Manifesto* and the 1853 India writings as a form of Orientalist knowledge fundamentally similar to the colonialist mindset.

Most of these critics have failed to notice that by 1853, Marx's perspective on Asia had begun to shift from the standpoint of the *Manifesto*, becoming more subtle, more dialectical. For he also wrote in the 1853 *Tribune* articles that a modernized India would find a way out of colonialism, which he now described as itself a form of "barbarism." Sooner or later, he argued, the end of colonialism in India would come about, either through the aid of the British working class, or by the formation of an Indian independence movement. As Indian scholars like Irfan Habib have pointed out, this aspect of Marx's 1853 writings on India constitutes the first instance of a major European thinker supporting India's independence.

By 1856–57, the anticolonialist side of Marx's thought became more pronounced, as he supported, also in the *Tribune*, the Chinese resistance to the British during the Second Opium War and the Sepoy Uprising in India. During this period, he began to incorporate some of his new thinking about India into one of his greatest theoretical works, the *Grundrisse* (1857–58). In this germinal treatise on the critique of political economy, he launched into a truly multilinear theory of history, wherein Asian societies had developed along a different pathway than that of the successive modes of production he had delineated for Western Europe—ancient Greco-Roman, feudal, and capitalist. Moreover, he compared and contrasted the communal property relations, as well as the broader communal social production, of early Roman society to those of contemporary India. While he had seen the Indian village's communal social forms as a prop of despotism in 1853, he now stressed that these forms could be either democratic or despotic.

During the 1860s, Marx concentrated on Europe and North America, writing little on Asia. It was in this period that he completed the first version of the first volume of *Capital*, as well as most of the drafts of what became volumes II and III of that work. However, it would be very wrong to think of Marx in this period as occupied solely with the capital relation and the class struggle, to the exclusion of nationalism, race, and ethnicity. In the period that he was completing *Capital*, he also concerned himself with the dialectics of race and class during the long years of the Civil War (1861–65). Although the North was a capitalist society, Marx threw himself into the antislavery cause, critically supporting the Lincoln government against the Confederacy. In his Civil War writings, he connected race to class in several important ways. First, he held that white racism had held back labor as a whole. Second, he wrote of the subjectivity of the enslaved Black laboring class as a decisive force in the war's favorable outcome for the North. Third, he noted—as an example of the finest internationalism—British labor's unstinting support for the North, despite the harsh economic suffering the Northern blockade on Southern cotton had unleashed on Manchester and other industrial centers. Finally, his First International warned presciently that America's failure to grant full political and social rights to the emancipated slaves would once again drown the country in blood.

Marx also supported the Polish uprising of 1863, which sought to restore national independence to that long-suffering country. Already in *The Communist Manifesto*, Marx and Engels had signaled their support for Polish independence as a core principle for the labor and socialist movements. Marx's writings on Poland and Russia were intimately connected. He and his generation viewed Russia as a malevolent, reactionary power, which constituted the biggest threat to Europe's democratic and socialist movements. He saw the Russian autocracy, which he considered to be a form of "Oriental despotism" inherited from the Mongol conquests, as rooted in that country's agrarian character, particularly in the communal forms and communal property relations that predominated in the Russian village. As with India and China, by 1858 Marx began to shift his view of Russia, taking note of the looming emancipation of the serfs and the possibility of an agrarian revolution, as seen in several of his articles on Russia for the *Tribune*. Since Russian-occupied Poland stood between Russia proper and Western Europe, Poland's revolutionary movement represented a deep contradiction within the Russian Empire, one that had hampered its efforts to intervene against the European revolutions of 1830 and to an extent, those in 1848 as well. At the same time, Marx severely critiqued French and other Western democrats for having failed to reciprocate by adequately supporting their Polish allies. Moreover, these betrayals of Poland weakened the Western democratic and socialist movements, contributing to their defeat through Russian intervention, as had occurred on a major scale in 1849. Toward the end of his life, Marx began to emphasize anticapitalist strains within the Polish revolutionary movement.

As a result of working-class support for the Northern cause in the Civil War and then the 1863 uprising in Poland, an international network of labor activists came into being. This network—chiefly British, French, and German—joined together in 1864 to form the International Working Men's Association (later known as the First International), for which Marx came to serve as chief organizer and theorist. In this way, Marx's most sustained involvement with labor during his lifetime occurred under the backdrop of struggles against slavery, racism, and national oppression. Moreover, within a few years of the founding of the International, it became caught up in the Irish independence movement. The International's involvement with Ireland began in 1867, the very year that *Capital* came off the press in its first German edition. To their immense credit, and with no small amount of theoretical and political argument on Marx's part, the British labor leaders of the International initially took a remarkably strong stance against British domination of Ireland. During the years 1867–70, when the Irish conflict was at a boil, Marx's arguments concerning the relationship between national emancipation and the class struggle were hammered out, not as pure theory, but as arguments within the largest labor organization of the era.

Over time, Marx worked out a new theoretical position on Britain and Ireland that had implications reaching far beyond this particular historical juncture. His theorization of Ireland in this period marked the culmination of his writings on ethnicity, race, and nationalism. Earlier, he had predicted in modernist fashion that the British labor movement, a product of the most advanced capitalist society of the time, would first take power and then enable Ireland to regain its independence, also offering the newly independent country both material and political support. By 1869–70, however, Marx wrote that he had changed his position, now arguing that Irish independence would have to come first. British workers, he held, were so greatly imbued with nationalist pride and great power arrogance toward the Irish that they had developed a false consciousness, binding them to the dominant classes of Britain, and thus attenuating class conflict within British society. This impasse could be broken only by direct support for Irish national independence on the part of British labor, something that would also serve to reunite labor within Britain, where Irish immigrant labor formed a subproletariat. British workers often blamed competition from the desperately poor Irish for lowering their wages, while the Irish immigrants often distrusted the British labor movement as merely another expression of the very British society that was ruling over them, both at home and abroad. On more than one occasion, Marx linked his conceptualization of class, ethnicity, and nationalism for the British and the Irish to race relations in the United States, where he compared the situation of the Irish in Britain to that of African Americans. He also compared the attitudes of the British workers to the poor whites of the American South, who had too often united with the white planters against their fellow Black workers. In this sense, Marx was creating a larger dialectical concept of race, ethnicity, and class. At the same time, he critiqued narrow forms of nationalism, particularly Irish versions that retreated into religious identities or remained so aloof from the British people that they failed to take account of the work of the International.

Almost all of these considerations found their way into Marx's most important theoretical work, *Capital*, albeit at times only as subthemes. In the 1872–75 French edition of *Capital*, the last one he prepared for publication, Marx not only corrected the translation by Joseph Roy, but also revised the entire book. Several of these revisions concerned the question of multilinear pathways of social development. Some key passages Marx changed for the French edition concerned the dialectic of capitalist development out of Western feudalism that was at the heart of the book's part eight, "The Primitive Accumulation of Capital." In direct and clear language, Marx now stated that the transition outlined in the part on primitive accumulation applied only to Western Europe. In this sense, the future of non-Western societies was open, was not determined by that of Western Europe.

India also figured prominently at various points in the text of *Capital*. The Indian village served as an example of precapitalist social relations, while the sharp decline of traditional Indian manufactures and the resultant starvation of these handicraft workers was used to illustrate the terribly destructive effects of capitalist globalization at a human level. In addition, Marx devoted a major section of the first volume of *Capital* to the ways in which British capitalist penetration had resulted in the destruction of the land and the people of Ireland. The forced immigration of millions of Irish to America, he concluded, showed the revenge of history, as Irish labor was helping to form the foundations of a new capitalist power that would soon challenge Britain's world dominance. Finally, he took up slavery and racism in *Capital*, showing the ways in which the extermination of the indigenous peoples of the Americas and the enslavement of Africans constituted major factors in early capitalist development. He also pointed at several key junctures to the deleterious effects of slavery and racism on the nascent labor movement in the United States, writing in *Capital* that "labor in a white skin cannot emancipate itself where it is branded in a black skin" (*Capital* I, 414). In addition, concluded that the end of slavery had opened up important new possibilities for American labor.

By the 1870s, Marx returned to his earlier preoccupation with Asia, while also deepening his studies of Russia. Whereas he had previously concentrated on Russian foreign policy, he now began to learn Russian in order to study its internal economic and social relations. Marx's interest in Russia increased with the publication of *Capital* in Russian in 1872, especially after the book generated more debate there than it had in Germany.

During the years 1879–82, Marx embarked upon a series of excerpt notebooks on current scholarship on a multifaceted group of non-Western and non-European societies, among them contemporary India, Indonesia (Java), Russia, Algeria, and Latin America. He also made notes on studies of indigenous peoples, such as Native Americans and Australian Aborigines. One core theme of these excerpt notebooks was the communal social relations and property forms found in so many of these societies. While these research notes on other authors contained only intermittent or indirect expressions of his own viewpoint, some broad themes could nonetheless be discerned. In his studies of India, for example, two issues emerged. First, his notes indicate a new appreciation of historical development in India, as against his earlier view of that country as a society without history. Although he still saw the communal forms of India's villages as relatively continuous over the centuries, he now noted a series of important changes within those communal forms, as they evolved from clan-based to residential communes. Second, these notes show his preoccupation, not with Indian passivity as in 1853, but with conflict and resistance in the face of foreign conquest, whether against the Muslim incursions of the medieval period or the British colonialists of his own time. Moreover, he noted, some of this resistance was based on clan and communal social forms.

In his studies of India, Algeria, and Latin America, Marx discerned the persistence of communal forms in the face of attempts by Western colonialism to destroy them in favor of private property forms. In some cases, like Algeria, these communal forms were directly tied to anticolonial resistance. By this time, Marx's earlier notions of the progressiveness of colonialism had also fallen away, replaced by a harsh and unremitting condemnation.

As had been the case in some of his earlier writings, especially in the 1840s, gender was a prominent theme in Marx's 1879–82 notes on indigenous peoples like the Iroquois, as well as on Roman society. Here it is possible to compare Marx and Engels directly on gender, since Marx's notes on the anthropologist Lewis Henry Morgan's *Ancient Society* were composed in 1880 or 1881. Engels discovered them after Marx's death and used them as background for his own study, *The Origin of the Family, Private Property, and the State* (1884). While Engels's book has many flaws, it stands out in a positive sense as a ringing defense of women's equality, the only full-length book on that topic by a major theoretician of the early socialist movement. As against Engels, however, Marx tended to avoid any idealization of the gender relations of preliterate societies like the Iroquois. Always the dialectician, Marx followed Hegel in discerning dualities and contradictions within each social sphere, even that of egalitarian and communal preliterate societies. Nor did he seem to share Engels's simplistic view that a "world-historic defeat of the female sex" had occurred in Europe and the Middle East during the transition from preliterate clan societies to class ones. As against Engels, it is likely that Marx was looking at these alternate forms of gender relations for his own time, not merely as a consideration of the origins of class society, but also as potential sources of resistance to capital.

If Marx's theorization of nationalism, ethnicity, and class culminated in his 1869–70 writings on Ireland, those on non-Western societies reached their high point in his 1877–82 reflections on Russia. In a series of letters and their drafts, as well as the 1882 preface to the Russian edition of *The Communist Manifesto* he coauthored with Engels, Marx began to sketch a multilinear theory of social development and of revolution for Russia. These writings built on multilinear themes from the French edition of *Capital*. In his Russia writings, Marx repeatedly and emphatically denied that the argument of *Capital* offered any clear-cut prediction about Russia's future. He noted that the social structure of the Russian communal village differed markedly from that of the precapitalist village of Western feudalism. This difference between Western and Russian precapitalist social structures suggested the possibility of an alternate form of social development and modernization for Russia, if it could avoid absorption by capitalism. Since Russia's rural communes were contemporaneous with industrial capitalism in the West, a village-based social revolution in Russia might be able to draw upon the resources of Western modernity while avoiding the pain of capitalist development. Marx was in no way proposing an autarky or a socialism in one country for Russia, however, which would have meant a socialism based on a low level of economic and cultural development, a notion he had critiqued as early as 1844 as "crude communism." For as Marx and Engels argued in their 1882 preface to the Russian edition of the *Manifesto*, a radical transformation on the basis of Russia's rural communes would be possible only if accompanied by parallel revolutionary transformations on the part of the working class movements of Western Europe. In their preface, they also averred that such a Russian revolution could have a communist basis. Earlier, Marx had viewed anticolonial movements in China and India as allies of the Western working classes; he had viewed national movements in Poland and

Ireland in a similar light. Here, in the late writings on Russia, he went further, arguing that a communist development was a real possibility in noncapitalist Russia, if a Russian revolution could link up with its counterpart based in the Western labor movement.

In sum, I have argued in this study that Marx developed a dialectical theory of social change that was neither unilinear nor exclusively class-based. Just as his theory of social development evolved in a more multilinear direction, so his theory of revolution began over time to concentrate increasingly on the intersectionality of class with ethnicity, race, and nationalism. To be sure, Marx was not a philosopher of difference in the postmodernist sense, for the critique of a single overarching entity, capital, was at the center of his entire intellectual enterprise. But centrality did not mean univocality or exclusivity. Marx's mature social theory revolved around a concept of totality that not only offered considerable scope for particularity and difference but also on occasion made those particulars—race, ethnicity, or nationality—determinants for the totality. Such was the case when he held that an Irish national revolution might be the "lever" that would help to overthrow capitalism in Britain, or when he wrote that a revolution rooted in Russia's rural communes might serve as the starting point for a Europe-wide communist development.

On the one hand, Marx analyzed how the power of capital dominated the globe. It reached into every society and created a universalizing worldwide system of industry and trade for the first time, and with it a new universal class of the oppressed, the industrial working class. But on the other hand, in developing this universalizing theory of history and society, Marx—as emphasized in this book—strove to avoid formalistic and abstract universals. Again and again, he attempted to work out the specific ways in which the universalizing powers of capital and class were manifesting themselves in particular societies or social groups, whether in non-Western societies not yet fully penetrated by capital like Russia and India, or in the specific interactions of working-class consciousness with ethnicity, race, and nationalism in the industrially more-developed countries.

*

Another question arises, however. What does Marx's multicultural, multilinear social dialectic reveal about today's globalized capitalism? Does his multilinear perspective on social development concerning Russia—and other noncapitalist lands in his own time—have any direct relevance today? Here I would argue that this is so today only to a limited degree. There are of course some areas of the world—like Chiapas, Mexico, or the highlands of Bolivia and Guatemala, or similar communities across Latin America, Africa, Asia, and the Middle East—where indigenous communal forms survive. But none of these are on the scale of Russian or Indian communal forms during Marx's day. Nonetheless, vestiges of these communal forms sometimes follow peasants into the cities and in any case, important anticapitalist movements have developed recently in places like Mexico and Bolivia, based upon these indigenous communal forms. On the whole, however, even these areas have been penetrated by capital to a far greater degree than was true of the Indian or Russian village of the 1880s. Marx's multilinear approach toward Russia, India, and other noncapitalist lands is more relevant for today at a general theoretical or methodological level, however. It can serve an important heuristic purpose, as a major example of his dialectical theory of society. Therein, he worked on the basis of the general principle that the entire world was coming under the domination of capital and its value form, while at the same time analyzing very concretely and historically many of the major societies of the globe that had not yet come fully under that domination.

At the level of the intersectionality of class with race, ethnicity, and nationalism, many of Marx's theoretical conclusions are more directly relevant to us today. In all of the major industrial countries, ethnic divisions, often sparked by immigration, have transformed the working classes. Here, the principles underlining Marx's writings on the relationship of race and class in Civil War–era America, on that of the struggle for Polish independence to the wider European revolution, or on that of the Irish independence movement to British labor, have a more obvious continuing relevance. Marx's writings on these issues can help us to critique the toxic mix of racism and prisonization in the United States, or to analyze the Los Angeles uprising of 1992, or to understand the 2005 rebellion by immigrant youth in the Paris suburbs. Again, the strength of Marx's theoretical perspective lies in his refusal to separate these issues from the critique of capital, something that gives them a broader context, without collapsing ethnicity, race, or nationality into class.

Whether (1) as a multilinear dialectic of social development or (2) as a heuristic example that offers indications about the theorization of today's indigenous movements in the face of global capitalism or (3) as a theorization of class in relation to race, ethnicity, and nationalism, I believe that the writings by Marx that have been the focus of this book offer some important vantage points for today.

APPENDIX:
THE VICISSITUDES OF THE
MARX-ENGELS GESAMTAUSGABE
FROM THE 1920S TO TODAY

To this day there are a significant number of writings by Marx, especially on the themes of this study, which have never been published in any language. Why this is still the case over a century after Marx's death?

The problem really began with Engels and continues today. While he labored long and hard to edit and publish what he considered to be a definitive edition of volume I of *Capital* in 1890, and brought out volumes II and III of that work in 1885 and 1894 by carefully editing and arranging Marx's draft manuscripts, Engels did not plan or even propose the publication of the whole of Marx's writings. Under the post–Engels Second International, little more was done.

RIAZANOV AND THE FIRST
MARX-ENGELS GESAMTAUSGABE

It took the Russian Revolution of 1917 to break the impasse. With the strong encouragement of Lenin and the financial backing of the new Soviet state, the distinguished Marx scholar David Riazanov and his colleagues began the first *Marx-Engels Gesamtausgabe* (hereafter MEGA[1]) in the Soviet Union in the early 1920s. Since the non-Communist Second International still owned the manuscripts and letters of Marx and Engels, the director of the newly established Frankfurt School, Carl Gruenberg, who had relations with both Communists and Socialists, became the go-between. It was the Frankfurt School's staff that was charged, according to a formal agreement, with photocopying the papers of Marx and Engels in the German Social Democratic Party's archives in Berlin for Riazanov's Moscow-based Marx-Engels Institute "with a complete record of all peculiarities and special characteristics of the originals which cannot be recorded by photography" (cited in Wiggershaus [1986] 1994, 32). Riazanov established a far-reaching plan for MEGA[1], a small part of which was actually published during the years 1928–35. He divided MEGA[1] into three sections, each of which was to contain writings in the original language in which Marx or Engels had written them, usually German, English, or French, as well as a rigorous scholarly apparatus.

Section I. Philosophical, Economic, Historical, and Political Works

MEGA[1] eventually issued eight volumes of this section covering the years up to 1850, including most notably the *1844 Manuscripts* and the *German Ideology*, neither of which had been published by Engels or the Second International. Earlier, in 1927, Riazanov had published the *1844 Manuscripts* for the first time anywhere, in a Russian translation.

Section II. Capital *and Related Manuscripts*

This section was to comprise all editions of volume I of *Capital* as Marx wrote them or Engels edited them, from the first German edition of 1867 to Engels's "definitive" fourth German edition of 1890. It was also to include volumes II and III as edited by Engels, the original manuscripts for those volumes, plus other texts such as the *Grundrisse* and *Theories of Surplus Value*. None of this section of MEGA[1] was published, although the *Grundrisse* eventually appeared as a separate volume in 1939–41.

Section III. Letters between Marx and Engels

Only four volumes were actually published, covering all known letters of Marx and Engels to each other from 1844 to 1883, but not letters to or from third parties.

For all his commitment to publishing the whole of Marx, even Riazanov rejected the idea of publishing one type of writing by Marx: the excerpt notebooks—texts such as the *Ethnological Notebooks* in which Marx had copied extracts from, summarized, and commented on many of the texts he had studied throughout his life. In a 1923 report on his plans for MEGA[1] to Moscow's Socialist Academy, a report which was also published in Germany the following year by Frankfurt School Director Gruenberg, Riazanov referred to a fourth or "final group" of Marx's writings, "the notebooks," which he indicated would be of use mainly to Marx biographers. He mentioned in particular "three thick notebooks on the economic crisis of 1857 . . . , a chronological survey of world history up to the middle of the seventeenth century" as well as "some mathematical notebooks." He made an exception for the last of these, which were slated for publication.

In a surprising outburst of condescension toward Marx, this usually rigorous Marx editor added:

> If in 1881–82 he lost his ability for intensive, independent, intellectual creation, he nevertheless never lost the ability for research. Sometimes, in reconsidering

these Notebooks, the question arises: Why did he waste so much time on this systematic, fundamental summary, or expend so much labor as he spent as late as the year 1881, on one basic book on geology, summarizing it chapter by chapter. In the 63rd year of his life—that is inexcusable pedantry. Here is another example: he received, in 1878, a copy of Morgan's work. On 98 pages of his very miniscule handwriting (you should know that a single page of his is the equivalent of a minimum of 2.2 pages of print) he makes a detailed summary of Morgan. In such manner does the old Marx work.[1]

This attitude helps explain why Marx's notebooks were not slated to appear in MEGA[1].

An independent spirit, Riazanov averred publicly that he was a Marxist but not a Leninist. By the late 1920s, he began to feel the heavy hand of Stalin's regime. In 1931, Stalin had him arrested and deported to a forced labor camp, where he was executed in 1938. MEGA[1] ceased to appear in 1935, it too having become a victim of Stalinism.[2] For example, the publication of Marx's *Mathematical Manuscripts*, already edited by the young German mathematician Julius Gumbel (who had been recommended by Albert Einstein) and even set in proofs by 1927, did not appear until 1968. In Stalinist style, that 1968 edition did not mention Gumbel (Vogt 1995).[3]

THE *COLLECTED WORKS* OF MARX AND ENGELS

Riazanov also developed a plan for a more limited collected works of Marx and Engels, which was published in Russian during the years 1928–46. This edition became the basis for the German Marx-Engels *Werke* (1956–68) as well as other single-language editions, such as the English-language *Collected Works* of Marx and Engels (1975–2004). Taking the latter edition as our example, it also has three parts.

I. Volumes 1–27: Marx's and Engels's published and unpublished books, articles, and manuscripts
II. Volumes 28–37: Marx's major economic writings, from the *Grundrisse* to *Capital*
III. Volumes 38–50: Letters of Marx and Engels

Like all Stalinist editions, MECW has serious omissions as well as other problems. The prefaces and explanatory notes are often dogmatic and sometimes misleading. Divergences between Marx and Engels are sometimes covered over. Their sharp attacks on the Russian Empire's territorial ambitions, and their strong support for anti-Russian movements on the part of the Poles and the Chechens are sometimes concealed, or even ascribed to errors by Marx or Engels. But the biggest problem with MECW, MEW, and similar editions is that they are not the MEGA. For example, only a single version of *Capital*, volume I, is included, which leaves out the process by which Marx changed and developed it through its various editions, as well as important material from the French edition that was left out by Engels. Nor do they reproduce Marx's drafts for volumes II or III of *Capital*; only those volumes as edited by Engels are included. Additionally, very few letters to Marx or Engels are included. Finally, almost none of the excerpt notebooks appear in these additions.

MARX'S *OEUVRES*, AS EDITED BY RUBEL

During the long years before 1989, when the Soviet Union and East Germany exercised a near monopoly over the publication Marx's writings, the French Marxologist Maximilien Rubel's independent editions, chronologies, and biographies of Marx offered a libertarian alternative, albeit on a much smaller scale. In 1952, Rubel coauthored an attack on the Marx-Engels-Lenin Institute in Moscow for its "silence" regarding "the fate of Riazanov and his enterprise," adding that Stalin "could not tolerate the publication *in its entirety* of an oeuvre that stigmatized his despotism via the merciless struggle waged by Marx and Engels against police states: those of Louis Napoleon, of Prussia, of Tsarism" (Rubel and Bracke-Desrousseaux 1952, 113; original emphasis). A decade later, Rubel, who by then had gained financing from a French academic institute, began to issue his edition of Marx's *Oeuvres* with France's most prestigious publisher, Éditions Gallimard. From 1963 to 1994, four large volumes appeared, each containing about 1,500 pages of Marx and 500 pages of Rubel's scholarly prefaces and footnotes. Unlike in Stalinist editions, differences between Marx and Engels were noted, especially with regard to *Capital*.

Rubel's commentary was often marred by a virulent anti-Hegelianism, however (K. Anderson 1992, 1997a). Another problem was that Rubel was also opposed to publishing the excerpt notebooks. Just before his death in 1996 he gave a surprisingly negative response to an interviewer's question on whether we could expect to see any important new material from Marx in the coming years as a result of the second MEGA, discussed below: "Frankly, I do not believe so. Riazanov only wanted to publish forty volumes quite simply because he thought it useless to publish the whole of the excerpt notebooks (more than two hundred!)" (Weill 1995).

THE SECOND *MARX-ENGELS GESAMTAUSGABE*: BEFORE AND AFTER 1989

In 1975, MEGA[2] was begun from Moscow and East Berlin. In pure Stalinist style, its editors made no reference to the pioneering work of Riazanov, their illustrious and martyred predecessor. As with MECW and other similar editions, the prefaces and notes had a dogmatic character, although the actual editing of Marx's texts was quite meticulous.

Following the collapse of East Germany and the Soviet Union in 1989–91, MEGA[2]'s funding was severely undermined. After a period of difficulty, it began to receive new funding from Western foundations, in recent years mainly through the International Institute of Social History in Amsterdam and the Berlin-Brandenburg Academy of Sciences. While the current level of funding is much more limited than before 1989, and the edition has been very slightly scaled back, editorial control has passed to a varied group of mainly Western Marx scholars. For example, the post-1989 advisory board has included internationally known figures like Shlomo Avineri, Iring Fetscher, Eric Hobsbawm, the late Eugene Kamenka, Bertell Ollman, the late Maximilien Rubel (who resigned just before his death), and Immanuel Wallerstein. Overall editorial control is in the hands of the International Marx-Engels Foundation, an affiliate of the International Institute of Social History, and the Berlin-Brandenburg Academy of Sciences, while editing groups are functioning in Germany, Russia, France, Japan, the United States, and other countries.

MEGA² includes four sections,[4] the last of these the excerpt notebooks:

Section I. Works, Articles, and Drafts

Of thirty-two volumes now planned, seventeen have appeared. Especially notable in this section is volume I/2, which includes Marx's *1844 Manuscripts*. Here, for the first time, two versions of these manuscripts are published, the one established by MEGA¹ that has been the basis for the English translations up to now, and a new version, this one rougher in form but closer to the original. Interestingly, in the first 10 pages of the new version, Marx is writing three essays at once, in separate vertical columns. MEGA² I/2 shows that Marx composed what is known today as the "Critique of the Hegelian Dialectic" of 1844 in at least two parts, with the part on Feuerbach separated from the text in which Marx extols "the dialectic of negativity as the moving and creating principle" of Hegel's *Phenomenology of Spirit* (MEGA² I/2, 292).

Section II. Capital *and Preliminary Studies*

Of fifteen volumes now planned, thirteen have been published, making this the most complete section of MEGA². What has already been published includes all the editions of volume I of *Capital* that either Marx or Engels prepared for publication. Important here is MEGA² II/10, a reprint of Engels's 1890 fourth German edition, but with an important addition: an appendix that gathers together sixty pages of text, much of it very significant, from Marx's 1872–75 French edition of volume I. This material was not included by Engels in volume I and has yet to appear in standard German or English editions of that volume. Other volumes include Marx's draft manuscripts for what became volumes II and III of *Capital*, which can now be readily compared to the versions published by Engels.[5]

Section III. Correspondence

Of thirty-five volumes planned, twelve covering most of the years through 1865 have been published. MEGA² includes all surviving letters by Marx and Engels, as well as those written to them.

Section IV. Excerpt Notebooks

Of thirty-two volumes planned, eleven have been published. What is most notable here are the texts that have never been published before in any language. Although Marx's "Notes on Bakunin's 'Statehood and Anarchy'" and his "Notes on Adolph Wagner" are included in the MECW, and parts of the 1879–82 notebooks on non-Western and precapitalist societies and the *Mathematical Manuscripts* have been published separately, a vast array of new material awaits publication in section IV. Among the volumes already published is MEGA² IV/3, which appeared to great acclaim in 1998 as the first volume produced under the new editorial guidelines, as edited by Georgi Bagaturia, Lev Curbanov, Olga Koroleva, and Ljudmilla Vasina, with Jürgen Rojahn. It contains Marx's 1844–47 notebooks on political economists such as Jean-Baptiste Say, Jean-Charles-Leonard Sismondi, Charles Babbage, Andrew Ure, and Nassau Senior. None of these texts had been previously published in any language.[6] Excerpt notebooks from Marx slated for eventual publication include, besides considerable material on political economy, the following: (1) notes from 1853 and 1880–81 on Indonesia, the latter to appear fairly soon in MEGA² IV/27 and in Marx's "Commune, Empire, and Class: 1879–82 Notebooks on Non-Western and Precapitalist Societies" (forthcoming); (2) 1852 notes on the history of women and gender relations; (3) many notes from the 1870s and 1880s on agriculture in Russia plus some on prairie farming in the United States; (4) notes on Ireland from the 1860s; (5) notes on agriculture in Roman and Carolingian times; and (6) a massive chronology of world history composed during the 1880s.

In this way, the publication of a complete edition of Marx's writings is continuing, having survived both Stalinism and Nazism. The ongoing work on MEGA² stands on the shoulders of those who, during the tortured twentieth century, worked to collect, preserve, and edit Marx's original writings, sometimes at the cost of their lives.

INTRODUCTION

1. Here and elsewhere, I have capitalized "Black" and "African American," as these refer to a specific ethnic group, as I have done with "Irish" or "Polish," while leaving the less-specific term "white" lowercased.

2. To be sure, such an historical approach to Marx's thought runs the risk of discovering changing perspectives where only different emphases are at work. This problem has been articulated most forcefully by the political theorist Bertell Ollman, who warns us in his *Dialectical Investigations* (1993) that many seeming differences or inconsistencies in Marx's formulations are the result of different levels of generality (a narrow focus on Russian or British society, one on global capitalism, one on human history as a whole, etc.) or of different intended audiences (himself only as in his drafts and notes, the Socialist movement as in his polemical writings, both the scholarly community and the latter as in *Capital*, etc.). Keeping such warnings in mind, I have tried to be cautious when referring to change or evolution in Marx's thought. Nonetheless, I believe that the preponderance of the evidence shows important change and evolution in Marx's treatment of a number of societies, especially India, Russia, and Ireland. I have tried to be cautious about ascribing changed positions to Marx for another reason as well: I see Marx's most fundamental concepts—his notion of dialectics, his theory of alienation and fetishism, his concept of capital and the exploitation of labor—as ones that run fairly consistently through the whole of his work, from the 1840s to the 1880s. In this sense, my discussion of change and development in Marx's work has little in common with attempts to locate "epistemological breaks" in his thought, as seen most prominently in Louis Althusser's structuralist Marxism.

3. To date, no comprehensive intellectual biography of Marx has been published in any language. Such a study would obviously have to run several volumes to do justice to the topic. In writing this book, I have found the single-volume biographies by Maximilien Rubel and Margaret Manale (1975), David Riazanov ([1927] 1973), David

McLellan (1973), Jerrold Seigel (1978), Saul Padover (1978), Franz Mehring ([1918] 1962), and Francis Wheen (2000) to be especially helpful. I have also found very useful Hal Draper's *Chronicle* (1985a) and *Glossary* (1986), the two Marx bibliographies by Rubel (1956, 1960), that by Draper (1985b), and the annotated bibliography of the interpretive literature in Barbier (1992). The often-anonymous reference notes and glossaries in the Moscow-edited *Collected Works* of Marx and Engels (MECW) are also very valuable, but they often exhibit an extremely ideological character. In the 1920s, before Stalin came to power, the Russians produced high-quality editions of Marx's work under the overall editorship of David Riazanov, who was executed in the 1930s. Subsequent Soviet editions of Marx sometimes covered up controversial issues for Stalinist orthodoxy such as differences between Marx and Engels, Marx's relation to Hegel, or Marx's strong critiques of Russia. These problems persisted long after Stalin's death, all the way until the collapse of the Soviet Union in 1991. For more discussion of the history of the various editions of Marx's collected works, see the appendix.

CHAPTER 1

1. While it is true that Marx and Engels are both listed as authors, Engels himself acknowledged in an 1888 preface that although the *Communist Manifesto* was "a joint production . . . the fundamental proposition which forms its nucleus belongs to Marx" (MECW 26, 517).

2. Evidently embarrassed by the ethnocentric term "barbarian," the Marx scholar Terrell Carver unjustifiably softens Marx and Engels's "most barbarian [*barbarischsten*]" to "most primitive" in what is in many other ways a valuable new translation of the *Manifesto* (Marx 1996, 5).

3. In January 1848, during the same period in which Marx was polishing the final text of the *Manifesto*, Engels published an article in the Chartist paper the *Northern Star*, in which he declares that the French "conquest of Algeria is an important and fortunate fact for the progress of civilization" (MECW 6, 471). Although I will usually be giving page references to Marx and Engels, *Collected Works*, I have also consulted two useful one-volume collections of Marx's writings on non-European societies, one of them edited with a scholarly introduction by the Israeli political theorist Shlomo Avineri (Marx 1968) and the other with comprehensive footnotes but no introduction by anonymous editors in Moscow (Marx and Engels 1972a). While Avineri features the above cited article by Engels on Algeria rather tendentiously as the first selection in his volume, the rival volume edited in Moscow fails to include it at all.

4. The translation of this passage has been altered slightly. Marx and Engels write, "den Menschen an seinen natürlichen Vorgesetzten knüpften," which the existing English translations render as "bound man to his 'natural superiors,'" but I have, here and elsewhere in this book, often rendered the German word *Menschen* as "human beings" or "people" rather than the more gendered "man." Fortunately, the German

language allows one to modernize the translation of Marx in this manner without violating the spirit of his text. In fact, "human beings" is a more literal translation for "Menschen" than "men" or "man," since German also possesses the words *Männer* or *Mann*. Elsewhere in this book, I have sometimes silently altered translations of Marx after consulting the German (or French) originals, while citing the most accessible or generally best English translation. If the original is in German and in the Marx-Engels *Werke* (MEW), I will not usually cite it, but I will do so more often if it is in French.

5. Throughout this book, I use the term "non-Western" in a broad sense to designate not only the economically underdeveloped non-European societies of the time (Latin America, Africa, the Middle East, and Asia), but also some of the economically underdeveloped areas of Europe (Poland and Russia).

6. As will be discussed in chapter 5, another element to consider here is *The German Ideology* (1846), in which Marx and Engels sketched four universal stages of development, from stateless clan societies, to the slave-based economies of the Greco-Roman world, to European feudalism, and to modern capitalist society, all of this without taking into account what Marx would later consider as a separate "Asiatic" mode of production.

7. Engels also wrote for the *Tribune*, but his articles appeared under Marx's name, or anonymously, as did many of Marx's, as well. Over the years, the editors of the writings of Marx and Engels have usually been able to pinpoint which were written by Marx and which by Engels.

8. A recent attempt to overcome this misperception has been carried out in Marx 2007, a one-volume collection of selected *Tribune* writings. Editor James Ledbetter notes "that there is considerable and important overlap" between Marx's *Tribune* articles and his "serious" writings (2007, xxii; see also Taylor 1996). The first substantial collection of writings by Marx and Engels for the *Tribune*, which stressed their articles on non-Western societies, appeared in a volume edited by the liberal journalist Henry Christman, with a scholarly introduction by Charles Blitzer (Marx and Engels 1966).

9. I discuss the French edition of *Capital* in chapter 5. More broadly, I would like to question the usual notion of Marx as a German thinker rather than a Western European one. Marx actually spent more years of his life in England (1849–83) than in Germany (1818–43, 1848–49). Concerning the lifetime writings of Marx and Engels, the Marx scholar Gerd Callesen estimates that "60 percent are in German, 30 percent are in English, 5 percent in French" (2002, 79). A prominent text Marx composed and published in English was his analysis of the Paris Commune, "The Civil War in France" (1871). Besides the last version of *Capital* I, other important Marx texts for which the French version is the original are *The Poverty of Philosophy* (1847) and the letter to Vera Zasulich and its drafts (1881).

10. Marx occasionally discusses colonialism in these early *Tribune* articles, however. In "The Chartists," a remarkable piece published in 1852, he recounts in great detail a speech by his friend the Chartist leader Ernest Jones to a wildly cheering crowd of twenty thousand workers in Halifax. While Jones aimed most of his thunder at the

exploitation of labor in England, his denunciations of what Marx terms "Whiggery and class rule," also included attacks on British colonialism, as Marx is careful to report: "*Who voted for Irish coercion, the gagging bill, and tampering with the Irish press? The Whig! There he sits! Turn him out! . . . Who voted against inquiry into colonial abuses and in favor of Ward and Torrington, the tyrants of Ionia and Ceylon? . . .* Who voted against shortening the nightwork of bakers, against inquiry into the condition of frame-work knitters, against medical inspectors of workhouses, against preventing little children from working before six in the morning, against parish relief for pregnant women of the poor, and against the Ten Hours Bill? The Whig—there he sits; turn him out!" (MECW 11, 340; emphasis added). For a recent discussion of Marx's relation to Chartism, see Black 2004.

11. Marx had begun to study the social structures of non-Western societies in the 1840s, as can be seen in parts of his massive 1846–47 excerpt notebook on Gustav von Gülich's five-volume history of trade and agriculture. Marx's notes, which were first published in the new MEGA², IV/6 in 1983, comprise over nine hundred printed pages and cover most areas of the globe, including substantial treatments of the Middle East, Africa, Asia, and Latin America. For a description of MEGA², see the appendix.

12. Engels, who had trained as a Prussian artillery officer and had taken part in the armed resistance to the Prussian army during the 1848–49 revolution in Germany, often wrote articles on military and geographic subjects, which Marx submitted to the *Tribune* as his own.

13. In part, this letter is a response to one from Engels discussing the clan-based social structures of the ancient Jews and Arabs.

14. Ian Cummins also attacks Marx's "fundamentally Eurocentric approach," again ascribing it to Hegelian influence (1980, 63).

15. As Hegel scholar Peter Hodgson notes, the German philosopher's "general assessment of Hinduism . . . was intended as a deliberate corrective to what he took to be uncritical enthusiasm in German intellectual circles," particularly in the writings of Friedrich Schlegel (Hodgson 1988, 46).

16. Of course, even this acknowledgement of Indian accomplishments was a two-edged sword for Hegel, who disparaged mathematical reason as far inferior to philosophical reason.

17. A number of scholars have overplayed the similarity between Hegel's views of India and Marx's 1853 writings. For example, the sociologist Daniel Thorner attributes to Hegel the notion that "Indian villages were fixed and immutable," even though Hegel had not analyzed the Indian village (Thorner [1966] 1990, 444; see also Nimni 1994). Marx drew these ideas from other sources.

18. Marx sent his articles to New York by sea, which took nearly two weeks. This one was datelined June 10, but here and below, I have cited the actual date of publication.

19. Western intellectuals of the 1850s viewed Indian society as in many respects an earlier form of European society that had been preserved because of its extreme traditionalism. Thorner points out that the relationship between Sanskrit and most

European languages had been recently discovered, and "it was widely held that Indian origins could be found for many aspects of European social history, forms of the family, the commune, etc." ([1966] 1990, 450). This colored Marx's perceptions of India and Indonesia.

20. Marx's use of the term "revolution" to describe the effects of colonial rule, so jarring today, but even so in 1853, was deliberate. As he wrote to Engels on June 14, 1853, this phrase, which he predicts that the *Tribune* editors "will find very shocking," was part of a "clandestine campaign" against the left-of-center American economist Henry Charles Carey, whose protectionist views the paper was touting. This protectionist slant, which dovetailed with that of northern capital, Marx writes, "is also the key to the mystery why the *Tribune*, despite all its 'isms' and socialist flourishes, manages to be the 'leading journal' in the United States" (MECW 39, 346; see also Perelman 1987).

21. According to contemporary historians of India, including Irfan Habib (2006; see also P. Anderson 1974), this is at best an exaggeration. The Indian village was neither as isolated nor as free of private property as Marx suggests here. Nonetheless, it was a more collectivist institution than the medieval European village, let alone that under modern capitalism. I would like to thank the economist and Marx scholar Paresh Chattopadhyay for discussing this issue with me.

22. The most problematic of Marx's India writings, it is the one most often cited and anthologized. It is the only article on India included in the best-known anthology of Marx's writings, the liberal political theorist Robert Tucker's *Marx-Engels Reader* (1978).

23. Said's error here highlights a more general problem with *Orientalism*, where literary and cultural expressions are seen as constitutive of economically based social structures like imperialism.

24. On this point, see the editorial notes by Erich Trunz to the German edition of Goethe's writings (Goethe 1949) as well as Edward Dowden's translator's notes in an early English translation of the *Divan* available at the time of Said's writing, one that is unfortunately quite loose (Goethe 1914).

25. None of this means that the poem has nothing to do with Timur—in fact, it continues a trend in European attitudes toward Timur beginning in his own time, when France and other European powers sought alliances with him because he had challenged from the East their most feared enemy, the Ottomans, thus interfering with their drive into central Europe (Rubel, in *Oeuvres* 4).

26. Although he makes it clear that he is quoting a poem, Marx does not mention Goethe's name, presumably because his German readers would have been familiar with these lines. An earlier implicit reference to the Goethe stanza can be found in Marx's "Alienated Labor" from the *1844 Manuscripts* (Marx [1844] 1961, 104; see also MECW 3, 278).

27. While part of these 1861–63 manuscripts are known as the *Theories of Surplus Value*, the passage in question is from an earlier part of the text, not published in English until 1988, when it appeared in MECW 30.

28. Marx's use of the phrases "individual development" and "general men" suggests strongly that the humanist themes of the 1840s were still central to his thinking. No alternate translation into English is possible since, as the editors of MECW note, most of this large passage, including these phrases, is in English in Marx's manuscript. Engels incorporated an abbreviated version of this passage into *Capital* III (182), but without the Goethe stanza. Marx's original draft for volume III, which does feature these passages, can be found in MEGA² II/4.2, 124–25, as discussed recently by Paresh Chattopadhyay (2006).

29. For a contrary view, see Chattopadhyay 2006, who holds that Marx maintained the same dialectic of progress throughout his writings.

30. For defenses of Said's critique of Marx, see Inden 2000 and Le Cour Grandmaison 2003.

31. In a letter of October 18, 1853, Marx complains of the *Tribune* editors "watering down" this passage by changing the word "revenge" to "ravages" (MECW 39, 390).

32. I owe this point to a conversation with Raya Dunayevskaya.

33. Krader offers some context for this remark: "The 'invariant law of history' to which Marx made allusion has been assimilated in recent times to the theory of ethnology, whereby the more highly developed culture is ultimately the conqueror, regardless of whether it has gained the initial military victory. Thus China conquered its conquerors, the Manchus" (1975, 81).

34. *Jats* are a mainly peasant caste with a martial tradition, who were a source of resistance against the Mughal Empire.

35. This procedure resembles the dialectical structure of Hegel's *Phenomenology of Spirit*, where each stage of consciousness is introduced as superior to the previous one, but is itself torn apart by its internal contradictions, which leads to the next stage, etc.

36. While I am giving page references in the margins to Raffles's text, for Marx's actual excerpt notes I am using the handwritten notes in the Amsterdam archives of the International Institute of Social History (Karl Marx, Excerpt notes on Thomas Stamford Raffles, *The History of Java*. Marx papers, Box 65 (Heft LXVI), pp. 3–7. Amsterdam: International Institute for Social History, 1853). I would like to thank Rolf Hecker for his assistance in obtaining a draft transcription.

37. Many of Marx's writings on China first reappeared in English in a one-volume collection edited by Dona Torr (Marx 1951), together with Torr's scholarly apparatus. A more complete one-volume collection of these writings, also with a good scholarly apparatus, was published later in Mexico under the editorship of Lothar Knauth (Marx and Engels 1975). See also the early discussion by Riazanov 1926.

38. Marx's frequent attacks on Palmerston are discussed in chapters 2 and 3.

39. "Intercourse," a parallel to the German word *Verkehr*, here in the nineteenth-century sense of economic relations, or communication across cultures.

40. Sepoy (also spahi, sepahi) is a Persian-Turkic term for soldier.

41. Most of these writings were collected with a brief introduction and notes by Marx editors in Moscow under the title *The First Indian War of Independence* (Marx and Engels 1959).

42. This may be changing. Whereas two older collections of Marx's writings include only 1853 articles on India (Tucker 1978, McLellan [1977] 2000), Robert Antonio's *Marx and Modernity* (2003) features two of these 1857 ones. Moreover, Ledbetter's 2007 one-volume selection of *Tribune* writings contains a full sampling of India articles, from 1853 to 1859. Another new collection recently published in India comprises the entirety of the *Tribune* articles on that country (Husain 2006). A reviewer in the *Hindu*, a large-circulation daily paper, found Marx's *Tribune* articles "strikingly relevant for contemporary times, as a critique of present-day neoliberalism" (Venkatesh Athreya, "Marx on India under the British," *Hindu*, December 13, 2006).

43. A reference to the Benthamite John Bowring, a British diplomat who played a prominent role in the decision to shell Canton in 1856, at the beginning of the Second Opium War.

44. A reference to General Aimable Pélissier's suffocation of a thousand Arab resistance fighters in Algeria in 1845, an action for which he was promoted. This passage suggests a different view of the French conquest of Algeria than that expressed by Engels in 1848. By 1857, Engels too had altered greatly his views, as can be seen in his article "Algeria" for the *New American Cyclopaedia*. Marx had been invited by *Tribune* editor Charles Dana to contribute to this encyclopedia, in part to defray the loss of income he was suffering as a result of cutbacks by the *Tribune* in its international coverage due to the economic depression of 1857. As with the *Tribune* articles, many of these encyclopedia entries were written by Engels, especially on military topics, but appeared over Marx's byline. Although Engels's encyclopedia article on Algeria, composed in the fall of 1857, contains a few extremely ethnocentric statements, its overall thrust is anticolonial. He writes that "the Arab and Kabyle tribes, to whom independence is precious, and hatred of foreign domination a principle dearer than life itself, have been crushed and broken by the terrible razzias in which dwellings and property are burnt and destroyed, standing crops cut down, and the miserable wretches who remain massacred, or subject to all the horrors of lust and brutality" (MECW 18, 67). Engels also expresses admiration for the resistance leader Abd-el-Kaber, referring to him as "that restless and intrepid chieftain" (68).

45. Characteristically, Marx seeks to link rather than to separate the experiences of oppressed groups across international divides. See also "The Punishment in the Ranks," an 1855 *Tribune* article by Marx and Engels attacking the common practice of severe flogging of enlisted men in the British army, at a time when most other Western armies had stopped the practice (MECW 14, 501–3).

46. A reference to the Haitian Revolution.

47. A reference to sixteenth-century Holy Roman Emperor Charles V's extremely harsh penal code, enacted as he was attempting to suppress the Reformation.

48. A reference to Blackstone's *Commentaries on the Laws of England*.

49. A reference to the carrying of a statue of Juggernaut, an incarnation of Vishnu, in a chariot as part of a Hindu festival in which impassioned worshippers sometimes committed suicide by jumping under the wheels of the giant chariot.

50. Ferdinand Freiligrath, Marx's close friend, a poet who had been active in the Communist League.

51. Unfortunately, the parts of this well-known letter on Hegel, economic theory, and Jones were first published in English in a general volume of Marx and Engels's correspondence ([1934] 1965), but without the sentence on India. The latter was published separately in Marx and Engels (1959)! This chopping up of Marx into different topic areas obscures the multidimensionality of his worldview.

CHAPTER 2

1. This attitude would persist into the early twentieth century, as can be seen in a well-known literary work, Joseph Conrad's *The Secret Agent* (1907). Conrad, who was descended from Polish revolutionaries, portrays the Russian diplomat Vladimir as the manipulator of a spectacular terrorist plot by anarchists, through which Russia aims to shock the West into a crackdown on the revolutionary movement.

2. See below for more on Engels and Pan-Slavism. Although Marx and Bakunin had important differences from the 1840s onward, this did not stop Marx from publicly defending Bakunin in letters to English newspapers in 1853 against charges that he was a Russian agent (MECW 12, 284–86, 290–91). These charges were leveled by followers of David Urquhart, a virulently anti-Russian British aristocrat and former diplomat. The Urquhart group, which controlled several small newspapers and other outlets, published a number of Marx's writings on Russia during the 1850s.

3. A reference to the February 1853 uprising in Milan, then still under Austrian rule, by followers of the Italian democrat Giuseppe Mazzini. The rising, on which Marx also wrote for the *Tribune*, drew strong support from both Italian workers and Hungarian refugees, but was crushed by the Austrian army.

4. Here Marx is summing up in positive terms a parliamentary speech by Richard Cobden, a liberal of the Manchester School.

5. The text, originally written for the *Tribune*, was published there only in abbreviated form.

6. David Riazanov, the outstanding Russian Marx editor of the 1920s who was later executed by Stalin, wrote that it was on Marx's part "an error . . . to make Palmerston into a principled friend of Russia. . . . His highest 'principle' was the interests of the English oligarchy." (Riazanov in Marx and Engels 1920, 1, 499).

7. August Nimtz (2000) and Terrell Carver (1996) have highlighted the involvement of Marx and Engels in democratic movements.

8. Along with Buda, Pesth [Pest] is one of the twin cities comprising Budapest.

9. Hal Draper (1996) argues unconvincingly on the basis of passages such as these that Marx and Engels never supported, even critically, the British and French war against Russia, but were only interested in how the war might spark a general European revolution. This obfuscates the depth of their view of Russia as the archenemy of all forms of democracy and revolution, and their willingness to support, albeit critically, its foes.

10. Volumes 16–21 of the MECW, covering the years 1858–70, were all published during the years 1980–85, while volume 15, which covers the years 1856–58, did not appear until 1986. Curiously, an earlier edition of the *Secret Diplomatic History* had appeared in Britain and the United States under Communist Party auspices (Marx 1969).

11. Not only is their introduction marred by such expressions as Russian "barbarism," but they also edit heavily one key text, Marx's four drafts for a letter to Vera Zasulich of 1881, which they synthesize into a single draft, rather than letting Marx speak for himself. Despite these flaws, however, the Blackstock and Hoselitz edition made many Marx and Engels texts available in the English-speaking world, texts that had been omitted from more widely circulated Communist Party editions. See also Joseph Baylen, who writes in Cold War terms of Marx's *Tribune* articles on Russia "as a lesson to the West on how to deal with the threat from the East that has much validity today" (1957, 23). For their part, Maximilien Rubel and Margaret Manale view the *Secret Diplomatic History* in a surprisingly uncritical fashion, as a "well-documented study" in which Marx "exposed the expansionist plans of the Russian Czar" and also the complicity of British leaders with Russia (1975, 129).

12. One could compare Marx's portrayal here of the "abject" ex-slave, who retains many slave attitudes even as master, to Friedrich Nietzsche's concepts of the slave morality and of *ressentiment*, to the Frankfurt School's notion of the authoritarian personality, or to Julia Kristeva's writings on the "abject."

13. Roman Rosdolsky (1986) offers a detailed discussion of this strange episode.

14. See Marx's letter of April 17, 1855 to *Neue Oder-Zeitung* editor Moritz Elsner submitting Engels's articles on Pan-Slavism for publication (MECW 39, 534–35); his letter to Engels of May 18 complaining bitterly that the *Tribune* had not published them in full (MECW 39, 536); and his letter to Engels of June 26 reporting on efforts to find a German publisher for a pamphlet by Engels on Pan-Slavism (MECW 39, 538–39). In 1852, Marx had allowed a series of articles by Engels, later collected in the book *Revolution and Counter-Revolution in Germany*, to appear in the *Tribune* under his own name. This series also included an ethnocentric attack on Pan-Slavism. In criticizing Marx on this point, Nimni fails to notice that *Revolution and Counter-Revolution in Germany* was authored by Engels, not Marx (Nimni 1994, 31, 200). For a response to Nimni's critique of Marx, see Löwy 1998.

15. By the 1870s, Engels had changed his position on the Slavic peoples of southeastern Europe. In "The Workingmen of Europe in 1877," he refers to "the awakening of the smaller Slavonic nationalities of Eastern Europe from the Panslavist dreams fostered among them by the present Russian government" (MECW 24, 229).

16. This attitude was common among nineteenth-century Western intellectuals, who according to historian Ronald Suny dwelled upon what they saw as "the patience, submissiveness, lack of individuality and fatalism of the Russians" (2006, 7).

17. Although Shamil was regarded as an anti-tsarist hero in the early years of the Soviet Union, this position was later reversed (Henze 1958).

18. Padover has created a convenient digest of the problematic discussions by Marx on Judaism and Jews (KML 5, 169–225). Padover errs, however, when he attributes to Marx "The Russian Loan," a particularly noxious *Tribune* article about Jewish bankers published on January 4, 1856 (KML 5, 221–25). In "Die Mitarbeit von Marx und Engels an der 'New York Tribune'" (2001), an illuminating essay that forms part of the apparatus to MEGA I/14, the volume's editors (Hans-Jürgen Bochinski and Martin Hundt, with Ute Emmrich and Manfred Neuhaus) write that the earlier attributions of "The Russian Loan" to Marx can "definitely be ruled out," this on the basis of a close textual analysis (903).

19. Concerning Marx's "On the Jewish Question" and the vast debate around it, see especially Ingram 1988 and Megill 2002.

20. Traverso (1994) and others have argued persuasively that later theorists in the Marxian tradition such as Leon Trotsky and Walter Benjamin did so, under the impact of Nazism.

21. Qualifying immediately what may have come as a shock to Engels, Marx adds ironically that "Herzen, of course, has discovered afresh that 'liberty' has emigrated from Paris to Moscow" (MECW 40, 310).

22. Two years before these articles focusing on the Russian peasantry, in a letter of April 16, 1856, to Engels, Marx had shown renewed interest in the revolutionary potential of the German peasantry: "The whole thing in Germany will depend on whether it is possible to back the Proletarian revolution by some second edition of the Peasants war," an allusion to Engels's book on sixteenth century peasant uprisings (MECW 40, 41).

23. An allusion to the "sham" character of the Crimean War, as discussed above.

24. Some of Luxemburg's writings against Polish national independence can be found in Hudis and Anderson 2004; I have previously discussed Lenin and "national liberation" in K. Anderson 1995 and K. Anderson 2007.

25. Despite clarifications of this issue in respected scholarly studies dating as far back as Solomon Bloom's *The World of Nations* (1941; see also Lichtheim 1961), the historian Andrzej Walicki has lamented the "stubborn vitality" of a "classic misreading" of Marx on nationalism. According to this misreading, prevalent even today, writes Walicki, Marx held to "a standpoint of total indifference toward the national problems as having, allegedly, no relevance to the real situation or class interests of the industrial working class of Europe" (1982, 358). The dismissive response by Harvard historian Roman Szporluk (1997) to the careful scholarly treatment of Marx on nationalism by Erica Benner (1995) illustrates the persistence of this problem.

26. Although I cite MECW as usual, I have amended the MECW translation based upon the French originals of their speeches, as published in Marx's *Oeuvres* 4 999–1004, edited by Rubel.

27. Even accounts of Marx and Engels on Poland that steer clear of the pitfall of class reductionism sometimes overestimate this momentary lapse by Engels in order to jump to the conclusion that their support of Polish national emancipation in 1848–49

was a merely tactical expediency aimed at securing allies against conservative Russia for the communist movement (MacDonald 1941, Hammen 1969).

28. Bem's name remained important in both Poland and Hungary. In November 1956, Hungarian revolutionaries held their first gathering around a statue of Bem in Budapest.

29. Marx's views of Palmerston and Britain's attitude toward the Civil War in the United States are discussed in the next chapter.

30. Marx's notes and drafts run over a hundred pages; they have been published in their original languages (German, English, and French) with a translation into Polish (Marx 1971).

31. Fox was a leader of the British National League for the Independence of Poland, a group formed during the 1863 uprising. Philosophically, he was an advocate of atheism and a follower of the French positivist Auguste Comte. During the 1860s, a more prominent Comtist, Professor George Spencer Beesly, a friend of Fox and a prominent supporter of Poland, was also close to Marx, although he seems to have worked with but never formally joined the First International. Given Marx's own hostility to positivism, this is perhaps surprising, unless one realizes that the International was a rather heterogeneous organization.

32. Marx's term for the wars following the French Revolution, 1792–1815.

33. The notes, mainly in English but with some passages in French and German, have been published in Marx 1971. A fairly substantial excerpt was included in a footnote to MECW 20 (490–94), which is the version cited here, with the translation occasionally amended.

34. Pierre Joseph Proudhon, *Si les traités de 1815 ont cessé d'exister? Actes du futur congrès* (1863).

35. Could also be translated as "fellows."

36. In addition to forceful repression, Russia undermined the Polish uprising of 1863 by emancipating the Polish peasantry from serfdom. This drove a wedge between the peasants and the leaders of the uprising, some of whom were members of the gentry (Blit 1971).

37. A reference to the *Neue Rheinische Zeitung*.

38. See also the French original in MEGA I/25, 211–12. The 1880 address was signed by Marx, Engels, Paul Lafargue (Marx's son-in-law), and Friedrich Lessner (a colleague of Marx since the 1840s).

CHAPTER 3

1. He saw it as a deeply democratic revolution, but not as one aimed at bursting the bounds of capitalism. In this sense, the sociologist Barrington Moore's characterization of the Civil War as "the last capitalist revolution" (1966, 112) is compatible with Marx's standpoint. The historian Malcolm Sylvers (2004) has provided an overview

of Marx's writings on the United States, including notebooks that will appear for the first time in MEGA².

2. At the same time, Schlüter's book steered clear of the economic reductionism prevalent in American socialist writing on the Civil War (Kelly 2007).

3. Three decades earlier, in *The Souls of Black Folk*, Du Bois already links the Civil War to his famous statement about the color line: "The problem of the twentieth century is the problem of the color-line—the relation of the darker to the lighter races of men in Asia and Africa, in America and the islands of the sea. It was a phase of this problem that caused the Civil War; and however much they who marched South and North in 1861 may have fixed on the technical points of union and local autonomy as a shibboleth, all nevertheless knew, as we know, that the question of Negro slavery was the real cause of the conflict" ([1903] 1961, 23).

4. Dunayevskaya analyzed race and class in the United States in depth in *American Civilization on Trial* ([1963] 2003) and *Philosophy and Revolution* ([1973] 1989). Besides the present study, other writings that have picked up these threads from Dunayevskaya include Turner and Alan 1986 and Alan 2003.

5. Later on, Genovese's sympathy for Southern planter culture would become more apparent, as he moved from the Far Left to neoconservatism. For a critique that links Genovese's differences with Marx and his fundamental Stalinism to this shift, see Roediger 1994.

6. See also Runkle 1964, who offered a detailed analysis of the Civil War writings but downplayed their importance in Marx's overall work, seemingly unaware that concepts from these writings found their way into *Capital*.

7. This is part of a critique of Proudhon, whom Marx accused of misusing Hegel's concept of contradiction by speaking of "the good side" as well as "the bad side of slavery," attempting thereby to find "the synthesis of freedom and slavery, the true golden mean, in other words the balance between slavery and freedom" (MECW 38, 101–2.) Soon afterwards, in *The Poverty of Philosophy* (1847), he reworked and sharpened this attack, accusing Proudhon of wanting to "save slavery" (MECW 6, 168).

8. Although I have referenced the MECW, here (and sometimes elsewhere) I have actually quoted the clearer translation in Saul Padover's edition of Marx's writings on the Civil War (KML 2) or modified the translation myself in consultation with the German original in the MEW (Marx-Engels *Werke*).

9. Nor was there a German-language socialist organ that would publish Marx during this period. A letter of March 11, 1861, from Jenny Marx to her "loyal fellow fighter and sufferer" in America, Louise Weydemeyer, the wife of Joseph Weydemeyer, who had joined the Union army, refers to efforts by Marx during his "clandestine trip to Berlin" that spring to "arrange for a monthly or weekly publication." "Should Karl succeed in setting up a new party organ," she adds, "he will assuredly write to your husband, asking him to send reports from America" (MECW 41, 574–75). That effort was not successful.

10. Prominent here as a military leader was Weydemeyer, who had served in the German army as an artillery officer in the 1840s before joining the Communist League (Roediger 1978). Weydemeyer was also among the German American socialists who organized public meetings in 1860 to thwart efforts by New York manufacturers to drum up working class support for the South by pointing to impending layoffs, were cotton supplies to be cut off by war (Mandel [1955] 2007).

11. In English in the original.

12. Although he wrote this letter in German, Marx used the English phrase "border ruffians," the abolitionist term for the pro-slavery elements in Kansas.

13. Marx's information on these controversies came to him from Weydemeyer, who was serving as an aide to Frémont. Marx praises Frémont in these writings, without mentioning his repression of Native Americans and Mexican nationals in California.

14. Given the fact that Marx gave no sources for these quotes, as he often did in his dispatches from London, it is possible that he attended the meeting and was reporting from his own notes.

15. An allusion to William Makepeace Thackeray's 1841 story, "The Yellowplush Papers." Prawer writes, "From Thackeray Marx borrows Yellowplush, the West-End footman with a lackey's outlook on life" (1976, 252–53).

16. An apparent reference to the *Economist*.

17. "Catholic Emancipation" refers to an 1829 decision by Parliament, under pressure from a mass movement in Ireland, to grant limited political rights to Catholics; the 1832 Reform Act extended the suffrage to the upper middle and manufacturing classes; the protectionist Corn Laws, which had placed tariffs on imported agricultural products, were repealed in 1846; the Ten Hours Bill of 1847 limited the working day for women and children (Marx was to detail the movement to reduce the hours of labor in *Capital* I); the Conspiracy Bill, voted down in 1858, would have facilitated the extradition of political refugees to the Continent.

18. The officer in question was Colonel Charles Jennison of the Kansas "Jayhawkers," a volunteer regiment that traced its origins to John Brown's campaigns against pro-slavery forces during the 1850s. In his recent study of Marx, Kansas, and the Civil War, the Germanist Charles Reitz sums up Jennison's career: "Col. Jennison was appointed acting brigadier general for his valiant 1862 activities dramatically liberating slave 'property' in Missouri, but was passed over for the official commission to this rank. When Jennison's ferocious military form of 'practical abolitionism' was criticized by conservatives as 'premature interference with slavery' and his tactics as too much committed to foraging (decried as plunder by Missourians), he resigned from the military believing he was being slandered and that he could not conduct the war with honor under a high command hostile to Jayhawker radicalism. . . . In the view of many, Gen. William T. Sherman's scorched earth policies in his famed March to the Sea vindicated the ruthlessness with which both Jennison and John Brown, Sr. prosecuted the campaign for a slavery-free America" (2008, 9).

19. Engels's articles for the *Volunteer Journal* (MECW 18, 525–34), published in December 1861 and March 1862, were a version of a military analysis he had apparently sent at Marx's suggestion to the *Tribune*, which did not print it. Engels's articles are rather technical and make few larger political points. The surviving documentation does not tell us about the specific role of Marx in developing them into the more expansive ones that appeared in *Die Presse*, but one can surmise that these changes were more the work of Marx than of Engels.

20. In English in the original.

21. Few Marx scholars have noted these differences, with Dunayevskaya ([1958] 2000) and Henderson (1976) as exceptions.

22. In this often-cited letter, Marx also makes some very problematic personal remarks, referring to "the Jewish nigger Lassalle" (*der jüdische Nigger Lassalle*) and writing as well that "the impertinence of the fellow is also niggerlike" (*niggerhaft*) (MECW 41, 389, 390). That Marx was capable of making such racist remarks in private should not obscure the fact that a major part of what had made him so angry with Lassalle was the latter's indifference to the Civil War and the issues of slavery and racism in America.

23. John Breckinridge, who ran against Lincoln in 1860, became a Confederate general and cabinet member.

24. Marx's occasional use of the "n" word for dramatic effect was covered up in Marx and Engels, *The Civil War in the United States* (1937), but the word could subsequently be found in Padover's KML 2 and in MECW. The relevant MECW volumes are 19 (1984) and 41 (1985), whose Moscow-based "scientific editor" was the late Norair Ter-Akopian. Also a specialist on Marx's 1879–82 notebooks on non-Western and precapitalist societies, Ter-Akopian later participated in preparing these notebooks for publication in MEGA².

25. During this period, Marx hoped to become a paid correspondent for the *Evening Post*, something that never came about.

26. Recent treatments of Lincoln by Black and leftist historians have been much harsher; see, e.g., Bennett 2000.

27. The full text can be found in Phillips 1969, 448–62.

28. "Niggers" in English in the original, again an instance of Marx using a racist word to make an antiracist point. Filibusterers were military adventurers, usually from the South. Among them was the Tennessean William Walker, who invaded and briefly took over Nicaragua in the 1850s, where he reestablished slavery.

29. Two years later, in a letter to Weydemeyer of November 24, 1864, Engels writes: "Of the Germans who have joined in the war, Willich appears to have given the best account of himself" (MECW 42, 40). A Prussian officer who joined the revolutionary cause, Willich took part in the 1848–49 German Revolution, where he worked closely with Engels. Not long after Marx dissolved the Communist League in 1852, in large part to keep what he regarded as Willich's ultra-leftist faction from taking control, the latter emigrated to the United States, where he edited a newspaper for the sizable German community of Cincinnati, Ohio.

30. "See, it moves" is what Galileo purportedly muttered under his breath after recanting to a religious court his discoveries about the rotation of the earth; "reason in history" is a reference to Hegel.

31. In fact, Lincoln had claimed to be a "rail-splitter" and had been not a senator but a congressman from Illinois (1847–49).

32. It was in this period of what was probably the most explicit political disagreement between Marx and Engels in their lifetimes that one also sees a personal conflict, what Draper terms "the first and last episode of coolness between the two" (1985a, 115). In a letter of January 7, 1863, Engels informed Marx of the death of his longtime companion, Mary Burns. Marx, drowning in a sea of financial woes, responded perfunctorily in a letter of January 8 that spoke mainly of his own troubles. In a letter of January 13, Engels expressed his bitter disappointment at his friend's insensitivity, to which Marx replied on January 24 with an apology. (These letters can be found in MECW 41.)

33. In this same letter, as discussed in chapter 2, Engels enthusiastically praises the Polish revolutionaries for their uprising against Russia.

34. A reference to the radical wing of Puritanism, which became part of the English Revolution of the 1640s.

35. Although some sources assert that Marx helped to organize the meeting, historians of the International Henry Collins and Chaim Abramsky dismiss this as a "legend" (1965, 30; see also Foner 1981).

36. As discussed in this volume, p. 67.

37. Curiously, this important text was not included in the appendix of the Moscow-edited volume 20 of MECW covering the years 1864–68 and published in 1985. This may reflect an effort to downplay the cordial relations between the International and the Lincoln's government. (Adams's letter was subsequently included in MEGA² II/20, published in 1992.) It has long been accessible in English in the two collections of Marx's writings on the Civil War (Marx and Engels 1937, KML 2).

38. In English in the original. The Emancipation Society, founded in 1862 by English radicals, included John Stuart Mill and Marx's friend George Spencer Beesly among its leading members. It had cooperated with the London Trades Council in organizing pro-America meetings.

39. Here Marx refers to the 1337–1453 dynastic war between England and France, the European war of 1618–48 during the Reformation, and finally to the European wars of 1792–1815, following the French Revolution.

40. The *Workmen's Advocate* article about the meeting is reprinted in MEGA² I/20, 1524–28).

41. The September 1865 "Address" was not included in either of the two English-language collections of Marx's writings on the Civil War (Marx and Engels 1937, KML 2), nor was it published as a document of the First International in either MECW or MEGA², despite the fact that these editions include in their appendices many major documents from the International, some of them not written by Marx. I have cited

it from the rather obscure seven-volume series of minutes of the First International published in Moscow; more recently, it has been reprinted as an appendix to Dunayevskaya (1963) 2003.

42. But although he reprinted the entire "Address," Schlüter failed to recognize the significance of its attacks on Johnson's policies. Writing in 1913, at the height of Southern segregation and lynch law, he comments blandly that "the constitutional amendments affirming the political equality of the Negroes were steps in accordance with the address which the conference of the International Workingman's Association directed to the people of the United States" ([1913] 1965, 201). Schlüter fails to mention that by 1913, these amendments had been a dead letter in the South for decades. Nor does he grasp the contemporary relevance of the International's dire warnings about race relations in America.

43. After 1867, as the struggle over Reconstruction and within U.S. labor over the color bar was raging, Marx moved on to other issues, never again addressing in a substantial way the dialectics of race and class in America (Foner 1977).

44. The minutes of the General Council of the International for 1864–67 have been reprinted in MEGA^2 I/20.

CHAPTER 4

1. Although I have not found these kinds of pejorative statements in Marx's writings on Ireland, this should not obscure the fundamental congruence of Marx's and Engels's views on Ireland and the Irish.

2. This book, published when the author was only twenty-four, was to be the one by Engels that Marx cited most often in *Capital*.

3. In his study of Engels's book, the American literary critic Steven Marcus focuses almost exclusively on the dimension of class. Although Marcus acknowledges that "in 1840 about 20 percent of Manchester's working class were Irish" (1974, 5), he misses completely the book's interweaving of class and ethnicity. In a more recent treatment of *The Condition*, Anne Dennehy takes note of this, arguing that the situation of the Irish as described by Engels can be connected to "similar conditions experienced by ethnic minority groups in Britain today" (1996, 114).

4. This notion of a labor reserve, here linked to immigrant labor, anticipates Marx's discussion in *Capital* I, of a reserve army of labor, the vast unemployed and underemployed sector of the working class, which undermines the employed workers because its very existence "puts a curb on their pretensions," thus strengthening the hand of capital (*Capital* I, 792).

5. Only two of the major Marx biographies, Mehring [1918] 1962 and Rubel and Manale 1975, devote much space to his intense involvement with Irish issues during the years 1867–70. See also the brief but useful discussion in Hal Draper's 1978 study of Marx's theory of revolution. Draper overemphasizes Marx's critique of "bourgeois

liberal-national leadership" in Ireland, however, which obscures Marx's new thinking after 1867 (1978, 400).

6. The green, white, and orange Irish tricolor symbolized the eventual unity of Protestant and Catholic. It had been unveiled for the first time in a ceremony in Paris presided over by French president Alphonse de Lamartine during the 1848 Revolution.

7. The text, drawn up by Fox and signed by International Working Men's Association president George Odger, "The Irish State Prisoners. Sir George Grey and the International Working Men's Association," was published on March 10, 1866, in the *Commonwealth*, a London newspaper connected to the International. It is reprinted in Marx and Engels 1972b, 361–67.

8. The complexity of Marx's view of the state could also be noted here. He held that the London government of the day, led by the Tory Edward Derby, was unaware of the radical changes taking place in Irish agriculture, which were presumably being carried out by forces that were to some degree separate from it and its class base. A better-known evocation of the relative autonomy of the state can be found in the *Eighteenth Brumaire of Louis Bonaparte* (1852).

9. It is not clear if Engels wrote this review, never mentioned again in their correspondence. During this period, he published a number of reviews of *Capital* in German newspapers and attempted without success to get one placed in an English periodical as well.

10. As Kapp (1972) notes, fourteen-year-old Eleanor had also stayed in the Engels household in Manchester for some months, where Elizabeth Burns filled her with stories about the Fenians and other Irish rebels.

11. These notes, which Marx drew from the historian Ernst Wachsmuth's 1833 book on the history of European mores, are to appear in full in MEGA² IV/11.

12. The Korean scholar Jie-Hyun Lim offers a subtle analysis of this change, also relating Ireland to India: "It should be kept in mind that Ireland in the later 19th century was located in the periphery of the capitalist world system; Marx in fact saw India as the Ireland of the East" (1992, 170–71).

13. For general background to the beginning of the Marx-Bakunin dispute, see especially Stekloff 1928, Braunthal [1961] 1967, Rubel 1964, and Rubel 1965. None of these sources, however, takes up Ireland as a major issue in the controversy.

14. In contrast to Proudhon, however, it should be noted that Bakunin had strongly supported Poland, even participating in the 1863 uprising.

15. The entire program, along with Marx's marginal notes, is reprinted in MECW 21, 207–11.

16. It is unclear if an English version was available before the vote. The French original of this text can be found in *General Council of the First International* 1966, 354–63.

17. Again, as in several passages in his writings on the Civil War, Marx is using a racist term to make an antiracist point. More problematic here is Marx's relative

inattention after 1867 to race in America. Philip Foner complains, with some justifica-tion, that Marx's "failure to make the analogy" between the Irish in Britain and Blacks in the United States "clear to his American correspondents" through further elabora-tion shows "that the issue of black-white relations was a minor one in his mind at that time" (1977, 41).

18. Recently, in a discussion of Marx on race and ethnicity, the Canadian politi-cal theorist Abigail Bakan has noted the non-economic aspects of this process: "The sense of privilege cultivated among one section of workers over another may or may not be accompanied by material benefit, and the nature of that material benefit is vari-able. . . . Maintaining that sense of superiority is part of how oppression operates in capitalist society, and part of the contested terrain in the battle for ruling-class he-gemony" (2008, 252).

19. Barbier, who has closely analyzed some of these texts, nonetheless reads them too narrowly, through the lens of class alone, when he writes that they illustrate Marx's "instrumental conception of national independence," in which "the independence of Ireland is not presented as an end in itself, but as a necessary means for realizing the proletarian revolution in England" (1992, 300, 302).

CHAPTER 5

1. Rubel ([1973] 1981) has argued that Marx stuck to the longer 1859 plan of six books on political economy, and therefore completed only a small portion of his plan, volume I of *Capital* and the draft material for volumes II and III. It is possible, how-ever, that Marx altered his plan, since in 1867 he gave another list, this in the preface to *Capital*. In this 1867 list, volume I of *Capital* would have been followed by volume II, comprising book II on circulation and book III on "the process of capital in its totality," and then by volume III, comprising book IV on the history of theory. This 1867 list was the model Engels followed in publishing Marx's manuscripts on capital, with volume II on circulation and volume III on the whole process, while what was to be published after Engels's death as *Theories of Surplus Value* was comparable to book IV. Some of this material, like the long discussion on landed property in what became volume III, suggests that Marx had come closer to covering the topics outlined in 1859 than Rubel held. In any case, one should not reify the 1859 list, since focusing too narrowly on it could obscure changes Marx's project underwent from 1859 to 1867 and after.

2. The best-known account of Marx on the Asiatic mode of production is the rather tendentious one by Wittfogel (1957; see also Gluckstein 1957, Bahro 1978), which at-tempts to link it ahistorically to later Stalinist systems. More balanced discussions can be found in Lichtheim 1963, Krader 1975, and some of the essays in Musto 2008. Krader attempts to view the whole of Marx's writings on non-Western societies under the rubric of the Asiatic mode of production, which is problematic given Marx's own failure to delineate specifically what he meant by the concept. Critics like Heinz Lubasz have pointed this out, arguing: "What the concept 'Asiatic mode of production'

conceptualizes is not Asian society, which Marx knew very little about and never attempted to theorize, but the hypothetical origins of modern bourgeois society" (1984, 457). Lubasz goes too far, however, given the scope and quality of Marx's writings on India and China in the 1850s, not to mention the late writings on Asian societies in the 1879–82 notebooks. In fact, Marx wrote much more on Asian societies than on ancient Greece or Rome, or European feudalism, yet the Eurocentric Lubasz, who wishes to see the Asiatic mode of production "laid to rest" (1984, 457), does not advocate any such laying to rest of the feudal or ancient (slave) modes of production. Rather than an overarching concept through which to order Marx's multifaceted writings on non-Western societies, I view his references to an Asiatic mode of production as merely one among many indicators of the multilinear perspective on historical and social development that he had begun to work out by the late 1850s.

3. For a careful refutation of Rosdolsky on this point, see Krader 1975, 174–75.

4. Here and below, I refer to the page numbers in the English translation of the *Grundrisse* by Martin Nicolaus, the best one to date (Marx [1857–58] 1973). I have occasionally altered the translation, however, after consulting the German original (MEW 42). I have also consulted the English translation in MECW 28–29, as well as Hobsbawm's influential edition of this section on precapitalist formations (Marx 1965).

5. Again, Marx is using a racist term to make an antiracist point. Both of the existing English translations cover this up by rendering this parenthetical passage as "the free blacks of Jamaica" (*Grundrisse*, 325; MECW 28, 251). For the German original see MEW 42, 245 or MEGA^2 II/1.1, 242.

6. Could also be translated as "primitive" or "naturally evolved."

7. Marx indicates that this material is to be "brought forward," which suggests that these final thoughts would have been important to any further development of the *Grundrisse*.

8. Marx's likely target was August Haxhausen's writings on the Russian village, although he does not mention him.

9. Could also be translated as "traced back" or "deduced."

10. At one point in the drafts for the *Critique of Political Economy*, Marx mentioned that both the Inca Empire and the traditional Indian village had a complex division of labor. This was not, however, "a division of labor based on exchange value," the hallmark of capitalism. Instead, it was "a more or less direct communal production" (MECW 29, 464).

11. In elaborating his concept of contradiction, Hegel writes that "intelligent reflection . . . consists . . . in grasping and asserting contradiction," this versus commonsense thinking, in which contradiction "remains an external reflection which passes from likeness to unlikeness" without grasping "their transition" into each other, with the latter constituting "the essential point" ([1831] 1969, 441). As mentioned in chapter 1, Marx was studying Hegel's *Science of Logic* during the very weeks that he was writing the section on precapitalist formations in the *Grundrisse*.

12. These were first published in full in English in MECW 30–34, from 1988 to 1994.

13. For those who would argue that the Asiatic mode of production was a chronological category intended to precede the more advanced ancient mode of production, I call attention to the fact that in the above passage, Marx listed the "ancient" ahead of the "Asiatic." Unfortunately, but all too typically, this Moscow-based volume, published as late as 1994, does not mention the "Asiatic mode of production" in the index. Under "modes of production," it lists only "slaveowning," "feudal," and "capitalist" (MECW 34, 538), part of a long Stalinist cover-up of the issue of a separate Asiatic mode of production in Marx's work.

14. At another point, Marx links India and precolonial Peru, referring to "the naturally arisen Indian communities or the more artificially developed communism of the Peruvians" (*Capital* III, 1017). Elsewhere, he mentions as well "the old system of communal property in land" in Poland and Romania (939).

15. In Western Europe, whenever precapitalist forms were dismantled through the pressures of mercantile capital, but without moving fully toward industrial capitalism, Marx saw the result as almost as bleak. For example, French silk workers and English lacemakers coming under the domination of mercantile capital were still "working in their old fragmented manner": "Without revolutionizing the mode of production, it simply worsens the conditions of the direct producers, transforms them into wage-laborers and proletarians under worse conditions than those directly subsumed by capital" (*Capital* III, 452, 453).

16. This in the parts later published as *Theories of Surplus Value*.

17. Lukács wrote famously that "the whole of historical materialism" could be found there ([1923] 1971, 170).

18. To date, there has been no truly systematic comparison of the French edition with the German one established by Engels. Besides the editorial apparatus to the MEGA² editions mentioned above, previous work pointing to the importance of the French edition has included Dona Torr's appendices to a pre–World War II edition of *Capital* (Marx 1939), Dunayevskaya's discussions of the changes Marx made in the French edition in her *Marxism and Freedom* ([1958] 2000) and *Rosa Luxemburg, Women's Liberation, and Marx's Philosophy of Revolution* ([1982] 1991), Rubel's editorial notes to volume I of his Marx *Oeuvres* (1963–94), and a short intervention by Christopher Arthur (1990). For more details on key passages left out by Engels, see also my two previous treatments of this topic (K. Anderson 1983, 1997b).

19. Marx's critique of John Stuart Mill's explanation of profit at the end of the chapter on "Absolute and Relative Surplus Value" was added in the French edition, now also in the standard English edition (*Capital* I, 652–54).

20. In 1969, going further than Engels, the structuralist Marxist Louis Althusser wrote that in the French edition, "Marx, who was uncertain of the theoretical capaci-

ties of his French readers, sometimes dangerously compromised the precision of the original conceptual expressions" (Althusser 1971, 90). Althusser did so in a preface to what is to date one of the most widely circulated versions of *Capital* in France, a reprint of the Marx-edited Roy translation from Éditions Flammarion (Marx [1872–75] 1985a, [1872–75] 1985b). Eventually, the situation in France concerning *Capital* became almost comical. On the one hand, the prestigious publisher Éditions Gallimard's La Pléiade series of great books continues to reprint Maximilien Rubel's edition of the 1872–75 French edition as the definitive text, an edition that is marred by the editor's decision to change the order of some parts of Marx's text; and Éditions Flammarion's more faithful version of the same translation is still in print with Althusser's preface attacking the text. On the other hand, the Communist Party publishing house Messidor/ Éditions Sociales published a careful translation of the Engels-based 1890 edition into French in 1983. The publishers claimed on the jacket that that this translation, carried out by a committee led by Jean-Pierre Lefebvre, had finally resulted in a "definitive" French edition (Marx 1983). (Since my concern is with alternate texts, not translation issues per se, I will not take up issues such as their decision to change *plus-valeur*, the Marx-sanctioned translation of his "surplus value [*Mehrwert*]," to *survaleur*, as discussed by their French critics such as Pierre Fougeyrollas ["Aventures et mésaventures de Marx 'en français,'" *Le Monde*, October 28, 1983].) This new edition was later reissued by the prestigious Presses Universitaires de France. In an erudite but ultimately tendentious introduction, Lefebvre stressed the limitations of Roy as translator, never managing in forty-four pages to quote Marx's statement in the 1875 afterword that the French edition had "a "scientific value independent of the original." Instead, Lefebvre characterizes that afterword, without actually quoting it, as "an indirect critique of Roy's work," because Marx had also referred to the French edition's possible "literary defects" (Lefebvre in Marx 1983, xxx). Lefebvre writes further, here without citing any evidence and merging uncritically the sometimes differing views of Marx and Engels into one, that although they had initially thought highly of the French edition, "Marx and Engels gradually changed their minds and came to the idea that in all those passages containing important theoretical issues, it was necessary to take the German edition as the point of departure" (Lefebvre in Marx 1983, xli). In 1989, such attempts to push aside the 1872–75 French edition were seriously undercut when the third German edition of 1883, edited by Engels, was reprinted as MEGA² II/8. The extensive editorial apparatus included Marx's own "List of Changes" from the French edition that he specifically wanted included in subsequent editions. The editors—Rolf Hecker et al.—were careful to indicate which of these changes, some of them important, had not been carried out by Engels. Two years later, Engels's fourth German edition appeared in MEGA² II/10, with its sixty-page list of passages from the French edition that Engels had left out, as mentioned above.

21. In the 1873 second German edition, the sixth chapter was "Constant and Variable Capital," which is chapter 8 in English editions.

22. In the original German, this reads: "Das industriell entwickeltere Land zeigt dem minder entwickelten nur das Bild der eignen Zukunft" (MEGA² II/10, 8).

23. "The tale is told of you," from Horace, *Satires*, Book I, Satire 1—based on notes in *Capital* I.

24. Elsewhere, Trotsky writes even more forcefully concerning this sentence from the preface to *Capital*: "Under no circumstances can this thought be taken literally" ([1939] 2006, 39).

25. In the original French, this reads: "Le pays le plus développé industriellement ne fait que montrer à ceux qui le suivent sur l'échelle industrielle l'image de leur propre avenir" ([1872–75] 1985a, 36; see also *Oeuvres* 1, 549 and MEGA² II/7, 12). This change is not noted either in MEGA² II/7 or in MEGA² II/10.

26. In the original German, this reads: "Die Expropriation des ländlichen Producenten, des Bauern, von Grund und Boden bildet die Grundlage des Ganzen Processes. Ihre Geschichte nimmt in verschiedenen Phases in verschiedener Reihenfolge und in verschiedenen Geschichtsepochen. Nur in England, das wir daher als Beispiel nehmen, besitzt sie klassische Form" (MEGA² II/10, 644).

27. Marx did so twice in his correspondence with Russians, as will be seen in the next chapter. In addition, in an outline he made in the fall of 1882 for a new German edition, he had specifically indicated that this passage was "to be translated from the French edition" (MEGA² II/8, 17). (I would like to thank Rolf Hecker for pointing this out and for also showing me Marx's handwritten notes on this issue [personal communication, Moscow, May 29, 1998]). Engels's omission may well have been deliberate, since he indicated that he had consulted "notes left by the author" in preparing the 1883 German edition (*Capital* I, 110).

28. In the original French, this reads: "Mais la base de toute cette évolution, c'est l'expropriation des cultivateurs. Elle ne s'est encore accomplie d'une manière radical qu'en Angleterre: ce pays jouera donc nécessairement le premier rôle dans notre esquisse. Mais tous les autres pays de l'Europe occidentale parcourent le même mouvement, bien que selon le milieu il change de couleur locale, ou se resserre dans un cercle plus étroit, ou présente un caractère moins fortement prononcé, ou suivre un ordre de succession différent" (Marx [1872–75] 1985b, 169; see also *Oeuvres* 1, 1170–71 and MEGA² II/10, 778).

29. In MEGA², the page numbers of the general introduction to a volume are marked with asterisks.

30. It should be underlined that this reference to the Asiatic mode of production occurs in the most-discussed part of *Capital,* that on commodity fetishism. Perry Anderson writes imprecisely that Marx referred to the Asiatic mode of production "for the first and only time" in the *Critique of Political Economy,* this as part of his often-cited plea to give it "the decent burial it deserves," (1974, 478, 548). This leads Perry Anderson into an interpretive error when he writes: "In *Capital,* on the contrary, he substantially reverted to the earlier position," i.e., historical stages without a separate Asiatic mode of production (1974, 479). At the same time, the renowned British historian counters with some justice the too-sweeping use of the concept of the Asiatic

mode of production when he writes that "Asian development cannot in any way be reduced to a uniform residual category, left over after the canons of European evolution have been established" (1974, 549).

31. This fourth noncapitalist form roughly paralleled the first phase of communism in Marx's *Critique of the Gotha Program* (1875), not the "higher phase" of "from each according to his abilities, to each according to his needs" (MECW 24, 87).

32. He may also have been distancing himself from the growing brutality of the Taiping rebels, as discussed in chapter 1. For a discussion of the history of Voltaire's phrase in legal and military discourse—and its connection to the notion of punishment "to set an example"—see Bowman 2004.

33. In his descriptions of Indian craft workers, Marx makes some analogies that sound ethnocentric and condescending to contemporary ears, at one point comparing these craft workers to bees in a hive (*Capital* I, 452), and at another likening their skills to those of spiders (460). The contemporary reader should be aware, however, that Marx made a similar analogy when he described the Western European guild member as "like the snail with its shell," this as against the modern worker (480).

34. Marx's notion of the changes introduced during this period is theorized in an original manner in the chapter "Abstract Time" in Moishe Postone's *Time, Labor, and Social Domination* (1993).

35. As noted earlier, Marx tended to exaggerate the premodern Indian village's isolation from wider commerce.

36. Even at the end of his discussion of the Indian village system, when Marx addresses its negative features, his focus is not on despotism but on its essential conservatism: "The simplicity of the productive organism in these self-sufficing communities . . . supplies the key to the riddle of the unchangeability of Asiatic societies, which is in such striking contrast with the constant dissolution and refounding of Asiatic states, and their never-ceasing changes of dynasty. The structure of the fundamental economic elements of society remains untouched by the storms which blow up in the cloudy regions of politics" (*Capital* 1, 479). As I will argue in chapter 6, he would move away from these notions of "unchangeability" in his 1879–82 notebooks.

37. To Marx, this illustrated the underlying drive by capital to maximize value no matter the human cost. Where modern capital and its ideologists viewed technology as a means toward that end, he argues that ancient thinkers saw things differently: " 'If each tool' dreamed Aristotle, the greatest thinker of antiquity, 'if each tool, when summoned, or even by intelligent anticipation, could do the work that befits it, . . . if the weavers' shuttles were to weave of themselves, then there would be no need either of apprentices for the master craftsmen, or of slaves for the lords.' And Antipater, a Greek poet of the time of Cicero, hailed the water-wheel for grinding corn, that most basic form of all productive machinery, as the liberator of female slaves and the restorer of the golden age. Oh those heathens! They understood nothing of political economy and Christianity. . . . They did not, for example, comprehend that machinery is the surest means of lengthening the working day" (*Capital* I, 532–33).

38. In the French edition, Marx dropped the longer German title "So-Called Primitive Accumulation," still retained in the standard edition. In addition, as mentioned earlier, he demarcated these chapters as a separate part on primitive accumulation for the first time in the French edition.

39. This is not a standard English term, but a common enough one in German [*Schwarzhäute*] or French [*peaux noires*], both of them analogous to the English term "redmen," the latter a less pejorative term than "redskins." I owe this point to Charles Reitz.

40. The 1976 Fowkes translation (*Capital* I) was the first English edition to include this paragraph, added for the French edition, here following the earlier MEW 23, 662. It had not been included by Engels.

41. The last phrase was a quote from political economist Constantin Pecquer.

42. Marx added this passage about centralization to the French edition, which Engels fortunately included in the standard edition.

43. In fact, Ireland later developed a major industrial center at Belfast, as pointed out by Ellen Hazelkorn in her discussion of Marx on Ireland (1980).

44. Actually, Wade was president *pro tempore* of the Senate. Constitutionally, he was next in line to succeed President Andrew Johnson, who was almost removed from office by the radical Republicans through impeachment in 1868. Wade was mentioned in a July 1867 address published by the International's General Council. Drafted by Lafargue and edited by Marx, it mentioned, in language quite similar to Marx's 1867 preface, Wade's proposals concerning capital and landed property, also calling him a representative of "the radical party." Additionally, the address noted that the "the working class ... has compelled several state legislatures to accept the bill for an eight-hour workday" (*General Council of the First International* 1964, 289). Du Bois describes Wade as "one of the extreme leaders of abolition democracy" and a representative of "Western radicalism" ([1935] 1973, 199).

45. It also should be noted that at as late as the 1870s, as discussed in chapter 3, most working-class men were still denied the franchise in Britain. On the Continent, the situation was even worse, with only the United States allowing anything approaching universal male suffrage, and that confined to white males until 1870. No country enacted women's suffrage until the twentieth century, and the United States did not truly enforce voting rights for African Americans until 1965.

46. In a letter of February 10, 1866, Marx writes Engels that since the year began, he had "elaborated the section on the '*Working-Day*' from the historical point of view, which was not part of my original plan" (MECW 42, 224).

CHAPTER 6

1. The liberation theologian Bastiaan Wielenga argues plausibly that one factor here was Marx's renewed interest in the peasantry of these non-Western societies, this after the Paris Communards failed to spread the revolutionary movement into rural

France, thus sealing their fate: "The Paris Commune led to the insight that the working class needs an alliance with the peasantry, based upon the latter's 'living interests and real wants'" (2004, 913). The quoted phrase within the sentence is from Marx's drafts for "The Civil War in France" (MECW 22, 493).

2. These notes, the whole of which will appear in MEGA² IV/27, and most of which are being published in English in Smith (forthcoming) and Marx (forthcoming), were not the only excerpt notebooks Marx made during the years 1879 to 1882. But they are especially significant because they show how Marx was moving into new areas of research. As Grandjonc and Rojahn (1995) reported in their comprehensive report on the editing of MEGA², excerpt notebooks on other topics have also survived from the years 1879 to 1882. Except where noted in the following list of MEGA² volumes, these have not yet been published: MEGA² IV/28 (Marx on Russian and French history, especially agrarian relations, and Engels on the history of landed property, both from 1879 to 1882), MEGA² IV/29 (Marx's chronology of world history, composed in 1881–82); MEGA² IV/30 (Marx on mathematics from 1863, 1878, and 1881); MEGA² IV/30 (Marx on chemistry and Engels on natural sciences and history, already published).

3. Thus, many of these notes refer to peasant societies. As the American anthropologist Christine Ward Gailey holds, "the common assumption that Marx was scornful of the peasantry, seeing them solely as ignorant or reactionary . . . simply cannot be born out in the Notebooks" (2006, 38).

4. Dunayevskaya calls attention to this lapse by the great Marx editor, writing of "the superficial attitude Ryazanov displayed toward the epoch-making Notebooks which rounded out Marx's life's work" ([1982] 1991, 178). As will be discussed in the appendix, Riazanov also made the unfortunate decision to exclude the excerpt notebooks in their entirety from the first MEGA.

5. For example, in an otherwise incisive biographical entry on Marx, Eric Hobsbawm writes that the 1870s "brought to an end his theoretical work" (*Oxford Dictionary of National Biography*, Vol. 37, s.v. "Marx, Karl Heinrich").

6. An all-English edition with a far more extensive editorial apparatus is also in the works (Smith forthcoming).

7. For premodern stateless, classless societies usually based upon clans, I will usually be using use the term "preliterate" in place of "primitive" or "tribal," both nowadays considered pejorative. Another possibility would have been "first peoples."

8. They are to be published in full in the next few years in MEGA² IV/27 in their original multilingual form, usually a mixture of German and English, but with significant portions in Latin, Spanish, and Russian. The editing group for MEGA² IV/27 has included Kevin B. Anderson (U.S.), Georgi Bagaturia (Russia), Jürgen Rojahn (Germany), David Norman Smith (U.S.), and the late Norair Ter-Akopian (Russia). An all-English volume containing much of the material from MEGA² IV/27 that Krader did not include in his *Ethnological Notebooks* is also in the works (Marx forthcoming).

9. Peter Hudis (1983) related the notebooks to Marx's writings on the Third World and Franklin Rosemont (1989) commented on their relevance to Native Americans,

while David Norman Smith (1995) connected them to Rosa Luxemburg's work, and Paresh Chattopadhyay (1999) referred to them extensively in a defense of Marx's stance on gender. (See also Levine 1973, Ito 1996, and Vileisis 1996).

10. This was not the first time Engels had drawn too easy a parallel between Marx and another thinker. At his friend's graveside in 1883, Engels had famously done so with regard to Charles Darwin, ignoring Marx's strictures concerning the English biologist in the first volume of *Capital*.

11. Marx never wrote a book on gender, although as will be discussed below, his 1880–82 *Ethnological Notebooks* give great attention to gender and the family. The other period in which Marx devoted a certain degree of attention to gender and the family was the 1840s, when he was formulating his core concepts of dialectic and historical materialism, as can be seen in passages from the *1844 Manuscripts*, his little-known essay/translation on suicide from 1846 (Plaut and Anderson 1999), and the following texts co-authored with Engels: *The Holy Family* (1845), *The German Ideology* (1846), and *The Communist Manifesto* (1848). During the 1850s, some of Marx's *Tribune* writings take up the oppression of both working- and middle-class women in Britain, while some passages in *Capital*, volume I, discuss the conditions of working women, as well as the radical transformation of the family that was being engendered by capitalism. For overviews of Marx's writings on gender, some of which draw contrasts with Engels, see Dunayevskaya 1985, [1982] 1991; Rich [1991] 2001; Rubel 1997; Chattopadhyay 1999; K. Anderson 1999; and Leeb 2007.

12. Unless otherwise noted, italics within passages from Marx's notebooks represent his underlining. Marx's use of the term "modern" in the first sentence is not very clear, but it seems to refer to the last three millennia, this in contrast to the far longer sweep of prehistory. This particular passage is entirely in German, but many of Marx's remarks (and summaries) are in a mixture of German and English, and sometimes entirely in English; here and below, I have generally followed the careful translation in Smith (forthcoming). The Krader edition (Marx [1880–82] 1974) reproduces all the original languages, since it is a transcription, not a translation.

13. See also Morgan 1877, 455.

14. Here and below, double square brackets represent Marx's own bracketing; single brackets are my interpolations.

15. See also Morgan 1877, 474–75.

16. See also ibid., 477–78.

17. Marx had already covered women's changing position in much more detail in his 1879 notes on Ludwig Lange's *Römische Alterthümer* (Ancient Rome), which are to appear in MEGA² IV/27 and Marx (forthcoming).

18. He did so only in a brief footnote.

19. Here and below, Marx's parenthetical page numbers usually refer the book he is annotating.

20. Maine also fell into the notion of "Aryanism" common at the time, which irritated Marx: "This ass imagines that '*modern research . . . conveys a stronger impression*

than ever of a wide separation between the Aryan race and races of other stocks' (!)" (Marx [1880–82] 1974, 290 [Marx's emphasis]; Maine 1875, 96).

21. Evil custom.

22. Smith (forthcoming) calls attention to this passage from Maine. While it does not appear in Marx's notes, it is crucial for the understanding of the attack that follows.

23. Ivan the Terrible (r. 1547–84).

24. Most of Marx's letters to Kovalevsky, which would likely have illuminated the issues under discussion here, were burned in Russia by Kovalevsky's friends, for fear that they would have been incriminating in the eyes of the police (White 1996).

25. Although I am citing—here and below—the only published English translation of the major part of Marx's notes on Kovalevsky, that of Krader (Marx [1879] 1975), I have also consulted the new annotated transcription by Norair Ter-Akopian and Georgi Bagaturia (with Jürgen Rojahn) that will appear in MEGA² IV/27, as translated and annotated further by Charles Reitz, Lars Lih, and me for Marx (forthcoming). Marx's notes are mainly in German, with some passages in Russian.

26. A contract that changed a property relationship from free and clear to conditional ownership.

27. More commonly transliterated as *waqf*: land set aside as a Muslim religious endowment.

28. For example, when he discusses Mexico, Morgan criticizes the Spanish colonialists only for having "lost" a "golden opportunity" to record and preserve "information" about indigenous cultures for science (1877, 184).

29. This was a year or two after the notes on Kovalevsky, but probably not long after those on Morgan, which precede those on Phear in the same notebook.

30. See also Sewell 1870, 6. I am citing the only published translation of these notes, which appeared in Moscow in 1960. However, I have also consulted the newer transcription by Norair Ter-Akopian and Georgi Bagaturia (with Jürgen Rojahn), which will appear in MEGA² IV/27, and the English translation of it by Ashley Passmore and me in Marx (forthcoming).

31. See also Sewell 1870, 66.

32. The Moscow translation of 1960 renders *Stammvater* somewhat less precisely as "forefather."

33. See also Sewell 1870, 33.

34. Unfortunately, in his enthusiasm over this resistance to India's Muslim rulers, Marx makes the erroneous assumption that the small Indian kingdoms fighting against the Delhi Sultanate were led by Hindus. In fact, their rulers were Muslim as well.

35. See also Sewell 1870, 32.

36. Again, however, the challengers to Delhi were not Hindu princes, but members of the Sharqi sultanate based in Jaunpur.

37. As mentioned above, he had incorporated more extensive material from Sewell on this point in his Kovalevsky notes, especially the description of Cornwallis's "permanent settlement of 1793," which set up the *zemindars* as landlords.

38. English moneylenders.

39. See also Sewell 1870, 145.

40. See also ibid., 268.

41. Here again, I am citing the most accessible English version of Marx's notes on Kovalevsky, that of Krader (Marx [1880–82] 1975). But I have also consulted the new transcription by Norair Ter-Akopian and Georgi Bagaturia (with Jürgen Rojahn) that will appear in MEGA² IV/27, as translated and annotated by Charles Reitz, Lars Lih, and me for an all-English edition of same.

42. This part of the Kovalevsky notes has not yet been published in English. Therefore, I am referencing the German edition (Harstick 1977). However, I am actually quoting the newer transcription by Ter-Akopian and Bagaturia for MEGA², in the translation by Annette Kuhlmann, Charles Reitz, Lars Lih, and me, with C. J. Pereira di Salvo (for the Spanish) that will appear in Marx (forthcoming).

43. This material is slated to comprise the entirety of MEGA² IV/22.

44. A liberal supporter of capitalism, Zhukovsky had attacked the labor theory of value, among other things.

45. I would like to thank Lars Lih for translating this material from the Russian.

46. Marx's letter, drafted in French, but with a few lines in Russian, was never completed; Marx decided not to send it, apparently because Kovalevsky warned him that this would endanger the journal.

47. Although I am referring to the Shanin collection, the best-known English edition of Marx's late writings on Russia, I have sometimes slightly revised that translation on the basis of the French original, as published in MEGA² I/25, 112–17, 655–77 (apparatus).

48. This refers primarily to land in the possession individual peasants in the precapitalist order.

49. My translation from the French edition. See also the slightly different version in the standard English edition (*Capital* I, 929).

50. For example, in his 1969 preface to the French edition of *Capital*, Althusser calls it "an imprudent formulation," adding that "Stalin was right, for once, to suppress 'the negation of the negation' from the laws of the dialectic" (Althusser in Marx [1872–75] 1985a, 22; English translation in Althusser 1971, 95).

51. Could also be translated as "was deployed."

52. In fact, Marx's 1879 notebook on non-Western and precapitalist societies, the one that included the notes on Kovalevsky on communal forms and the chronological notes on Indian history based on Sewell, also contained notes on the work of four historians of ancient Rome, in which these very questions were examined. These are to appear in MEGA² IV/27 and in Marx (forthcoming).

53. Could also convey the notion of a frame or framework.

54. Commentators since the 1980s have differed strongly concerning the newness of Marx's 1877 rejection of unilinear and deterministic frameworks. Some have viewed

it as a break with his past in too one-sided a fashion: Shanin characterizes it as a move away from the "unilinear determinism" of *Capital* (1983b, 4); Haruki Wada argues that Mikhailovsky was "not entirely mistaken" to see such a framework operating in *Capital*, because Marx "underwent significant change after he wrote the first German edition of *Capital*" (1983, 59–60); James White claims extravagently that it "imposed retrospectively on *Capital* an interpretation completely at variance with the spirit in which it was conceived" (1996, 242). In an equally one-sided fashion, other scholars have held that no fundamental change occurred: Sayer and Corrigan argue persuasively that "Shanin overstates . . . the extent of the break between the 'late Marx' . . . and what went before" (1983, 79). But then they minimize these changes as "not so much a radical break as a *clarification* of how his 'mature' texts should have been read in the first place" (1983, 80). In a recent erudite analysis, Chattopadhyay (2006) makes some astute criticisms of Shanin and Wada, while also minimizing the scope of the changes Marx introduced in his late writings. Dunayevskaya points beyond these dichotomies, stressing both newness and continuity: "It was clear that Marx was working out new paths to revolution, not, as some current sociological studies would have us believe, by scuttling his own life's work of analyzing capitalism's development in West Europe" (1985, 190).

55. As with the 1877 letter, Marx wrote both his reply to Zasulich and the drafts in French. Again, although I give page references to the Shanin collection, I have sometimes revised the translation on the basis of the original, as published in MEGA² I/25, 219–42 (text) and 823–30, 871–77, and 911–20 (apparatus).

56. That is, even more decisively.

57. Lit. "Caudine forks," a reference to a humiliating 321 BCE defeat suffered by the Roman army, which was forced to march under the "forks" of the victors at the Caudine pass.

58. Here, Marx crossed out some language referring to the important role of the Russian intelligentsia in this process.

59. Lit., "free soaring" or "flight."

60. Plekhanov, a staunch unilinearist, was probably disconcerted by the preface (White 1996). It also appeared in German in 1882, but largely has been ignored by Western Marxists ever since. The only important Marxist thinker in the generation after Marx who showed much interest in precapitalist, communal societies was Rosa Luxemburg, who covered them extensively in her lectures at the German Social Democratic Party School. These reflections—on the Incas, the Russian village, the Indian village, Southern Africa, and the ancient Greeks—appeared posthumously in her unfinished book, *Introduction to Political Economy.* One of its chapters, "The Dissolution of Primitive Communism," is translated in Hudis and Anderson (2004). Luxemburg, whose approach was more historical, noted that these communal forms put up a stubborn resistance to the penetration of the modern capitalist mode of production. She did not, however, seem to have shared Marx's view that contemporary

communal forms—as in Russia—could form a basis for a positive, emancipatory type of resistance to capital that could ally with the Western labor movement.

61. Wada (1983) argues unconvincingly that Engels must have introduced this condition into the 1882 preface and that Marx signed onto a text with which he did not agree. But as shown above, it is already implicit in Marx's drafts of the letter to Zasulich.

62. In his generally careful examination of these texts, Chattopadhyay stumbles over this point when he asserts that the late writings on Russia "contain no reference to a 'proletarian' or 'socialist' revolution in Russia," but only refer to "the 'Russian Revolution' *tout court*" (2006, 61). Chattopadhyay also mounts a strong but ultimately unconvincing case for a sort of Russian exceptionalism, wherein in Marx's late writings on communal forms and revolution apply solely to the "unique" case of Russia. In contrast, the American anthropologist Thomas Patterson concludes, "The possibility of alternative trajectories of development in the future was one of the reasons why Marx devoted so much time and energy to his anthropological studies" at the end of his life (2009, 131).

63. There is no record of the deliberations, if any, between Marx and Engels over their 1882 preface. It should be mentioned, however, that Engels had written on some of these same issues in his pamphlet *Social Relations in Russia* (1875). The main thrust of this pamphlet was against Russian Populist and Bakuninist arguments to the effect that the Russian people could easily move to a modern form of communism without going through a capitalist phase, because they were instinctively communistic, as shown by the structure of the Russian village community. Engels argued that these communal structures were a long distance from a modern form of communism and that they were rapidly disintegrating as Russia modernized. As a subordinate point, however, he acknowledged that "the possibility undeniably exists of raising this form of society to a higher [communist] one," on condition that "a proletarian revolution is successfully carried out in Western Europe, creating for the Russian peasant the preconditions requisite for such a transition" (MECW 24, 48). While in congruence with some of these themes, the 1882 preface differs from Engels's 1875 article in two respects. (1) It emphasizes the potential of the village commune as a source of revolution, not the problems with such notions. (2) Rather than making the Western European proletarian revolution a precondition for a Russian revolution, here it is stated that the Russian revolution might come first, might give the "signal" for the Western one. What is unchanged from 1875, however, is the notion that a Russian revolution could not achieve a modern form of communism without the assistance of a contemporaneous communist revolution in the industrialized West.

APPENDIX

1. Most of these citations from Riazanov's report are translated in Dunayevskaya [1982] 1991, 177–78. For the full report in German, see Riazanov 1925.

2. For their part, the German Social Democrats had to scramble to save the original handwritten manuscripts of Marx and Engels from the flames of Nazism. They were sent to the Netherlands and later to Britain for safekeeping. Today they are at the International Institute of Social History in Amsterdam, which holds about two-thirds of the handwritten originals. Most of the rest of the originals of Marx's writings are in Moscow, at the Russian State Archive for Socio-Political History (formerly the Marx-Engels-Lenin Institute).

3. For an English translation, see Marx [1968] 1983.

4. For an overview of the changed state of MEGA^2 after 1991, see especially Grandjonc and Rojahn 1995, and in English, Rojahn 1998, Hecker 1998, Wendling 2005, and Musto 2007. The *Marx-Engels Jahrbuch* (Berlin), *MEGA-Studien* (Amsterdam), and the *Beiträge zur Marx-Engels-Forschung* (Berlin) each carry regular reports and scholarly discussions of the MEGA project and its history.

5. For some discussions of this, see Bellofiore and Fineschi 2009.

6. For a discussion of this volume, see Chattopadhyay 2004.

REFERENCES

Adler, Victor. 1954. *Briefwechsel mit August Bebel und Karl Kautsky*. Vienna: Verlag der Wiener Volksbuchhandlung.

Ahmad, Aijaz. 1992. "Marx on India: A Clarification." In *In Theory: Classes, Nations, Literature*, 221–42, 337–39. London: Verso.

Alan, John. 2003. *Dialectics of Black Freedom Struggles*. Chicago: News & Letters.

Althusser, Louis. 1971. *Lenin and Philosophy and Other Essays*. Trans. Ben Brewster. New York: Monthly Review Press.

Anderson, Kevin B. 1983. "The 'Unknown' Marx's *Capital*, Vol. I: The French Edition of 1872–75, 100 Years Later." *Review of Radical Political Economics* 15, no.4: 71–80.

———. 1992. "Rubel's Marxology: A Critique." *Capital & Class* 47:67–91.

———. 1995. *Lenin, Hegel, and Western Marxism: A Critical Study*. Urbana: University of Illinois Press.

———. 1997a. "Maximilien Rubel, 1905–1996, Libertarian Marx Editor." *Capital & Class* 62: 159–65.

———. 1997b. "On the MEGA and the French Edition of *Capital*, Vol. I: An Appreciation and a Critique." *Beiträge zur Marx-Engels Forschung*. Neue Folge 1997: 131–36. Berlin: Argument Verlag.

———. 1999. "Marx on Suicide in the Context of His Other Writings on Alienation and Gender." In *Marx on Suicide*, ed. Eric A. Plaut and Kevin Anderson, 3–27. Evanston, IL: Northwestern University Press.

———. 2007. "The Rediscovery and Persistence of the Dialectic: In Philosophy and in World Politics." In *Lenin Reloaded: Toward a Politics of Truth*, ed. Sebastian Budgen, Stathis Kouvelakis, and Slavoj Zizek, 120–47. Durham, NC: Duke University Press.

Anderson, Perry. 1974. *Lineages of the Absolutist State*. London: New Left Books.

Antonio. Robert. J., ed. 2003. *Marx and Modernity: Key Readings and Commentary*. Malden, MA, and Oxford: Blackwell.

Arthur, Christopher J. 1990. "*Capital*: A Note on Translation." *Science & Society* 54, no. 2: 224–25.

———, ed. 1996. *Engels Today: A Centenary Appreciation*. London: Macmillan.

Avineri, Shlomo. 1968. *The Social and Political Thought of Karl Marx*. Cambridge: Cambridge University Press.

Bahro, Rudolf. 1978. *The Alternative in Eastern Europe*. Trans. David Fernbach. London: NLB.

Bakan, Abigail. 2008. "Marxism and Antiracism: Rethinking the Politics of Difference." *Rethinking Marxism* 20, no. 2: 238–56.

Barbier, Maurice. 1992. *La pensée politique de Karl Marx*. Paris: Éditions L'Harmattan.

Baylen, Joseph O. 1957. "Marx's Dispatches to Americans about Russia and the West, 1853–56." *South Atlantic Quarterly* 56, no. 1: 20–26.

Beauvoir, Simone de. [1949] 1989. *The Second Sex*. Trans. H. M. Parshley. New York: Vintage.

Bellofiore, Riccardo, and Roberto Fineschi, eds. 2009. *Re-reading Marx: New Perspectives after the Critical Edition*. Basingstoke, UK: Palgrave Macmillan.

Benner, Erica. 1995. *Really Existing Nationalisms: A Post-Communist View of Marx and Engels*. New York: Oxford University Press.

Bennett, Lerone Jr. 2000. *Forced Into Glory: Abraham Lincoln's White Dream*. Chicago: Johnson Publications.

Black, Dave. 2004. *Helen Macfarlane: A Feminist, Revolutionary Journalist, and Philosopher in Mid-Nineteenth Century England*. With a reprint of Macfarlane's 1850 translation of *The Communist Manifesto*. Lanham, MD: Lexington Books.

Blit, Lucjan. 1971. *The Origins of Polish Socialism: The History and Ideas of the First Polish Socialist Party 1878–1886*. New York and London: Cambridge University Press.

Bloom, Solomon F. 1941. *The World of Nations: A Study of the National Implications of the Work of Marx*. New York: Columbia University Press.

Bowman, Frank O. III. 2004. "*Pour encourager les autres?* The Curious History and Distressing Implications of the Sarbanes-Oxley Act and the Sentencing Guidelines Amendments That Followed." *Ohio State Journal of Criminal Law* 1, no. 2: 373–442.

Bourdieu, Pierre. 1977. *Outline of a Theory of Practice*. Trans. Richard Nice. Cambridge and New York: Cambridge University Press.

Braunthal, Julius. [1961] 1967. *History of the International, Volume One: 1864–1914*. Trans. Henry Collins and Kenneth Mitchell. New York: Praeger.

Bright, John. [1865] 1970. *Speeches on the American Question*. With an introduction by Frank Moore. New York: Kraus Reprint Co.

Callesen, Gerd. 2002. "A Scholarly MEGA Enterprise." *Tijdschrift voor de Geschiednis van Soziale Bewegingen* 4:77–89.

Carver, Terrell. 1996. "Engels and Democracy." In Arthur 1996, 1–28.

Chandra, Bipan. 1980. "Karl Marx, His Theories of Asian Societies and Colonial Rule." In *Sociological Theories: Race and Colonialism*, 383–451. Paris: UNESCO.

Chattopadhyay, Paresh. 1999. "Review Essay: Women's Labor under Capitalism and Marx." *Bulletin of Concerned Asian Scholars* 31, no. 4: 67–75.

———. 2004. "On 'Karl Marx—Exzerpte und Notizen: Sommer 1844 bis Anfang 1847,' in *Gesamtausgabe (MEGA)*, vierte Abteilung, Band 3." *Historical Materialism* 12, no. 4: 427–54.

———. 2006. "Passage to Socialism: The Dialectic of Progress in Marx." *Historical Materialism* 14, no. 3: 45–84.

Collins, Henry, and Chimen Abramsky. 1965. *Karl Marx and the British Labour Movement: Years of the First International*. London: Macmillan.

Cummins, Ian. 1980. *Marx, Engels and National Movements*. London: Croom Helm.

Curtis, Michael. 2009. *Orientalism and Islam*. New York: Cambridge University Press.

Debs, Eugene V. 1908. "The American Movement." In *Debs: His Life, Writings and Speeches*, 95–117. Girard, KS: The Appeal to Reason.

Dennehy, Anne. 1996. "The Condition of the Working Class in England, 150 Years On." In Arthur 1996, 95–128.

Derrida, Jacques. 1994. *Specters of Marx*. Trans. Peggy Kamuf. New York: Routledge.

Draper, Hal. 1978. *The Politics of Social Classes*. Vol. 2 of *Karl Marx's Theory of Revolution*. New York: Monthly Review.

———. 1985a. *The Marx-Engels Chronicle*. Vol. 1 of *The Marx-Engels Cyclopedia*. New York: Schocken.

———. 1985b. *The Marx-Engels Register*. Vol. 2 of *The Marx-Engels Cyclopedia*. New York: Schocken.

———. 1986. *The Marx-Engels Glossary*. Vol. 3 of *The Marx-Engels Cyclopedia*. New York: Schocken.

———. 1996. *War and Revolution. Lenin and the Myth of Revolutionary Defeatism*. Ed. Ernest Haberkern. Atlantic Highlands, NJ: Humanities Press.

Du Bois, W. E. B. [1903] 1961. *The Souls of Black Folk*. New York: Fawcett.

———. [1935] 1973. *Black Reconstruction in America: An Essay Toward a History of the Part Which Black Folk Played in the Attempt to Reconstruct Democracy in America, 1860–1880*. New York: Atheneum.

Dunayevskaya, Raya. [1958] 2000. *Marxism and Freedom. From 1776 until Today*. With a preface by Herbert Marcuse and a new foreword by Joel Kovel. Amherst, NY: Humanity Books.

———. [1963] 2003. *American Civilization on Trial: Black Masses as Vanguard*. 5th ed. Chicago: News & Letters.

———. [1973] 1989. *Philosophy and Revolution: From Hegel to Sartre and from Marx to Mao*. With a preface by Louis Dupré. New York: Columbia University Press.

———. [1982] 1991. *Rosa Luxemburg, Women's Liberation, and Marx's Philosophy of Revolution*. 2nd ed., with additional material by the author and a foreword by Adrienne Rich. Urbana: University of Illinois Press.

———. 1985. *Women's Liberation and the Dialectics of Revolution: Reaching for the Future*. Atlantic Highlands, NJ: Humanities Press.

———. 2002. *The Power of Negativity: Selected Writings on the Dialectic in Hegel and Marx*. Ed. Peter Hudis and Kevin B. Anderson. Lanham, MD: Lexington Books.

Dupré, Louis. 1983. *Marx's Social Critique of Culture*. New Haven, CT: Yale University Press.

Eaton, Henry. 1980. "Marx and the Russians." *Journal of the History of Ideas* 41, no. 1: 89–112.

Ellis, Peter Berresford. 1996. *A History of the Irish Working Class*. London: Pluto.

Fetscher, Iring. 1971. *Marx and Marxism*. Trans. John Hargreaves. New York: Herder and Herder.

———. 1991. *Überlebensbedingungen der Menschkeit*. Berlin: Dietz Verlag.

Foner, Philip S. 1973. *When Karl Marx Died: Comments in 1883*. New York: International Publishers.

———. 1977. *American Socialism and Black Americans: From the Age of Jackson to World War II*. Westport, CT: Greenwood Press.

———. 1981. *British Labor and the American Civil War*. New York: Holmes & Meier.

Gailey, Christine Ward. 2006. "Community, State, and Questions of Social Evolution in Karl Marx's *Ethnological Notebooks*." In *The Politics of Egalitarianism: Theory and Practice*, ed. Jacqueline Solway, 32–52. New York: Bergahn Books.

General Council of the First International, 1864–1866, Minutes. 1962. Moscow: Progress Publishers.

General Council of the First International, 1866–1868, Minutes. 1964. Moscow: Progress Publishers.

General Council of the First International, 1868–1870, Minutes. 1966. Moscow: Progress Publishers.

Genovese, Eugene. [1968] 1971. "Marxian Interpretations of the Slave South." In *In Red and Black: Marxian Explorations in Southern and Afro-American History*, 315–53. New York: Pantheon.

Gluckstein, Ygael [Tony Cliff]. 1957. *Mao's China*. London: Allen & Unwin.

Godelier, Maurice. 1970. Preface to *Sur les sociétés précapitalistes: Textes choisis de Marx, Engels, Lénine*, 13–142. Paris: Éditions sociales.

Goethe, Johann Wolfgang von. 1914. *West-Eastern Divan*. Trans. Edward Dowden. London: J. M. Dent & Sons.

———. 1949. *Gedichte und Epen*. Vol. 2 of *Werke*. With editorial notes by Erich Trunz. Hamburg: Christian Wegner Verlag.

Gouldner, Alvin W. 1980. *The Two Marxisms*. New York: Oxford University Press.

Grandjonc, Jacques, and Jürgen Rojahn. 1995. "Aus der MEGA-Arbeit. Der revidierte Plan der *Marx-Engels-Gesamtausgabe*." *MEGA-Studien* 2 (1995): 62–89.

Habib, Irfan. 2006. "Introduction: Marx's Perception of India." In *Karl Marx on India*, ed. Iqbal Husain, xix–liv. New Delhi: Tulika Books.

Hammen, Oscar. 1969. *The Red '48ers. Karl Marx and Friedrich Engels*. New York: Scribner's.

Harstick, Hans-Peter, ed. 1977. *Karl Marx über Formen vorkapitalistischer Produktion*. Frankfurt: Campus Verlag.

Hazelkorn, Ellen. 1980. "*Capital* and the Irish Question." *Science & Society* 43, no. 3: 326–56.

Hecker, Rolf. 1998. "The MEGA Project: An Edition Between a Scientific Claim and the Dogmas of Marxism-Leninism." *Critique* 30–31:188–95.

Hegel, G. W. F. [1807] 1977. *Phenomenology of Spirit*. Trans. A. V. Miller. New York: Oxford University Press.

———. [1831] 1969. *Science of Logic*. Trans. A. V. Miller, with a foreword by J. N. Findlay. London: Allen & Unwin.

———. 1956. *Philosophy of History*. Trans. J. Sibree. New York: Dover.

Henderson, F. O. 1976. *The Life of Friedrich Engels*. 2 vols. London: Frank Cass.

Henze, Paul B. 1958. "The Shamil Problem." In *The Middle East in Transition: Studies in Contemporary History*. Ed. Walter Z. Laquer, 415–43. New York: Praeger.

Hodgson, Peter. 1988. "Editorial Introduction" to *Lectures on the Philosophy of Religion*, by G. W. F. Hegel, 1–71. One vol. ed. Berkeley: University of California Press.

Hudis, Peter. 1983. *Marx and the Third World*. Detroit: News & Letters.

———. 2004. "Marx Among the Muslims." *Capitalism Nature Socialism* 15, no. 4: 51–67.

Hudis, Peter, and Kevin B. Anderson, eds. 2004. *The Rosa Luxemburg Reader*. New York: Monthly Review Press.

Husain, Iqbal, ed. 2006. *Karl Marx on India*. With an introduction by Irfan Habib. New Delhi: Tulika Books.

Inden, Ron. 2000. *Imagining India*. Bloomington: Indiana University Press.

Ingram, David. 1988. "Rights and Privileges: Marx and the Jewish Question." *Studies in Soviet Thought* 35:125–45.

Ito, Narihiko. 1996. "Überlegungen zu einem Gedanken beim späten Marx." In *Materialien zum Historisch-Kritischen Wörterbuch des Marxismus*, ed. Frigga Haug and Michael Krätke, 38–44. Berlin: Argument Verlag.

Jacobs, Jack. 1998. "Friedrich Engels and 'the Jewish Question' Reconsidered." *MEGA-Studien* 2:3–23.

James, C. L. R. 1943. "Negroes in the Civil War: Their Role in the Second American Revolution." *New International* 9, no. 11: 338–42.

Jani, Pranav. 2002. "Karl Marx, Eurocentrism, and the 1857 Revolt in British India." In *Marxism, Modernity, and Postcolonial Studies,* ed. Crystal Bartolovich and Neil Lazarus, 81–97. New York: Cambridge University Press.

Kapp, Yvonne. 1972. *Eleanor Marx.* Vol. 1. New York: Pantheon.

Kelly, Brian. 2007. Introduction to *Labor, Free and Slave: Workingmen and the Anti-Slavery Movement in the U.S.,* by Bernard Mandel, xi–lxix. Urbana: University of Illinois Press.

Kiernan, Victor G. 1967. "Marx and India." In *The Socialist Register,* ed. Ralph Miliband and John Saville, 159–89. New York: Monthly Review Press.

Krader, Lawrence. 1974. Introduction to *Ethnological Notebooks,* by Karl Marx, 1–93. 2nd ed. Assen: Van Gorcum.

———. 1975. *The Asiatic Mode of Production: Sources, Development and Critique in the Writings of Karl Marx.* Assen: Van Gorcum.

Krings, Torben. 2004. "Irische Frage" In *Historisch-kritisches Wörterbuch des Marxismus.* Vol. 6:2, 1505–518. Hamburg: Argument Verlag.

"Le Conseil Général." 1869. *L'Égalité* 47 (December 11).

Le Cour Grandmaison, Olivier. 2003. "F. Engels et K. Marx: le colonialisme au service de 'l'Histoire.'" *Contretemps* 8:174–84.

Ledbetter, James. 2007. Introduction to Marx 2007, xvii–xxvii.

Leeb, Claudia. 2007. "Marx and the Gendered Structure of Capitalism." *Philosophy & Social Criticism* 33, no. 7: 833–59.

Lenin, V. I. [1916] 1964. "The Discussion of Self-Determination Summed Up." In *Collected Works* 22:320–60. Moscow: Progress Publishers.

Levine, Norman. 1973. "Anthropology in the Thought of Marx and Engels." *Studies in Comparative Communism* 6, nos. 1 & 2: 7–26.

Lichtheim, George. 1961. *Marxism: An Historical and Critical Study.* New York: Praeger.

———. 1963. "Marx and the 'Asiatic Mode of Production.'" *St Antony's Papers* XIV: 86–112.

Lim, Jie-Hyun. 1992. "Marx's Theory of Imperialism and the Irish National Question." *Science & Society* 56, no. 2: 163–78.

Löwy, Michael. 1996. "La dialectique du progrès et l'enjeu actuel des mouvements sociaux." In *Congrès Marx International. Cent ans de marxisme. Bilan critique et perspectives,* 197–209. Paris: Presses Universitaires de France.

———. 1998. *Fatherland or Mother Earth? Essays on the National Question.* London: Pluto Press.

Lubasz, Heinz. 1984. "Marx's Concept of the Asiatic Mode of Production: A Genetic Analysis." *Economy and Society* 13, no. 4: 456–83.

Lukács, Georg. [1923] 1971. *History and Class Consciousness.* Trans. Rodney Livingstone. Cambridge, MA: MIT Press.

———. [1948] 1975. *The Young Hegel.* Trans. Rodney Livingstone. Cambridge, MA: MIT Press.

MacDonald, H. Malcolm. 1941. "Marx, Engels, and the Polish National Movement." *Journal of Modern History* 13, no. 3: 321–34.

Maine, Henry Sumner. 1875. *Lectures on the Early History of Institutions*. New York: Henry Holt and Co.

Mandel, Bernard. [1955] 2007. *Labor, Free and Slave: Workingmen and the Anti-Slavery Movement in the U.S.* Urbana: University of Illinois Press.

Marcus, Steven. 1974. *Engels, Manchester and the Working Class*. New York: Random House.

Marcuse, Herbert. [1948] 1972. "Sartre's Existentialism." In *Studies in Critical Philosophy*, 157–90. Trans. Joris de Bres. Boston: Beacon Press.

Marx, Karl. [1843] 1994. "On the Jewish Question." In *Early Political Writings*. Ed. and trans. Joseph O'Malley, 28–56. New York and Cambridge: Cambridge University Press.

———. [1844] 1961. "Economic and Philosophical Manuscripts." Trans. Tom Bottomore. In *Marx's Concept of Man*, by Erich Fromm, 85–196. New York: Ungar.

———. [1857–58] 1973. *Grundrisse: Foundations of the Critique of Political Economy (Rough Draft)*. Trans. Martin Nicolaus, with notes and index by Ben Fowkes. New York: Penguin.

———. [1872–75] 1985a. *Le Capital. Livre I. Sections I à IV*. Traduction de J. Roy. Préface de Louis Althusser. Paris: Éditions Flammarion.

———. [1872–75] 1985b. *Le Capital. Livre I. Sections V à VIII*. Traduction de J. Roy. Préface de Louis Althusser. Paris: Éditions Flammarion.

———. [1879] 1975. "Excerpts from M. M. Kovalevskij (Kovalevsky)." In *The Asiatic Mode of Production: Sources, Development and Critique in the Writings of Karl Marx*, trans. Lawrence Krader, 343–412. Assen: Van Gorcum.

———. [1879–80] 1960. *Notes on Indian History (664–1858)*. Moscow: Progress Publishers.

———. [1880–82] 1974. *Ethnological Notebooks*. Second Edition. Ed. Lawrence Krader. Assen: Van Gorcum.

———. [1884] 1978. *Capital*. Vol. 2. Trans. David Fernbach, with an introduction by Ernest Mandel. London: Penguin.

———. [1890] 1976. *Capital*. Vol. 1. Trans. Ben Fowkes, with an introduction by Ernest Mandel. London: Penguin.

———. [1894] 1981. *Capital*. Vol. 3. Trans. David Fernbach, with an introduction by Ernest Mandel. London: Penguin.

———. [1897] 1969. *The Eastern Question*. Ed. Eleanor Marx Aveling and Edward Aveling. New York: Augustus Kelley.

———. 1939. *Capital: A Critical Analysis of Capitalist Production*. Vol. 1. With a supplement edited and translated by Dona Torr. New York: International Publishers.

———. 1951. *Marx on China, 1853–1860*. Ed. Dona Torr. London: Lawrence and Wishart.

———. 1963–94. *Oeuvres*. 4 vols. Ed. Maximilien Rubel. Paris: Gallimard.

———. 1965. *Pre-Capitalist Economic Formations*. Ed. Eric J. Hobsbawm. New York: International Publishers.

———. 1968. *Karl Marx on Colonialism and Modernization*. Ed. Shlomo Avineri. New York: Doubleday.

———. [1968] 1983. *Mathematical Manuscripts*. Trans. C. Aronson and M. Meo. London: New Park.

———. 1969. *Secret Diplomatic History of the Eighteenth Century and The Story of the Life of Lord Palmerston*. Ed. Lester Hutchinson. New York: International Publishers.

———. 1971. *Przyczynki do historii kwestii polskiej (Rekopisy z lat 1863–1864)*. With an introduction by Celina Bobinska. Warsaw: Ksiazka i Wiedza.

———. 1971–77. *The Karl Marx Library*. 7 vols. Ed. and trans. Saul K. Padover. New York: McGraw-Hill.

———. 1983. *Le Capital*. Livre 1. Traduction de la 4e édition allemande sous la responsabilité de Jean-Pierre Lefebvre. Paris: Messidor/Éditions Sociales.

———. 1996. *Later Political Writings*. Ed. and trans. Terrell Carver. New York and Cambridge: Cambridge University Press.

———. 2007. *Dispatches for the New York Tribune: Selected Journalism of Karl Marx*. With an introduction by James Ledbetter and a foreword by Francis Wheen. London: Penguin.

———. 2008. *Capital*. Vol. 1 [Persian]. Trans. and with a preface by Hassan Mortazavi. Tehran: Agah Publishing. [Preface, trans. Frieda Afary, available at http://iranianvoicesintranslation.blogspot.com/2009/07/translators-preface-to-new-persian.html (accessed July 31, 2009)].

———. Forthcoming. "Commune, Empire, and Class: 1879–82 Notebooks on Non-Western and Precapitalist Societies." Ed. Kevin B. Anderson, David Norman Smith, and Jürgen Rojahn. With Georgi Bagaturia and Norair Ter-Akopian.

Marx, Karl, and Frederich Engels. 1920. *Gesammelte Schriften 1852 bis 1862*. 2 vols. Ed. David Riazanov. Trans. Luise Kautsky. Stuttgart: Dietz Verlag.

———. [1934] 1965. *Selected Correspondence*. 2nd ed. Ed. S. Ryazanskaya. Moscow: Progress Publishers.

———. 1937. *The Civil War in the United States*. Ed. Richard Enmale [Richard Morais]. New York: International Publishers.

———. 1952. *The Russian Menace to Europe*. Ed. Paul W. Blackstock and Bert F. Hoselitz. Glencoe, IL: The Free Press.

———. 1956–68. *Werke*. 42 vols. plus 2 suppl. vols. Berlin: Dietz Verlag.

———. 1959. *The First Indian War of Independence 1857–1859*. Moscow: Progress Publishers.

———. 1966. *The American Journalism of Marx and Engels*. Ed. Henry M. Christman, with an introduction by Charles Blitzer. New York: New American Library.

———. 1972a. *On Colonialism: Articles from the New York Tribune and Other Writings*. New York: International Publishers.

———. 1972b. *Ireland and the Irish Question*. Moscow: Progress Publishers.

———. 1975. *China. Fósil viviente o transmisor revolucionario?* With an Introduction and notes by Lothar Knauth. Mexico City: Universidad Nacional Autonoma de Mexico.

———. 1975–. *Gesamtausgabe*. Sections I–IV. Berlin: Dietz Verlag, Akademie Verlag.

———. 1975–2004. *Collected Works*. 50 vols. New York: International Publishers.

McLellan, David. 1973. *Karl Marx: His Life and Thought*. New York: Harper & Row.

———, ed. [1977] 2000. *Karl Marx: Selected Writings*. 2nd ed. New York: Oxford University Press.

Megill, Allan. 2002. *Karl Marx: The Burden of Reason (Why Marx Rejected Politics and the Market)*. Lanham, MD: Rowman & Littlefield.

Mehring, Franz. [1918] 1962. *Karl Marx: The Story of His Life*. Trans. Edward Fitzgerald. Ann Arbor: University of Michigan Press.

Mikhailovsky, Nikolai Konstantovich. [1877] 1911. "Karl Marks pered sudom g. Yu. Zhukovskogo" [Karl Marx Before the Tribunal of Mr. Yu. Zhukovsky]. In *Polnoe Sobranie Sochinie*, 4:165–206. St. Petersburg: M. M. Stasiulevich.

Moore, Barrington. 1966. *Social Origins of Dictatorship and Democracy: Lord and Peasant in the Making of the Modern World*. Boston: Beacon.

Morgan, Lewis Henry. 1877. *Ancient Society*. New York: Henry Holt & Co.

Musto, Marcello. 2007. "The Rediscovery of Karl Marx." *International Review of Social History* 52, no. 3: 477–98.

———, ed. 2008. *Karl Marx's* Grundrisse: *Foundations of the Critique of Political Economy 150 Years Later*. New York: Routledge.

Newsinger, John. 1982. " 'A Great Blow Must Be Struck in Ireland': Karl Marx and the Fenians." *Race & Class* 24, no.2: 151–67.

Nimni, Ephraim. 1994. *Marxism and Nationalism: Theoretical Origins of a Political Crisis*. With a preface by Ernesto Laclau. London: Pluto Press.

Nimtz, August H. 2000. *Marx and Engels: Their Contribution to the Democratic Breakthrough*. Albany: State University of New York Press.

Ollman, Bertell. 1993. *Dialectical Investigations*. New York: Routledge.

Padover, Saul K. 1978. *Karl Marx: An Intimate Biography*. New York: McGraw-Hill.

Patterson, Thomas C. 2009. *Karl Marx, Anthropologist*. Oxford: Berg.

Perelman, Michael. 1987. "Political Economy and the Press: Karl Marx and Henry Carey at the *New York Tribune*." In *Marx's Crises Theory: Scarcity, Labor, and Finance*, 10–26. New York: Praeger.

Phillips, Wendell. 1969. *Speeches, Lectures & Letters*. New York: New American Library; Negro Universities Press.

Plaut, Eric A., and Kevin Anderson, eds. 1999. *Marx on Suicide*. Trans. Eric Plaut, Gabrielle Edgcomb, and Kevin Anderson. Evanston, IL: Northwestern University Press.

Postone, Moishe. 1993. *Time, Labor, and Social Domination: A Reinterpretation of Marx's Critical Theory*. New York: Cambridge University Press.

Prawer, S. S. 1976. *Karl Marx and World Literature*. London: Oxford University Press.

Raffles, Thomas Stamford. [1817] 1965. *The History of Java*. 2 vols. With an introduction by John Bastin. Kuala Lumpur: Oxford University Press.

"Refléxions." 1869. *L'Égalité* 47 (December 11).

Reitz, Charles. 2008. "Horace Greeley, Karl Marx, and German 48ers: Anti-Racism in the Kansas Free State Struggle, 1854–64." In *Marx-Engels Jahrbuch 2008*, 1–24. Berlin: Akademie Verlag.

Resis, Albert. 1970. "*Das Kapital* Comes to Russia." *Slavic Review* 29, no. 2: 219–37.

Riazanov, David. 1925. "Neueste Mitteilungen über den literarischen Nachlass von Karl Marx und Friedrich Engels." In *Archiv für Geschichte des Sozialismus und der Arbeiterbewegung*, 11:385–400.

———. 1926. "Karl Marx on China." *Labour Monthly* 8:86–92.

———. [1927] 1973. *Karl Marx and Friedrich Engels: An Introduction to Their Lives and Work*. New York: Monthly Review.

Rich, Adrienne. [1991] 2001. "Raya Dunayevskaya's Marx." In *Arts of the Possible: Essays and Conversations*, 83–97. New York: Norton.

Robinson, Cedric. [1983] 2000. *Black Marxism*. Chapel Hill: University of North Carolina Press.

Roediger, David, ed. 1978. *Joseph Weydemeyer: Articles on the Eight Hour Movement*. Chicago: Greenleaf Press.

———. 1994. *Towards the Abolition of Whiteness: Essays on Race, Politics, and Working Class History*. London and New York: Verso.

Rojahn, Jürgen. 1995. "Parlamentarismus-Kritik und demokratisches Ideal: Wies Rosa Luxemburg einen 'dritten Weg'?" In *Die Freiheit der Andersdenkenden: Rosa Luxemburg und das Problem der Demokratie*, ed. Theodor Bergmann, Jürgen Rojahn, and Fritz Weber, 11–27. Hamburg: VSA Verlag.

———. 1998. "Publishing Marx and Engels after 1989: The Fate of the MEGA." *Critique* 30–31:196–207.

Rosdolsky, Roman. [1968] 1977. *The Making of Marx's "Capital."* Trans. Pete Burgess. London: Pluto Press.

———. 1986. *Engels and the "Nonhistoric" Peoples: The National Question in the Revolution of 1848*. Glasgow: Critique Books.

Rosemont, Franklin. 1989. "Karl Marx and the Iroquois." In *Arsenal: Surrealist Subversion*, 201–13. Chicago: Black Swan Press.

Rubel, Maximilien. 1956. *Bibliographie des Oeuvres de Karl Marx. Avec en appendice un répertoire des oeuvres de Friedrich Engels*. Paris: Marcel Rivière.

———. 1960. *Supplément à la Bibliographie des Oeuvres de Karl Marx*. Paris: Marcel Rivière.

———. 1964. "Marx et la Première Internationale. Une Chronologie." *Études de Marxologie* 8 (August): 9–82.

———. 1965. "Marx et la Première Internationale. Une Chronologie. Deuxième Partie." *Etudes de Marxologie* 9 (January): 5–70.

———. [1973] 1981. "The Plan and Method of the 'Economics.'" In *Rubel on Karl Marx: Five Essays*, ed. Joseph O'Malley and Keith Algozin, 190–229. New York: Cambridge University Press.

———. 1997. "L'Emancipation des femmes dans l'oeuvre de Marx et d'Engels." In *Encyclopédie politique et historique des femmes*, ed. Christine Faure, 381–403. Paris: Presses Universitaires de France.

Rubel, Maximilien, and [Alexandre] Bracke-Desrousseaux. 1952. "L'Occident doit à Marx et à Engels une édition monumentale de leurs oeuvres." *La Revue socialiste* 59 (July): 113–14.

Rubel, Maximilien and Margaret Manale. 1975. *Marx without Myth: A Chronological Study of His Life and Work*. New York: Harper & Row.

Runkle, Gerald. 1964. "Karl Marx and the American Civil War." *Comparative Studies in Society and History* 6, no. 2 (January): 117–41.

Said, Edward. 1978. *Orientalism*. New York: Vintage.

San Juan, E. Jr. 2002. "The Poverty of Postcolonialism." *Pretexts: Literary and Cultural Studies* 11, no. 1: 57–73.

Sartre, Jean-Paul. [1949] 1962. "Materialism and Revolution." In *Literary and Philosophical Essays*, 198–256. Trans. by Annette Michelson. New York: Collier.

Sayer, Derek and Philip Corrigan. 1983. "Late Marx: Continuity, Contradiction, and Learning." In Shanin 1983a, 77–93.

Schlüter, Hermann. [1913] 1965. *Lincoln, Labor and Slavery: A Chapter in the Social History of America*. New York: Russell and Russell.

Schumpeter, Joseph A. 1949. "*The Communist Manifesto* in Sociology and Economics." *Journal of Political Economy* 47, no. 3: 199–212.

Seigel, Jerrold. 1978. *Marx's Fate: The Shape of a Life*. Princeton, NJ: Princeton University Press.

Sewell, Robert. 1870. *Analytical History of India: From the Earliest Times to the Abolition of the Honourable East India Company in 1858*. London: W. H. Allen & Co.

Shanin, Teodor, ed. 1983a. *Late Marx and the Russian Road: Marx and the 'Peripheries' of Capitalism*. New York: Monthly Review Press.

———. 1983b. "Late Marx: Gods and Craftsmen." In Shanin 1983a, 3–39.

Slater, Eamonn, and Terrence McDonough. 2008. "Marx on Nineteenth-Century Colonial Ireland: Analysing Colonialism as a Dynamic Social Process." *Irish Historical Studies* 23, no.142: 153–71.

Smith, David Norman, 1995. "The Ethnological Imagination." In *Ethnohistorische Wege und Lehrjahre eines Philosophen. Festschrift für Lawrence Krader zum 75. Geburtstag,* ed. Dittmar Schorkowitz, 102–19. New York: Peter Lang.

———, ed. Forthcoming. *Patriarchy and Property: The Ethnological Notebooks of Karl Marx.* New Haven, CT: Yale University Press.

Spence, Jonathan. 1996. *God's Chinese Son: The Taiping Heavenly Kingdom of Hong Xiuquan.* New York: Norton.

Stekloff, G. M. 1928. *History of the First International.* Trans. Eden and Cedar Paul. London: Martin Lawrence.

Suny, Ronald Grigor. 2006. "Reading Russia and the Soviet Union in the twentieth century." In *The Cambridge History of Russia.* Vol. III. *The Twentieth Century,* ed. Ronald Grigor Suny, 8–64. New York: Cambridge University Press.

Sylvers, Malcolm. 2004. "Marx, Engels und die USA—ein Forschungsprojekt über ein wenig beachtetes Thema." In *Marx-Engels-Jahrbuch 2004,* 31–53.

Szporluk, Roman. 1997. Review of *Really Existing Nationalisms,* by Erica Benner. *American Journal of Sociology* 102, no. 4: 1236–38.

Taylor, Miles. 1996. "The English Face of Karl Marx." *Journal of Victorian Culture* 1, no. 2: 227–53.

Thorner, Daniel. [1966] 1990. "Marx on India and the Asiatic Mode of Production." In *Karl Marx's Social and Political Thought: Critical Assessments,* ed. Bob Jessop and Charlie Malcolm-Brown, 3:436–65. New York: Routledge.

Tichelman, Fritjof. 1983. "Marx and Indonesia. Preliminary Notes." In *Marx on Indonesia and India,* 9–28. Trier: Schriften aus dem Karl-Marx-Haus.

Traverso, Enzo. 1994. *The Marxists and the Jewish Question: History of a Debate, 1843–1943.* Trans. Bernard Gibbons. Atlantic Highlands, NJ: Humanities Press.

Trotsky, Leon. [1933] 1967. "Appendix II: Socialism in a Separate Country?" In *The History of the Russian Revolution,* 3: 349–86. London: Sphere Books.

———. [1939] 2006. "Presenting Karl Marx." In *The Essential Marx,* ed. Leon Trotsky, 1–43. New York: Dover (originally published as *The Living Thoughts of Karl Marx,* 1939).

Tucker, Robert, ed. 1978. *The Marx-Engels Reader.* 2nd ed. New York: Norton.

Turner, Lou, and John Alan. 1986. *Frantz, Fanon, Soweto & American Black Thought.* 2nd ed. Chicago: News & Letters.

Vileisis, Danga. 1996. "Engels Rolle im 'unglücklichen Verhältnis' zwischen Marxismus und Feminismus." *Beiträge zur Marx-Engels Forschung.* Neue Folge 1996: 149–79.

Vogt, Annette. 1995. "Emil Julius Gumbel (1891–1966): der erste Herausgeber der mathematischen Manuscripte von Karl Marx," *MEGA-Studien* 2 (1995): 26–41.

Wada, Haruki. 1983. "Marx and Revolutionary Russia." In Shanin 1983a, 40–75.

Walicki, Andrzej. 1982. "Marx, Engels, and the Polish Question." In *Philosophy and Romantic Nationalism: The Case of Poland,* 359–91. Oxford: Oxford University Press.

Weill, Nicolas. 1995. "Un penseur du XXe siècle et non du XIXe. Un entretien avec Maximilien Rubel." *Le Monde des Livres*, Sept. 29, viii.

Welsh, John. 2002. "Reconstructing *Capital*: The American Roots and Humanist Vision of Marx's Thought." *Midwest Quarterly* 43, no. 3: 274–87.

Wendling, Amy E. 2005. "Comparing Two Editions of Marx-Engels Collected Works." *Socialism and Democracy* 19, no. 1: 181–89.

Wheen, Francis. 2000. *Karl Marx: A Life*. New York: Norton.

White, James D. 1996. *Karl Marx and the Intellectual Origins of Dialectical Materialism*. New York: St. Martin's.

Wielenga, Bastiaan. 2004. "Indische Frage." In *Historisch-kritisches Wörterbuch des Marxismus*, Vol. 6:2, 904–17. Hamburg: Argument Verlag.

Wiggershaus, Rolf. [1986] 1994. *The Frankfurt School: Its History, Theories, and Political Significance*. Trans. Michael Robertson. Cambridge, MA: MIT Press.

Wittfogel, Karl A. 1957. *Oriental Despotism*. New Haven, CT: Yale University Press.

Wolfe, Bertram D. 1934. *Marx and America*. New York: John Day.

Wood, Ellen Meiksins. 2008. "Historical Materialism in 'Forms which Precede Capitalist Production.'" In Musto 2008, 79–92.